A MODERN HISTORY

THE CREATION OF A NEW TIER IN THE INFRA-STRUCTURE
OF PROFESSIONAL FOOTBALL

BY ROGER READE

EMPIRE
PUBLICATIONS

First published in 2021

EMPIRE PUBLICATIONS

1 Newton Street, Manchester M1 1HW

© Roger Reade 2021

ISBN: 978-1-909360-83-9

Cover photograph: "The United Colours of Football in the Community" was the caption for this iconic photograph taken at the Pizza Hut launch event at Arsenal's Highbury in 1993 when virtually every professional club's Community Officers was photographed together in one picture wearing their own club colours... for full details see page 301.

CONTENTS

APPENDICES

OTHER NOTES

ABOUT THE AUTHOR

ROGER READE began his career in football administration at Manchester City Football Club in 1975 when he was appointed as an administrative assistant working in the club's main office – though he had also been working alongside the club as a voluntary Secretary – and later chairman - of the club's young supporters club, the Junior Blues Club. In 1979 he was appointed as the youngest Secretary in the Football League when he became Club Secretary at Doncaster Rovers. He returned to work at Manchester City as an Assistant to City's long-serving Club Secretary – Bernard Halford – in 1983.

In 1986, Roger was appointed as General/Chief Administrator to the new 'pilot' Community Programme in Professional Football where he eventually worked alongside over 100 community schemes linked with professional football over the next 21 years. He qualified as a member of the Institute of Chartered Secretaries and Administrators during this time and became and remains a Fellow of the Institute. He was also awarded an Honorary Doctorate from Buckinghamshire Chilterns University for services to football in 2003.

Since 2007 he has held positions at Manchester CFA (Chief Executive), Blackpool FC Community Trust (Director of Strategic Development) and at Sheffield & Hallamshire CFA (Company/General Secretary), the latter of which he left after serving for just under six years in 2018. He is a lifelong Manchester City supporter and has a season ticket for the Etihad.

ACKNOWLEDGEMENTS

I WOULD LIKE TO THANK all those people who have helped and encouraged me during the compilation of this book. Without their help and their contributions, it would have been impossible to have written this book in such detail. First and foremost, I would like to thank my partner, Julie, for her patience and tolerance whilst I have been engaged in undertaking the extensive research necessary to complete the book. Thanks too to Tom and Laura for all their encouragement and support.

May I also take the opportunity to thank my sisters, Vicki and Lindsay, for their considerable help, and support not forgetting my brother-in-law, Graham, for his extensive input, expertise and frequent encouragement (and to Mike from IMA too). Thanks to my former colleague, Richard Finney, for his backing, input and positive energy throughout the writing of this book. He has personally contributed enormously to the contents, kindly putting me right where necessary and helping to ensure the chronological sequence of events.

My thanks too to many individuals who have kindly spared the time to speak to me including Mickey Burns, Mike Evans (EFL Trust), Mike Foster (PL), Gordon Taylor (PFA), Michael Tattersall and Susan O'Brien (National League) and to John Platt, Tony Currie, Tommy Spencer, Dick Krzywicki, Bob Oates, Kath Boullen, Graham Moran, Keith Daniell, Kevin Glendon, Ian Lees, Nigel Rothband, Kay McKechnie, Derek Allan, John Relish, Dave Edmundson, Rick Fenoglio and John Shiels. Thanks to them for their generous advice, support and contributions during the completion of the book. In addition, they have, of course, also all played key parts in ensuring the development and long-term sustainability of "Football in the Community" schemes at clubs at various different stages since 1986.

May I also say a huge "thank you" to John and particularly to Ash at Empire Publications for all their hard work and support in getting this book 'out there'.

In closing, I must also apologise in advance for any errors or mistakes that I may have made. I am responsible for the writing of the book and it is almost inevitable that in the course of all my research, I may have got the odd fact or date wrong, but the vast majority of the book has been thoroughly checked – and checked again. Someone once said that there hasn't been a football book produced yet that hasn't got at least one mistake in it! I have written this book predominantly as a record of facts, so I really hope that there aren't too many mistakes in it! I don't believe there will be.

*"I am of the opinion that my life belongs to the whole community,
as long as I live, it is my privilege to do for it whatever I can"*

GEORGE BERNARD SHAW

"Nothing great was ever achieved without enthusiasm"

RALPH WALDO EMERSON

FOREWORD BY GORDON TAYLOR OBE

A S I REFLECT on the last four decades of achievement at the PFA and what the Football in the Community Scheme has meant to so many people from diverse backgrounds, with different ideals, different motivations, and from different cultures, the PFA membership boasts professional players from all over the globe, demonstrating that irrespective of culture, race, creed, religion or politics, we are an open and welcoming country.

Casting my mind back three decades, and when we at the PFA sat down in the middle of the 1980's and started to talk about where football in England was, and what a battering it was taking, the scene was unremittingly bleak.

I had taken over from Cliff Lloyd as the Chief Executive in 1981 eager to build on so much of the excellent work of the Association in so many ways. The working conditions for players had gradually improved, the maximum wage had been abolished and at the advent of TV coverage in the 1950's, Cliff had negotiated with the television companies to protect payments to the Union on behalf of the players. We were in a good place, but we knew there were several daunting challenges ahead.

Then the going got really tough. Football was being used for political reasons, extreme groups latched on to it, we experienced pitch invasions, racism, the horrors at a number of stadiums, notably Heysel and Valley Parade at Bradford before the Hillsborough tragedy concluded an appalling decade.

Prime Minister Margaret Thatcher pinned the blame on football and there was talk of identity cards just to get into stadiums; Sir Bert Millichip and Ted Croker, the Chairman and Secretary of the Football Association, insisted it was a societal problem and it seemed impossible to resolve the differences between politicians and the football authorities.

We at the PFA felt we had to take the initiative. We said there was no use playing a blame game and that if football was our major spectator and participant sport, then it was clearly a vital part of our social fabric and we needed to use it for the greater good. Some threw up their hands and said "there's nothing you can do about it, it's just the way society is".

If we had done nothing, there was every chance the game could have died on its feet. We got all the staff together - Mickey Burns, our Education Officer, to the fore - and discussed how we could make football a force for good. We decided that, by asking our members to agree to a clause in their contracts to work a few hours a week on community work, they would be showing an enormous degree of social responsibility. They would go into the schools and the rundown areas around our grounds, where so many homes were boarded up, and preach a gospel of better behaviour, how important it was that people were involved with their local football club, to extol equality schemes and diversity, discuss crime in inner cities, talk about the benefits of sport for health reasons, promote the virtues of education if kids were playing truant, and teach them about their local club and the history of the game. People looked at us - frowned may be a better description - and wondered if we could ever change it.

We said we'd try a pilot scheme in the North West, at six clubs, Manchester United, Manchester City, Oldham Athletic, Preston North End, Bury and, my old club, Bolton Wanderers, providing jobs for ex-players. What was looked at very dubiously in its initial period, then extended and extended and is now not only established in this country but also sets a great example to the rest of the world extolling football's contribution to social responsibility.

There has been a massive change in the intervening years to the extent that it is one of the major reasons why football, instead of dying on its feet, regained its popularity attracting people who had never been before, more women, youngsters, family stands, all-seater stadia, it was the game to be at.

I like to think from that particular acorn a lot of oak trees have grown and football set that in motion and set the standard. We have conferences here at the PFA where countries from around the world come to wish to know what we do and what effect it has.

Several images spring to mind. I particularly remember talking to local police officers who said what a difference it was making to their job to see the football club embracing the community and having players going out and speaking against knife crime and hooliganism and the letters we had by the dozen from schools saying how good it was players could come out to their schools and get the message across. The teachers would simply not have had the same impact.

There was the time I visited a centre in Liverpool where disabled youngsters were playing our game at a community function. One of the parents approached me and said I had no idea what a difference had been made to the quality of life of her son and herself because unless he was playing with other handicapped children, he felt so disadvantaged, that the level we had found was perfect, her son so loved the interaction with players and it gave her such peace of mind that she was able to bring him to these sessions and talk to other parents of disabled children and share their stories.

We also funded a programme for young offenders to take coaching courses in Wigan. I went there with Chris Kirkland, Brett Emerton and Kevin Davies representing their respective clubs. It was quite an intimidating atmosphere but the lads did great and I'll always remember the response of one of the lads in there when he started to coach. I told him who I was, that we helped with the funding, and said we just wanted the lads in here to do well, and for them to be able to engage in something meaningful when they were released. He said: "Mr Taylor, all my life I've been told what to do, what to do, what to do. For the first time, I'm running a course and the youngsters are asking ME what to do." It was a humbling moment.

So, here we are. Thirty plus years down the road. Football in this country is thriving. It is a £7 billion dollar industry worldwide, thanks to the remarkable success of the Premier League, the bolstering of the English Football League and the fact we have a Conference in which over half the players are full-time. People who once ran scared of football, now need to be there. The change has been phenomenal. But we do need to remember where it was to truly appreciate where it is now.

There have been a whole lot of issues we have addressed, we have been open and inviting, we have women on our Management Committee, the women's game is flourishing; we're getting to the stage where Football League clubs will introduce an open and fair recruiting system for all its coaching staff. These are massively important steps forward.

There are still many things in football that aren't perfect but what we started in the 80's has had a real and lasting impact, no doubt about it. We don't sit back, there are always new challenges. And with any cause, the longer it runs, the more you need to keep it fresh. You want to do better and better because these issues need to be addressed in whatever way is appropriate for this digital age.

We are all one football family and if one particular tribe wants to be divisive and only think about itself that will be self-defeating. We know the issues out there; racism, homophobia, anti-Semitism, anti-Islamism and all the gender issues – they haven't gone away, they' re always below the surface if you're not careful but the message from football is more important than ever because our country has assimilated more nationalities than any other country in the world which is to our credit.

Roger Reade has created an impressive and chronological analysis of the development and progression of the national Community Programme over the past thirty years, and we should be enormously proud of the positive influence and contributions made by so many to effect positive change in our society. The book is a tribute to the thousands of people involved in football's social responsibility programme and to all PFA Community personnel from Mickey Burns at the outset, Roger who took over the reins and John Hudson who has impressively accelerated the programme with his colleagues to its eminent place in football's culture in the present day.

CHAPTER 1 – INTRODUCTION

WHEN **MICKEY BURNS** first took up his post as the new Chief Education Officer of The Footballers Further Education and Vocational Training Society (FFE&VTS) in 1983, following the sad death of the previous officer **Bob Kerry**, he could not possibly have realised what a huge influence he would have on the game of football during the remainder of his working life. Not only that, but he could not have fully appreciated the wonderful 'legacy' that he would leave for the game following all his early endeavours.

An ex-England amateur, Mickey played for Skelmersdale United as an amateur in the 1960's before turning professional when he signed for Blackpool in 1969 eventually spending five successful years there and helping the club to win promotion in 1970 and also to win the Anglo Italian Cup in 1972. He then moved to Newcastle United in 1974, appearing in the 1976 League Cup Final at Wembley against Manchester City. Following a short spell with Cardiff City, Mickey spent his final years as a player with Middlesbrough. Based on his playing experience and, also his experience as a former teacher, he had a clear appreciation and understanding of the importance of the wider role that the FFE&VTS might play in supporting current and former professional footballers to 'expand their horizons', given the right support and funding.

The FFE&VTS that he inherited was run at the time by a Board of Trustees comprising representatives from the Professional Footballers' Association (PFA) and the Football League (FL).

It was a very small operation when compared to the one that he was able to build up over a period of just under 25 years, especially as the growth of the organisation was based around Mickey's driving and abiding ambition to provide increased opportunities for footballers coming out of the game (at all age groups), through injury, retirement or having been released by their clubs.

His first challenge was to attempt to understand the extremely complicated arrangements made by his predecessor, most notably with colleges, in support of Youth Training (YT) that had been introduced into professional football in the early 1980's. The YT programme provided opportunities for vocational training to 16-17-year-old young people not in full-time education or employment. Mickey then had to investigate if better and more relevant qualifications (and 'A' Levels too where necessary) for young players could be introduced so that the large numbers of 18/19-year-olds who dropped out of the game would then be better qualified and better equipped to find alternative work elsewhere. Ultimately, Mickey would also be personally responsible for the introduction of the 'scholarship' programme into the game many years later, which would fundamentally change and improve the status and prospects for huge numbers of young footballers in this age group. Mickey would also grow and develop a source of funding for former players so that a much broader range of possible second career options would become available for players coming out of the game.

Arguably his greatest achievement, and one that has not only endured to this day but one that is also likely to continue to develop and grow in future years, was his introduction of "**The Community Programme in Professional Football**" whereby 'Football in the Community' schemes became established at professional clubs. In turn, the game and, indeed, all the professional clubs, have experienced the benefits that these super successful and now highly professional and polished community-based organisations have brought with them over the years.

What drove him on, following a series of regional meetings with current professional players around the country in 1983/4 (all held within 12 months of his appointment), was that it had become clear that players were worried about what second career/job opportunities might be available for them once their playing careers came to an end. This was especially the case as there was very little in the way of direct training support for other careers at the time. This troubled Mickey. He felt that it was his responsibility to see what he, and the FFE&VTS, could come up with in terms of being able to offer alternative solutions. Arguably Mickey's biggest success was in creating so many new jobs in the years to follow for former professional footballers.

An opportunity arose in 1984 when Mickey attended an open meeting of several different employers across a number of different industries when the Manpower Services Commission (MSC) outlined to employers (i.e. possible future partners) how they could support not only their YT Programme (the reason he was attending the meeting) but also the Government's 'Community Programme' initiative that had just been launched. Mickey met and talked at some length with **Pat Buckmaster** from the MSC who confirmed that, as a job creation scheme, the 'Community Programme', could well be applied to football. Mick invited her to the FFE&VTS office at the Corn Exchange in Manchester in order to exchange ideas and to pass on more information. In turn, Pat brought with her some application forms together with sound advice suggesting that a "pilot" initiative in the North West of England (i.e. where it could be more easily and locally controlled by the Manchester-based FFE&VTS) could represent the best way forward.

Pat also passed on advice about the completion of the application forms (single applications would have to go for consideration by each pre-selected local MSC agency). Mickey was also advised about the preparation of suitable aims and objectives for the proposed football scheme. He said:

> "Pat felt that a 6-club pilot scheme would allow things to be properly tested. Her support and encouragement were obviously key, but her advice was clearly appropriate, especially when you consider how the aims and objectives have stood the test of time and are still relevant even today. I certainly felt that the Community Programme could become a vehicle for helping players to move into second careers following the end of their playing careers."

Less supportive at the time, however, were the football authorities. Representatives of the FL were sceptical, and even the normally supportive PFA representatives needed convincing of the potential merits. Indeed, it took several meetings, and the not-inconsiderable support of the then chairman of the FFE&VTS, **Professor Sir John Wood** (who understood the 'vision' and its potential and the benefits all round), to secure its approval as a pilot venture. Mickey said of his chairman:

> "Without his involvement, it is extremely unlikely that approval for the pilot venture would have been forthcoming. Without question, he helped get the concept accepted by the Board."

The world of professional football had long been notorious for not wishing to embrace new ideas and/or for taking its time to support new ventures. Indeed, by Mickey's own admission, at the very first meeting there was, to say the least, a 'lukewarm' reception. If the people attending that meeting had known then what the future of football-related community involvement was to hold, they would have overwhelmingly approved the idea without any of the delays that subsequently ensued, for sure. One of Mickey's key hopes was for clubs to open their doors more than once a fortnight and to embrace the idea of becoming more involved in their local communities.

Gordon Taylor (Chief Executive of the PFA) confirmed that it was, in the end, changing circumstances in football that convinced the Board to reconsider:

> "There were so many factors at the time, but the big turning point for the Board followed the Bradford City fire and the Heysel disaster (both in May 1985) when it was unanimously agreed that football had to take action."

Gordon Taylor was born in Ashton-Under-Lyne near Manchester, enjoying a successful playing career as a winger with Bolton Wanderers (who he joined from non-league Curzon Ashton), Birmingham City, Blackburn Rovers, Vancouver Whitecaps and Bury. He became Chief Executive of the PFA in 1981, having taken over from **Cliff Lloyd.** He was also awarded the OBE in 2008.

The discussions with **Pat Buckmaster** had led to the selection by Mickey of six suitable clubs (Bolton Wanderers, Bury, Manchester City, Manchester United, Oldham Athletic and Preston North End) that were local to the Manchester-based FFE&VTS's office for the pilot venture. That said, he did let it be known that the list hadn't originally included Preston North End (instead, it included another Greater Manchester-based club). Mickey said:

> *"The idea was that the six clubs included large and small clubs that spanned the then four divisions of the Football League, though the positive interest and support of officials at Preston North End ultimately merited their inclusion ahead of one of the other smaller Greater Manchester clubs."*

Mickey, who in later years would be appointed as Chief Executive of the FFE&VTS, then attended a meeting in Rochdale attended by representatives of the six local MSC agencies, in order to present his ideas for the proposed new football initiative. After impressing with his presentation about the impact football could make, all six agencies unanimously agreed to support the new programme.

Following this landmark initial meeting, and after many years' hard work and endeavour by literally thousands of people, professional football club based community work has developed significantly. This work is now known and respected across the world and has contributed in so many ways towards, amongst other things:
-   better education
-   increased employment opportunities
-   better social cohesion
-   improved health and well-being etc.

To emphasise the growth of the club-based community operations over the years, it should be noted that turnover across 98 charitable Foundations and Trusts established by PL, FL and some non-league clubs was estimated to be over £125 million for year-end accounts in 2017 (see Appendix I). Given the information to follow in this book, the growth of the community scheme in financial terms alone is simply incredible!

This book provides the first comprehensive record of:
-   how, when, where and why community projects were established in conjunction with professional football clubs
-   where funding came from (and when)
-   the critical 'step-changes' in strategically and politically taking forward the work
-   the moves towards the creation of the original 'football family' supporting the scheme
-   who were the key 'activators'
-   the first, and later, national sponsorship arrangements

More details about the many former professional footballers who were to play such a significant part in driving things forward is also provided. Indeed, in the early days there was a clear objective to ensure that former professional players were appointed as Community Officers, thus providing useful employment (and training) for former players (in line with the hopes of **Mickey Burns**). Their appointment was, in the end, even more significant than that, as someone who was to play a key role in the growth of Community Schemes over the next 20 years or so, **Richard Finney,** explained:

> *"What was important was that, wherever possible, the ex-player selected to become the first Community Officer had some affinity with the club, the town and area, was someone that was recognised as an ex-player."*

Rotherham-born, Richard Finney made his debut for his local town club, Rotherham United, at the age of 18, scoring in a 1-1 draw against Brentford in March 1974. As a youngster, Richard was also selected to play for the England Youth team. Sadly, a more than promising career was tragically cut short after serious injury sustained in 1980 when he was only 24. A Testimonial match was held for him in 1982 when the Millers played Aston Villa (then holders of the European Cup). Richard is now an ambassador for the town of Rotherham.

CHAPTER 2 – EARLY DAYS

THE WORDS "FOOTBALL" AND "COMMUNITY" have never been strangers to each other. Indeed, it would be fair to say that many professional football clubs, as we know them today, have their roots firmly entrenched in their local communities. Times have, of course, changed considerably since the 1950's when football players and fans were known to arrive at matches having travelled together by bus. It is only in recent years, however, that clubs have recognised the importance of playing more active roles in their local communities.

This new role was first identified sometime before Football in the Community schemes of the 1980's and 1990's were introduced. Indeed **John Harding**, in his excellent official history of the PFA, *For the Good of the Game*, comments that the idea and potential of clubs becoming more involved in their local communities:

> *"Had its philosophical roots back in the 1968 Chester Report, the opening up of clubs to involve local people, young and old, and had been given extra impetus in the seventies and eighties by the despair of not knowing what to do about hooliganism. The tragedies of Heysel and Bradford, as well as the losing battle against crowd disorder, threatened to sever the public's links with the national game."*

The Sir Norman Chester Report of 1968 came about when **Sir Norman Chester** was invited by the Football League to analyse the problems in the game, most notably including the growing financial problems being experienced by League clubs. He was also invited to recommend solutions to the problems and difficulties encountered. As far as the wider community was concerned, the Report included comments such as:

> *"Women provide a major and largely untapped source of potential support."*

and considered the possibility of a football future with a

> *"more integrated relationship between The FA and The Football League."*

That said, the term *"football and the community"* (as it was referred to) was first recognised as part of the then Sports Council initiative developed by **Denis Howell** (Minister of Sport at the time) in the late 1970's and early 1980's (The Sports Council was originally formed in 1972 and was succeeded in 1997 by the operation of "UK Sport" in the various home countries of the UK, and in England by "Sport England"). The Minister stated that the idea behind the new proposals was:

> *"for football clubs to give a lead to young people and encourage them to make more positive use of their time."*

The 'Football and Community' projects part funded by the Sports Council at this time were, however, largely restricted to the capital funding of projects only - i.e. they were building projects such as the one established at Plymouth Argyle where a number of small sided pitches were built at the club's Home Park ground for use by the local community. Another example was the erection of a full-size floodlit shale football pitch at Ipswich Town's Portman Road ground. In total, 29 professional clubs benefitted. It was, though, recognised at a later stage that, in the absence of additional local investment in appropriate manpower resourcing (and forward planning) in the longer-term to ensure the sustainability of the projects, most of these ground-breaking football and community projects were simply, and sadly, destined to fail.

The game of football in England during the 1970's and early 1980's was suffering not only from the fact that grounds at the professional clubs were becoming unsafe and outdated but also from the blight of hooliganism and vandalism. Attendances at FL matches, then consisting of 92 clubs across 4 divisions, were plummeting. In fact, having reached a peak of well over 40 million people attending matches during season 1948/49 (i.e. just after the Second World War), FL attendances had reached an all-time low point of around 16.5 million people during season 1985/86 (see Appendix II). Not only that, but there were three separate major occurrences in the Spring of 1985 that had dire consequences for the game.

Firstly, on the 13th March 1985, Luton Town played Millwall at Kenilworth Road and the scenes of Millwall fans ripping up seats and hurtling them, and other missiles, at home supporters and the police were captured on television for all to see. To make matters worse, television also captured a pitch invasion of supporters. (These pictures also led to the Government inspired and generally unwelcome "membership scheme" being adopted by Luton Town in the 1986/87 season).

Secondly, on the 11th May 1985, at a FL match at Valley Parade between Bradford City and Lincoln City, a fire in the main stand at the ground broke out which saw 56 people lose their lives and 265 people injured. Many of those who perished were attempting to get out of the burning stand, only to find the exit gates locked.

Finally, in 1985, on the 29th May, and prior to the start of the European Cup Final between Liverpool and Juventus, hooliganism erupted on the terraces at the Heysel Stadium in Brussels, Belgium. Football fans attempting to escape from the problems on the terraces caused a wall to collapse. Tragically, 39 people lost their lives and over 600 more people were injured.

1985 also saw the sporting authorities taking a long hard look at football's woes to the extent that two potential embryonic 'community schemes' started to be developed at one and the same time. "Action Sport" (driven forward by **Joe Patton** from The Sports Council) and "Football and the Community" were two very different schemes to be taken forward. **Mickey Burns** himself spent many months liaising with the MSC to set up what was to be a ground-breaking new £300,000 one year 'pilot' initiative based around using the power of football clubs to engage with their local communities. The schemes main aims and objectives were eventually finalised as follows:

1.   To provide temporary employment and training for unemployed people and, if possible, to enhance skills and future employment prospects.

2.   To promote closer links between professional clubs and the community by organising activities, participation in sport and inter-club activities. This should involve players and workers organising coaching sessions in football. Developing the promotion of other sports subject to the needs of the community. The workers will identify the needs of the community and utilise the resources available to meet these. The development of leagues, coaching sessions, social events, involving as many sports as possible, will be part of the main brief.

3.   To involve minority and ethnic groups in social and recreational activities. Particular emphasis will be put on people from disadvantaged areas. This will involve contacting local community leaders to identify desires and aspirations. This will be the responsibility of the Supervisor at the club and he/she will respond by organising such events as are requested e.g. six-a-side competitions, basketball, coaching and competitions.

4.   To attempt to prevent acts of hooliganism and vandalism by a programme of talks and visits involving professional players aimed at educating and influencing young people. The players will be very much involved in this capacity, using their influence as

players to develop a better understanding of community appreciation. This will be done through contacting schools, youth clubs, soccer organisations and industry. It is hoped that these will be carried out on a weekly basis at varying venues.

5.   To maximise the facilities of the club, i.e. training stadium facilities such as gymnasiums, indoor sports facilities and social facilities. To use outside facilities that are available for events. The Club Doctor and Physiotherapist or other qualified staff may also be introduced to give advice on health and safety.

In addition, it was noted that the workers will co-ordinate "match day" schemes, bringing in families and organising inter-club events and that clubs will offer access to their facilities for use by the scheme.

The key objective for MSC was, of course, the first objective listed as above. The "driver" for them was the proposal, particularly for young people, who were out of work, to be able to enter full-time employment. If successful as a job creation scheme, it was made clear by the MSC that there would be additional funds available for an expansion of the pilot. Going forward for the game itself, it was more important for all 5 objectives to be met.

Some professional football clubs during the previous 10-20 years had introduced a variety of different ways of engaging with their local community. Possibly the most active club in this aspect of work was Watford FC who were managed by **Graham Taylor** and supported by the dynamic Chief Executive **Eddie Plumley** under the Chairmanship of **Elton John**. Graham Taylor's whole intention was for the club to become part and parcel of the fabric of the whole town and surrounding area. The club created the first "family enclosure" and encouraged their players to visit local schools and to 'build bridges' with local community organisations. It was also no coincidence that gates at the club rose throughout the Taylor years.

At that same time, the former Greater London Council also offered funding to certain London-based clubs to set up community initiatives. The first of these to be established was set up at Millwall under the careful supervisory watch, drive and energy of **Gary Stempel** who, like many Community Officers after him, would go on to become a successful football coach in later years. In Gary's case this would be as an international coach in his native Panama. In the early days, it is also worth noting that Gary was greatly encouraged and supported by someone who was destined to become the Scheme Chairman, **Fred Nind**. (Fred once spoke passionately at a meeting of London-based officers about the importance of organisations not standing still and aiming to progress, particularly by looking at wider opportunities to develop; e.g. in anti-racism, the Duke of Edinburgh's Scheme, college work and training etc.)

Meanwhile, back in Manchester, plans to take the 6 club 'pilot' venture forward led to interviews for the newly created post of "General Administrator" (the role was to oversee the pilot scheme, albeit only for a guaranteed 12-month period at the start). The interviews were held in the late spring of 1986 at The Britannia Hotel in Manchester and a total of six candidates were invited for interview. What was interesting about the format for the day was that all six candidates were able to meet each other, spend lunch together and share a briefing about the future plans to operate and develop the scheme through the FFE&VTS. As explained, the FFE&VTS was a registered charity and an ideal 'vehicle' for introducing the community scheme as it was then jointly operated by the PFA and the FL. It is also fair to say that given the interest in the new scheme, some candidates retained a keen interest in what was to unfold and kept in touch following the conclusion of the interviews.

The successful candidate for the "General Administrator" post was **Roger Reade** based on his first-hand experience not only of community involvement but also on his contacts at many of the professional clubs following his previous work experience with Manchester City and Doncaster Rovers. Within a year or so, one of the other six candidates, **Richard Finney,** would be appointed as a Regional Manager in Yorkshire and the North East. Richard was to become one of the key influencers and a member of the senior management team responsible for overseeing the development of the whole scheme.

CHAPTER 3
THE START OF THE COMMUNITY PROGRAMME IN PROFESSIONAL FOOTBALL

THE NEWLY APPOINTED "General Administrator" of 'The Community Programme in Professional Football' under the auspices of the FFE&VTS saw his first day in post on June 16th, 1986. The induction was brief and to the point. Six brown cardboard files were passed on, each relating to the proposed new projects to be set up at Bolton Wanderers, Bury, Manchester City, Manchester United, Oldham Athletic and Preston North End. Each file contained details of the local budget and staffing support structure to be put in place at each club.

The original scheme structure was set out as follows:

BOARD OF DIRECTORS (FL AND PFA)

EDUCATION OFFICER

GENERAL ADMINISTRATOR (PLUS ADMINISTRATION SUPPORT)

3 SUPERVISORS (2 CLUB SCHEMES EACH)

6 FULL TIME ACTIVITY ORGANISERS (1 AT EACH CLUB)

36 PART TIME ACTIVITY ORGANISERS (6 AT EACH CLUB)

12 PART TIME CLERICAL (ADMINISTRATION) OFFICERS (2 AT EACH CLUB)

In addition, it was noted that:

- Manchester City, as a club, was keen to offer community access to their Platt Lane Training Ground (which included a small sided all-weather pitch).

- Manchester United generously provided access to their Cliff Training Ground in Salford.

- Oldham Athletic and Preston North End were ideally placed to encourage greater community participation following the installation of all-weather pitch surfaces at Boundary Park and at Deepdale (their respective grounds). At Boundary Park, Oldham Athletic were also able to provide community access to their Clayton Arms Sports Hall adjacent to the main stadium.

The new General Administrator's first day at work also included a brief tour of the offices of the FFE&VTS, together with the offices of the PFA. Both organisations were then based at the

Corn Exchange Building in central Manchester.

As already stated, the FFE&VTS were already leading the way in delivering the new Government YT programme for players between 16 and 18 years of age at professional clubs (first set up in 1982/83). Indeed, because of the high "drop out" rate of footballers in this age group, it was felt (rightly) that it was appropriate to provide these young men with additional skills to help them find alternative employment should they not be able to pursue a career in the game at such a young age.

Originally established by The PFA and The FL in 1980 to support current and former professional players with any training needs which might assist them to move into second careers after their playing days were over, the FFE&VTS was clearly in a strong position to be able to take forward the proposed new community project in conjunction with FL member clubs.

Meetings with representatives of the six 'founding' clubs were arranged. In addition, meetings with job centre officials at Bolton, Bury, Oldham, Preston and several in Manchester (Fountain Street, Moss Side and Stretford amongst others) were also lined up.

Amongst those seen in the early meetings with football club representatives were:

- **Des McBain** (Secretary, Bolton Wanderers) who was extremely supportive in the early days of the community scheme whilst the club was based at their former Burnden Park ground.
- **John Heap** (Secretary), **Ian Pickup** (Director) at Bury and, later, **Terry Robinson** (Chairman).
- **Bernard Halford** (popular and long-serving Club Secretary), **Phil Critchley** (Commercial Manager) and **Richard Hodgson** (Manager of the Platt Lane Community Complex near the club's Maine Road ground) at Manchester City.
- **Les Olive** (Secretary), **Danny McGregor** (Commercial Manager) and **Barry Moorhouse** (Assistant Secretary) at Manchester United, who kindly arranged for the topic of 'Football and the Community' to be added to the agenda for a Board Meeting to be held on the 16th July 1986. The Board Meeting was chaired by **Martin Edwards** and saw fellow Directors **Bobby Charlton**, **Michael Edelson** and **Maurice Watkins** in attendance alongside the Club Secretary.
- **Ian Stott** (Chairman) and **Tom Finn** (Secretary) at Oldham Athletic (and, following Tom's departure to join West Ham United as Secretary, the new Secretary at Latics, **Phil Hough**).
- **Barney Campbell** (Director) and **Derek Allan** (Club Secretary) at Preston North End (together with **Brian Hall** who was then working with Preston Council) and, at a later stage, Manager **John McGrath**, and Assistants **Les Chapman** and **Walter Joyce.**

Brian Hall secured a degree in mathematics at Manchester University before signing for Liverpool FC initially as an amateur before signing professional forms in 1968. He made his debut against Stoke City in 1969 and played for the club up to 1975 when he moved to Plymouth Argyle for one season. He then moved nearer home to play for Burnley where his playing career ended in 1980. Brian sadly passed away in July 2015.

The first appointed Supervisors (Community Officers) were all well-known ex-players:

- **Pat Howard,** who took up his new duties at the end of July 1986.
- **Brian Kidd,** who also commenced his new duties at the end of July.
- **Dennis Leman** who started work during early August 1986.

Born in Dodworth, Barnsley, **Pat Howard** began his playing career with his local club before moving to Newcastle United in 1971 where he played for the club in the 1974 FA Cup Final against Liverpool and in the 1976 League Cup Final against Manchester City. A central defender, Pat later played for Arsenal, Birmingham City and Bury where he finished his career in 1982. He also played briefly for Portland Timbers in the NASL in 1978.

Brian Kidd played as a striker for Manchester United between 1967 and 1974 before later moves to Arsenal, Manchester City, Everton and Bolton Wanderers. He famously scored one of United's four goals on his nineteenth birthday in their European Cup Final victory of 1968. He then spent some time with NASL clubs in America before joining Barrow and Preston North End in a managerial role. He also later enjoyed huge success as a coach with Manchester United, Leeds United, Sheffield United and Manchester City.

Born in Newcastle, **Dennis Leman** began his career as an apprentice with Manchester City where he played as a midfield player between 1973 and 1976. He then moved to Sheffield Wednesday between 1976 and 1982 under Jack Charlton. His playing career ended in 1984 following short term spells with Wrexham (on loan) and Scunthorpe United.

All three supervisors were in post in good time for the start of the new 1986/87 football season. Under the structure for the pilot scheme at the time (see above) Pat, Brian and Dennis were appointed as 'supervisors' overseeing two clubs each. Pat oversaw developments at Bolton Wanderers and Bury (Pat had recently finished his playing career at Bury); Brian at Manchester United (his former club) and at Oldham Athletic; Dennis at his old club, Manchester City and at Preston North End.

At the clubs, **Kevin Glendon** left Manchester City's Community Programme scheme (where he had been a part time activity officer for a short spell) to be appointed as the first full time "Activity Organiser" at Bolton Wanderers. Kevin was a former Manchester City apprentice who moved to Crewe Alexandra in 1980 where he made his league debut. He also played for Burnley between 1983-84 but then moved into non-league football with Hyde United and Mossley before finishing his career with Macclesfield Town in 1990. He was later to become Manager of Radcliffe Borough for a twenty-year spell between 1990 and 2010.

Kevin was soon succeeded as Bolton's Full Time Activity Organiser by **Jim Caffrey** in September 1987, and then by **Tommy Booth** in November 1987 when Jim left.

Born in Middleton, Manchester, **Tommy Booth** was a popular and successful centre half with Manchester City and Preston North End. At City, Tommy played his part in helping City to win three major trophies in 1969 and 1970 – and again in 1976 when the club won the League Cup. He was also briefly Manager of Preston North End between 1985 and 1986.

Gary Pierce took up the full-time role at Bury Football Club. A popular ex-goalkeeper, Bury-born Gary made a name for himself when he played for Wolverhampton Wanderers in the 1974 League Cup Final against Manchester City, making a string of outstanding saves to help Wolves win the Cup. Gary's professional career started at Huddersfield Town in 1971 who he joined from non-league Mossley. He also later played for Barnsley and Blackpool.

Eugene "Gus" Wilson, brother of former City player **Clive Wilson**, took on the Full Time Activity Organiser role at Manchester City. Gus had previously worked closely in a coaching capacity alongside **Richard Hodgson** at City's Platt Lane Training Complex.

Former Manchester United player **Danny Healey** was appointed as full-time Officer at Old Trafford. Manchester-born Danny played for Manchester United as a youth player and later moved to Bolton Wanderers and Workington where he played a small number of matches in 1974/5.

John Platt returned to Boundary Park to take on the full-time role there (at the same time, he also took over bookings for the club's newly installed all-weather pitch). Born in Ashton-Under-Lyne, John's goalkeeping talents were spotted whilst he was playing for his local club, Ashton United, by scouts from Oldham Athletic. He went on to spend several years with Oldham between 1971 and 1981. Before taking up his duties as the club's first ever community officer in 1986, John also played briefly for Bury, Bolton Wanderers, Tranmere Rovers (on loan) and Preston North End.

Following his appointment at Oldham Athletic, **John Platt** said:

> *"Job opportunities for ex-players in the game were limited at the time, so, it was the next best thing to get the chance to still be involved in the game and to work in and amongst football people. Having been at the club as a player between 1973 and 1981, when I received the opportunity to come back as Community Officer it was superb, even though I did view the job with some trepidation during the first few months."*

Once a centre back with Preston North End and later with Middlesbrough, **Mick Baxter**, went back to Deepdale as Preston North End's new full-time activity officer. Born in Birmingham,

Mick had begun his playing career with Preston North End where he went on to make over 200 full league appearances between 1974 and 1980. He then moved to Middlesbrough where he was encouraged by Manager/Coach Malcolm Allison to develop his talents as a 'footballing' centre half, playing over 120 games for the club up to 1984.

The 'back up' team at the Corn Exchange also started to take shape with the appointment of administrators **Kate Bateman, Amelia Coppage** and **Tracey Paul**. Tracey would eventually join the PFA and become an important member of the PFA's admin team in future. **Louise Pearson** was appointed following Kate's decision to leave early in 1987 and she, like Tracey, was later to become a long serving and popular figure at the PFA.

Work in recruiting the part time activity organisers and administrative assistants to each of the clubs continued into the autumn of 1986. Indeed, interviews were organised at all the clubs in conjunction with the jobcentres in each area for the various available positions. Amongst those appointed were:

- **Graham Gill** at Bolton Wanderers (Graham would later become a senior administrator within the North West regional support team).
- **Dave Bell** at Bury (Dave would play a key role at several clubs in future).
- **Kevin Jardine** and **Derek Clydesdale** at Manchester City. Kevin and Derek would play important roles in the future development of the Community Programme scheme. Indeed, Derek was offered the opportunity to set up the community scheme at Crewe Alexandra as the club's first Full Time Activity Organiser during the summer of 1987. Derek then moved to the United States in the summer of 1988 before returning to the UK during the winter of 1988/89 where he was then also kind enough to agree to set up the Darlington community scheme before returning to the United States once again in the summer of 1989. He also then went on to play other important roles in the scheme in the future.
- **Pat Mallinson** and **David Hanson** at Manchester United. Pat would later become Mrs Pat Wilkinson and go on to become a loyal and long-serving member of the PFA's administrative team. David was a former Manchester United apprentice who was released by the club in 1986. He later played briefly for Bury, Leyton Orient, Chesterfield (on loan) and Halifax Town between 1993 and 1998.
- **Janet Baxter** (Mick's wife), **Ian Johnstone, Alan Kershaw, Peter "Leo" Sayer** and **Andy Welsh**, all at Preston North End. Andy took up the important role of full-time activity organiser at Blackpool FC when the new community scheme started there in 1987.

Alan Kershaw was a former Preston North End apprentice who moved to Southport in 1974 where he made several league appearances for the Haig Avenue side between 1974 and 1975. He went on to play in Scotland and then in Australia and Sweden.

Born in Cardiff, **Peter "Leo" Sayer** played for his local club, Cardiff City (at the club's former Ninian Park ground) between 1974 and 1978. He then played for Brighton and Hove Albion and Preston North End before moving back to Cardiff on loan in 1981 before ending his league career with Chester City in 1985.

Andy Welsh was a Blackpool apprentice who played briefly at Bury, and who went on to great things in later years as a coach at Blackpool and Manchester United after having coached the Elite Development Squad and Reserve teams at Manchester City.

The official launch of the Community Programme in Professional Football was held at Oldham Athletic's Boundary Park ground on Wednesday the 3rd September 1986. Significantly, the launch was attended by the Minister of Sport, **Dick Tracey,** and the Minister of Employment, **Ian Lang**. This underlined the importance of the new scheme both as a sports operation *and* as provider of new employment opportunities.

Dick Tracey, in his capacity as Minister of Sport, stated in a letter to **Gordon Taylor** later that year:

> *"I firmly believe that schemes like yours are absolutely essential for the future well-being of football. Youngsters and families must be made to feel that the game presents safe and enjoyable entertainment; projects which involve them, and which*

*make them feel that they have a stake in the club, must be the right way to achieve
that aim."*

Gordon also held the view that football needed to develop much closer links with the Government and with MPs in particular. Indeed, he believed that this was essential. This view was endorsed within a couple of years when the Government, led by Prime Minister, **Margaret Thatcher**, attempted to introduce the ill-fated "ID cards/membership scheme" into football in the late 1980's. Gordon's hopes were to ensure that such action could not happen again in future, especially if MPs were given more regular information and therefore a better understanding of how football worked.

The day after the launch, the well-known and highly-respected sports journalist, **Simon Barnes**, wrote an article in *The Times* (4.9.1986) entitled "Send-Off for the Titanic's Lifeboat" in which he said:

*"Football needs people. It needs to be accepted, it needs to be loved again. This
is an economic necessity. "Football in the Community" is full of honest, earnest
endeavour to be just that. In the words of Tom Lehrer, "doing well by doing good."
Perhaps the whole thing is best regarded not as a pint pot bailer on the Titanic but
as a lifeboat. Well, if so, God Bless all who sail in her."*

Key to supporting these initial appointments were North West based MSC officers **John Gray** and **Gary Naven**. Also involved was **Angela Harrison,** whose work mainly related to overseeing the financial aspects of operating the fledgling 'pilot' scheme. Gary played an important supporting role in the early days and would go on to play a leading role within the 'Football and Community' scheme in later years.

John Ainsworth, Gordon Shaw, **Chris Curry**, **Kath Boullen** and **Jan Harwood** (like Angela, Jan was to be involved in financial matters), together with **Sue Fletcher** and **Janice Savage**, were also to become key link personnel and important supporters of the scheme on behalf of the new Training Agency (replacing the MSC) effective from 1987/88. Meetings with them were regular and plentiful. As much as anything else, it was clear that their necks were also on the blocks if things went wrong with the 'pilot' scheme. Monitoring visits were eventually arranged during the autumn months when all Football and the Community staff were interviewed by MSC officials.

Each local club budget allowed for the installation of new, direct telephone numbers at each club, together with the purchase of desks and typewriters (they didn't have PCs or lap top computers in those days) at each of the clubs. The only thing the club had to provide was some office space.

Regarding the establishment of new offices at the clubs, **John Platt** (Community Officer at Oldham Athletic) said:

*"At my first meeting with Football in the Community officials I was handed a
typewriter and a load of A4 paper to take to my new office at Boundary Park. I
thought "What do I do with this?"*

Umbro and Adidas (thanks to a key member of staff at Umbro, **Maggie**) became the first providers of tracksuits and clothing for the activity organisers (also part of the budget).

These were exciting times, though not without initial 'teething' difficulties. Memorably, for example, one club secretary (who shall remain nameless) announced that if the community scheme at his club added even one single extra piece of work for him, he would make immediate arrangements for the scheme to be closed down!

Additionally, recruitment at Manchester United was slow. This was understandable, to a certain extent, as it was vital to ensure that the name and reputation of the club was protected at all costs, though the delay in recruiting new personnel didn't help in relation to the possible wider expansion of the scheme across the North West and the rest of the country.

The beginning of November 1986 also saw the first organised event of any substance when a team of unemployed young people from the Manchester City area were invited to play a team of unemployed youngsters from Preston. The match was played on North End's all-weather pitch. In January of 1987, Manchester City's Community staff invited young, unemployed people from Oldham Athletic's community scheme to play in a similar fixture.

School work in offering coaching/playing support for pupils both in school time (i.e. during Physical Education lessons) and after school was offered once approval had been given by Schools Inspectors from each local authority involved. Added to this, and with the generous support of the clubs, complimentary tickets were increasingly made available to schools to attend matches at their grounds. These tickets, in the main, went to children who had never attended a football match before.

The first six months saw significant success. Not only was it clear that several part time activity organisers moved on to full time employment (therefore meeting the MSC's requirements) but it was also true that the clubs were experiencing an upturn in interest and support. Discussions concerning the possible expansion of the scheme across Lancashire and Merseyside therefore followed as early as November/December 1986.

In addition, a preliminary and exploratory meeting with **Richard Faulkner** and **Pat Finney** from The Football Trust was held. Their positive interest in future developments would prove to be of great significance in the near future.

The success of the six club 'pilot' programmes (particularly in relation to helping previously long-term unemployed people into more permanent employment) saw early support from MSC for the proposed expansion. Meetings with several new FL clubs were held as early as December 1986/January 1987 including meetings involving:

- Representatives of Blackburn Rovers, including Chairman **Bill Fox** (then a powerful influence within the FL), popular Club Secretary **John Howarth**, Manager **Bobby Saxton** and **Jim Furnell** (coaching staff), who collectively confirmed the club's keen willingness to become involved at the earliest possible opportunity.

- **David Johnson** (Secretary at Blackpool, where a formal invitation had been extended to present more information at a full Board of Directors meeting).

- **Albert Maddox** (Club Secretary at Burnley).

- **Albert Eckersley** (Secretary at Chester City).

- Crewe Alexandra initially through Manager **Dario Gradi**, and later through Club Secretary, **Gill Palin.**

- Everton via **Jim Greenwood** (Chief Executive/Secretary).

- Liverpool through Chief Executive/Secretary **Peter Robinson.**

- Rochdale via Secretary **Tom Nicholl**, Manager **Eddie Gray** and an enthusiastic Marketeer who would later become Club Secretary, **Jackie Armstrong.** Sometime later, Director **David Walkden** also became involved when he became the Club's Vice Chairman (in January 1989, he would lead the club's moves towards securing Sports Council funding support for a new 5-a-side pitch at Rochdale's Spotland ground).

- **Norman Wilson** (Secretary) at Tranmere Rovers.

- **Bryan Hamilton** (Chief Executive) at Wigan Athletic.

The second phase or "roll-out" was therefore intended to embrace a further ten more clubs from around Lancashire and Merseyside. MSC officials were especially keen to see the scheme expand into the Merseyside area where they felt it would capture the imagination of local people given the huge passion for football that existed there.

It should be noted that several clubs from Yorkshire were also in touch at this time to confirm that, if the 'pilot' was successful, they too would be interested in being part of any potential "roll out" of the MSC funded scheme.

New supervisors appointed to oversee affairs at the new North West clubs included **Duncan McKenzie,** who was to oversee the schemes at Liverpool and Everton (before the two schemes were re-structured in the early 1990's).

Born in Grimsby, **Duncan McKenzie** began his league career with Nottingham Forest where he played between 1969 and 1974 when he moved to Leeds United and, later, Everton. He played briefly for Anderlecht in Belgium before his return to England to play for Chelsea and Blackburn Rovers where his playing days finished. He also briefly played in the USA for Tulsa Roughnecks and Chicago Sting. In later years, Duncan became a popular and entertaining after-dinner speaker.

Also appointed around the same time was **Mike Bernard**, who took up the role of Supervisor of the two community projects at Chester City and Crewe Alexandra. Mike had been an extremely successful midfield player during his playing career which began with Stoke City in 1965. He helped Stoke win the Football League Cup in 1972 before moving on to, firstly, Everton where he spent a further five years and then Oldham Athletic (a further two years).

Mike was a popular and upbeat Supervisor within the Community Programme who was always happy to support other Community Officers where he could. He eventually left the Community Programme to become Assistant Commercial Manager at one of his former clubs, Stoke City.

Indeed, **John Platt** (Community Officer at Oldham Athletic) also tells a tale about Mike from his early days in past at Boundary Park:

> *"Mike Bernard very kindly came across to show me how to organise a bingo session for one of my senior citizens tea dances, leaving me to host the bingo session the following week. So, I purchased an old bingo number machine where the numbers appeared in sequence on ping pong balls that were fed up a tube. I bought over 250 bingo cards from the local newsagents and I was ready to go. Unfortunately, when the bingo started, it seemed to go on and on without anyone calling house. When I was reaching the last of the ping pong balls in the machine, I realised that all the bingo cards were numbered from 1 to 100 whilst the ping pong balls only went up to 90! There were no winners that day!"*

Appointments made at the clubs included **Simon Whittle** and, later, **Mick Heaton** (at Blackburn Rovers). **Mick Heaton** was born in Sheffield and began his league career as an apprentice with local club Sheffield United before moving to Blackburn Rovers in 1971. He made just under 170 league appearances for the Ewood Park club.

Andy Welsh was also appointed as a Community Officer at Blackpool (having been promoted from his former part time role at Preston North End) as was **Ronnie Evans** at Burnley (though this was for all of three days before he was approached by Oldham Athletic Manager, **Joe Royle**, to become the club's Medical Officer).

Manchester-born **Ronnie Evans** was an apprentice with Manchester City before signing as a professional with the club, becoming a regular in the club's reserve side. Following Ronnie's departure, **Brian Flynn** was appointed as Community Officer at Burnley.

Born in Port Talbot, Brian was a Welsh international with 66 full international caps. He began his career with Burnley before moving to Leeds United in 1977. He then returned to Burnley (initially on loan) before later moves took him to Cardiff City, Doncaster Rovers and Bury. He finished his league career with Wrexham in 1993. He later went on to have a successful career as a manager with Wrexham, Swansea City and Doncaster Rovers.

Other Community Officers appointed included **Mike Rigg** (at Chester City), **Alan Whittle** (at Everton), **Brian Kettle** (at Liverpool), **Keith Hicks** (Rochdale), **Steve Williams** (Tranmere Rovers) and **Tony Allan** (Wigan Athletic). Tony would go on, in later years, to become Club Secretary with Wigan and, later, with Port Vale.

Born in Liverpool, **Alan Whittle** played professionally for Everton between 1967-1972 before later moves to Crystal Palace, Orient and AFC Bournemouth where he ended his career in 1981. He also played for Persepolis in Iran between 1977 and 1978.

Liverpool through and through, **Brian Kettle** signed professional forms with Liverpool in 1973 making just 3 appearances over a seven-year period. He eventually moved for a short time to Houston, USA before moving back to England to spend a season with Wigan Athletic. He also managed several non-league clubs before returning to his beloved Liverpool in a coaching capacity.

Keith Hicks was born in Oldham and began his career as a central defender with his local club, Oldham Athletic, in 1971, moving to Hereford United in 1980 and to Rochdale in 1985. He then played non-league football with Hyde United, Mossley and Radcliffe Borough.

Interest in the scheme's potential was growing. A keen interest in what the community schemes might be likely to offer in the longer term was shown by **John Williams** from The University of Leicester. John wanted to explore the sociological aspects of the community scheme, especially in the early years in relation to how it may help to solve the issues of hooliganism in football (as a social problem).

A meeting with **Paul Robinson** from the Gateway Clubs (Mencap) in early 1987 led to football being made available to young people with learning difficulties for the first time at Bolton Road playing fields in Salford. This was ground-breaking work for the fledgling community scheme which represented the first organised footballing involvement for people with disabilities.

The start of February 1987 saw the first "review" meeting looking at how things in the community scheme were progressing. Club chairmen and secretaries were invited to attend a meeting which took place on the top floor of the PFA's plush new offices in Oxford Court, Manchester based to the south of the city centre (staff from the PFA and from the FFE&VTS had moved from the old office at the Corn Exchange in Manchester, located to the north end of the city centre near to Victoria Station, at the end of the previous year).

Close links were being successfully forged not just with club directors and staff but also with MSC and local Jobcentre personnel. Amongst those who were extremely supportive were:

- **Dorothy Livesey** (Blackburn Link Officer)
- **Carol Carless** (Bolton Job Centre)
- **John Conway** (Bury)
- **Manhur Ranhat** (Merseyside). Manhur was in close contact with scheme officials throughout the early operation of the Everton, Liverpool and Tranmere Rovers schemes.
- **Jill Saxon** (Oldham)
- **Doreen Mercer** (Preston Office Link Officer).

Doreen wrote to **Mickey Burns** in February 1987 to say:

> *"I was impressed by the enthusiasm shown by the participants, members of the public, officials and players of the club. All objectives of the scheme are being met and the success can be measured by the numbers of people involved in sporting activities, including a good percentage of people from ethnic groups, and the overwhelming number of letters of appreciation from the public."*

One phrase regularly used in conjunction with the Community Programme scheme is that it was always "ahead of the game". In later years, for example, the PL achieved significant success with the "*Kickz*" (later "*Kicks*") scheme that was established with the support of the Metropolitan Police. The Community Programme scheme, however, set up initial local meetings with Greater Manchester Police as far back as 1987 when police support was confirmed by Inspector **John Bateman**. Follow up support also followed from Lancashire Police.

Similarly, meetings were regularly held with **Bob Perkins** from the Association of Metropolitan Authorities (AMA) in order to explore the possibilities of working more closely with local authorities. Indeed, Liverpool City Council even managed to make contact about the scheme's expansion into Merseyside before either of the professional clubs.

For the very first time, and thanks to the generosity of the PFA, who were still the driving force behind the scheme's advancement, scheme officials were invited to attend the PFA's annual "Player of the Year" Awards Dinner held at the Grosvenor House Hotel in London in early April 1987.

The end of July 1987 saw a first ever women's match organised by the scheme between

Oldham Athletic and Bolton Wanderers which went ahead with the blessing of **Linda Whitehead**, the hard-working Secretary of the Women's Football Association (WFA). The WFA was formed following an upsurge in interest in the game from women and girls. In relation to the women's game, *Football Nation – Sixty Years of the Beautiful Game* (Ward and Williams) states:

> *"The World Cup (in 1966) stimulated women's interest in football but a great opportunity was missed had English grounds been more conducive to females, many more fans could have been cultivated. Instead the women's football revolution took another direction. More women started to play the game."*

Bolton Wanderers women's team also hosted a match against a Crewe Alexandra women's team soon after that. The following year (1988), matches between women's teams increased significantly – much to Linda's delight. Indeed, the Oldham Athletic women's team also hosted a team from Manchester City on Boundary Park's all-weather pitch (with a return match also arranged at the Platt Lane Training Ground).

Linda, in fact, was a keen supporter of the early embryonic scheme. Her view (quite rightly) was that the scheme could facilitate greater interest amongst young girls to play and to watch the game. The following year (1988), Linda took the decision to relocate the WFA to the Corn Exchange offices in Manchester, thereby bringing it closer to the fledgling 'Football and Community' scheme, and to the PFA and to the FFE&VTS as a whole. Linda worked for the Women's FA between 1980 and 1993 with a great deal of distinction. She was also voted *Sunday Times* Sportswoman 'Administrator of the Year' in 1989.

June 1987 saw **Brian Kidd** attend the FA's full badge course (then held at Lilleshall) which he was successful in securing. July saw an important football conference held at Keele University. In attendance was a particularly enthusiastic **Jimmy Hill,** who expressed his positive hopes for the future, which also included his strong support for the scheme going forwards. An ex-player with Brentford and Fulham between 1949 and 1960, Jimmy was also a former Chairman of the PFA and a leading light and Chairman of Coventry City when the club moved into prominence in the 1960's and 1970's.

The new 1987/88 football season kicked off at a time when the fledgling 'Football in the Community' scheme was beginning to make its mark in the football world. The Sports Council (now Sport England) generously pledged significant support to the scheme for the purchase of some short mat bowls mats (kindly 'housed' by Burnley Football Club in the short term) and minibuses. The capital purchase of three super new Vauxhall Midi minibuses was organised through **Jeff Ball**, Manager of a Manchester-based Vauxhall dealer, Syd Abrams. Whilst the purchase of the minibuses and mats saw little change from an original investment of approaching £50,000, it did prove to be successful in broadening the reach of the North West based community operations and in allowing regular transport of new football supporters (families and children) to football matches.

Another local supporter of the scheme was former Manchester City player **Fred Eyre**, owner of a Manchester-based stationery company. Fred Eyre Stationery and their staff **Beth** and **Jane** (not to forget Fred himself!) provided that reliable stationery support service throughout this early phase of the Community Programme scheme. Fred Eyre had been an apprentice footballer with Manchester City in the early 1960's, moving to Lincoln City and Bradford Park Avenue in later years.

The new season saw **Brian Kidd** appointed to a club coaching position at Manchester United. His departure also brought with it the decision made by Manchester United's Board of Directors to "shelve" their partnership with the FFE&VTS in community work. The United scheme was to finish once **Danny Healey** completed his full year in post as Full Time Activity Organiser in October 1987.

Manchester City's talented Activity Organiser, **Eugene "Gus" Wilson**, was also offered a contract to play professionally at Crewe Alexandra where he played for three years, making over 100 league appearances between 1991 and 1994.

One of the first Football Association (FA) Preliminary Coaching Courses exclusively for Community Officers was held at Preston North End's Deepdale ground between the 12th and 16th October 1987, when **Mick Wadsworth** (then working for the FA as a Regional Coach) was kind enough to offer to run the course. This followed an initial meeting in January of the same year when it was recognised that close working and support links with the FA could be beneficial for all concerned. Indeed, the first FA Preliminary Coaching course exclusively for Community Programme workers had been held in March 1987.

October 1987 also saw the three Midi minibuses make their respective "debuts" at a football match when some 40 or so young people were taken to a league match at Portman Road between Ipswich Town and Manchester City. The buses left Manchester at 7.00 a.m. and travelled in convoy to and from the match. Ipswich Town were generously supportive with tickets, and the whole day proved to be an unparalleled success, not least in encouraging new interest amongst the young people themselves, many of whom had never ever been to a football match in their lives.

The same month brought the scheme's first moves into ensuring that appropriate training for all community staff was "joined up" when the post of "Training Officer" was created and interviews held. **Kevin Jardine**, previously a part time Activity Organiser at Manchester City and a recent graduate, had proved himself to be extremely capable and a worthy successful candidate. Kevin took up his new role in November 1987.

The end of October 1987 saw many of the clubs organising "soccer schools" (or "soccer camps") during the school half-term. Numbers of attendees were high, even more so as the courses were offered on a "turn up and play" basis at no cost whatsoever to the participants (Football in the Community schemes in these early days were under instructions not to charge at any of their activities in order to ensure that no-one was turned away because of the cost.)

Christmas 1987, and the New Year in 1988, heralded a fresh impetus in terms of the growing status of a community scheme that most people felt would ultimately move towards becoming nationwide across the whole of the FL. As an example, even at this early stage, representatives of sports retailer, Puma, recognised the early potential of a link with the scheme. Led by **Ian "Spider" Mellor** and ably assisted by **Dorothy** and **Vera**, Puma put down a marker for their future interest in working alongside the scheme, once it reached a certain number of clubs, by offering their support with kit and equipment as required.

Ian Mellor began his league career as a left winger at Manchester City who he joined having once been a postman. He moved on to Norwich City in 1973 before later moves to Brighton and Hove Albion, Chester, Sheffield Wednesday and Bradford City.

As a gesture of goodwill, Puma also kindly donated a full kit (in England colours) for the blossoming charity team put together for certain matches comprising many well-known former professional footballers. The first ever Community Scheme charity match took place at Salford's Albert Park against a police representative XI. The match even saw "Spider" himself make an appearance for the team. Further matches also took place, for example, against Greater Manchester Transport, British Airways and the Stockport and Cheadle Sunday League, later in the season. Additional charity matches were held at Glossop and at Crewe Alexandra. All funds raised were donated to local charities.

The scheme was also becoming more and more high profile. Granada Television presenter and music entrepreneur, **Tony Wilson,** "fronted" a short promotional video kindly put together by experienced photographer/film and movie maker **Richard Cooper** from a film company called Photoflex. The video featured community action from all six of the pilot club schemes and saw Tony himself come up with the closing line about the scheme's work:

"doing good for people, doing good for the community and doing good for football."

Other meetings with long term 'Football and the Community' supporters were held during the season. The first was with **Brian Lee** (at the time connected with the then Non-League Wycombe Wanderers Football Club and later to become a successful, popular and influential

Chairman of the National League) who wrote the first book about football and the community called "*Twin Strikers*". This was a well-researched and well written account of how the original community schemes had got underway, and what important work was being delivered. Brian announced in his book that Football in the Community schemes,

"may well be the only route to survival for the future of clubs."

Brian also highlighted that Football in the Community schemes were,

"uncoordinated from the FA and Football League point of view and a coordinated national approach would be in the best interest of the game, the clubs and the communities."

A meeting with **Gerry Stewart** and **John Sutherland** was positive as they agreed to undertake the first important and factually recorded research into the community scheme. This was an important milestone, and there would be plenty more research undertaken as the scheme grew.

The 1987/88 season also saw an important "review" meeting with **Lynda Bloomfield** and **Pat Buckmaster** from the MSC at Manchester City so that a 'flavour' of the successful work being delivered could be seen. The meeting was aimed at reviewing what was felt to be a rapid expansion of the scheme to set up community schemes at so many professional clubs so swiftly. The meeting also endorsed the idea of a further expansion into the Yorkshire and Humberside area when MSC officials stated that they were genuinely delighted with the success of the scheme so far.

The proposed further expansion into other football "hot-bed" areas of Yorkshire and the North East made a great deal of sense not only for football and for the clubs in these areas, but also for MSC who were conscious of the issues of unemployment and the demand for re-training opportunities for many people. This was especially so in the towns where the closure of the pits had seen a profound impact on local working populations (e.g. in South Yorkshire).

To facilitate the expansion into Yorkshire and the North East, it was agreed with the MSC at an early stage that Football's Community Programme staffing structure would have to change to accommodate regional support offices aimed at facilitating the continued growth of the programme. This meant that "Regional Managers" and "Assistant Regional Managers" would soon be required either side of the Pennines.

The first regional office was established on Queen Street in Barnsley, South Yorkshire. This was selected because it was central to the newly defined Yorkshire and the North East region (and comparatively inexpensive!) Furniture was ordered and a regional office telephone was installed early in November.

The appointments east of the Pennines were straight forward. **Richard Finney** had proved to be a more than interested person in the future expansion of the Community Programme scheme following his original application for the post of General Administrator in 1986, and, given his knowledge of the game and his background in the Yorkshire and North East area, it was agreed that he was the ideal candidate to take on the senior role of Regional Manager. Richard said at the time:

"I was obviously thrilled to be offered the opportunity to become part of the management team that would develop and expand the Football in the Community scheme. Opening the door to the empty room in Barnsley that would become the first base, the first regional office for the 30 or so club projects on the Eastern side of the country from Newcastle to Peterborough and across to Norwich, was exciting"

His assistant was well known in Yorkshire and continued to play football on a part time basis for some time following his appointment. **Ray McHale** proved to be an excellent choice given his knowledge and enthusiasm for supporting the expansion of the scheme in the East.

Sheffield-born Ray began his league career with nearby Chesterfield in 1971 where he made 123 league appearances in a three-year spell. He then played for Halifax Town, Swindon Town, Brighton and Hove Albion, Barnsley, Sheffield United, Bury (on loan), Swansea City, Rochdale and Scarborough.

Full briefings and an induction were held with Richard and Ray in October 1987 even though they eventually took up their appointments officially on the 2nd November 1987. They were quickly "off the mark" with meetings arranged with clubs across South Yorkshire (to run through the criteria). Many would-be-officers were already waiting in the wings ready to take up their new roles at clubs. Richard and Ray were also supported by two administrative assistants recruited under the Community Programme scheme.

With the benefit of hindsight, it is easy to say that the introduction and establishment of inter-schools competitive small sided tournaments was an important and positive step forward for the Football in the Community scheme at this time. Not only did the involvement of local professional clubs encourage and stimulate the involvement of huge numbers of Primary and Junior Schools (and, in later years, Secondary Schools), but it also led to a guaranteed opportunity for the finalists to play at Wembley (or at Cardiff's national stadium whilst the new Wembley was being built). The chance for school children to play in a national tournament and to play at either Wembley or the Millennium Stadium in Cardiff was, of course, simply awesome!

The first tournament came about entirely due to the support and encouragement of officials at the Football League and linked in closely, in the case of the initial tournament for sure, with sponsors Guinness. Unfortunately, some local community projects were already extremely busy delivering activities, meaning that total support for this brand-new concept was somewhat restricted. In future years, however, the realisation dawned on most Community Officers that participation in the national competition was an opportunity to stimulate interest from people in local areas. In addition, and as **Richard Finney** outlined:

> *"What was always important in the national six-a-side competitions was that children, teachers and parents all had a positive experience. In the final stages of tournaments at regional finals and the grand final, before the games started, we spoke to the children and teachers explaining that at the end of the games it was important for the children to 'win modestly and lose graciously' and always shake hands with the match officials and players from the opposing team at the end of the games"*

The Guinness competition was eventually first staged in December at the Greater Manchester Exhibition Centre (or GMEX, previously Manchester's Central Railway Station, now called the Manchester Central Convention Complex) in 1987. This became the forerunner for the extremely successful national six-a-side competitions that would be run every season. Whilst only North West club community schemes took part in this inaugural tournament, the success of the competition was directly responsible for and led to the swift growth of the competition across the country. Many thanks were also extended to **Dave Bell** and **Billy Margetts** for kindly refereeing all matches in the first Competition.

Between 1987 and 1990, the competition was open only to FFE&VTS-supported Community Programme schemes (mainly in the North and some in the Midlands), so it could be argued that these competitions weren't in fact fully national, even though increasing numbers of schools and clubs took part each year.

In advance of the next phase of growth of the Community Programme itself, various meetings were also established with MSC officials in and around the Yorkshire area regarding developments east of the Pennines:

- **Ron Mason** and **John Lucas** (Sheffield)
- **Richard Atack**, **David Gibson** and **Lynn Heyes** (Barnsley)
- **Jenny Scott** (Grimsby)
- **Carol Bradburn** (Hull)

- **Angela Dobson**, **Trevor Ellis** and **Marion Stevenson** (Bradford)

These meetings were obviously important in terms of ensuring that the Community Programme requirements were met. So, the next significant phase of expansion into Yorkshire and then into the North East of England, saw the following clubs establish community projects: Barnsley, Bradford City, Doncaster Rovers, Grimsby Town, Halifax Town, Huddersfield Town, Hull City, Leeds United, Rotherham United, Scunthorpe United, Sheffield United and Sheffield Wednesday (all were underway early in 1988). Initial approaches were also made to the North East clubs, Darlington, Hartlepool United, Middlesbrough, Newcastle United and Sunderland (four out of these five projects got underway later in the year).

Appropriate meetings were established with interested club officials including:

- **Mike Spinks** (Secretary) at Barnsley.
- **Terry Newman** (Secretary) at Bradford City, with a further meeting, at the club's request, with **Howell Williams** and **Martin Hunter** from Bradford City Council in view of the close links between the club and the Local Authority.
- **Dave Mackay** (Manager) and later **Bernie Boldry** (Chairman) and **Joan Oldale** (Secretary) at Doncaster Rovers.
- **Ian Fleming** (Secretary) and, later, **Peter Furneaux** (Chairman), **Brian Glover** (Associate Director) and **Tom Lindley** (Managing Director) Grimsby Town.
- **Billy Ayre** (Manager) and **Carol Bell** (Club Secretary) at Halifax Town, plus a further meeting with **Dr Mike Blanch**, **Graham Nash**, **Raymond Attiwell** and **Rod Thomas,** all of whom represented the Local Authority who, uniquely, had taken a key stake holding in the club.
- **George Binns** (Secretary) and **Keith Hanvey** (Commercial Executive) at Huddersfield Town.
- **Christopher Needler** (Chairman) at Hull City.
- **David Dowse** (Secretary) Leeds United and, later, **Bill Fotherby** (Managing Director), **Nigel Pleasants** (Secretary) and **Alan Roberts** (Safety Officer).
- **Norman Darnill** (Secretary) at Rotherham United.
- **Don Rowing** (Secretary) at Scunthorpe United.
- **Dave Capper** (Secretary) and **Andy Daykin** (Marketing Executive) at Sheffield United
- **David Richards** (Chairman. He would later become Chairman of the PL and, later still, Sir David Richards) and **Graham Mackrell** (Secretary) at Sheffield Wednesday.

Many of these meetings, of course, were arranged, and involved, the new Yorkshire Regional Managers **Richard Finney** and **Ray McHale**.

The first appointed officers in the East were **Derrick Parker** and **Eric McManus**. **Derrick Parker** was appointed as Supervisor of affairs at Barnsley and Doncaster Rovers. Derrick was a product of the Wallsend Boys Club, beginning his league career as an apprentice with Burnley, although after playing only a few games for the club he moved to Southend United in 1977 where he became a regular first team choice. He then moved to Barnsley, Oldham Athletic and Doncaster Rovers (on loan) before returning to Burnley. He finished his career in England with Rochdale following which he spent a short spell in Finland with Haka Valkeakoski.

Eric McManus was appointed to oversee things at Bradford City and Leeds United. Eric was born in Northern Ireland and began his league career with Coventry City following a move from Coleraine. He then moved to Notts County in 1972 where he spent the next seven years. He then moved to Stoke City and Lincoln City (on loan) before a lengthy spell with Bradford City. He also enjoyed short loan spells at Middlesbrough and Peterborough United before finishing his playing career at Tranmere Rovers.

Derrick and Eric were the first officers to be appointed in Yorkshire, taking up their new duties on the 1st February 1988.

Former Rotherham United centre back **Tommy Spencer** was soon chosen to oversee the community projects at Rotherham United and Sheffield United. Glasgow-born, Tommy Spencer made his league debut for Southampton as a striker in 1965 before converting to become a central defender. He later moved to York City, Workington, Lincoln City and Rotherham United where he finished his league career in 1978.

Sheffield-born **Charlie Williamson** took up the reigns as Supervisor overseeing developments at Sheffield Wednesday and Scunthorpe United. Charlie's playing career began as an apprentice with Sheffield Wednesday before loan moves to Lincoln City and Southend United, finally moving to Chesterfield where he played between 1985-1987.

Former Scotland international, **Jim McCalliog**, became overseeing supervisor of the Halifax Town and Huddersfield Town community projects. In a hugely successful playing career, Jim played for several clubs starting at Chelsea in 1963. He then made 150 league appearances for Sheffield Wednesday during a four-year spell before moves to Wolverhampton Wanderers, Manchester United and Southampton (also playing for Chicago Sting in the USA) before finishing his playing career with Lincoln City in 1979. Jim was also a Scottish international.

At the clubs, well known former players such as **Dave Wilkes** (Barnsley), **Willie Boyd** (Doncaster Rovers), **Bobby Mitchell** (Grimsby Town), **Dick Krzywicki** (Huddersfield Town), **Cyril "Ces" Podd** (Leeds United), **Ian "Chico" Hamilton** (Rotherham United), **John Dungworth** (John left on 30th June 1989 in order to take up the post of Youth Team Coach at Sheffield United) and, later, **Steve Cammack** at Scunthorpe United (Steve was appointed just before John Dungworth's departure in June 1989). Also appointed as full time Activity Organisers were **Tony Currie** (Sheffield United) and **Steve Adams** (Sheffield Wednesday).

Dave Wilkes was born in Barnsley and played for his local club side between 1981-1984 despite suffering injury problems, going on to play briefly for Halifax Town (on loan), Stockport County, Harps and Carlisle United in the league, though he also spent short spells with several non-league clubs such as Frickley Athletic, Guiseley and Bridlington.

Born in Bellshill, Glasgow, **Willie Boyd** won international recognition as a schoolboy footballer and as a former Scottish youth international goalkeeper. He made his debut for Doncaster Rovers in 1980 against Peterborough United and helped Rovers to win promotion to the then Third Division in 1981. Willie was forced to retire from playing due to a knee injury in 1983.

Bobby Mitchell was born in South Shields and began his playing career as an apprentice at Sunderland before moving to Blackburn Rovers in 1976. He then moved to Grimsby Town in 1978 where he played for the next four years. He also played for Carlisle United, Rotherham United and Lincoln City before spending a year with Maltese side Hamrun.

Born in Penley, **Dick Krzywicki** began his career as an apprentice with West Bromwich Albion where he made his debut before moving to Huddersfield Town in 1970. He played briefly on loan at Scunthorpe United and Northampton Town before moving to Lincoln City in 1974. Dick was also a full international with Wales with whom he made his debut in 1969.

Cyril "Ces" Podd made just under 500 league appearances for Bradford City between 1970 and 1984 before moving to Halifax Town. He also moved to Scarborough with whom he secured promotion to the Football League in 1987. He later went on to manage the St Kitts and Nevis national team between 1999-2002.

Born in Streatham, **Ian "Chico" Hamilton** began his career as an apprentice with Chelsea before moving to Southend United. The nickname, 'Chico', came from the well-known American jazz drummer and bandleader. Arguably Ian's most successful period as a player was whilst he was with Aston Villa where he helped the club to become champions of the Third Division in 1971/72 and where he appeared in two League Cup Finals, losing one (against Tottenham Hotspur in 1971) and winning one (against Norwich City in 1975). He also played for Sheffield United, finishing his playing career in the USA with Minnesota Kicks and San Jose Earthquakes.

John Dungworth was born in Rotherham and began his playing career as an apprentice with Huddersfield Town, making his debut for the club in 1972. He then went on to play for several clubs including Barnsley (on loan), Oldham Athletic, Rochdale (on loan), Aldershot, Shrewsbury Town, Hereford United (on loan) and Mansfield Town before finishing his career, as a central defender, with his home town club, Rotherham United. Later in his career he would also become Youth Team Coach at Sheffield United, also coaching at Leeds United, Huddersfield

Town and Sheffield Wednesday.

Born in Sheffield, **Steve Cammack** began his career as an apprentice with Sheffield United before moving to nearby Chesterfield. He then made a name for himself by scoring goals-a-plenty whilst with Scunthorpe United in two separate spells between 1979-1980 and 1981-86. He also played briefly for Lincoln City in 1981-82 and had short loan spells with Port Vale and Stockport County.

Tony Currie was born in Edgware, North London and joined Watford as an apprentice. He moved to Sheffield United in February 1968, scoring on his debut and going on to become the club's greatest ever player. He played for the Blades between 1968-76 before later moves took him to Leeds United, Queens Park Rangers and Torquay United. He was also capped for England on 17 occasions.

Born in Sheffield, **Steve Adams** spent most of his playing career in non-league football, though he also played professionally for Scarborough and Doncaster Rovers whilst they were both in the Football League. Later on he set up his own coaching business entitled "Tricky Wingers". Steve very sadly passed away on the 3rd March 2017.

Richard Finney commented at the time:

> *"Football in the Community provided an ideal opportunity for ex-professional footballers to give something back to the game"*

Tony Currie went further than that. "TC" (as he is almost always known) said about his appointment as a Community Officer, having tried various other career opportunities after his playing career had ended:

> *"It may be an exaggeration to say that it saved my life but there's no doubt it was a life saver... I wasn't qualified to do anything. I'd been out of the game for five years. I didn't have any coaching badges. I was just feeling very sorry for myself. This really did put me back on my feet."*

Swift progress in Yorkshire, particularly in relation to the establishment of the Yorkshire-based regional support office, meant that it was essential for a North West regional office to be established. Consequently, interviews were held for the post of North West "Regional Administrator" early in January 1988. **Graham Gill** was appointed to the newly created post based on his previous administrative experience and, of course, his direct experience of the Community Programme scheme as an Activity Organiser at Bolton Wanderers. Graham took over a new office based in the Corn Exchange in Manchester (where the very first Community Programme office had originally been first established in 1986). Graham's assistant was the well-known and popular ex-Welsh international footballer, **Brian Flynn**, who had done such a great job as Community Officer at Burnley and who very ably continued to combine his duties with a highly successful playing career.

The new set up in having regional operations either side of the Pennines also meant that regular weekly meetings of officers and supervisors could be held on a regional basis (usually on Fridays).

One meeting of Yorkshire-based Supervisors held at Doncaster Rovers former ground at Belle Vue saw a certain Supervisor manage to firmly wedge his scheme minibus under the iron entrance gateway to the Belle Vue car park, an incident that was witnessed by virtually all the other Yorkshire Supervisors who then, understandably, spent most of the meeting laughing about what they had just witnessed. Said Supervisor was also unsure as to how to remove the minibus from the gateway (especially as it was blocking access to the club's car park for other users) until one other Supervisor wisely suggested to him that he should simply let some of the air out of his tyres (which worked a treat!).

As already mentioned, approaches were made to the five North East based professional clubs in February 1988, following local approaches to MSC officials in the North East including:

- **Jan Scott** and **Dave McClelland** (Darlington)

- **Bob Little** and, separately, **Carole Wright** (Hartlepool)
- **Roy Brown** (Middlesbrough)
- **Terry Cahe** (Newcastle)
- **Jules Preston** (Sunderland)

Following on from these meetings, included amongst those club representatives seen in the early meetings with the North East clubs were:

- **Alan Heaton** (Chairman) at Darlington
- **Malcolm Kirby** (Secretary) at Hartlepool United
- **Tom Hughes** (Secretary) and, later, **Keith Lamb** (Chief Executive/Secretary) and **Jack Ord** at Middlesbrough
- **Russell Cushing** (Chief Executive) at Newcastle United. The initial meeting with Russell led to the whole idea of Newcastle's potential involvement in the scheme being endorsed at a Board of Directors meeting in July 1988.
- **Alec King** (Commercial Director) and **Geoff Davidson** (General Manager/Club Secretary) at Sunderland. Interestingly enough, Sunderland Club Chairman **Bob Murray** also paid early attention to the idea of supporting the development (and growth) of the club's community scheme. Bob's involvement and support would ultimately lead in later years to Sunderland's community scheme receiving much wider recognition both for the club and for Bob himself.

CHAPTER 4
'EMPLOYMENT TRAINING' AND FURTHER GROWTH

IT BECAME VERY CLEAR, in the spring of 1988, that the Government's "Community Programme" initiative was to change. Having met with such unprecedented success in the football-based programme, scheme officials were more than a little disappointed to discover that the Government's Community Programme venture had not been as successful elsewhere as the football-based Community Programme scheme. That said, it was replaced by a new programme entitled (appropriately enough) "Employment Training" ("ET"). The new programme was launched simultaneously in the North West at Manchester University; in Yorkshire in Bradford and in Scunthorpe on the 1st September 1988. Details were first flagged up at a meeting with **Chris Curry** and **Eric Finch** from the MSC and saw the announcement of completely new and very different criteria which had to be adapted to all the existing football club projects.

The fundamental change was for participants in the scheme (the longer term unemployed) to be offered training and qualifications. In other words, the emphasis would move towards participants gaining recognisable training qualifications rather than purely work experience.

As a former teacher himself, **Mickey Burns** delivered the first ever Community Sports Leaders Award course in Bolton for community officers at the start of the year in 1988. Opportunities would also present themselves for participants to join pre-existing training opportunities where youth trainees were already attending courses around the country. Amongst the training courses provided for Community Officers and trainees alike were:

-    FA Preliminary, Intermediate and Advanced (Full Badge) Coaching Certificate courses.
-    National Examination Board Supervisory Management courses (in recreation and leisure).
-    City & Guilds Recreation and Leisure courses (parts I and II).
-    City & Guilds Adult Trainers Award courses.
-    Central Council for Physical Recreation Community Sports Leadership awards.
-    St. John Ambulance First Aid courses (and/or alternative first aid courses – e.g. Red Cross, St Andrews).
-    Royal Life Saving Society Bronze Medallion courses and Resuscitation Awards courses.
-    Other sports courses (e.g. Basketball, Volleyball, Canoeing etc.)

Access to these courses was important, of course, as many former players joined the scheme without any qualifications at all. As **Richard Finney** explained:

> *"The management team knew that many of the officers being ex-players would not have many qualifications, educational or sporting, so it was important to provide the opportunity to gain relevant qualifications. For example, working with the FA, officers were encouraged to take the FA Preliminary Coaching qualification and then move on to the FA Full Badge."*

Job search training was also included as part of the original Community Programme scheme. This embraced job interview techniques, the completion of Curriculum Vitaes (CVs), how to write to apply for vacant job posts etc.

Kath Boullen (in later years Kath would receive an MBE for her work as Chief Executive of St Helens Chamber) was a key figure supporting the Community Programme's moves into ET. She was one of the Senior Managers working under **John Ainsworth** at the Large Companies

Unit at the former office on Matilda Street in Sheffield. She recalls:

> *"Following the Community Programme scheme, the Government needed a new, bigger programme to cope with increasing unemployment, together with less cost. Employment Training 'fitted the bill' and was duly introduced, even though it didn't really fit with many providers. In view of the success of the Community Programme in professional football, coupled with its high profile, it meant that there was a strong desire to make it work."*

One of the main "ground breakers", **Pat Howard,** left the scheme in August 1988 in order to take up a new position as Football Development Officer with Salford Council. This was an important move at the time, firstly as it confirmed that, even at supervisor level, there was still a general feeling of a lack of long-term employment security for these positions. Secondly, it showed that with genuine work experience gained, high ranking positions elsewhere were attainable by Community Officers.

Mickey Burns said of this important development (and the departure of **Brian Kidd** to join Manchester United in a coaching capacity the previous year):

> *"I welcomed the fact that Pat, and Brian the previous year, had taken the opportunity to move into better/more important posts as these represented positive outcomes for us. This not only underlined the fact that we could be successful in providing the relevant work experience for people to move on to other roles but it also then provided additional opportunities for former players to potentially come into the roles they had vacated."*

Dennis Leman, quoted in the PFA's "Celebrating 30 years of the PFA's Community Programme", said:

> *"We always felt the community scheme could be a stepping-stone for players to take on more challenges once their playing days were over. That was part of the plan, to up-skill them. It has been a real success."*

Purely for the record, another officer who made a key contribution to the scheme's success, particularly towards the growth of the female game at Manchester City as a coach, **Neil Mather**, also left just before the turn of the year.

On March 27th, 1988, the FL were generous enough to offer the scheme the opportunity to put on a display on the pitch at Wembley as part of the pre-match entertainment at the Simod Cup Final between Reading and Luton Town (which Reading won 4-1). What happened was that all twenty participating clubs at the time, including the fledgling Yorkshire clubs, were invited to take part in a co-ordinated coaching display on the Wembley pitch. Six local children from each club were invited and transported to Wembley using the fleet of minibuses (the fleet had now reached a total of 10 thanks to further support generously provided by the Sports Council). The coaching display was put together and coordinated by **Andy Welsh**.

On pitch, all children wore their local club colours and took part in a display that was soundly 'choreographed' (from an on-lookers perspective) and very well organised. This also saw the first national event coordinated by scheme officials, headed up by someone who over the years became something of an expert in the field of "event management", **Richard Finney**.

May 1988 saw steps taken by the Football Trust to introduce their first "Community Awards" (or "Centenary Awards" as they were to be referred to) during season 1988/89. The first meeting was held at the Waldorf Hotel and saw regular panel meetings introduced to consider the awards. It was very strongly felt that the Football Trust should take a lead and introduce worthwhile community awards to stimulate and encourage clubs to play greater roles in their local communities and to recognise and reward those clubs that were 100% behind the principle of community engagement.

It was agreed that clubs that were genuine about their community involvement should again be recognised and rewarded. Prize money set aside of £125,000 would cover what would be 4 Divisional winners awards (£20,000 each) and 8 runners up awards (£5,000 each. An additional £5,000 would also be set aside to cover the costs of awards and trophies). The first overall Football Trust Community Awards Scheme winners (awarded at the end of the 1988/89 season) were Millwall and Preston North End. The winners (announced in 1989) were:

	FL DIVISION ONE	FL DIVISION TWO	FL DIVISION THREE	FL DIVISION FOUR
Winners	Millwall	Manchester City Watford	Preston NE	Crewe Alexandra
Special Commendation	Arsenal			
Commendations	Aston Villa Derby County Sheffield W Southampton	Bradford City Leeds United Oldham Ath.	Brentford Reading Sheffield United	Colchester U Doncaster R Grimsby T Tranmere R
Other Entries	Coventry City Everton Liverpool Luton Town Newcastle Utd Norwich City Nottingham F Queens Park R Tottenham H West Ham Utd	Barnsley Bournemouth Crystal Palace Ipswich Town Leicester City Oxford United Portsmouth Shrewsbury T Stoke City Sunderland Swindon T Walsall	Blackpool Bolton Wanderers Bristol R Bury Huddersfield T Notts County Port Vale Southend U	Burnley Exeter City Halifax Town Rochdale Rotherham U Scarborough Scunthorpe U

There was also a very special personal award made to **Mick Baxter** (Preston North End).

The summer of 1988 saw the commencement of the Port Vale Community Programme following discussions with club representatives (including **Derek Barber** and **Andy Waterhouse**) when former goalkeeper **Alex Williams** was appointed as the club's first ever Community Officer. Born in Manchester, Alex was "understudy" to Manchester City goalkeeper Joe Corrigan before establishing himself as a first team regular between 1980 and 1986, helping City to secure promotion to the First Division at the end of the 1984/85 season. He then spent brief spells with Queen of the South and Port Vale before retiring from the game as a player in the autumn of 1987 due to injury.

The brief experience gained by Alex at Port Vale set him up for his later appointment as Community Officer at his beloved Manchester City a year or so later, where he would be gainfully employed over many years and where he would receive an MBE for services to the community and young people in 2001/2.

The new 1988/89 season started with 28 community projects live and active. There were also clear plans to continue the growth into the Midlands with additional clubs who hadn't already been approached in the North to be added as their interest was confirmed.

Senior officers, plus several Community Officers, were encouraged to attend a dedicated City and Guilds Adult Trainers Award course held in Frodsham in Cheshire and led by an inspirational tutor in **Colin Hendry** (not to be confused with the former Blackburn Rovers player). The highly successful course was held over several weeks between July and October

1988. This was an important step for the FFE&VTS Community Programme not just because of the cost (it was expensive) but also as it was a clear sign of its commitment to ensure that officers were properly and appropriately qualified.

Further meetings with would-be new clubs continued – e.g. with Carlisle United (**Gordon Butterfield, Alison Moore** and, later, **Clive Middlemass**, Club Manager at the time. Board approval for the scheme was eventually forthcoming in February 1989) and Stockport County (Secretary, **Terry McCreery** and **John Simpson**).

September 1988 also saw the Sir Norman Chester Centre for Football Research at Leicester University, led by **Eric Dunning** and **John Williams** and ably supported by **Janet Tiernan**, organise a football dedicated conference entitled "*Football into the 1990's*". **Mickey Burns** and **Roger Reade** were invited to speak on behalf of the scheme at the conference about the potential hopes and aspirations for "Football in the Community" and the achievements to date.

In terms of activities, some of the pioneering six North West community schemes that were established in 1986 were starting to develop and expand their community involvement. Manchester City's well-respected Community Scheme, for example, staged three separate successful community nights at City's Social Club on Maine Road which saw different parts of the community engaged. Firstly, there was a "Ladies Presentation Night" for the female players who took part in the women's 5-a-side competition held at the Platt Lane Training Complex on the 5th September. This was a huge success with lots of women attending who had never played football at all before. Next up was a social evening "Trivia Quiz" for people living near the ground at Maine Road. Finally, there was a commercially driven "Sportsman's Dinner" aimed at raising funds for the club's community scheme.

Memorably, on one of these Social occasions, one of the City community scheme's coaching staff, **Ian Lees**, went on stage to tell the audience more about City's community work, describing it as:

"a scheme that teaches little kids how to dribble"

Plans to support the expansion of the scheme continued towards the end of the year as new projects were considered and separate meetings with MSC staff were held, including meetings with **John Thompson** (Workington office) following up on the interest shown by officials from Carlisle United, which looked at the possibility of establishing a new scheme at Brunton Park, and **Graham Smith** (Stoke office) also following up on Stoke City's interest in joining the scheme.

Employment Training (ET) was officially underway with effect from the 4th September 1988. In order to help boost the promotion of the new Government scheme, the newly established Training Commission chose to sponsor a couple of football matches. First up was the Newcastle United versus Coventry City fixture on the 8th October, followed by the Hartlepool United versus Grimsby Town match on the 12th November. Both matches heralded the launch in the North East of the new club-based community initiatives. As a new venture, ET brought with it much needed funding to continue to help propel the expansion of the community scheme, but it also brought with it a whole new way of doing things. The new forms alone took some getting used to!

Records show that the new ET2 and ET9 forms were causing problems simply by regularly going missing! The demands of the new scheme were also noted to be considerably greater than the previous 'Community Programme' scheme. Amongst other things, additional requirements included the need for formal and individual development plans, training information and action plans for all trainees which outlined their planned training programme during their stay with club schemes.

One issue that **Mickey Burns** was particularly aware of, when formulating the new scheme, was the lack of community accessible facilities at football grounds. His view was that facilities such as the creation of changing rooms and all-weather turf pitches would not only encourage more people (participants) to play the game but also encourage them to feel completely comfortable about visiting football grounds and to create new employment opportunities. Indeed, this became part of the new Football Trust funded initiative that got underway in the early 1990s (see later). As such, the launch of Bolton Wanderers new "kick about area" at Burnden Park (on the opposite side of the ground to the main stand but still easily accessible by the local community) in November 1988 provided much inspiration for the future.

Following his house move from Brighton to his native North East, **Mick Ferguson** took up his new supervisory duties, looking after the projects at Newcastle United and Sunderland at this time.

Beginning his career with Coventry City, Mick scored an average of just under a goal every two games during his first spell at Highfield Road, later moving to Everton and Birmingham City (initially on loan) before returning to his first club on loan in 1984. He finished his career with spells at Brighton and Hove Albion and Colchester United.

Jeff Cook also took up his new duties as supervisor, overseeing the more southerly North East club projects at Darlington and Hartlepool. A native of Hartlepool, Jeff played for South African side Hellenic (where the coach was former Stoke City player **George Eastham**) between 1975-1977 before being brought back to England by Eastham to play for Stoke City. After loan spells with Bradford City and then Plymouth Argyle (where the move became permanent), he moved to Halifax Town where he played between 1983-1985.

Newcastle United's new Activity Officer (soon to be confirmed as "Community Officer") was **Jeff Clarke**, who commenced his new duties in early October 1988 when he secured the FA Preliminary Coaching Award. Born in Hemsworth, Yorkshire, Jeff's career began with Manchester City before he moved to Sunderland as part of the deal that took Dave Watson to City. He made just under 180 full league appearances for the club over a seven-year period before moving to North East rivals Newcastle United in 1982. He also served Newcastle well, making over 120 league appearances between 1982-1986.

Tony McAndrew took up the role of Full Time Activity Officer at Darlington (briefly). Glasgow-born Tony began his football career as a central defender with Middlesbrough where he made 245 full appearances up to 1982 before moving to Chelsea. He re-signed for 'Boro in 1984 making a further 66 league appearances. He then enjoyed brief spells with Darlington and Hartlepool United.

Vic Ferguson was also appointed at Hartlepool United. The legendary former Newcastle and Sunderland striker **Bryan 'Pop' Robson** was also at one point a contender for the Sunderland full time post. Bryan "Pop" Robson enjoyed a wonderful career with several clubs and most memorably with Newcastle United between 1964 and 1970. He also played for West Ham United (twice), Sunderland (three spells), Carlisle United (twice) and Chelsea.

The proposed Middlesbrough project was put 'on hold' on a temporary basis following a meeting held in November that involved **Gordon Bates** from the Training Commission and **Keith Lamb**, **Colin Henderson**, **Tom Hughes** and Manager **Bruce Rioch** from the football club. This wasn't a major issue other than the unused places allocated under ET had to be returned (a few months later in February 1989) to the Cleveland office for use by another training provider.

At this point in time, the introduction of new club-based schemes across the North and Midlands had moved at a terrific pace with new Community Officers, local Training Commission staff and senior Community Programme Officers generally forming very positive working relationships to help individual local schemes move forwards. Inevitably along the way, however, there were occasional difficulties concerning how best each local scheme could fulfil all the varying needs and requirements of clubs, the Training Commission, the FFE&VTS Community Programme and those of the local community. One Training Commission Officer, **Jane Kitching**, who oversaw schemes at Grimsby Town and Scunthorpe United, was particularly helpful following certain difficulties that had arisen in late 1988 concerning the scheme at Grimsby. Indeed, it is fair to say that Jane's positive input, help and guidance was very much appreciated at the time and helped to smooth things over for all concerned.

Other new appointments during late 1988 included **Brian Taylor** as Community Officer at Burnley and **Eric Randerson** as Community Officer at Doncaster Rovers.

Brian Taylor began his career with Middlesbrough as an apprentice, going on to make 18 league appearances before moving to Doncaster Rovers in 1975. He then moved to Rochdale in 1978 where he served the club for a period of five years making over 150 league appearances.

John Hudson also started work as an activity assistant at Manchester City's Community Programme in December 1988. (In later years, John would become a Regional Director and, much later, leader of the PFA's Community Operations). Middleton-born, John was an apprentice at Manchester City who moved to Oldham Athletic where he made his name as a full back whilst **Joe Royle** was Manager. He moved to Rochdale during 1986/87 and was only prevented from a longer career in the game due to a serious knee injury.

At this point, changes were introduced to the staff structure which meant that supervisors previously overseeing two clubs were now re-allocated to manage one club only. Inevitably, this did lead to some officers being slightly uncertain about the future following their respective moves. Looking back, however, it is very much to the credit of those officers affected that the clear majority acted so positively in agreeing to the change. Indeed, **Mickey Burns** was particularly praiseworthy for the fact that officers in post at the time were so flexible, willing and open to change:

> *"The passion and enthusiasm shown by all the Community Programme staff was what carried us through those uncertain times. Without this clear commitment and enthusiasm, I seriously doubt whether the scheme would have been as successful as it clearly was in the end."*

These changes now allowed for one dedicated community officer at each club. So, for example, moving from the post of Supervisor overseeing two separate club schemes were:

- **Eric McManus,** who took up the new post at Bradford City
- **Kevin Reeves,** who took up the new post at Crewe Alexandra. Kevin began his playing career as an apprentice with Bournemouth, going on to make over 60 appearances for the club before moving to Norwich City. After a successful spell with the Canaries, he then moved to Manchester City in a big-money transfer in 1980. Sadly, he was forced to retire from the game whilst with Burnley in 1984 due to a hip injury. He also played for England at Under 21, "B" and full international level. After leaving the Community Programme, Kevin worked in the professional game with Wrexham, Swansea City, Stoke City, Wigan Athletic and as Chief Scout at Everton.
- **Jim McCalliog,** who took up the new post at Halifax Town.
- **Jeff Cook,** who took up the new post at Hartlepool United.
- **Mick Ferguson,** who took up the new post at Sunderland.

The new structure was as follows:

BOARD OF DIRECTORS
(FA, FL AND PFA ALL REPRESENTED ON THE BOARD OF THE FFE&VTS)

CHIEF EXECUTIVE

CHIEF ADMINISTRATOR (PLUS DEPUTY AND TRAINING OFFICER)

REGIONAL MANAGERS

COMMUNITY OFFICERS (1 AT EACH CLUB)

TRAINEES (AVERAGE OF 10 AT EACH CLUB)

The adoption of the new structure also saw the appointment of **Dennis Leman** as "Deputy Chief Administrator". Dennis went on to do a terrific job over many years, working across many different aspects of the FFE&VTS Community Programme and taking responsibility for specific projects along the way. **Tommy Spencer** also took on the role of working alongside Training Officer, **Kevin Jardine**.

Christmas 1988 brought with it the payment of "Christmas bonuses" for all Community Officers for the first time. Incredibly, given the nature of the funding available within the game today, it should be noted that individual bonuses of around £40 were paid to office, administrative and management staff!

The new year of 1989 brought with it several exciting new opportunities which would ultimately support an even faster expansion of the scheme across the country.

A further meeting with **John Thompson** (Workington office) led to the creation of the new community project at Carlisle United, available places having already been confirmed by the Training Commission. The intention was for the new scheme to be headed up by well-known former Carlisle player, **Billy Rafferty**. Billy was a former player of some note whose career began with Coventry City though he enjoyed playing for several clubs during his career including Blackpool, Plymouth Argyle, Carlisle United, Wolverhampton Wanderers, Newcastle United, Portsmouth and AFC Bournemouth.

Billy had been in touch with the PFA and with scheme officials during the previous year and his contact details had been retained in case a community project at Carlisle was ever to get underway. Unfortunately, in the end, it took some time for progress to be made concerning the possibility of the appointment of an officer at the club (because of this delay, the decision was made to return the ET places allocated by the Workington office in May 1989 and the opportunity for Billy was eventually lost altogether).

A training seminar held at Leeds United's Elland Road ground also proved to be popular with Yorkshire based Community Officers.

Sadly, January 1989 brought with it the first major tragedy in the scheme's history with the death of Preston North End's very popular and very successful Community Officer, **Mick Baxter,** on the 14th January. This was devastating news for his family (he was a much-loved family man with wife Janet, who worked at Deepdale alongside Mick, and two young children, and for everyone at Preston North End FC and all those involved with the scheme.

Popular Club Secretary at the time was **Derek Allan**:

> *"It was a huge honour for Preston North End to be chosen as one of the initial six football clubs to take part in the Community Programme in Professional Football 'pilot' scheme in 1986. We were extremely lucky to be able to appoint our former player, Mick Baxter, as our Community Officer. He quickly adapted to the role and was very much responsible for establishing the scheme at PNE and overseeing its spectacular growth and popularity. Tragically, Mick passed away in January 1989 but his enormous contribution to the scheme's continued success will never be forgotten"*

Mick's death did, however, act as something of a 'catalyst' for people, the club and the PFA to pull together to see if they could support the family most notably via a fund-raising match at Deepdale held eventually at the beginning of March. Out of tragedy, however, there did arise a worthwhile 'legacy' for the scheme which saw a new life-assurance scheme established for all community officers, which hadn't been in place previously. **Ian Johnstone**, previously a part time activity organiser at Deepdale, kindly agreed to take up the post at Preston on a temporary, 'caretaker' basis.

A low-point for the whole of football followed three months later when, at the FA Cup Semi Final on the 15th April 1989 held at Hillsborough between Liverpool and Nottingham Forest, 96 people tragically lost their lives. The events at Hillsborough that day would fill newspaper columns for the best part of the next 30 years.

For the Community Programme, work undertaken up to November 1989 saw various club scheme collections made in support of the families of the victims of the Hillsborough disaster, all of which were added together and then forwarded to people dealing with the donations. Several hundred pounds in total was collected by Community Programme schemes from all around the country in a clear illustration of support, unity and sympathy from them all.

Also, in January, **Ray McHale** announced that he was to leave the scheme in order to take up a playing contract with Scarborough FC (Ray was also later to become the club's manager) thus leaving a vacancy as assistant to **Richard Finney** in the Yorkshire/North East area. Interviews for the Assistant Regional Director's post were held on January 19th and former Huddersfield Town player and Community Officer at the club, **Dick Krzywicki**, was appointed to the role. Dick's promotion also allowed for the later appointment of former Terriers player **Bobby Hoy** to come in as Community Officer following interviews held in May at the club. Born in nearby Halifax, Bobby began his league career with Huddersfield Town as a striker where he stayed until 1975. He then played for Blackburn Rovers, Halifax Town, York City and Rochdale before moving into non-league football.

The full-time officer post at Wigan Athletic, vacated by **Tony Allan** in January, was filled by former Blackburn Rovers player **Pete Devine** following interviews held in early February. The interviews were led by Regional Administrator, **Graham Gill**.

Pete Devine was born in Blackburn and his playing career started with Bristol City in 1981 before moving to Vancouver in Canada. He then signed for his home-town club, Blackburn Rovers, in 1982. He eventually moved on to Burnley where he made 56 appearances between 1984 and 1986 before moving into non-league football with Chorley and Lancaster City amongst others. Pete also has the dubious 'honour' of taking (allegedly!) the worst-ever penalty kick for Lancaster City in a match against Whitley Bay in 1991 (still available on You Tube!).

Also in January **Joe Patton** made contact, once again, to confirm that further Sports Council funding had generously been made available, which would allow the purchase of 3 more minibuses, to add to the 12 already being used.

March 1989 saw The University of London host a conference (attended largely by academics but also by some football personnel) entitled "The People's Game", when the FFE&VTS Community Programme scheme was widely lauded as an initiative "for the future". Also, in March, scheme officials were thrilled and delighted to have been asked to attend the All-Party Football Committee of MPs at Westminster. The briefing given to **Mickey Burns** was to focus on three aspects of the game that were "current" being:

1. Discipline in the game/misbehaviour
2. The new Community Programme initiative
3. ID cards and the fact that professional players were against their use

The presentation saw **Mickey Burns** cover items 1 and 3, whilst **Roger Reade** provided more information about item 2 including:

-   The success of the local community schemes so far (including the attention given to encouraging more opportunities for girls and women, minority ethnic communities, disabled people, senior citizens etc.)
-   The success of the schemes in reducing recorded arrests at matches, and the huge increase in average attendances at clubs where community initiatives were underway.
-   The success in creating new jobs and in providing new (leisure based) qualifications for trainees recruited through the local schemes.
-   The success of the 'schools programmes' across the North.

April 1989 saw Preston North End contact FFE&VTS officials with a view to making a permanent Community Officer appointment after **Mick Baxter** had passed away in January. Interviews were held at the club and amongst those interviewed was current North End player **Oshor Williams.**

Born in Stockton-on Tees, Oshor served his apprenticeship with nearby Middlesbrough before moving to Southampton, Exeter City (on loan), Stockport County, Port Vale and Preston North End for whom he signed in 1986. As a contracted player at the club who was retiring from playing at the end of the 1988/89 season, Oshor was able to take up the post of Community Officer once all the club's fixtures had been completed.

North End Manager, **John McGrath**, Community Director, **Barney Campbell,** and Club Secretary, **Derek Allan,** all played a part in supporting the necessary 'transition' from player to Community Manager that Oshor went through. To assist him in his entirely new role, it was agreed that the experienced **Ian Johnstone** (who had acted as a "caretaker" community officer since Mick Baxter's death) would continue in the new role of Administrative Supervisor. Derek Allan would move on to Blackpool and Brighton & Hove Albion as Club Secretary in later years and he remained extremely supportive of those club's respective community operations.

Meetings with **Peter Coates** (Chairman) and **Mike Potts** (Secretary) at Stoke City, held over the previous nine months or so, helped to 'pave the way' for the introduction of the community scheme at the old Victoria Ground. Peter, especially, was keen to support a community venture at the club at the earliest opportunity. This was further helped following a positive meeting with former Stoke striker, **Brendan O'Callaghan**, who was automatically lined up for the new role at Stoke in view of his industry experience (he had been working in ceramics for some time since he had hung up his boots). Brendan made his league debut for Doncaster Rovers in 1973 and became a key player alongside **Peter Kitchen** in scoring plenty of goals for the Rovers. Brendan moved on to Stoke City in 1978 where the goals continued. He was also capped for the Republic of Ireland on six occasions whilst with Stoke. He finished his career with Oldham Athletic in 1986.

Employment Training (ET) places ultimately became available for both the Stoke City project and the Stockport County project in April 1989. Indeed, interviews for the Stoke position were eventually held at Stoke's former ground (the Victoria Ground) the following month and Brendan O'Callaghan was finally able to take up his new post as Community Officer at the end of July 1989.

A candidate for the Stockport post was also put forward during April 1989. **Carl Halford** had been an extremely popular player at the club during his playing days in the late 1970's, having joined the club in 1977 from Manchester City where he had served his apprenticeship. He also moved as a player to Bury playing at full back at Gigg Lane for one season in 1979/80. Carl later moved to Australia where he played for South Melbourne for six seasons up to 1987 before moving into coaching.

It is also, at this point, worth noting that **Gordon Shaw**, on behalf of the Training Commission, confirmed that a total of 326 ET places had been made available to the FFE&VTS which covered club projects across the North West, North East and Yorkshire. With an average of 10 places available at each club, this meant that a total of 32 club schemes were underway at this time.

Under ET, each new trainee would be issued with a "National Record of Vocational Achievement" (NROVA). The costs of each NROVA (at between £6 - £7 each) had to be factored into the overall budget costs. It is important to understand that, at this time, the success of the Community Programme scheme was almost completely dependent on the success of ET and, in turn, income generated under that programme, together with any savings that could be made in expenditure.

The Spring of 1989 saw the establishment of more meetings with club officials aimed at a further expansion of the Community Programme venture into the East Midlands with initial meetings arranged during late March, April and early May. Meetings were held with:
- **Bob Pepper** (Secretary, Chesterfield)

- **Michael Dunford** (Secretary, Derby County)
- **Allan Bennett** (Long-serving Club Secretary at Leicester City)
- **Joe Eaton** (Secretary, Mansfield Town)
- **Dr John Evans** (Secretary, Northampton Town). For the record, the first meeting took place at the offices near the County Tavern at the old County Ground. Close links between the club and their local authority also required a follow-up meeting with representatives of the local Council that was eventually arranged during June 1989.
- **Neal Hook** (Chief Executive/Secretary at Notts County). Neil had already been in touch with scheme officials to ask if County could be considered as part of any proposed expansion into the East Midlands region.
- Exploratory contact was also made via **Paul White** (Club Secretary) with representatives of Nottingham Forest following an enquiry made by **Allan Clarke** (not the former Leeds United and England player!) from the club, who suggested that it would be advisable to meet with the club's manager, **Brian Clough** at the first possible opportunity. This meeting was, of course, hastily convened!

In some cases, follow up meetings were also convened with club officials (including directors) as necessary. Plans to include Lincoln City as part of this phase of the expansion were thwarted, however, as it became very clear that ET places would not be available in the Lincoln area.

Sometime later than all the other meetings in the East Midlands, a meeting was also arranged with **Arnold Blades** (Club Secretary at Peterborough United) following an enquiry made in early 1990.

It must be stressed that all club officials contacted were highly positive and supportive of the proposed plans for community engagement as presented to them. All Club Secretaries responded positively and secured the support of their various Boards of Directors.

An idea being explored at this time by scheme officials was to establish a further Midlands-based regional office. Indeed, various visits were made to the area of Stone (near Stafford) where it was felt that its location and excellent motorway access could provide sound access to both the West and East Midlands. At the same time, the operation of the North West regional support unit was unfortunately suffering from the absence of Regional Administrator **Graham Gill** through illness.

The idea of a Midlands-based regional office was, in the end, never taken forward when the discussions concerning the new Football Trust criteria, facilitating the further rapid expansion of the scheme into the South of England, commenced at the beginning of 1990 (see later). Indeed, in May 1989 the decision was made to give six months' notice on the property being used as the North West Regional Office in the Corn Exchange in Manchester.

Next on the agenda for the FFE&VTS were discussions with various people, mainly former professional footballers, about the vacant posts that were to become available in the East Midlands. **Mike Raynor** was put forward as a possible candidate by Nottingham Forest and his appointment was duly confirmed. Mike started his new job on the 3rd July.

Also starting work on the 3rd July was **Neville Hamilton** at Leicester City. Neville began his playing career as an apprentice with Leicester City, making his debut against Manchester United at the end of 1977. He then moved on to play for Mansfield Town and Rochdale. He retired from the game as a player due to ill health in 1983. Neville sadly passed away on 9th February 2009.

Paul Curtis, whose name had initially been put forward in April by Town's **Mark Underwood**, commenced work as Northampton Town's Community Officer on the 3rd July. Once on Charlton Athletic's books as an apprentice, Paul Curtis later played for Northampton Town as a right sided defender. In his later career, Paul spent time coaching in the professional game and in non-league football.

Mike, Neville and Paul all worked ever so hard to build up their respective community schemes and Neville was quickly able to build a team of dependable assistants that developed a range of new opportunities for the wider Leicester community.

Back in Yorkshire, and following a meeting with **Keith Usher** (Secretary at York City),

Richard Finney met up with former York and Plymouth midfield player, **Gordon Staniforth,** about the new post at the club (ET places were made available effective from the 1ˢᵗ June 1989) and he swiftly took up his new duties at Bootham Crescent (future Regional Director in the South, **John Relish**, had kindly put forward Gordon's details in May). As a player, **Gordon Staniforth** had played for several clubs having commenced his league career as an apprentice with his local club Hull City. He then enjoyed moves to York City, Carlisle United and Plymouth Argyle (playing for them in their run to the FA Cup Semi-Final in 1984), Newport County and with York City once again.

By coincidence, the FA had confirmed the attendance of several Community Programme Personnel at their summer Full Badge training course due to commence in June 1989 at Lilleshall. Those put forward to take the course at Lilleshall included: **Dave Bell**, **Alan Kershaw**, **Jim McCalliog**, **Eric McManus**, **Bobby Mitchell**, **Cyril "Ces" Podd**, **Kevin Reeves**, **Andy Welsh**, **Alan Whittle**, **Dave Wilkes** and **Alex Williams**.

July 1989 saw the first ever 'team photograph' taken at Preston North End's Deepdale ground. This included *all* club officers and trainees, together with supervisory management staff, all photographed together for the first time.

Even at the time this photograph was taken, plans were in hand for yet more new appointments.

Well-known former player **Alan Young** who, by coincidence, lived literally 'around the corner' from Notts County's Meadow Lane ground at the time, also took up his new duties as Community Officer at Notts County with effect from the start of August 1989. Alan's professional career began with Oldham Athletic in 1974 and took him to Leicester City, Sheffield United, Brighton and Hove Albion, Notts County and, finally, in 1986, to Rochdale.

Ray Hankin, took up his new duties as Community Officer at Darlington in August 1989 following the appointment of former Community Officer **Tony McAndrew** as Darlington's new Youth Development Officer (Tony had undertaken the role of Community Officer, literally, for just a few weeks between June and July).

Ray Hankin was born in Wallsend, and signed apprentice forms with Burnley with whom he made his debut as a striker as a 17-year-old in 1973. He went on to play for several English clubs during his career, perhaps most notably with Leeds United (1976-80). He also played for Arsenal, Middlesbrough, Peterborough United and Wolverhampton Wanderers in England and for Vancouver Whitecaps in the USA.

As if to illustrate the high calibre of persons interviewed, other unsuccessful candidates interviewed for the position at Darlington were still able to secure employment elsewhere. Amongst them was **Tony King,** who was appointed later in August 1989 as Community Officer at Scarborough where he became the club's first ever Community Officer.

The 1989/90 season started full of promise for the now fast-growing Community Programme, most notably as plans had already been agreed with the Training Commission for places to be made available in conjunction with West Midlands based football clubs. The new places would become available with effect from September 1ˢᵗ and would be available from their local offices at Birmingham (for Aston Villa and Birmingham City), Coventry (for Coventry City), Dudley (for West Bromwich Albion), Telford (for Shrewsbury Town) and Wolverhampton (for Walsall and Wolverhampton Wanderers). Added to this, once new ET year negotiations were underway, interest was expressed by the Worcester ET Training Agency Officer in starting a new project at Hereford United. Meetings with club representatives in the West Midlands region were arranged with club officials as follows:

-   Long-serving Club Secretary, **Steve Stride,** at Aston Villa in mid-September. A follow up visit with Club Chairman, **Doug Ellis,** was also held the following March.
-   New Owner and Chairman at Birmingham City, **Samesh Kumar.** A later follow-up meeting with **Rick Bailey** from Birmingham City Council was also held.
-   **John Peacock** and **Graham Hover** (Club Secretary) at Coventry City.
-   **David Vaughan** at Hereford United based on the availability of ET places.
-   **Malcolm Starkey (**Club Secretary) at Shrewsbury Town in early October.

- Long-serving and well-respected Walsall Club Chief Executive and Secretary, **Roy Whalley**, at the Post House Great Barr in early September.
- Newly appointed Club Secretary at West Bromwich Albion, **Dr John Evans** (who knew of the Community Programme scheme from his previous post as Secretary at Northampton Town), and Manager **Brian Talbot** (who also knew of the Community Programme scheme from his time as Chairman of the PFA). A follow up meeting aimed at outlining plans with representatives of Sandwell Council was also held at the club's request.
- Secretary **Keith Pearson** at Wolverhampton Wanderers.

Brian Caswell was appointed as the first ever Football in the Community Officer at Birmingham City in October 1989. Originally hailing from the West Midlands, Brian began his career as an apprentice with nearby Walsall where, having made his debut in 1972, he went on to serve the club mainly as the club's regular full back for a further 13 years before later moves to Doncaster Rovers, Leeds United and Wolverhampton Wanderers (on loan).

Mick Kearns also took up the post of Club Community Officer at Walsall from the 1st December 1989. Mick was a popular goalkeeper wherever he played. He started his career as an apprentice with Oxford United before loan moves to Plymouth Argyle and Charlton Athletic. He then moved to Walsall where he made just under 250 league appearances between 1973 and 1979 and then to Wolverhampton Wanderers. He returned to Walsall where he finished his career between 1982-1985. He also played for the Republic of Ireland on 18 occasions.

Interviews were held at West Bromwich Albion on the 18th October, and **Dennis Mortimer** was successful in being appointed. Liverpool-born, Dennis began his career as an apprentice with Coventry City in 1969 before moving to Aston Villa in 1975. He spent the next ten years with Villa and was Club Captain when they won the European Cup by beating Bayern Munich 1-0 in 1982. Dennis had an illustrious playing career, also playing for Sheffield United (on loan), Brighton and Hove Albion and Birmingham City.

As an 'aside' at this point, it is perhaps worth noting the "briefing' offered to all interview candidates at the time which included the following:

- 'Football in the Community' is all about offering activity opportunities literally "from the cradle to the grave" – i.e. for toddlers through to senior citizens.
- Successful officers are likely to have considerable natural enthusiasm for the scheme, not to mention a belief in the work leading to bigger and better things for football.
- The wages payable are not going to be the best in the world, at least in the beginning, so application and enjoyment for the work is going to be essential.

By June 1989, it had become evident that the previous decline in club attendances (up to 1985) had been arrested and that there was now strong evidence in place to show that attendances at matches were increasing, especially at most of those clubs that operated community schemes.

PFA Chief Executive, **Gordon Taylor,** speaking in the summer of 1989 said:

> *"At all clubs where the scheme has been introduced, attendances have increased and the behaviour of the crowd has improved dramatically. The concept of bringing club and community together is one that will benefit the game in the long term."*

The very end of July saw **Dave Ryan** take up the post of Community Officer at Stockport County having been interviewed at Edgeley Park in May that year. A popular figure wherever he played, Dave began his goalkeeping career with Manchester United, though he made his league debut whilst on loan with Port Vale in 1976. That same year he signed for Southport whilst they were still a League club, though he later became a loyal servant for non-league clubs Northwich Victoria and Chorley.

Details of contractual arrangements made with the Training Commission for the new ET year (4th September 1989 to 31st August 1990) confirmed that places had been made available at a total of 50 club community schemes, who were "pencilled in" to start the new ET year as follows:

LOCAL TRAINING AGENCY	CLUB-BASED COMMUNITY SCHEMES
Barnsley/Doncaster	Barnsley, Doncaster Rovers
Birmingham	Aston Villa, Birmingham City
Cheshire	Chester City, Crewe Alexandra
Cleveland	Hartlepool United
Coventry	Coventry City
Derby	Chesterfield, Derby County
Dudley/Sandwell	West Bromwich Albion
Durham	Darlington
Halifax	Halifax Town
Humberside	Grimsby Town, Scunthorpe United
Lancashire	Blackburn Rovers, Blackpool, Burnley, Preston North End
Leeds/North Yorkshire	Leeds United, Scarborough, York City
Leicester	Leicester City
Manchester Central	Manchester City
Manchester East	Oldham Athletic, Stockport County
Manchester North	Bolton Wanderers, Bury, Rochdale, Wigan Athletic
Merseyside	Everton, Liverpool, Tranmere Rovers
North Tyne	Newcastle United
Northampton	Northampton Town
Nottingham	Mansfield Town, Nottingham Forest, Notts County
Sheffield	Rotherham United, Sheffield United, Sheffield Wednesday
South Tyne	Sunderland
Staffordshire	Port Vale, Stoke City
Telford	Shrewsbury Town
West Yorkshire	Bradford City, Huddersfield Town,
Wolverhampton	Walsall, Wolverhampton Wanderers
Worcester	Hereford United

Clearly the plans were there for all to see to support a total of fifty club schemes. The support of the MSC in the early days and, later, The Training Commission, facilitated the rapid expansion of the Community Programme scheme. This, in turn, owed a great deal to the spirit and endeavour of the original "ground-breaking' Community Officers whose collective enthusiasm had helped to achieve so much success originally. That said, due to developments at certain clubs, some changes were made in the months ahead to this list including:

As Coventry City officials hesitated about starting a project at their Highfield Road ground, the proposed community project at the club was temporarily "shelved" and places allocated under ET were returned to the Training Commission to be used with other providers.

Places allocated at Wolverhampton Wanderers were also returned as the club, like Coventry City, made the decision to delay further consideration of the possibility of starting a community scheme at their Molineux ground. Similarly, the places available by offices in Derby and Telford (the latter for Shrewsbury Town) were put on hold as Derby County and Shrewsbury Town officials expressed the view that they would prefer to wait to launch their local community project (Shrewsbury Town's decision was entirely based around the very limited amount of room available at their old Gay Meadow ground).

However, in order to preserve the targeted 50 community schemes, new places would again be made available at Carlisle United, even though the club had previously put 'on hold' their plans to become involved in the scheme. New places would also become available at Wrexham, which meant that these new projects could get underway straight away. Additional places would also become available from Humberside, following an application that had been submitted in March 1990 in support of a new project at Hull City. A new appointment would be made in the near future.

It should also be noted that places made available by Worcester (for Hereford United) meant that the proposed new Hereford United project, when it was finally established, would become the most southerly based of community schemes to be supported from the FFE&VTS Manchester base.

Great credit must be made to all those people involved in this extremely complicated process which eventually saw around 10 ET places allocated at each club at an average income of just under £18 each. Some of the Training Agency[1] officers who were particularly supportive during this 'renewal' process included: **Tony Griffin**, **Rita McLoughlin** and **Lesley Bird** (Birmingham), **Keith Ditchfield** (Cheshire), **Keith Boynton** (Cleveland), **Gary Ledger** (Coventry) **Sue Peake** and **Pauline Kirkland** (Derby), **Margaret Robinson** (Dudley/Sandwell), **Dave McClelland** (Durham), **Geraldine Williams** and **Kevin Corbett** (Humberside), **Geoff Brocklehurst** (Lancashire), **John Dyer** (Manchester Central), **Jack Holt** (Manchester East), **Roy Holmes** and **Linda Gibson** (Manchester North), **Elaine Lloyd** (Merseyside), **Mike Hawkins** (North Tyne), **Claire Bloom** (Northumberland), **Alan Parry** (Nottingham), **Richard Percival** and **Geoff Fieldsend** (Sheffield), **Ron James** (Shropshire), **David Oliver** (South Tyne), **Joy Appleton** (Staffordshire, previously Stoke Training Agency), **Trevor Ellis** (West Yorkshire), **Kevin Ashford** (Wolverhampton).

As things progressed, more and more dealings occurred with representatives of the TECs. For example, new ET contracts were signed during April/May 1990 with TECs at Bradford, Calderdale and Kirklees, Cumbria, South and East Cheshire, Teesside, Tyneside and Wearside. Thanks for their support must also be extended at this point to **Ann Collins** (Bradford), **John Howard**, **Rhodda Berry**, **Ian Sidcup** and **Ajaz Shah** (Calderdale and Kirklees), **Carol Watson** (Cumbria), **Viv Gee** and **Les Cooper** (South and East Cheshire) and to **Alan Wallace** (Teesside).

After three years of growth and development, there was some inevitability that certain difficulties would start to arise, not least out of the ET programme. For example, the new ET scheme requirements regarding paperwork were significantly more demanding than its predecessor, the Community Programme scheme. Amongst the much more detailed requirements were stock control books, induction checklists, action plans, trainee reviews, exit interview forms, timesheets and many other forms, not to mention the requirement for full college liaison concerning the provision of courses. In addition, there were recruitment problems in certain areas. Recruitment was massively important in generating the necessary funding to pay officers at the clubs.

A meeting with **Glyn Williams** and **Gordon Shaw** from the Training Commission (held in the Autumn) flagged up several important issues for scheme officials going forwards including:

- Negotiations with the new TECS would be for the FFE&VTS to take forward (noting that from a national perspective, ET recruitment levels were plummeting).
- The status of the comparatively new National Vocational Qualifications (NVQs) was

---

1. *It should be noted that plans were afoot during early 1990 to reorganise the Training Agencies into Training and Enterprise Councils (TECs) and that some re-organisation of area offices was to follow. Indeed, during February 1990,* **Chris Curry,** *from the Training Commission, advised that certain TECs had already been set up and that future liaison would 'transition' the current Training Agencies into becoming TECs.*

It also became clear that the previous weekly allowances ("supplementary grants") paid by Training Agencies were to be merged into a more generic payment of "unit costs" which would become payable via the new TECs for the new contract year which began on the 30th April 1990. The unit costs would include a basic allowance plus travel, childcare and costs for the purchase of outfits. This meant that managing agencies would, in future, be forced to handle their own budgets and to take responsibility for the payment of travel, childcare and outfit costs to trainees from within the overall unit costs (monies) received.

being reviewed; educationalists and practitioners apparently disagreed about the future!

-   TECs were new and individual organisations that may, or may not, choose to support the Community Programme scheme on a local basis.

-   A national Development Plan had identified that there were quality assurance demands that might be forthcoming from local TECs which may become a requirement for all would-be providers in future (see later).

These were important issues for the national programme to take on board that ultimately supported the move towards introducing dedicated ET support officers when the new Football Trust funded Community operation got underway.

In addition, the fleet of minibuses, which had now reached 15 in total (thanks to Sports Council support), were taking some managing. Difficulties had arisen such as trainees driving buses inappropriately, missing petrol vouchers, unauthorised purchases of fuel, increasing costs of repairs and maintenance, occasional accidents (nothing too serious - fortunately!). In addition, the Shell sponsored "Gold Cards" (which provided central funding for fuel) were not been used properly and it became clear that the minibuses themselves were also not being used solely for authorised trips in certain areas!

One or two officers were also realising that community work was not their "cup of tea". For example, it was very much to the credit of **Mick Heaton** at Blackburn Rovers that he admitted that he was finding the work 'tough' and that he was going to look for work back in professional club management if he could.

On 21st November 1989, a Committee of The Football Trust met, and recommendations were made to approve a significant grant for the FFE&VTS Community Programme, though it was, in the end, referred for final approval to a further meeting of the trust to be held on the 13th December. The very good news received in time for Christmas that year, however, came when the Football Trust agreed to offer the scheme a grant of £150,000 to purchase a further 10 minibuses (bringing the total number of minibuses within the FFE&VTS Community Programme fleet to 25 minibuses) to support a total of 50 existing and proposed new club community schemes in the North and Midlands.

Re-organisation saw yet another new structure introduced. Basically, the country was divided into two distinct areas of approximately 25 clubs in each region, the West and the East. In addition, new posts as Regional Managers (West and East) were created for each region. The Western region would cover from Carlisle United in the north right down to Hereford United in the south.

Interviews were held at the end of November and after much deliberation, **Kevin Glendon** was selected as the successful candidate given his huge community experience at several levels. At the same time, **Richard Finney** was elevated to the new post of Regional Manager covering clubs across the Eastern region from Newcastle United in the north down to Peterborough United in the south.

Dedicated assistants were also appointed to support Kevin in the West, being **Graham Gill** (in the North West) and **Derek Clydesdale** (in the West Midlands). In the East, Richard would be assisted by **Dick Krzywicki** (Yorkshire and the North East) and **Tommy Spencer** (East Midlands).

Also, around this time, approaches were made by both the BBC and by Granada TV (separately) for information about the successful work of the FFE&VTS Community Programme scheme to date. **Mickey Burns** was, however, keen to ensure that no-one interviewed was put in the position of having to announce future plans for growth prematurely.

The Granada enquiry (*World in Action*) was based around the scheme's growth to date (50 clubs, plus independent schemes that were at this point underway at Millwall, Arsenal, Brentford and Leyton Orient based on access to funding made available by the former Greater London Council).

Christmas 1989 saw great care taken in deciding to offer Community Officers the chance to receive a bottle of whisky each (or, alternatively, brandy) as a "thank-you" to them for all their hard work during the year. Wine and boxes of Roses were provided for additional staff and trainees!

The Christmas senior management meeting recorded thanks and best wishes for their future careers to **Brian Flynn** and **Kevin Reeves** who had just left to take up new posts in professional football. Brian had taken up the role of Manager at Wrexham Football Club, a terrific opportunity for him, and a position that he would hold for a total of twelve years until 2001. Kevin joined him as Assistant Manager at the Racecourse ground. Kevin was replaced as Community Officer at Crewe by **Derek King** who started work in November 1989.

Interest in the scheme from Wrexham (expressed via new manager Brian Flynn) was noted, and a follow up meeting was promptly arranged when it became clear that officials of Wrexham Football Club were keen on setting up their own community scheme at the earliest opportunity (application forms were eventually submitted to the Training Commission in February 1990). The new management team at Wrexham were also soon to play a key role in recommending the recruitment of their first Community Officer being **Mike Rigg,** who was recruited from nearby Chester City. In turn, **John Kerr** took over from Mike as Community Officer at Chester City. John served his football apprenticeship with Tranmere Rovers and stayed with the club as a professional until 1983 when he moved to Bristol City. He also played briefly for Stockport County and for Bury.

The turn of the year from 1989 into 1990 saw several more changes, this time at Community Officer level, including the following:

Former Scottish international **Jim McCalliog** left Halifax Town in January to go back into the licensing trade. He was replaced at the end of the month by former Manchester United and Halifax Town goalkeeper **Paddy Roche**. Born in Dublin, Paddy played for Shelborne before moving to Manchester United in 1973. He made 46 appearances for the Old Trafford club before leaving in 1982 to join Brentford. He joined Halifax Town in 1984 and made 189 appearances for the club up to 1989. Paddy was also capped for Ireland on 8 occasions.

It is also worth noting that very soon after this, **Jim McCalliog** was appointed as Manager of Halifax Town (in March 1990) and he, in turn, appointed former Community Officer **Brian Taylor** as his Assistant Manager. Sadly, both club appointments proved to be only short-lived, as both Jim and Brian left the club at the start of the new 1990/91 season.

As had been expected, **Mick Heaton** left Blackburn Rovers at the end of January 1990 and he was replaced by **Pete Devine**, who left Wigan Athletic and who was, in turn, replaced at Wigan by **Peter Cunningham**.

Steve Cammack chose to move to Chesterfield from Scunthorpe United as the club's new Community Officer to set up the Spireites new community scheme. In turn, of course, this created a vacancy at Scunthorpe United.

Alex Williams moved to Manchester City as Community Officer and, following interviews held in January, **Ray Train** was appointed to the post vacated by Alex at Port Vale. Ray's career began with Walsall (where he was an apprentice) before a successful move to Carlisle United where he helped the club to gain promotion to the First Division of the Football League in 1974. He then played for Sunderland, Bolton Wanderers, Watford and Oxford United. A loan move to AFC Bournemouth then followed and Ray ended his playing career with short spells at Northampton Town, Tranmere Rovers and Walsall once again. After leaving the Community Programme, Ray enjoyed a successful career in coaching and scouting, most notably with Middlesbrough.

Former Rotherham and Doncaster Rovers midfield player **Dave Bentley** took up the new post of Community Officer at Mansfield Town, following the club's confirmation, also in January, that their Board of Directors wished to join the scheme. Dave was a left sided midfield player who had played for Rotherham United, Mansfield Town, Chesterfield and Doncaster Rovers during a successful career that saw him help Rotherham and Doncaster to achieve promotion whilst he was with them. He took up coaching in 1980 and became Assistant Manager alongside Manager **Billy Bremner** at Doncaster Rovers during the early 1980's.

Ron Wylie was appointed as the first ever Community Officer at Aston Villa (following a successful interview in mid-January). Glasgow-born Ron was a former player who had first joined Notts County as a midfield player from Clydesdale Juniors in 1950 and went on to play for County, Aston Villa and Birmingham City in a successful playing career that finally ended in 1970. He had also held coaching and managerial positions with Coventry City, West Bromwich Albion and Aston Villa.

In July 1989, **Dave Wilkes** was made an offer of a terrific 'package deal' to become Carlisle United's new Youth Team Officer (with a guaranteed two-year contract). Dave was to work closely with the Carlisle Manager, **Clive Middlemass,** in relation to work in local schools, the club's School of Excellence and he was even to play for the Reserve team on the odd occasion if required! After his departure from Barnsley, his replacement at Oakwell was another former player in **Colin Walker** who actually played for the Reds in the early 1980's. Rotherham-born Colin Walker played for several Yorkshire clubs during a successful playing career including Barnsley, Doncaster Rovers and Sheffield Wednesday. He also played for Gisborne City in New Zealand where he acquired New Zealand citizenship. After leaving the Community Programme, he moved successfully into coaching and management in 1988.

Following the departure of **Gary Pierce** to take up a commercial post at Bolton Wanderers, **Dave Bell** took over as Community Officer at Bury.

Following the departure of **Tommy Booth** to set up his own trophy business, and after a formal interview process involving a total of five candidates, the successful candidate appointed as Community Officer at Bolton Wanderers was former Manchester City player **Geoff Lomax**. Droylsden-born Geoff began his career as an apprentice with Manchester City, moving on to Wolverhampton Wanderers (on loan in 1985), Carlisle United and Rochdale before retiring from playing through injury in 1988.

Will Foley was appointed as Community Officer at Hereford United. Born in Bellshill, near Glasgow, Will made a handful of appearances for Swansea City before moving to non-league Frickley Athletic. Will also played briefly for Cardiff City.

In November 1989, having served the Community Programme scheme so well for approximately four years, **Louise Pearson** was offered the position of Office Manager at the PFA. This was a fantastic move for her even if she was much missed by scheme senior managers after she left.

Mark Holroyd had also taken over as the Scheme's accounts officer. Allied to his work with the Scheme, Mark was to spend the next four years studying so that he would eventually qualify as an Associate Member of the Charter of Management Accountants

Eric McManus left Bradford City to take up the vacant Youth Development Officer position with Walsall in mid-January. His post as Community Officer was taken up by **Richard Angus**, who had been working closely with him at Valley Parade for some considerable time.

The early part of the new year 1990 also saw a visit by the then Minister for Employment, **Michael Howard MP**, to view for himself Leeds United's successful Community Programme scheme, then being overseen by **Ces Podd**.

At Community Officer level in April 1990, it was noted that, in the Western region, Port Vale's Community Officer, **Ray Train**, was to move on to a Youth Development Officer post at Middlesbrough and that **Brian Taylor** had left Burnley having been offered a coaching position at Halifax Town alongside Manager **Jim McCalliog**. Former Burnley player, **Terry Pashley,** was appointed as Community Officer at Burnley. Born in Chesterfield, Terry began his league career as a defender with Burnley before moving to Blackpool in 1978 where he made 201 league appearances for the Seasiders. He then moved to Bury in 1983 where he made a further 217 league appearances before finishing his playing career in 1990.

In the Eastern region, **Tony King** left Scarborough and **Vic Ferguson** left Hartlepool United. Although temporary supervisory arrangements were made in each case, new officers were soon appointed at the clubs being **Ian Kerr** at Scarborough and **Terry Bainbridge** at Hartlepool United. Born in Hartlepool, Terry was a former central defender with Hartlepool United between 1981 and 1983, making 34 appearances and scoring one league goal.

Having moved into the Cheshire area, **John Seasman** took over the vacant post at Crewe Alexandra that had been created because of the departure of **Derek King**. This matter had been fully discussed at a meeting with **Dario Gradi**, **Bill Prendergast** and **Gill Palin** at Crewe Alexandra in early May.

A cultured midfield player, **John Seasman** enjoyed spells with several league clubs as a player having begun his career as an apprentice with Tranmere Rovers. He moved to Luton Town in 1975 though his longest spells were with Millwall (1976-1980) and Rotherham United (1980-1984). He also played for Cardiff City, Rochdale (on loan), Chesterfield and Rochdale again.

The now monthly senior management team meetings (or "administration meetings" as they were referred to then) provided regular updates for all involved, and, in the case of the end-of-season May 1990 meeting, also provided the opportunity to comment further on the successes and failures of existing programmes aimed at informing the proposed new Business Plan for what would become a fully amalgamated scheme that was still to be discussed at Board level.

In addition, careful consideration was given towards the organisation and professionalism of the recent Easter soccer schools and the integration and involvement of community officers with junior *and* senior club-based supporters' clubs. Linked to this, there would be much closer monitoring of the quality aspects of delivery at club level – i.e. there would be a greater emphasis on ensuring quality delivery.

For the summer 1990 FA full badge, it was noted at the meeting that a total of 15 people (mainly club-based Community Officers) had been put forward to the FA by the FFE&VTS.

Bizarrely, one notable issue reported at the management meeting was that, whenever it rained, the roof over the office provided by Wigan Athletic at their Springfield Park ground leaked! It was unanimously agreed that this matter needed to be raised and sorted with club officials immediately!

Soon after that there was another strange issue development. Given the onset of the Criminal Record checks about to be undertaken by all Community Officers, a club-based Community Officer resigned (in advance of undertaking a check) on the basis that he hadn't informed people at the time of his interview of a very serious conviction that would appear in his Criminal Record check.

CHAPTER 5
THE FOOTBALL ASSOCIATION, THE FOOTBALL TRUST AND A NEW BUSINESS PLAN

JANUARY 1990 STARTED WITH an early "tip off" that the FA appeared to be planning to set up their own independent community scheme. In a hastily arranged meeting involving **Joe Patton** from the Sports Council with **Gordon Taylor**, **Mickey Burns** and **Roger Reade**, Joe kindly explained that the FA's proposals appeared to be aimed at grass roots football and that they didn't seem to represent any sort of "rival" scheme. Gordon and Mickey expressed their concern, however, as it appeared that, despite the now spectacular success, development and growth of club-based community projects at professional clubs over the past three and a half years under the FFE&VTS Community Programme, the FA at least appeared to have chosen to go forward with their own ideas about setting up their own national community scheme.

A further meeting, involving Gordon Taylor, Joe Patton and the Football Trust's **Richard Faulkner,** shed new light on what was happening and led to the staging of an emergency FFE&VTS Board of Directors meeting at Preston North End's Deepdale ground at the end of February 1990. PFA Chief Executive **Gordon Taylor** seized the initiative at the start of the meeting by reminding all present that, some twelve months earlier at a meeting held in January 1989, the FA had promised to keep other parties informed of any community-related developments (which appeared not to have happened) and that, a year on from that initial meeting, rumours about the proposed FA "community scheme" had been picked up. Those rumours had also been confirmed following contact with the Sports Council and the Football Trust.

At the Board Meeting, Gordon expressed his delight that the Football Trust had recently chosen to provide grant support for the FFE&VTS scheme for the purchase of ten new minibuses but, on the other hand, he felt that the PFA and the FL had been treated "*in an offhand way*" in view of the lack of communication from the FA during the last year. In addition, given the significant community development work that had been undertaken by the professional clubs with the support of the PFA and the FL, he stressed that he felt that it was vital that *all* the football authorities worked together in the long-term best interests of the game.

In response, the FA confirmed that their aim was to increase the number of boys and girls playing football *and* to increase the numbers of people watching the game. It was noted that gates at league matches had increased over the past three seasons as a result of the combined efforts of the many and various schemes undertaken by many people working in the game and that there were approximately 65 Football Development Officers in post across the country that were doing similar work to that being undertaken by local community schemes. This work was underway in places such as Brighton, Ipswich and Wolverhampton where club-based community schemes that could be set up in those areas might 'duplicate' a provision that already existed. The FA felt that they should provide the necessary "broad base" for the development of such community schemes.

There then followed a lengthy discussion about the merits of work undertaken by Football Development Officers and the existing work being undertaken by club-based Community Officers.

It was noted that the community work undertaken by club schemes with the backing of the FFE&VTS "Community Programme in Professional Football" to date embraced work with schoolchildren (emphasising that this comprised boys *and* girls), people from ethnic minority groups, people with disabilities, senior citizens, women and girls, people who were out of work and a terrific added-value involvement of current players in attending community activities. Indeed, the scheme operated literally "from the cradle to the grave" and the desire by a huge majority of professional clubs to play an increased role (and to be seen to be playing such a role) in their local towns and cities was clear. **Gordon Taylor** stressed that it was clear that the "broad base" previously mentioned was already in existence and that the 92 Football League (FL) clubs provided that base (or platform) for community engagement with the support of the FL and the PFA through the FFE&VTS.

This late February meeting proved to be of extreme importance, especially as it was subsequently recognised that the Football Trust would *not* provide funding for either the FA *or* the FFE&VTS working alone and/or independently. It therefore became essential for the FA *and* the FFE&VTS to agree to work together under a new 'management structure' that would work for all concerned.

A follow-up meeting was arranged in early March at the FA when discussions centred on possible working criteria that could work for all parties. In attendance were **Graham Kelly** (by now Chief Executive of the FA having previously been Chief Executive of the FL until 1989), **Frank Hannah**, **Charles Hughes** and **Robin Russell** from the FA; **Bill Fox** (Chairman of the FL) and FL Secretary, **David Dent** (who had been previously, of course, a highly popular and successful Secretary at Coventry City), and **Gordon Taylor** from the PFA; together with **Mickey Burns** and **Roger Reade** from the FFE&VTS.

On behalf of the FL, **Bill Fox** suggested that what he felt was essential for the future was "*amalgamation*" and not "*co-existence*". On behalf of the FA, **Charles Hughes** insisted that the FA reserved the right to undertake the technical direction of all football coaching within any community schemes. Whilst this may have seemed somewhat demanding at the time, it was fair to suggest that, ever since the scheme began, all Community Officers had been informed of the importance of holding the FA Preliminary Coaching course (as a minimum. Community Officers already holding the FA Preliminary Coaching award had also been encouraged to go on to take the FA's Full Badge).

The FA also set out that any Community Officers should be paid in accordance with the salary scale that applied for Football Development Officers in the "market-place" and that they should be referred to as "Football and Community Development Officers" in future. By coincidence, this latter requirement was something that scheme officials had been talking about since 1986, especially as it was very clear that wages payable to Community Officers (based on income from Government) were well below the level that was felt to be appropriate. As a key proposal, this was obviously welcomed!

One more requirement, demanded by the Football Trust, was for schemes to adopt the principle of charging for their activities and to aim to become financially self-sufficient. This was to be in much the same way that Football Development Officers within local authorities were aiming to preserve their respective futures by charging for the running of, for example, soccer courses, after school coaching sessions and other coaching involvement. In other words, generating income in future would be essential.

Finally, it was felt that the FA and the FFE&VTS needed to join up to work together in some sort of "national forum" that would oversee the Community Programme scheme. This forum would need to oversee the appointment of new Community Officers and the establishment and operation of some form of locally-based management committee or 'forum' at each local club community project.

It was noted that £2 million had already been "reallocated" by the Football Trust to support a possible new community venture. Interestingly, the view was expressed at the meeting that an amount of around £750,000 of this money could be made available for the development of community accessible facilities (on a similar basis to the former **Denis Howell** "Football and the Community" 'capital' initiative) with the remainder going towards the appointment of Community Development Officers. In the end, this figure was reduced to £460,000.

These two round-the-table meetings then triggered an avalanche of follow-up meetings both internally (involving scheme regional staff and Community Officers for necessary feedback) and externally (involving FA, FL, PFA and FFE&VTS officials) all of which were aimed at reaching final agreement on the criteria necessary to secure the Football Trust's approval to release their funding and supporting an expansion of the scheme that was supported by all of football's bodies. Initial internal meetings also, out of interest, involved several discussions about a possible budget which were essentially *"back of a cigarette packet"* calculations about how best any new monies could be utilised (this was when it became clear to all involved that it would be impossible to allocate as much as three quarters of a million pounds towards facilities).

The first of the 'follow-up' meetings, took place within a week at Lilleshall when the following suggestions were put forward in order to take things forward:

- The FFE&VTS Memorandum and Articles of Association should be amended so that, at Board level, instead of the current 5 PFA representatives, 5 FL representatives and 1 FA representative, there should be a proposed maximum of 3 representatives put forward by each organisation (to include Chief Executives) with equal funding to be paid by each organisation to the FFE&VTS. This would require approval for a funding contribution to be made by the FA Council. This 'coming together' was, of course, much in line with the original proposals put forward by the Sir Norman Chester Report of 1968.
- Working under the direction of the Board, there should be a national 'Working Party' comprising staff level representatives from each of the three organisations (this would later become the 'Staff Committee').
- Community Officers already in post should remain in post and be promoted to become "Football and Community Development Officers" with new job descriptions and higher salaries (in line with the salary scales for existing Football Development Officers – i.e. local Government scales which were, at that time, roughly between £11,000 and £13,000 per annum).
- Local management committees or 'forums' should be set up to oversee local operations. They should be chaired by a senior representative or Director of each 'host' club. Interestingly, it was agreed that local authority input should be "optional" and not "mandatory" at this stage.
- The FFE&VTS was to be put forward as the organisation that made the application/submission for the available funding of £2 million to the Football Trust. In addition, the FFE&VTS should hold the secretariat for the National Working Party.
- The timescale would be swift.
- The FA felt that it was appropriate for local County Football Associations (CFAs) to be encouraged to become involved, especially in areas where professional club involvement may not extend across local areas – e.g. in places like Devon and Cornwall. It was also felt that the English Schools Football Association (ESFA) should be contacted. This was something that the FFE&VTS were happy to do as very positive links with **Steve Allatt** and his colleagues at the ESFA were already in place.
- The FA wished to be offered the key role of chairing the 'National Working Party' (or 'Staff Committee' as it would become) for a minimum period of at least 12 months.
- Other ideas put forward also included:
- A national 'launch' event should be arranged.
- Regular "update" newsletters should be sent to clubs, press and media and all of football's many other organisations (leagues, associations, partner organisations etc.)
- Staff training should be encouraged (though this was already very much in place across the existing FFE&VTS funded schemes).
- The FFE&VTS and The FA should be represented at all future interviews, though, in practical terms, and in the longer term, this became impossible due to timescales, changes in dates for interviews, club staff availability, club requirements etc.

A post meeting discussion at the FFE&VTS confirmed that the conversations to date represented positive and acceptable progress. Indeed, it was felt that the key suggestions as outlined were perfectly in order. **Mickey Burns** was keen to ensure that the FFE&VTS Community Programme senior management team, particularly Regional Managers, were seen to be on an equal footing with FA Regional Directors in terms of their qualifications. As a result of all the discussions to date (and to ensure parity with FA Officers), Regional Manager, **Kevin Glendon**, was summarily instructed to attend a coaching preparatory course so that he could take the FA Full Badge course at the first possible opportunity!

The point was also made that FEE&VTS personnel were already well 'trained' in work within the Community Programme and Employment Training (ET). One thing that was recognised, however, was that the management structure was likely to change again and that a new structure would need to be put in place in the very near future.

A further meeting was held at the PFA's offices in Manchester on the 10th April involving **Robin Russell** from the FA and **Mickey Burns** and **Roger Reade** from the FFE&VTS. Yet another meeting was held on the 17th April at the FA at which those 3 Officers were joined by **Charles Hughes** (FA) and **Chris Whalley** (FL). This meeting was the first to be referred to as a meeting of members of staff from all the football organisations or, as it would become known, the 'Staff Committee'.

Both meetings had been aimed at running through some of the detail of the agreement reached at Board level. It was noted before both meetings that the Football Trust was to further consider the matter at the end of the month (April), so agreement was essential concerning the reorganisation of the FFE&VTS who, it was now acknowledged, would be the key player in taking community engagement forward.

Other issues agreed included:

- Officers recruited at all clubs would be employed by the FFE&VTS for a minimum period of three years before becoming employees of the local management forum or committee responsible for overseeing the local community project. This matter was to be discussed in conjunction with the adoption of local constitutions in due course (see later).
- Consideration was to be given to the possible issue of any significant surpluses being "capped" by being paid to a separate trust fund or directly into a contingency fund. This was aimed at ensuring that officers did not become "money driven".
- Local management forums (committees) and, importantly, bank accounts should be set up, allowing income to be paid in to a locally established, and community-exclusive, bank account.
- After lengthy discussion, and in order to recognise the FA's status in directing the coaching elements of the future scheme, the following wording was also agreed:

*"The FA reserves the right to retain all the content of the technical aspects
of football throughout the scheme"*

- Guidelines on possible charges (i.e. sources of income) would be drawn up
- The FA requested for a "bonus" structure to be drawn up, though the FFE&VTS expressed serious reservations about this, especially in view of the concern that had already been agreed concerning officers who might become "money driven".
- A formal Business Plan should be prepared for presentation to the Football Trust which outlined how the money would be spent (in a budget), the role of the various agencies involved and what would be achieved. Also, to be considered would be how the scheme could be "measured", in terms of targets set.
- The PR/Marketing of the new scheme needed to be carefully considered and, as already identified, a formal launch event should be arranged.
- The line management structure of the FA and the FFE&VTS Community Programme should be compared and contrasted so that technical line management could be introduced (the FA oversaw three distinct areas of England being the North, Midlands and South, whereas the FFE&VTS Community Programme structure split into two regions currently

(West and East), with plans to add a third region in the South in due course.

- The FFE&VTS scheme already embraced one area of Wales (Wrexham) and would need to embrace other areas of Wales, notably Cardiff and Swansea, too. These were areas overseen by the FA of Wales.

The FA representatives also expressed some concern about the local authority areas where Football Development Officers had already been appointed – e.g. in Bradford, Huddersfield, Leeds, Newcastle, Sunderland and Walsall. What was proposed, in the end, was that careful consideration should be given to some form of 'dovetailing' with each local club-based community scheme, where both football development and club-based community schemes existed.

The FA remained insistent that they wanted to permanently "chair" all future FFE&VTS meetings. Whilst this was discussed at length, it was finally agreed that the FA would chair Staff Committee meetings for the first year of operation before reviewing these arrangements.

The point was also stressed by FFE&VTS representatives that community schemes at clubs were involved in a whole host of other activities *other* than purely football - e.g. other sporting provision such as short mat bowls (mats had already been purchased from Sports Council funding), 'kwik cricket', short tennis plus social events such as tea dances for senior citizens.

Another meeting of all representatives was held at the FA in mid-May, attended by **Graham Kelly**, **Charles Hughes** and **Robin Russell** from the FA; **Gordon Taylor** from the PFA; **Mike Foster** and **Chris Whalley** from the FL and **Mickey Burns** and **Roger Reade** from the FFE&VTS. It proved to be a lengthy affair.

At the meeting, it was noted that the Football Trust had generously made available two years of funding at £2 million per year (rather than simply one year of funding) making a total of £4 million to be made available in total which, it was felt, would allow for any budget to be stretched to cover total costs over a three-year period, (i.e. ideally to cover the period from January 1991 to December 1993) especially when added to the already existing Government funding (via ET). In the end, the budgeted figures for expenditure included in the Business Plan for this period were as follows:

Detail of Expenditure	Amount	Percentage
Officers wages and grant aid	£3,806,510	69%
Management wages[2]	£1,107,139	20%
Marketing	£128,000	2.5%
Facility support	£460,000	8.5%
Total	£5,501,649	100%

It should be noted that budgeted income included £4 million from the Football Trust, PLUS an additional £1.5 million from other sources – i.e. (in the main) FFE&VTS contracts with Government (ET at the time). It should also be noted that some concern was expressed at the time about the high percentage of "management wages" in comparison to the total amount available. This was addressed by the FFE&VTS at the end of 1993 (see later).

It was also agreed that the following Aims and Objectives should be set in the Business Plan:

- To encourage more people (especially children) to play football

- To encourage more people (especially children) to watch football

- To encourage more people to become interested and support their local football club by forging closer links between them

- To improve the image of the game

- To improve atmosphere at matches

---

2. *Including travel expenses and pension contributions*

- To improve the behaviour of players and spectators

The main issue for discussion at the meeting, however, concerned that of the slightly different managerial structures in place at the FA and at the FFE&VTS Community Programme and how they would interact. Should difficulties arise, however, it was agreed that **Robin Russell** and **Roger Reade** should liaise together to come up with acceptable solutions. In the case of new appointments, the FA wanted to ensure that their Regional Managers would provide final approval. Whilst this was felt to be an unnecessary burden, it was agreed initially, subject to a review after at least a year of operation. It was also agreed that the two officers should work closely together to further consider and prepare the budget, which was to be included in the overall draft Business Plan covering the three-year period. In "ball-park" terms, for the Business Plan, it was noted that a new management structure needed to be introduced, together with at least an additional new 40 club-based Community Officers (based largely in the South).

In order to alert existing Community Officers of the proposed developments, a series of smaller, round-the-country meetings were held during July 1990 at Stockport County (10 officers attended including **Mike Rigg** on behalf of Wrexham[3]), Blackburn Rovers (7 officers including **Dave Wilkes** on behalf of Carlisle United), Newcastle United (4 officers), Huddersfield Town (8 officers), West Bromwich Albion (4 officers) and Mansfield Town (7 officers). Four officers were away on holiday at the time of these meetings and were to be updated later. It was also agreed that new officers soon to be appointed at Birmingham City (**Brian Caswell** had just left – see Chapter 6), Chesterfield, Port Vale and Scunthorpe United would be provided with these important details at their inductions. In addition, as already stated, there were no imminent appointments at Coventry City, Derby County, Shrewsbury Town or Wolverhampton Wanderers.

Whilst all details were properly announced and discussed, the main talking point at the meetings proved to be the issue of the need to generate income and for local community schemes to become self-sustainable by the end of 1993. Numbers would also be recorded, given that the likelihood was that national targets would be set. Targets set in the Business Plan included:

1. To introduce the game through coaching or other football involvement to 500,000 boys and 75,000 girls aged 6-16.
2. To involve 150,000 boys and girls in football club junior supporters' clubs.
3. To attempt to reduce indiscipline on and off the field in football.
4. To provide initiatives to involve the whole community in football club activities whether at the club or in "outreach work" including the following: The mentally/physically handicapped, Senior Citizens, Ethnic Minorities - statistics to be recorded in each of these groups.

These were, of course, giant steps for a scheme that had previously endeavoured to avoid cash handling at all and that was dealing already with huge numbers of people.

The Business Plan ended up being a thoroughly comprehensive document and it was interesting to note that even though agreement had been reached before that the FFE&VTS would not only provide the secretariat for future meetings but also be responsible for the preparation of the Business Plan, the FA still insisted on preparing their own version. This was sent through for further consideration on the 7th August. So that several matters identified by all parties could be further discussed, it was agreed that **Robin Russell** and **Roger Reade** should meet to 'thrash out' the details. Interestingly, even the venue for the meeting was debated at some length! In the end, curiously, a hotel in Matlock was identified as acceptable for the meeting as it was roughly half-way between the two respective officers' office bases!

It is fair to say that both officers were keen to reach agreement, especially having seen somewhat dogmatic positions adopted by others in the meetings leading up to the Matlock 'summit'. As such, the FA accepted the importance of Employment Training as a continuing part of the offer to clubs where available. In addition, it was agreed that a 'Critical Path' (or 'timeline' that identified separate phases of the introduction of the new scheme to clubs) should

---

3. Carlisle United and Wrexham were new club schemes that were not included in the original list of 50 club schemes listed on Page 46.

be prepared as a guide which would introduce clubs and other organisations as follows:

Phase I   36 0f the 50 existing FFE&VTS club-based community schemes
Phase II   The remaining 14 of the 50 existing FFE&VTS club-based community schemes in areas
               that may link into local authority or other existing (football development) schemes
Phase III 27 clubs currently without any local form of community scheme
Phase IV   15 clubs with some form of community scheme that already existed
Phase V   Certain Non-League clubs and/or County Football Associations (CFAs) identified in areas
               where there was currently no community provision and/or a clear need for some form
               of community engagement or liaison.

The Critical Path recognised that there were aspects where further discussions would be necessary notably in areas where CFAs had expressed an interest in taking up a 'community involvement' – i.e. (at that time) Avon, Lincolnshire, Oxfordshire, Sheffield & Hallamshire, Suffolk and Wiltshire.

Of the 14 areas identified in Phase II, it was also noted that discussions were already underway in the Leeds area involving **Colin Morris** (local Football Development Officer) and in the Bradford area involving **Mick Wood**.

Something of a sticking point, however, proved to be the issue of reaching agreement concerning the involvement of FA Regional Directors in undertaking technical monitoring inspections at the community projects. In the end, it was agreed that these visits would see liaison and co-operation between the FFE&VTS Community Programme Regional Managers (who would, in future, be referred as Regional Directors for the sake of parity) and FA Regional Directors.

The country was also to be split up into three regions. The existing two Regional Managers, **Kevin Glendon** and **Richard Finney**, would automatically transfer into the new Regional Director posts.

John Relish would eventually take over as Regional Director for the new FFE&VTS Community Programme Southern Region at the beginning of January 1991. John was born in Huyton and played for Liverpool's youth teams before joining Chester City as an apprentice where he made his league debut. He joined Newport County in 1974 going on to make well over 300 league appearances for the club before leaving in 1987. He briefly returned to the club in 1989/90 as player/manager. John was alerted to the concept of appointing former players wherever possible at an early stage:

> *"At that time I saw my role, wherever possible, as being to support the appointment*
> *of an ex-player to the role of Community Officer. However, this wasn't always*
> *possible and, in some cases, there was occasionally pressure from club personnel at*
> *local level to support their choice, whether it was a former player or not."*

In the new structure, there would be nine separate sub-areas (two of which would include North and South Wales). Each sub-area would be locally supported by an Area Manager and there would be three in each region who would be line-managed by the FFE&VTS Community Programme Regional Directors. The Area Managers were still to be appointed, though it was expected that at least one of the existing FFE&VTS managers would be transferred into one of the nine posts. The remaining vacant positions would be advertised nationally.

The issue of working with local authorities was addressed, notwithstanding, of course, that some professional clubs were adamant that they did NOT wish to work at all closely with their local authorities. Quite rightly though, common ground was reached with agreement on the following recommendation:

> *"it is recommended that either: 1. Local Authorities be invited to have a representative*
> *on the local Management Forum or 2. Approaches be made to Local Authorities to*
> *cooperate separately about the way forward via regular communication".*

It was also agreed that approaches should be made to representatives of the local police and Sports Council if felt appropriate.

In much the same way as offered by FFE&VTS to date, it was agreed that the minimum commitment from clubs would be the provision of an office at the ground (including the costs of lighting and heating that office) for the use of their local Community Officer(s).

To support these 'conditions', a draft formal agreement for signature by each professional club would be drawn up and schemes would only receive funding once the form of agreement had been signed.

A Staff Committee meeting took place in London in mid-September, chaired by **Graham Kelly** (Chief Executive of the FA), and attended by staff level representatives of the FA, the FL, the PFA and the FFE&VTS. The meeting was arranged to further discuss the details contained in the draft FFE&VTS Business Plan.

Final agreement was reached as follows:

- All income generated by local community projects would be paid into local community project bank accounts (to be opened if not already open) and all local projects should aim to be "financially self-supporting within three years" (this issue is considered further in Chapter 8).
- New scheme details should be presented to club Directors and Secretaries at a round of FL group meetings as soon as possible.
- The importance of primary club involvement was critical.
- The FA "syllabus" concerning their technical authority regarding coaching should be presented for further discussion and agreed by the Staff Committee.
- In the event of any disputes, matters would be referred to the full Board of Directors of the FFE&VTS.

The round-the-table meetings continued into the Autumn. Indeed, yet another meeting of the Staff Committee was held on the 16th October when it was clarified that the Staff Committee needed to report to the Board of Trustees of the FFE&VTS and that all minutes and reports needed to be copied to the Board (which would now, of course, include equal representation from the FA, FL and the PFA). In addition, it was confirmed that all parties were entitled to put forward, in advance and by giving proper notice, items for discussion at future meetings.

Various amendments or additions were raised in relation to the proposed 1991-1993 Business Plan: in relation to approaches to Welsh professional clubs, it was agreed that discussions needed to be held with representatives of the FA of Wales so that attention could be given to plans to embrace, at the very least, the more densely populated areas of Wales. It was also agreed that in addition to the 92 professional clubs, a further 8 community schemes should be established in densely populated areas, either in conjunction with non-league clubs (in certain areas) or with CFAs, or both. As a result, the target of 100 separate community schemes by the end of 1993 became clear for the new joint venture. Information from the 1981 Census revealed the following as key areas of population that could be included in the Plan

Population	Towns/Cities[4]
Over 500,000	Birmingham, Liverpool, London, Manchester and Sheffield
Over 200,000	Bradford, Bristol, Cardiff, Coventry, Derby, Hull, Leeds, Leicester, Newcastle, Nottingham, Plymouth, Portsmouth, Southampton, Stoke, Sunderland, Teesside, Wolverhampton
Over 100,000	Basildon, Birkenhead, Blackburn, Blackpool, Bolton, Bournemouth, Brighton, Cambridge, Dudley, Havant, Huddersfield, Ipswich, Luton, Newport, Northampton, Norwich, Oldham, Oxford, Poole, Reading, St. Helens, Solihull, South Shields, Southend, Swansea, Thurrock, Torquay, Walsall, York

4. *It is fair to say that this list may not be fully complete. Indeed, there may have been additional towns with populations in excess of 100,000 people that may not have been included in this table – e.g. Doncaster and Rotherham in South Yorkshire.*

The FFE&VTS was also 'tasked' with compiling, arranging and presenting a new pay structure for Community Officers that would work across existing Community Officers based on individual qualifications and including slightly increased salaries for Officers who held the FA Full Badge as against those Officers who held only the FA Preliminary Award.

In terms of management, the 3 FFE&VTS Regional Managers (now including **John Relish**) were to be confirmed as new scheme Regional Directors (with parity with the FA Regional Directors). In addition, existing Area Manager **Dick Krzywicki**, would automatically transfer to become the Yorkshire/North East new "Area Manager" (thus leaving eight Area Manager positions to be filled).

Financial information (including financial forecasts) needed to be introduced and include, for example, pension contributions for all managerial staff (this was way in advance of the Government's Pensions Act of 2008 when the 'Auto-Enrolment" scheme was first introduced).

FFE&VTS Community Programme Regional Directors met soon after this meeting to run through the various matters raised. All points were met with positive and, in some cases, enthusiastic responses. Details of the proposed pay structure for Community Officers were discussed and several ideas put forward as to how the structure could work. Also considered was how best officers at the lower end of the pay scale could be encouraged to aspire to higher wages.

It was noted at that meeting that, in addition to **Dick Krzywicki** transferring to become one of the nine new Area Managers, **Tommy Spencer** and **Derek Clydesdale** would move to become dedicated "ET liaison/quality assurance support officers" respectively in the East and in the West. Both would work under **Kevin Jardine** in his capacity as Training Officer (though Derek was to move on soon enough to take up a club-based Community Officer position).

The FA's **Robin Russell** and **Roger Reade** from the FFE&VTS met again at the offices of the National Coaching Foundation in Leeds in October 1990 to run through further details, mainly relating to the final preparation of the proposed new Job Descriptions and to attempt to finalise the draft Business Plan for 1991-1993. Their final detailed recommendations were then taken to a Staff Committee meeting at Lilleshall at the end of October. This meeting welcomed the proposed amendments incorporated in the Business Plan. Although it was recognised that, effectively, the three-year Business Plan would cover the period from the 1ˢᵗ January 1991 to the 31ˢᵗ December 1993, it was also agreed and recognised that it was important to start work as soon as possible. It was therefore agreed that approaches would be made to the existing 50 professional club schemes that already received FFE&VTS Community Programme support during November and December 1990.

It was agreed that the remaining eight Area Manager positions should be advertised so that a short-list of possible candidates for interview could be made available for further consideration by Staff Committee members before Christmas 1990. This would facilitate the process of interviews to be arranged in early January 1991.

In November, agreement was reached concerning the pay structure that would work for all existing FFE&VTS Community Programme Officers that was loosely based on Local Authority pay scales for equivalent posts. The range of salaries available was fixed as being between £11,000 and £13,000 per annum. As a result, levels were set whereby those Officers who held the FA's Full Badge *plus* appropriate Recreation and Leisure qualifications would be paid at the top end of the scale. Officers with fewer qualifications would be paid at the lower end of the scale, though they could work their way up depending on their achievement of qualifications. Effectively, and as a guideline for the future, the scales agreed were:

Salary	Suggested Qualifications
£11,000 per annum	FA Preliminary Coaching Award (only)
£11,500 per annum	FA Preliminary Coaching Award plus, for example, NEBSM award
£12,000 per annum	FA Full Badge (only)
£12,500 per annum	FA Full Badge plus, for example, NEBSM award
£13,000 per annum	FA Full Badge plus, for example, ILAM award and NEBSM award

It was also agreed that any existing Community Officers who didn't hold the FA Preliminary Coaching Award (as a minimum) should be encouraged to attend a course immediately. The FA had suggested that around 12 officers didn't hold this award at the time of the end of the year, although it was later confirmed that the correct number was only 6 officers, most of whom were newly appointed, and plans were already in-hand for them to attend FA Preliminary Award courses.

Interestingly, a further meeting of the Staff Committee in November 1990 saw **Joe Patton** from the Sports Council attend, when it was acknowledged and agreed that an appropriate amount from within the overall budget should be set aside for facility and equipment provision within the Business Plan (dependent on local community needs). Possible facilities would include all-weather pitches, changing rooms, classrooms and kickabout/multi-use areas. In addition, it was agreed that consideration could be given to supporting certain existing sites that were poorly managed and which could be better utilised. Use of the Sports Council/Football Trust funded minibuses was also discussed at the meeting, notwithstanding that it was accepted that Football Trust available funding was unlikely to be able to cover the costs of running the minibuses.

In relation to the new eight Area Manager positions, it was agreed that they should be advertised in the *Times Educational Supplement* (amongst other newspapers). Once placed, there was an expected deluge of enquires from many former players, teachers, existing Football Development Officers and Community Officers from all around the country. Interviews were arranged during the week commencing 7th January 1991 and an initial short list of 26 candidates for interview were invited. This shortlist was then reduced to an initial 15 candidates for interview. Three separate days interviewing were spent at the FA offices at Lancaster Gate with a further two days spent interviewing at The Football League (FL) office in Lytham St. Anne's. The interview panel included **Robin Russell** from the FA, **Mike Foster** from the FL, and **Mickey Burns** and **Roger Reade** from the FFE&VTS.

Discussions following the interviews were thorough and worthwhile and, in the end (and after some lengthy discussions on this subject alone!), it was agreed that there should only be 3 Area Managers appointed in each region (rather than 4 in each region as had originally been put forward). This would also support a more balanced budget as outlined in the Business Plan (which was already 'tight' to say the least!) Indeed, a revised budget was put forward for inclusion in the draft Business Plan soon after this decision had been confirmed. Agreement was soon reached that the following successful candidates would be invited to accept the respective posts of Area Managers:

Region	Area	Area Manager
Western	Lancashire & Cumbria	**Andy Welsh**
Western	Manchester, Merseyside, Cheshire & North Wales	**Paul Power**[5] 1986/7.
Western	Staffordshire & West Midlands	**Brendan O'Callaghan** (see Chapter 4 for Brendan's background)
Eastern	North East & North and West Yorkshire	**Dick Krzywicki** (already in post)
Eastern	South Yorkshire & Humberside	To be appointed
Eastern	East Midlands and Bedfordshire	**Gordon Coleman**[6]
Southern	South West & South Wales	To be appointed[7]

5. *Paul made his debut for Manchester City in 1975, going on to make 365 league appearances before joining Everton in 1986 where he helped the club to win the Championship in 1986/87.*
6. *Gordon began his playing career with Preston North End, making his league debut against West Bromwich Albion in 1973. He continued to play for the club over the next ten years, making over 300 appearances. He then played for Bury during the 1983/4 season before retiring from playing.*
7. *Initial offers made to successful candidates for one of the London positions and for the South West & South Wales positions were refused, leaving the FFE&VTS having to make alternative arrangements in these areas.*

Southern	South London & the South Coast	To be appointed[7]
Southern	North and East London & Essex	To be appointed

After further consideration, the London appointments of **Jim Hicks** (North and East London & Essex) and **Dave Palmer** (South London & the South Coast) were agreed.

Jim Hicks was a central defender with Exeter City (where he made his debut), Oxford United and Fulham (where he made 39 league appearances) before going on to play briefly in the USA. Jim would, in later years, go on to head up the PFA Coaching Department.

Dave Palmer was a former professional player with Wrexham who joined the Community Programme scheme having previously been involved as Crawley's Football Development Officer. Dave was able to start work in his new role on the 2nd April 1991.

In addition, it was agreed that the vacant post in the South Yorkshire & Humberside area would be considered further at a later date. Out of interest, it is worth noting that all these senior appointments were former players and/or former members of the PFA.

In the end, and after only a short period in post as Area Manager in Staffordshire & West Midlands, **Brendan O'Callaghan** also made the decision to move back into industry, leaving this position vacant once again. Interviews for all three vacant positions were then held in, of all places, Ross-On-Wye (Herefordshire) in May 1991 and at Bristol City Football Club in September 1991. After careful consideration, the new Area Managers appointed were **Peter Withe** (Staffordshire & West Midlands), **John Seasman** (South Yorkshire & Humberside) and **Dave Bell** (South West & South Wales).

Liverpool-born **Peter Withe** played professionally for several clubs during his league career but is probably best remembered for his days with Aston Villa (1980-1985) for whom he scored the winning goal in the 1982 European Cup Final when they beat Bayern Munich 1-0. He also played for Nottingham Forest when they won the First Division Championship and FL Cup in 1978.

The initial wave of Area Managers took up their new posts in March and early April 1991 and a formal induction was arranged for them between the 3rd and 5th April. Induction for the later appointments of the new Area Managers took place around the end of June.

As the newly amalgamated scheme was evolving, it became apparent that as **Graham Kelly** (FA), **Gordon Taylor** (PFA) and FL Secretary **David Dent** were FFE&VTS Board level representatives, they needed to be replaced on the Staff Committee by more permanent appointments (although it was agreed that they would also have the mandate to attend Staff Committee Meetings if necessary). **Mick McGuire** and **Brendon Batson** were swiftly appointed as PFA representatives on the Staff Committee whilst **Charles Hughes** and **Robin Russell** were appointed as representatives of the FA. **Mike Foster** and **Chris Whalley** would continue to represent the Football League (FL).

Mick McGuire's background as a professional footballer was that he began his league career with Coventry City where he made 72 league appearances for the club over a four-year period. He then moved to Norwich City where he played for eight years. He also played for Tampa Bay Rowdies, Barnsley and Oldham Athletic before moving into non-league football.

Born in Grenada, **Brendon Batson** began his football career as an apprentice with Arsenal before moving to Cambridge United under then manager Ron Atkinson where he made over 160 league appearances between 1973 and 1977. He then followed Atkinson to West Bromwich Albion. After retiring from playing in 1982, Brendon then spent many successful years working as Deputy Chief Executive of the PFA working alongside **Gordon Taylor**.

Mickey Burns would also now adopt the title of Chief Executive of the FFE&VTS overall. He was to be given the power of 'veto' should anything be brought forward by any of the partner organisations that might be unacceptable on the basis that the full board should then consider this matter further. This was a huge step forward for the FFE&VTS 'ownership' of the Community Programme scheme and one that prevented any further possible disruption in future years to come.

The Business Plan covering the period 1991-1993 was eventually adopted in February

1991.

Following hot on the heels of the successful schools Guinness six-a-side competition, the National Crime Prevention and Thorn Home Security Cup had been launched at the start of the 1990/91 season, linking in with key messages of home security for all participants and their parents. The final of the competition was played at Wembley, once again with the support of the Football League, prior to the Manchester United v Sheffield Wednesday Football League Cup Final match on April 21st 1991. Former Manchester United and England player **Bobby Charlton**, was kind enough to present the trophy and medals, alongside the English Schools FA Chairman, to the match officials and players. Several of the Manchester United and Sheffield Wednesday players also stood on the side-lines and watched the junior match prior to the main match.

In June 1991, the FA arranged for formal 'technical briefings' to be held for all Community Officers based at Phase I club projects when a total of 21 Community Officers from the 36 clubs attended.

Roger Reade's welcome speech at the technical briefings was notably sombre in mood. He spoke of the recent sad death of **Mick Baxter** who, *"had the greatest enthusiasm for the community scheme that I have ever known."* He went on to say that *"much of what has been achieved since his death has been done and achieved in his memory."* He also said that, *"whatever else may be happening in football, this scheme must thrive and continue expanding. There is now a new spirit of co-operation and trust to be built up."*

Mike Foster and **Chris Whalley** from the FL stated that one of the significant aspects for them was the fact that there was *"no direct cost to clubs"*. They also identified the importance of family and community initiatives merging together to create a new force for good.

Robin Russell from the FA spoke about the FA's document *"The Blueprint for the Future of Football"* and the fact that the FFE&VTS Community schemes had been referred to in the document (although it is also fair to say that the press and media were otherwise engaged principally by the idea put forward in the Blueprint of a new breakaway League).

What was notable from the various FA presentations (from well-known and respected officers such as **Alex Gibson, Jim Kelman, Helen Jeavons, Alex Welsh** and **Eric Williams**) was that the FA was increasingly moving towards embracing football for everyone – i.e. girls and women, disabled people, special needs children/children with learning difficulties etc.

Whilst it was clear that the technical authority of the FA was now in place, it was also clear that there were distinctly grey areas. As an example, the FA wanted all community projects to deliver the FA's 'fun-weeks' and 'soccer star scheme' courses for children. After some discussion, the FFE&VTS position was clarified to be:

> *"(Club-based local) Management forums can draw on the technical briefing aspects but may wish to run any elements from the technical briefing book."*

What became clear in later months was that whilst the FA offer of using the three lions logo, England posters, postcards and giveaways etc. was all very welcome, clubs were becoming increasingly adamant that the 'branding' of their own locally delivered courses should be undertaken in the name of their local club and that these courses would also be directly supported by the clubs – e.g. by encouraging local players to attend.

In the end, it became very clear that after what had clearly been incredibly lengthy (and sometimes heated!) discussions and what were, on occasions, undoubtedly difficult negotiations, very positive steps forward had been taken. This was especially true as the "football family" of all the then key football authorities (FA, FL and PFA – supported by the Football Trust) were now to come together, and work together, for the very first time in 1990 (a good 22 years after similar recommendations had been included in the Chester Report of 1968).

John Collier had been appointed as Community Officer at Scunthorpe United earlier on the year, but he left in the Spring after only a few months in post. **Rick Passmoor** was eventually appointed as the new Community Officer at the club at the end of June.

A meeting was arranged with **John Davies**, who expressed a keen interest in the soon-to-be created post of Community Officer at Hull City. John began his career as an apprentice goalkeeper with Cardiff City where he made his league debut before moving to Hull City. He also spent a short time on loan at Notts County in 1985/6. Following his appointment as Community Officer at Hull at the end of July 1990, John became a very popular figure who went on to successfully serve the club in this role for many years.

CHAPTER 6
GROWTH... AND A BROADENING EXPERTISE

THE NEW 1990/91 SEASON kicked off with plenty of optimism amongst Community Programme officials and 'business as usual' whilst discussions were ongoing about the proposed amalgamated scheme. In the meantime, local club-based community work continued to thrive and flourish with additional ideas for engaging with local communities being introduced on an almost on-going basis.

The success of the work already undertaken by **Brian Caswell** in his role as Community Officer at Birmingham City led to him being offered the post of Youth Team Coach/Youth Development Officer at the club in early July 1990. Indeed, Brian would go on to have a very successful career in coaching with Stoke City, Telford United, Northampton Town and Shrewsbury Town (amongst others) in future. Popular former Blues player, **Joe Gallagher,** took over as Community Officer from Brian at the beginning of August 1990 and his appointment was enthusiastically supported by new Club Secretary **Annie Bassett** at the club, partly in view of his hugely successful and long spell as a player with the club. Liverpool-born Joe was a loyal servant of Birmingham City as a central defender having played for the club between 1972 and 1981 (he made his debut in October 1973 against Arsenal). He also enjoyed short-term spells as a player with Wolverhampton Wanderers, West Ham United, Burnley and Halifax Town (on loan).

Richard O'Kelly was appointed at the start of August as Community Officer at Port Vale following the earlier departure of **Ray Train** to Middlesbrough as Youth Development Officer. As a player, Richard began his career at Walsall and helped the club to promotion in his first season (1979/80). He moved to Port Vale in 1986 but returned to Walsall two years later. He then moved to Grimsby in 1988 but retired through injury a year later. In later years, Richard went on in later years to have an extremely successful career as a coach with several clubs including Hereford United, Bournemouth, Doncaster Rovers, Brentford and Aston Villa.

Adrian Shaw was appointed as Community Officer at Chesterfield in September. Adrian began his playing career with Nottingham Forest as an apprentice before moving to Halifax Town, initially on loan, York City and Chesterfield where he was forced to end his playing days after a serious injury. He also enjoyed spells at non-league Bridlington and Gainsborough.

Dick Krzywicki met up with his former team-mate **Frank Worthington** at this time (Frank had called the office expressing interest in the post at Huddersfield Town that had been vacated by **Bobby Hoy** during early September). Frank Worthington's playing career began with Huddersfield Town in 1966 where he remained until he moved to Leicester City in 1972 with whom he won 8 England caps. A regular goal scorer with all his clubs, Worthington's next moves took him to Bolton Wanderers, Philadelphia Fury (USA), Birmingham City, and several more clubs before he finished his league career at Stockport County in 1988.

Frank was scheduled to commence his employment in early September though this was, in the end, delayed. After working only a few days, Frank expressed doubt as to whether the position was in fact the right move for him at that time. Whilst this was, to an extent at least, understandable, it was clearly a big loss for the club and for the local community as it was felt that Frank could well have gone on to become an excellent 'conductor' of local community initiatives in the Huddersfield area, in much the same way that former England international **Tony Currie** had 'orchestrated' things so successfully over many years at Sheffield United.

Interest in the scheme also came from north of the border. **Bobby Jenks**, then a Development Officer at Motherwell, expressed his delight with what he had heard about the scheme and promptly set about speaking to the Scottish FA to see if similar steps could be taken in Scotland. Indeed, a follow up call from **Jim Gardner** at the Motherwell Training Agency expressed interest in how Motherwell Football Club could help to deliver a community programme scheme in the area.

The Football Trust, who many people in the game felt were beginning to play a key role in the transformation of football in the late 1980's, convened a meeting held at Leicester University in September 1990 that was attended by a number of individuals[8] from different walks of football life. The meeting was aimed at considering a further round of Football Trust Community Awards. In the end, based on the extent of their involvement in their local communities at that time, the 1990/91 joint winners were Brentford and Sunderland.

"Business as usual" in the new season meant that the important senior management (monthly) meetings continued and whilst there were important "updates' about the proposed new scheme, there were also full (and much lengthier) 'updates' about monthly Officers reports (which were noted to be improving, especially as better statistics were now being produced for Training Agencies/TECs), ET in general, recruitment levels, Community project performance etc. As a result of discussions at the meetings, around twenty letters were sent to Community Officers about the low number of trainees in post at their respective community projects with a strong recommendation made that increased contact with their local jobcentres was essential if they were to improve their recruitment levels. That said, scheme officials were absolutely thrilled and delighted to find that 'Approved Training Manager' status had been awarded to the FFE&VTS Community Programme during the Autumn of 1990.

Figures made available by **Gordon Shaw** on behalf of the Training Commission at that time suggested that scheme performance within ET was good with a total of 303 trainees then in post.

In addition, there were more starters than leavers recorded and over 70% of trainees were noted to be in training towards achieving National Vocational Qualifications (NVQs) at Level II.

Raised, at the October management meeting, was a general update from all the Regional Managers about how football for women and girls was developing and growing. It was noted, for example, that women's teams had been formed at several professional clubs including Blackburn Rovers (who had successfully negotiated local sponsorship support from Whitbread and were in the process of looking to affiliate with the FA) , Blackpool, Bolton Wanderers, Burnley, Bury (whose team was already playing in the North West Women's League), Crewe Alexandra (linked to British Home Stores), Liverpool (who had played Crewe Alexandra recently), Manchester City, Nottingham Forest, Oldham Athletic, Rochdale (who had played several friendly matches already – the latest of which had been against Blackpool), Rotherham United, Sheffield Wednesday, Tranmere Rovers, Walsall and Wigan Athletic (whose team had applied to join the North West Women's League). Port Vale were in the process of affiliating their team with the FA and Stockport County were at an early stage in that, at this time, they had merely organised a few sessions for interested female players.

The bigger picture suggested that because of the fantastic success of the community schemes across the country, enquiries, of various types, started to be received from clubs from across the South of England. One such enquiry from **Neil Watson** at Leyton Orient even facilitated the supply of a Vauxhall Midi minibus (through the FFE&VTS Community Programme suppliers) at a substantially reduced rate than Orient representatives were able to negotiate in London.

John Adams, Chief Executive at Southend United, made contact to express a keen interest in establishing a community scheme at the club in June 1989 (a follow up meeting was eventually

---

8. *Individuals involved as part of the Judging Panel included:* **John Williams** *(University of Leicester),* **Jean Evans** *(Learning Through Football),* **John Maiden** *(Football's Family Face),* **Monica Hartland** *(Football Supporters Federation),* **Joe Patton** *(Sports Council),* **Linda Whitehead** *(WFA),* **Garth Crooks** *(PFA),* **Rogan Taylor** *(Independent Supporters),* **Bob Perkins** *(AMA),* **Peter Lee** *(new Secretary of the Football Trust),* **Roger Reade** *(FFE&VTS Community Programme),* **Jack Crawford, David Woodall, Dennis Artez** *and several others. Individuals were grouped into groups of three or four people for each of the divisional awards.*

held with him and Club Chairman, **Vic Jobson,** in October 1990. Following on from that meeting, John confirmed that he would be very keen to appoint a Community Officer at the first possible opportunity!) The Football League (FL) also reported at a Staff Committee meeting of an enquiry from **Jean Harrison** of Bristol City, which was to be followed up in time so that details of the new Football Trust-funded 'roll-out' could be passed on.

Discussions involving representatives of the FL then took place aimed at supporting a national 6-a-side competition, with exciting implications for the future given the FL commitment to make available grounds for staging certain matches, including Wembley Stadium on the occasion of FL fixtures, in future.

In mid-November, **Daral Pugh** was appointed as the FFE&VTS Community Programme Officer at Leeds Road, Huddersfield Town's former ground. Daral began his playing career as an apprentice at Doncaster Rovers, helping the club to win promotion from the old Fourth Division in 1982. He then had spells with Huddersfield Town, Rotherham United, Cambridge United (on loan) and, finally, with Torquay United. Since leaving the Community Programme, Daral has enjoyed coaching with several clubs including Leeds United, Hull City, Bury, Rotherham United and Sheffield Wednesday.

Daral's appointment was to become a topic of discussion as part of lengthy discussions about the merger of the Huddersfield Football Development scheme (headed up by Football Development Officer **Dai Jones**) with the Huddersfield Town Football in the Community Scheme (see later).

Cyril "Ces" Podd (then Community Officer at Leeds United) had flagged up that he was keen to arrange a Preliminary Coaching course for teachers in the Leeds area and the FA, through their Regional Director **Ted Copeland**, had confirmed that they would be happy to assist. This coming together had encouraging and positive overtones for the future of the new 'partnership'.

In terms of new appointments, **Domenico Genovese** was appointed as the first ever Community Officer at Peterborough United, the 50th club to join the scheme. Domenico was born in Peterborough and played non-league football for Boston United before joining Peterborough United in 1988 where he made his league debut in a 2-1 win over Exeter City. He later joined non-league clubs Cambridge City and Kettering Town.

Will Foley made the decision to resign from the post of Community Officer at Hereford United and was replaced in the New Year by **Brian Williams**, whose induction was held alongside **Craig Madden** (Community Officer at Blackpool) and **Paul Johnson** (new Officer at Stoke City) in May 1991. Following the promotion of Blackpool's Community Officer, **Andy Welsh**, to become an Area Manager, former Blackpool and striker **Craig Madden** had come forward to take over the role at the Bloomfield Road club. He was appointed and commenced his new duties at the beginning of April 1991. Similarly, the vacant position of Community Officer at Stoke City had been created as a result of the move by **Brendan O'Callaghan** to take up the position of Area Manager in Staffordshire and the West Midlands. The Stoke post had been widely advertised, with interviews held at the end of March 1991.

Born in Salford, **Brian Williams** began his playing days as an apprentice with Bury where he made just under 150 league appearances before later moves to Queens Park Rangers, Swindon Town, Bristol Rovers and Bristol City before a final move to Shrewsbury Town in 1987 where he finished his career.

Craig Madden was born in Manchester and became a true football hero with the club for whom he made his debut in 1977 – Bury. He went on to spend the next nine years with the Gigg Lane club and remains the club's all-time record goal scorer. He also played at West Bromwich Albion, Blackpool, Wrexham (on loan) and York City.

Stoke-born **Paul Johnson** served his apprenticeship as a footballer with Stoke City before making his debut in 1977. After four years he moved to Shrewsbury Town and then to York City. He then played non-league football for Macclesfield Town and Leek Town.

CHAPTER 7 – "CORE" ACTIVITIES

T HE DEVELOPMENT OF COMMUNITY 'expertise' was crucial to the Scheme's advancement and it is very much to the credit of the Community Officers in post that activity involvement at club level was beginning to grow and develop in the early 1990's. What would be defined as "core" activities at most club schemes saw an ongoing involvement throughout the year based on the following:

FOOTBALL ACTIVITY	
School term time (for boys AND (importantly) for girls too)	- In-school activity (mainly sports coaching in PE lessons) - Inter-school tournaments - After-school sessions - Ground tours/Training ground visits/coaching at club facilities (where possible) - Player visits (and talks/Question and Answer sessions) - Saturday club activities - Match day visits - Veterans football - Football sessions for unemployed young people - Football sessions for people with disabilities
School holidays/non-school time	- Holiday course 'soccer schools'/fun schemes (including player visits) - Girls only holiday courses - Saturday activities (including match day and exchange visits) - Veterans football - Football sessions for unemployed young people - Football sessions for people with disabilities

NON-FOOTBALL ACTIVITY	
General	- Social events such as quiz nights, tea dances (for the over 50's), bingo etc. - Football (sessions and matches) for girls and for women - Birthday parties - Ground tours - Learning Through Football (cross curricular work) - Keep fit activities (including other sports – e.g. basketball/tennis/netball/short mat bowls) - The development of junior and/or adult supporters clubs (linked in to existing clubs as appropriate)

It is also, of course, worth noting that statistical details for all these areas of activity were requested as part of a process whereby regular quarterly reports were completed by Community Officers and submitted to the FFE&VTS Community Programme office where they were recorded.

Activities were notably split into age groups: nursery age/primary school age/secondary school age/up to 35s/over 35's/Over 50's. In addition, there was much greater encouragement for girls to participate in community scheme activities rather than had been the case in Physical Education classes, for example, where lessons were often split into football for boys and either netball or hockey for girls.

As **Richard Finney** said:

> *"One important aspect was the decision to make sure there was whole class involvement in the school's programme activities. To include girls began to encourage their desire to play and potentially was the catalyst for the growth in girls and women's football."*

Reports submitted by Community Officers included numbers of those involved in these activities which were rated according to the amount of detail and information passed on. For example, the best and most informative reports were noted in early 1991 to have been received from Bradford City, Crewe Alexandra, Bury, Rochdale, Tranmere Rovers, Walsall, Aston Villa, Wrexham, Barnsley, Doncaster Rovers and Stockport County.

By the end of 1993 it was noted that there had been an average increase of approximately 2,000 new people to watch matches at each football club based on the involvement of their own local community schemes (i.e. a total of in excess of 190,000 nationally). This was largely facilitated through the popularity of "Saturday Club' activities which included coaching for children and young people, followed by attendance at matches.

It was, of course, recognised at an early stage that work undertaken by community schemes contributed to increasing attendances. **Gary Glendening**, Club Secretary at Stockport County, speaking in 1995, said:

> *"The number of school children visiting Edgeley Park has increased dramatically during the last twelve months, so much that the under 16's now make up just short of 25% of the average gate and this figure doesn't include the complimentary tickets we give to schools. This is a very positive sign."*

Key to much of the scheme's activities, of course, was the 'icing on the cake' of the involvement of current players. All activities were suitably enhanced if current players were also able to attend. One of the recognised ways of working was, for example, in schools where a programme of activity over a half term of six or seven weeks of coordinated activity in Primary/Junior schools finished with the attendance of one or two players in the school concerned. **Richard Finney** commented:

> *"Player visits to schools and local activities increased as clubs began to see the value of supporting their local communities"*

Schools saw the benefits too. Included amongst the many benefits were: support for their already extremely busy teachers, the introduction of a free, external expertise in sports (football) coaching for both boys and girls, greater interest in being at school and, as Richard also highlighted:

> *"One junior school in Sheffield told us that their attendances on Fridays had been at an all-time high when **Tony Currie** and the Sheffield United Community project visited the school for sessions on a Friday afternoon"*

There were many benefits of clubs running holiday courses of course including:
-   Closer identity with clubs for participating children (and, ultimately, the interest developing into children becoming supporters and/or season-ticket holders at clubs)
-   Increased revenue streams for Community Schemes
-   Improved skills and knowledge for children attending
-   Increased revenue for clubs via the purchase of souvenirs/mementos in club shops/stores

- Engaging with children during holidays, often providing parents with solutions to the age-old question of what to do for their children during holiday time

As the years rolled by, the 'core' of activities became greatly enhanced. In addition, as more and more partners came to work with local community schemes, there was more and more variety in what was being offered to the local community. The common factor in all activity provision, however, was always the football club and its community scheme, whether the activity was football related or not.

CHAPTER 8 – THE AMALGAMATED SCHEME 1991-1993

THE NEW YEAR 1991 kicked off with a round-the-table meeting at Liverpool Football Club's Anfield ground with the Chief Executives of Everton and Liverpool, **Jim Greenwood** and **Peter Robinson**, both of whom had recognised that the Merseyside clubs' community involvement needed re-structuring to facilitate the clubs' high expectations. The point was made that both clubs had been under pressure to 'step up' their community involvement, particularly since the Hillsborough disaster, and that, for the clubs, they felt that they needed to consider the appointment of higher profile community engagement officers who could be brought in and who could work closely with the existing officers being **Alan Whittle** at Everton and **Brian Kettle** at Liverpool. Follow up meetings at both clubs confirmed that the two clubs were looking to go in slightly different directions.

Everton representatives (**Jim Greenwood**, Commercial Manager **Derek Johnstone** and Youth Development Manager **Ray Hall**) were to place their Football in the Community scheme under the overall charge of the Youth Development section and place Club Director **Dr. David Marsh** at the head of the whole set-up. In the end, **Neil Dewsnip** was appointed as the club's new Senior Community Officer, taking up his new duties in 1991.

Liverpool, meanwhile, were looking to develop a more generic total 'community' scheme and interviewed for someone who could lead this new approach. From the club's point of view, the 'ideal' for them, and one that they hoped might be possible, was for someone with a background at the club to be appointed. In the end and following the abandonment of the ET scheme at Liverpool, **Brian Kettle** left the club (to become manager of nearby non-league Southport) and Liverpool's former midfield player, **Brian Hall**, took up his new post in August. Brian became an extremely popular, hard-working and successful PR and Community Liaison Officer at the club over the next twenty years or so (he sadly passed away in July 2015).

Individual meetings with senior club officials also commenced early in the New Year 1991 in accordance with the plans and phases identified in the 'Critical Path' that had been drawn up following the adoption of the agreed Business Plan for 1991-1993. So, as part of Phase I, meetings were held with 36 of the 50 existing clubs that were already successfully working with the FFE&VTS. The meetings (held mainly between February and April 1991) were thorough in that the new 'criteria' was fully explained and followed up with the presentation of a formal written agreement that the club had to sign in order to trigger the financial support that was to become available to them. To illustrate the commitment of the clubs to work with the FFE&VTS, club agreements from clubs in Phase I and Phase II were all returned by the Summer of 1991.

The 36 clubs in Phase I, once again, were: Barnsley, Blackburn Rovers, Blackpool, Bolton Wanderers, Burnley, Bury, Carlisle United, Chesterfield, Crewe Alexandra, Darlington, Doncaster Rovers, Everton, Halifax Town, Hartlepool United, Hereford United, Hull City, Leicester City, Liverpool, Mansfield Town, Northampton Town, Nottingham Forest, Notts County, Oldham Athletic, Preston North End, Port Vale, Rochdale, Rotherham United, Scarborough, Sheffield United, Sheffield Wednesday, Stockport County, Stoke City, Tranmere Rovers, Wigan Athletic, Wrexham and York City.

The new criteria presented to clubs included the provision of background information, together with details of the new requirement for clubs:

- Community schemes were to aim to become self-sufficient within three years of the commencement of the Project (without 'profiteering').

- Schemes should be supervised by a local management forum comprising representatives of the club (Chairman/Director or Chief Executive – as specified by the club), the FFE&VTS and others as necessary (e.g. local authorities).

- Schemes should establish a local bank account to be set up in the name of the club's community scheme with joint signatory control – i.e. all payments were to be authorised by representatives of both the club and the FFE&VTS.

- Football clubs were to provide an office and cover the costs of the lighting and heating of that office.

- Football clubs were to provide regular player support (in the form of player attendances) at events/activities, together with the use of club-based facilities where available.

- Football clubs were to agree to the proposed new level of salary for the officer based at their club.

Following the completion of the first phase of approaches to the 36 clubs, the second phase of meetings was then arranged with the remaining 14 clubs, who were already working alongside the FFE&VTS but where local authorities also had Football Development Officers in post and some form of 'liaison' was going to be necessary.

The 14 clubs in Phase II were: Aston Villa, Birmingham City, Bradford City, Chester City, Grimsby Town, Huddersfield Town, Leeds United, Manchester City, Newcastle United, Peterborough United, Scunthorpe United, Sunderland, Walsall and West Bromwich Albion.

The third and fourth phases of approaches to the remaining clubs effectively coincided, as it was clear that by May 1991 those clubs, who had community schemes *and* those clubs without any sort of community operation, were clamouring to arrange meetings as soon as possible, so that they could get things moving at their respective clubs. Clubs identified under Phase IV but keen to become involved at the earliest opportunity included Arsenal, Leyton Orient and Millwall (to name but three).

FFE&VTS Community Programme officials, led by the Regional Directors and the new Area Managers, set about the huge task of contacting the remaining 42 Phase III and IV FL clubs (plus 2 new clubs being Barnet, who were promoted to the FL in 1991 and Colchester United, who were promoted back to the FL in 1992, having been relegated at the end of season 1989/90), during the remainder of the year. Clubs were contacted as follows:

April 1991	Arsenal, Bristol City, Cardiff City, Norwich City, Wimbledon
May 1991	AFC Bournemouth, Aldershot, Cambridge United, Fulham, Southend United, Swindon Town, Wolverhampton Wanderers
June 1991	Chelsea, Coventry City, Middlesbrough, Millwall
July 1991	Brighton & Hove Albion, Manchester United, Swansea City, West Ham United
August 1991	Gillingham, Plymouth Argyle, Portsmouth
September 1991	Charlton Athletic, Exeter City, Reading
October 1991	Barnet, Bristol Rovers, Lincoln City, Maidstone United, Queens Park Rangers, Torquay United, Watford
November 1991	Tottenham Hotspur
December 1991	Oxford United
Early 1992[9]	Brentford, Colchester United, Crystal Palace, Derby County, Ipswich Town, Leyton Orient, Luton Town, Shrewsbury Town, Southampton

Additional approaches as part of Phase V of the Critical Path were made to non-FL clubs and CFAs in 1992 as follows:

---

9. *It was recognised that it might not be possible to offer funding covering a full three-year period to these clubs as they had been approached so late.*

Barrow AFC, possibly in conjunction with Lancashire County Football Association (CFA), Farnborough Town FC (to replace the former community scheme at Aldershot FC), Kidderminster Harriers FC, Merthyr Tydfil FC (South Wales), Weymouth FC (in conjunction with Dorset CFA) and Yeovil Town FC.

The following CFAs were also approached:

Cornwall CFA,
Durham CFA,
Kent CFA,
Norfolk CFA,
Nottinghamshire CFA and Sheffield & Hallamshire CFA.

The following tables outline approaches made to organisations and, where appropriate, the appointments made at Phase III, Phase IV and Phase V clubs and associations:

Phase III Club	Representatives of Club seen	Community Officer Appointed
AFC Bournemouth	Contact with the club arose out of an original enquiry from **Brian Tiler** (formerly Managing Director) and, later, **Norman Hayward** (Chairman) and **Annie Bassett** (Chief Executive)	**David Armstrong**. (David started work at Bournemouth in July 1991 but moved to Weymouth in 1992 and wasn't immediately replaced when he left). Born in Durham, **David Armstrong** played for Middlesbrough for most of his career (1971-81) before a surprise move to Southampton where he played for six seasons under Saints Manager **Lawrie McMenemy**. He also briefly played for Bournemouth in 1987/88. David made 3 appearances for England.
Aldershot	**Brian Talbot** (Manager)	**Geoff Noonan**
Barnet	**Barry Fry** (Manager), **Stan Flashman** (Chairman), **Malcolm Cohen** and **Ricky George.** Also (later) **David Buchler, Fenton Higgins, Geoff Cooper, Colonel Brian Edwards OBE and Tony Kleanthous**	**Geoff Cooper** had been undertaking community work on behalf of the club, though **Gary Phillips** was eventually appointed for a short period. Gary left in February 1995.
Bristol City	**Jean Harrison**	**Shaun Parker**

Bristol Rovers	**Bob Twyford** (Secretary) and **Ron Craig**	**Glyn Jones** (though he moved to Cardiff City after a short period in post). Glyn was born in Newport and began his playing career as a goalkeeper with Bristol Rovers before later moves to Shrewsbury Town and his hometown club, Newport County. He also played for several non-league clubs including Bath City and Gloucester City.
Cambridge United	**John Howard** (Director)	**Mike Cook** (started early August). Born in Stroud, Mike began his playing career as an apprentice with Coventry City. After a short-term loan with York City, he then joined Cambridge United as a midfield player between 1989-1991. Sadly, after a further loan spell at York, Mike was forced to retire due to a serious back injury.
Cardiff City	**Eddie Harrison** (Club Secretary. Eddie was also very supportive when he left to join Port Vale as Club Secretary).	**Glyn Jones** (appointed in December 1992)
Charlton Athletic	**Roger Alwen** and **Steve Dixon**	**Jason Morgan**
Chelsea	**Colin Hutchinson** (Managing Director) and **Sheila Marson** (Secretary)	**Shaun Gore** (started 19th October 1992). Born in West Ham, Shaun was a solid 6'4" central defender who played initially for Fulham between 1985–1991. He then played for Halifax Town on loan for a short spell. Sadly, injury curtailed Shaun's playing career.
Exeter City	**Michael Holladay**	**George Kent**
Fulham	**Brian Naysmith** and **Tom Enefer**	**Mick Gayle,** though he was soon replaced by **Gary Mulcahey** (in May 1992)
Gillingham	**Paul Scally** (Chairman)	**Phil Attfield**
Luton Town	**Ron Howard** and **Cherry Newbury** (Secretary)	**Gary Hooper**
Maidstone United	**Mickey Ambrose**	No appointment made. The club folded in the summer of 1992
Manchester United	**Ken Merrett** (Secretary)	**Dave Ryan** (Dave joined United from Stockport County)

Middlesbrough	**Keith Lamb** (Chief Executive/ Secretary) and, later, **Jack Ord**	**David Geddis** and, later, **Gary Gill.** **David Geddis** was born in Carlisle and began his playing career with Ipswich Town, playing in the club's famous FA Cup Final victory over Arsenal in 1978. After a loan spell at Luton Town, he then moved to Aston Villa before short-term spells with Barnsley, Birmingham City and Shrewsbury Town, eventually finishing his career with Darlington in 1991. David also became a successful coach in later years. **Gary Gill** was a Middlesbrough apprentice who played for the club between 1983-1989 and later had short spells with Hull City (on loan), Darlington and Cardiff City.
Norwich City Project merged with Norfolk CFA's community project	**Andy Neville** (Club Secretary, whose initial enquiry had been received back in October 1990) and **Robert Chase** (Chairman). Meetings with **Ros Watson** also proved to be very helpful	**Peter Mendham.** Peter was a midfield player of some note, making over 200 league appearances for the Canaries in nine years with the club before injury forced his retirement from the game. Peter also featured in the team that won the Football League Cup in 1985.
Plymouth Argyle	**David Tall** and **Graham Little** (Secretary)	**Steve Rogers**
Queens Park Rangers	**Richard Thompson** (Chairman) and **Sheila Marson** (Secretary, having joined the club from Chelsea)	**Josephine (Jo) Swift**
Reading	**Annie Bassett** (Secretary). Annie knew a great deal about the scheme having been previously working at Birmingham City)	**Richard Hill.** Richard played football professionally with Northampton Town, Watford and Oxford United and also played non-league football with several clubs including Nuneaton Borough and Kettering Town. When he was forced to retire from playing due to a knee injury, Richard moved into coaching, scouting and management.
Shrewsbury Town	**Malcolm Starkey**	**Dick Pratley.** Dick was a former central defender who helped his first league club, Derby County, to become Second Division Champions in 1986/87. He also played for Shrewsbury Town between 1987-89 and had a brief loan spell with Scunthorpe United.

Southend United	**John Adams** (Chief Executive/Club Secretary) and **Vic Jobson** (Chairman)	**Frankie Banks.** Frankie signed as a professional with Southend United at the age of 17 making 4 league appearances before moving to his home-town club, Hull City, at the age of 21. After making 284 league appearances for Hull, he moved back to play for the Shrimpers for the final few years of his playing career.
Swansea City	**Major Reg Pike** (who had previously overseen community matters at the club)	**Alan Curtis.** Alan was born in the Rhondda area and spent most of his career with Swansea City, playing in all four divisions of the then Football League during three separate spells with the club between 1972 and 1990. He also played for Leeds United, Southampton and Cardiff City, and on loan at Stoke City. Alan also earned 35 Welsh international caps.
Swindon Town	**Jon Pollard** (Secretary) and **Peter Day** (Chief Executive) and, later, **Bob Johnson** at Swindon Borough Council	**Leigh Barnard** and, later, **Jonathan Trigg.** Jonathan was a former apprentice with Swindon Town who went on, at a later stage in his career, to become the club's physiotherapist.
Torquay United	**David Turner** (Secretary) and **Mike Bateson** (Chairman)	**Frankie Prince.** Frankie was well known as a player having made over 360 league appearances for Bristol Rovers between 1967 and 1980. He moved to Exeter City for the 1980/1 season and then moved into non-league football.
Tottenham Hotspur	**Peter Barnes** (Secretary)	**Len Julians.** Born in Tottenham, Len never played for his local club, but he did make several appearances for London clubs Leyton Orient, Arsenal and Millwall. He also played for Nottingham Forest between 1960 and 1963.
Wimbledon	**Adrian Cook** (Club Secretary) and, later, **David Barnard** (Chief Executive) and **Steve Rooke** (Secretary)	**Jim Lowther**
Wolverhampton Wanderers	**Keith Pearson** (Secretary)	**Tony Evans.** Liverpool-born, Tony began his playing career at Blackpool where he made a handful of appearances before moving on to Cardiff City. From there, he moved to Birmingham City, Crystal Palace, Wolverhampton Wanderers, Bolton Wanderers (on loan) and, finally, Swindon Town where he finished his career in 1986.

Phase IV Club	Representatives of Club seen	Community Officer Appointed
Arsenal[10]	**Ken Friar** (Club Secretary), Vice-Chairman **David Dein** and senior Community Officer **Alan Sefton**	**Steve Bradshaw** funded as full time Assistant to existing Officer Alan Sefton
Brentford[10]	**Keith Loring** (Chief Executive), **Martin Lange** (Chairman) and **Polly Kates** (Club Secretary, previously the club's Marketing Executive)	**Lee Doyle** funded as full time Assistant to existing Officer **Martyn Spong**
Brighton & Hove Albion[10]	**Ron Pavey** (Chief Executive/Secretary)	**Julie Helmsley** funded as full time Assistant to existing Senior Officer **Steve Ford**
Colchester United	**Marie Partner** (Commercial Manager and, later, Club Secretary) and **Peter Powell** (Director)	**Mickey Cook.** Mickey was a true legend of Colchester United where he spent his entire playing career, making over 600 appearances for the club and scoring 21 goals. He also played for the club when they won the Watney Cup in 1971.
Coventry City	**Graham Hover** (Club Secretary) and **John Peacock**	**Barry Powell.** Barry began his playing career as an apprentice with Wolverhampton Wanderers before later moves to Coventry City, Derby County, Burnley and Swansea City, also taking in a couple of spells with Portland Timbers in the USA and with Bulova in Hong Kong. He was also capped for England Under 23 side.
Crystal Palace[10]	**Alan Leather** (Secretary), **Sue McCann** and **Tony Willis.**	**Nicky Johns** funded as full time Assistant to existing Officer **Jeff Hawkins.** (Nicky took over as Senior Officer from Jeff in April 1996) **Nicky Johns** enjoyed an impressive career as a goalkeeper with several clubs, beginning his career with Millwall, and then, after short spells at Sheffield United and in the USA with Tampa Bay Rowdies, he moved to Charlton Athletic (initially on loan) where he racked up just under 300 league appearances. He then finished his career with short spells at Queens Park Rangers and Maidstone United.

Derby County	**Michael Dunford** (Club Secretary) and **Stuart Webb** (Managing Director)	No appointment made early on (**John Jarman**, and later, **Steve Bradshaw** and **Mike Umphray**, oversaw community matters at the club)
Ipswich Town	**David Rose** (Secretary) and, later, **David Sheepshanks** (Director and, later, Chairman)	No appointment made early on
Leyton Orient[10]	**Carol Stokes** and **Frank Clark** (Manager)	**Grant Cornwell** funded as full time Assistant to existing Officer **Neil Watson**
Lincoln City	**Geoff Davey** (Managing Director/Secretary) and **John Reames** (Chairman)	**Dean Wheatley**
Millwall[10]	**Graham Hortop** (Secretary)	**Louise Waller** funded as full time Assistant to existing Officer **Gary Stempel**
Oxford United	Contact with the club arose out of an original enquiry from **Malcolm Elias** (who oversaw the club's community affairs) and, later, **Mike Brown** (Secretary)	**Malcolm Elias** and **Peter Rhoades-Brown** (Peter started on the 1st June 1992). Peter was a former Chelsea apprentice who made over 80 league appearances for the club before moving to Oxford United where he played between 1984-1988.
Portsmouth	**David Deacon** and **John Prevost** (Directors)	**Gary Holland**
Southampton	**Brian Truscott** (Secretary)	**Alan Smith**
Watford	**Eddie Plumley** (Chief Executive/ Secretary) and **Brian Blower**	**John McDermott**
West Ham United[10]	**Tom Finn** (Secretary) and **Terry Brown** (Chairman)	**Trevor Lewin** funded as full time Assistant to existing Officer **Roger Morgan**. A former player, Roger began his career as an apprentice with Queens Park Rangers in 1964, making his debut against Gillingham in October 1964. He moved to Tottenham Hotspur in 1969. Sadly, injury forced his early retirement in 1973.

10. *Several club-based community schemes identified in Phase IV were already operational before the FFE&VTS offer was made; hence FFE&VTS Community Programme funding went towards the appointment of a second officer at these clubs.*

Phase V Non-League Club/CFA	Representatives of Club or Association seen	Community Officer Appointed
Barrow AFC	**Jim Kenyon** (Lancashire CFA)	*Interest withdrawn after meeting Lancashire CFA in January 1993*
Cornwall CFA	**John Ryder**	*Withdrew their interest.*
Durham CFA	**Frank Pattison** (Chairman), **John Walsh** and **Joe Grainger**	**Keith Longstaffe**
Farnborough Town FC		**Geoff Noonan**
Kent CFA	**Barry Bright** (Chairman)	**Darren Hare**
Kidderminster Harriers FC	**Graham Allner**	**Nick Griffiths**
Merthyr Tydfil FC (with Taff Ely Council)	Club representatives and **Adrian Barrwood, Brian Davies** and **John O'Callaghan** from Taff Ely Council (who were keen to support the proposed project)	**Tommy Hutchison.** Tommy was a Scottish international winger of some repute. He played for Alloa Athletic in Scotland before moving to Blackpool in 1967. He then spent nine years at Coventry City before shorter spells with Seattle Sounders, Manchester City (playing in the 1981 FA Cup Final), Burnley, Bulova (Hong Kong) and Swansea City where he was still playing, aged 43, in 1991.
Norfolk CFA * *Project merged with Norwich City's community project	**Ray Kiddell**	**Jamie Houchen**
Nottinghamshire CFA		*Withdrew their interest.*
Sheffield & Hallamshire CFA	**Geoff Thompson** (Secretary)	**Jack Detchon**
Weymouth FC (with Dorset CFA)	**Peter Hough** (Dorset CFA)	**David Armstrong** (David joined Weymouth from AFC Bournemouth in September 1992)
Yeovil Town FC (with Somerset CFA)	**John Fry** (Chairman) and **Tony Williams** (Director)	**Chris Whalley**

★*Meetings with representatives of both Norwich City and Norfolk CFA (including the highly respected and* *long-serving **Ray Kiddell**) were held in the summer of 1992, leading to the merger of the two operations. The launch of the newly merged organisation was held on the 23rd November 1992.*

At the same time as approaches were being made to clubs about the newly amalgamated national community programme scheme, discussions were ongoing in relation to supporting the spread of the excellent *Learning Through Football* cross curricular support pack for Primary Schools which used football as a teaching resource. *Learning Through Football* had been developed at her local club, Aston Villa, by a much respected and well-loved former teacher, **Jean Evans**, and it was hoped that the resource pack could be taken across the country and delivered in primary schools.

The discussions concluded that the resources, newly sponsored and generously supported by British Gas (10,000 books were to be printed initially), should be officially launched in October and then made available to any/all clubs interested in promoting the use of the resource in their own local primary schools.

The resource pack itself was simply excellent. Great credit was properly due to the authors and particularly to Jean for all her hard and painstaking work in preparing work in a language to which teachers could relate, easily understand and therefore deliver as part of the curriculum.

Regular update meetings were then held with Jean aimed at ensuring that all parties were aware of the 'roll-out' of *Learning through Football* across the country; this included a meeting with FFE&VTS Community Programme Regional Directors and Area Managers in early September 1991. This also, of course, linked in with an increasing demand from clubs for financial support for custom-built classrooms to be built at grounds, so that school children could visit the club and undertake lessons at the ground too.

The official launch of the *Learning Through Football* resources took place on the 24th October 1991 at Aston Villa Football Club where the 'pilot' had been introduced locally. As these resources became more widely available across the country, and more widely accepted by teachers in primary schools, clubs themselves began enquiring if the resources could be adapted to meet their own local needs – i.e. containing data relating to their own clubs. As this demand increased, and as local resources started being developed, demand for *Learning Through Football* somewhat inevitably (and sadly) began to reduce.

The move towards the establishment of new Training and Enterprise Councils (TECs) having once operated as local Training Agency offices or branches, brought with it a reduction in available contracts and even, in some areas, a complete withdrawal of the offer of any Employment Training (ET) places at all. Areas affected by the complete withdrawal of places included Merseyside (Everton and Liverpool); Greater Nottingham (Mansfield Town, Nottingham Forest and Notts County); North Yorkshire (Scarborough and York City) and Staffordshire (Port Vale and Stoke City). Essentially, however, the hard work done in building closer working relationships with the MSC/Training Agency/TECs over previous years meant that the North and Midlands remained strong areas for the operation of ET. It was also clear at the time that completely new and successful links would have to be forged with TECs in the South East and South West for club schemes in these areas to have any chance of similar success.

It is also worth pointing out that the move to local TEC management of contracts (and the withdrawal of places in some areas) brought with it added challenges. **As Kath Boullen** explains:

> *"Some TECs went through the process of 'seconding' civil servants as staff and whilst we did all we could to 'broker' arrangements between larger providers and individual TECs, it was clear to us that some TECs were not even receptive to the idea of working with us, let alone national providers."*

In the areas where places were withdrawn, it soon became clear that there were no 'overlap' arrangements available for trustees in post from the previous contract year which, in turn, meant that trainees based at these clubs were forced to terminate their training at the end of March 1991. This caused all sorts of difficulties for locally based Community Officers in these areas. For example, there was a total of 15 trainees affected at just two clubs – Port Vale and Stoke City. This further illustrated some of the difficulties scheme officials were experiencing in being able to take a coherent 'offer' to clubs across the country.

Where offers were made, these were very different from what had gone before, *and* introduced for the first time a certain element of 'bonus', meaning that the amount of guaranteed basic funding was very much reduced from the previous year. Examples of these areas included Calderdale & Kirklees (affecting Halifax Town and Huddersfield Town) and Teesside (Hartlepool United).

The following list of clubs (linked to their nearest TEC) also shows the slight changes in the 50 clubs from when the Training Agencies were operating. For example, places were no longer available at Coventry City, Derby County, Shrewsbury Town and Wolverhampton Wanderers, but they were made available at Carlisle United, Hull City, Peterborough United and Wrexham.

TRAINING AND ENTERPRISE COUNCIL (TEC)	CLUB-BASED COMMUNITY SCHEMES
Barnsley/Doncaster	Barnsley, Doncaster Rovers
Birmingham	Aston Villa, Birmingham City
Bolton/Bury	Bolton Wanderers, Bury
Bradford & District	Bradford City
Calderdale & Kirklees	Halifax Town, Huddersfield Town
Chester/Ellesmere Port/Wirral (CEWTEC)	Chester City, Tranmere Rovers
County Durham	Darlington
Cumbria	Carlisle United
East Lancashire (ELTEC)	Blackburn Rovers, Burnley
Greater Nottingham	Nottingham Forest, Notts County
Greater Peterborough	Peterborough United
Hereford & Worcester	Hereford United
Humberside	Grimsby Town, Hull City, Scunthorpe United
Lancashire Area West (LAWTEC)	Blackpool, Preston North End
Leeds	Leeds United
Leicestershire	Leicester City
Manchester	Manchester City
Merseyside	Everton, Liverpool
Metro	Wigan Athletic
North Derbyshire	Chesterfield
North East Wales	Wrexham
North Nottinghamshire	Mansfield Town
North Yorkshire	Scarborough, York City

Northamptonshire	Northampton Town
Oldham	Oldham Athletic
Rochdale	Rochdale
Rotherham	Rotherham United
Sandwell	West Bromwich Albion
Sheffield	Sheffield United, Sheffield Wednesday
South & East Cheshire	Crewe Alexandra
Staffordshire	Port Vale, Stoke City
Stockport/High Peak	Stockport County
Teesside	Hartlepool United
Tyneside	Newcastle United
Walsall	Walsall
Wearside	Sunderland

In the support office, **Kay MacMillan** commenced her new duties as Secretary/Personal Assistant to the General Administrator (by now referred to as "Chief Administrator" following the creation of the two Regional Manager positions) and to the Deputy Chief Administrator at the end of February 1991. Once Secretary to the great **Bernard Halford** at Manchester City, Kay did an outstanding job over many years, eventually leaving the FFE&VTS Community Programme after giving sixteen years excellent and dedicated service in 2007.

After **John Seasman**'s appointment as Area Manager in South Yorkshire (John commenced his new duties at the end of June), the vacant position of Community Officer at Crewe Alexandra was advertised and appointed. A popular figure who was well-known in and around Crewe, **Chris Walters** duly took up the reigns after John's departure.

It was noted at a meeting of West Midlands based Community Officers held in mid-March 1991 that now that the newly amalgamated scheme was underway, enquiries would be made as to whether it might be possible to interest a national sponsor in supporting the scheme in future. This was something that the Community Officers themselves felt strongly about (including, for example, the vastly experienced **Ron Wylie** at Aston Villa, **Joe Gallagher** at Birmingham City, **Mick Kearns** at Walsall and **Dennis Mortimer** at West Bromwich Albion). This was also something that would happen not too long after the scheme had become fully established as a fully national operation across the whole of England (and parts of Wales). Indeed, Football League (FL) Commercial Director, **Trevor Phillips**, also became involved in this process in the spring of 1991.

Of interest at this point is the fact that what was also produced at this time, and well ahead of any sort of 'Respect' or 'Fair Play' schemes introduced into football in later years, was a printed booklet outlining 10 key points for spectators, players and officials.

1.   Applaud both teams when they first come onto the pitch. Do not jump up and down, act noisily or, in any way, upset any other spectators near you.

2.   Praise good play by either team and applaud both teams off the pitch at the end of the game. Show your appreciation for both teams.

3.   Never boo or hiss the referee, linesmen or any player.

4.   Do not swear or use bad language.

5.   Always accept the referee's decision – never argue.

6.   Do not support the use of any form of violence or misconduct.

7.   Study and learn the laws of the game to increase your understanding.

8.   Set high standards for yourself with your appearance. Look smart and be the part.

9.   Do not over-react or cause upset to other spectators if/when your team scores.

10.   Accept victory modestly and accept defeat graciously. You will be remembered by your behaviour.

Following the appointment of **Dave Ryan** as Community Officer at Manchester United in March 1992 (he was previously Community Officer at Stockport County), **Neil Mather** (once a Community Programme Activity Organiser at Manchester City) returned to the fold to replace him as Community Officer at the Edgeley Park club the following month. **Bobby Mitchell** made the decision to move to South Africa, thereby giving up his post as Community Officer at Grimsby Town. **Dave Wilkes** vacated the Community Officer post at Carlisle United in order to take up the post of Youth Team Officer at the club in the summer of 1991. His post initially went to **John Dutton** (who resigned after a short spell in post in June 1992) and then to **John Halpin** who started his new job in June 1992. John was a Scottish winger who was once on Celtic's books, moving to Carlisle United as a player in 1984 spending the next seven years with the club. He also played briefly for Rochdale in 1991/92. John Halpin proved to be a fantastic appointment within the club's community scheme, going on to give many years of service in two separate spells as the club's Senior Community Officer.

Following the departure of **Ray Hankin**, after his appointment as Youth Team Coach in June at Darlington, **Iain Leckie** was appointed as his successor as Community Officer at Darlington's former Feethams ground.

After the appointment of **Richard O'Kelly** as Youth Team Coach at Grimsby Town in the summer of 1991, the vacant post of Community Officer previously held by Richard at Port Vale went, firstly, to **Ian Miller** (who was to leave in April 1992 to become Youth Team Coach) and then to **Chris Hemming** (appointed in June 1992).

Ian Miller had earned the nickname of "Windy" as a player because of his speed on the wing. Ian began his career with Bury and, after a short spell with Nottingham Forest, he moved to Doncaster Rovers in 1975. He became something of a sensation for Rovers, being voted into the PFA Fourth Division team of the year for three years running. He then played at Swindon Town and Blackburn Rovers before brief spells with Port Vale and Scunthorpe United. On leaving the Community Programme, Ian moved into coaching and enjoyed spells with several league clubs, often working closely alongside **Simon Grayson**, whilst the latter was employed as manager.

Ian 'Chico' Hamilton resigned from his position as Community Officer at Rotherham United in March 1992 to move into coaching, leaving that post free. Interviews held also in March saw the appointment of former Millers apprentice, **Fraser Foster**, as his replacement. Fraser was always a popular figure at Rotherham United both as an apprentice at the club and as the club's Community Officer.

Having proved his own versatility and adaptability to new areas already, former Manchester City Activity Organiser **Derek Clydesdale** took over from **Joe Gallagher** at Birmingham City in September 1991 who had left in order to take over as manager of a local non-league club.

The summer of 1991 brought with it the opportunity for around 16 Community Officers (mainly former professionals) to attend the FA's Full Badge course at Lilleshall. This interest in securing the FA Full Badge coaching qualification was incentivised by the fact that, under the new pay structure identified in the Business Plan, all Community Officers would automatically qualify for a higher level of wages should they be successful in passing! Indeed, pay rises were noted to have been authorised for at least ten Community Officers following the results of this summer FA course later that year.

The new 1990/91 season got underway with the topic of the scheme minibuses becoming a key talking point at this time, not least because of the increasing and high costs of running what was effectively a fleet of 25 minibuses. As such it was agreed before the turn of the year that club schemes would be invited to take on the ownership and responsibility for running the minibuses (there would be no charge for the sale/transfer of ownership of each minibus).

However, it was also agreed that only the initial 50 clubs (i.e. clubs in Phases I & II) would be approached and that the minibuses would be transferred to clubs on a "first come first served" basis, and shared reasonably fairly and equitably across the whole of the North and Midlands. In the end it was agreed that the ownership of 22 of the 25 minibuses would be transferred to community schemes at clubs. The remaining three (which were slightly different to the other as they were adaptable for use by people in wheelchairs) would be retained by the FFE&VTS for a short period whilst remaining to be based at three of the clubs.

The 22 clubs to benefit were:

NORTH WEST	NORTH EAST & YORKSHIRE	WEST MIDLANDS	EAST MIDLANDS
Blackburn Rovers	Hull City	Aston Villa	Leicester City
Blackpool	Scarborough	Birmingham City	Mansfield Town
Bury	Sheffield United	Port Vale	Nottingham Forest
Carlisle United	York City	Stoke City	Notts County
Chester City		Walsall	Peterborough
Crewe Alexandra		West Bromwich	United
Wrexham		Albion	

The other 3 adaptable minibuses were to be based at Manchester City, Sheffield Wednesday and Sunderland. Area Managers would take responsibility for ensuring appropriate use of the minibuses by the clubs in future.

Season 1990/91 had seen the impact of the introduction of the FA's document "*The Blueprint for the Future of Football*" and the separate responses of the FL and the PFA to the FA proposals. It also saw a mobilisation of various Football Supporters groups (including the official Football Supporters Association) to consider very carefully whether a brand new and independent top division (to replace the existing First Division of the FL) might be a good thing or not. Indeed, the FSA expressed their doubts:

> "*There are too many competing and conflicting interests, too many compromises to be made and too many people unwilling to do as they are told by the Blueprint's Authors*"

A PFA Management Committee meeting held in October 1991 recognised the threat to the PFA given the 10% cut of the existing domestic television deal that was being paid to the PFA to support their programmes in:

- Accident insurance
- Benevolent purposes
- Education and training

Indeed, the very real possibility of strike action by all players was raised should any new league be formed and then decide not to support at the very least the payment of the existing percentage.

As identified in the Blueprint, a new top league, the FA Premier League, formally got underway at the start of the 1992/93 season with Manchester-based accountant **Rick Parry** appointed as the League's new Chief Executive. The PL therefore took up seats on the FFE&VTS Board of Trustees and were to play a key role in community developments in future.

To be fair to the new Chief Executive of the PL, on whose shoulders rested a great deal of expectation from PL member clubs, it became very apparent early on that he was genuinely interested in supporting the FFE&VTS as a whole (i.e. across the 16-18-year olds programmes at clubs *and* across the Community Programme schemes set up at clubs).

Rick Parry continued to be very supportive and remained in contact with scheme officials on a regular basis with contacts/advice and/or information aimed at helping to grow and develop the Community Programme scheme throughout his term in office. In the autumn of 1995, Rick even outlined that he would be comfortable to be personally involved in further discussions concerning possible new sponsorship arrangements. This was most welcome and flagged up the fact that the PL were going to be comfortable working with the FFE&VTS in the longer term.

In mentioning Area Managers, it should be noted that a meeting with all the new Area Managers in early September 1991 proved to be a busy affair with as many as 26 separate items on the agenda for consideration! Included amongst the agenda items was the issue of the production of interim 'plans' covering the period from October to December 1991 which essentially picked up on the following:

- The make-up of each club's local Management Forum.

- Potential local liaison with local authorities.

- Consideration of other possible local support/partners and/or expertise.

- The adoption of local aims and objectives (and targets).

- Which community groups/age groups would be approached (and what activities would be available – i.e. football and/or non-football activity).

- Support from the host club.

- A financial plan including financial targets.

At a Staff Committee meeting held in September 1991, it was agreed that all organisations should be notified of the advertisement of vacant Community Officer positions and of the appointment of new Community Officers. A request from one of the newly appointed Area Managers to be allowed to continue playing football at non-league level was also supported. Thereafter, Staff Committee meetings were held on a regular quarterly basis. Indeed, the next two meetings were held in December 1991 and March 1992. Amongst decisions reached at the December meeting were the following:

- The FFE&VTS Community Programme were to assume responsibility for finding potential funding partners (e.g. would-be sponsors).

- Further consideration was to be given towards the criteria necessary for offering funding to clubs in connection with the building of possible community facilities.

- The FA would arrange a joint meeting with **Mick Parry** from Wiltshire CFA (where **Jimmy Shoulder** had been appointed as the local Football Development Officer) so that discussions could be taken further.

- Individual scenarios concerning Phase II clubs (and their local authorities) were fully discussed. Examples of Phase II clubs included Wolverhampton Wanderers (where, by coincidence, former Wolves hero **John Richards** now worked for the local authority) and Sunderland (with local liaison in place through **Paul Gowans**). A meeting also took place in Huddersfield in September 1991, attended by representatives of the club including **Paul Fletcher** (Chief Executive) with **Ted Copeland** (Regional Director the FA), **Neil Jenkinson** (Kirklees Council) and **Dick Krzywicki** (FFE&VTS Community Programme). The Huddersfield Town Kirklees Community Development Scheme was born as a single entity to embrace the former Kirklees Football Development Scheme and the Huddersfield Town Football in the Community Development Scheme and which would operate under a local Management Forum. This decision also brought together **Dai Jones** (Football Development Officer) and **Daral Pugh** (Community Officer). After lengthy discussion, it was agreed that Dai would take senior responsibility for the operation of the new project. The merger proved to be essential for the football club, given the discussions at that time that were ongoing concerning the club's new ground and its future operation.

- Note was made that the Sports Council had offered funding support towards several Football Development projects across the country, hence why Phase II approaches were so important. In line with agreement reached at a previous Staff Committee meeting, very positive meetings were held with representatives of the various regional offices of the Sports Council. An excellent example of this new-found liaison took place with **Steve Hurd** and **Chris Cutforth** from the Sports Council, Eastern Region. In essence, the possibilities at ALL clubs based in the Eastern Region were fully considered and helpful advice and information was offered by the Sports Council officers relating to the proposed 'roll out' of the new scheme into this area. Clubs affected included Barnet, Cambridge United, Colchester United, Ipswich Town, Luton Town, Norwich City, Peterborough United, Southend United and Watford. Perhaps the most positive Sports Council regional office support, however, came from **George Reynolds** in the South West region. George kindly offered significant funding support for the proposed projects to be set up in the area in conjunction with Cornwall CFA and the Yeovil Town/Somerset CFA project. Regional Director, **John Relish**, stated:

> "I had attended a couple of meetings with representatives of the Sports Council (as it was then) and I can well recall meeting with a very supportive George Reynolds at his office in Crewkerne (Somerset) who offered financial support not only for the community schemes in the area but also for two festivals – one for girls and women and the other for people with disabilities"

The March 1992 Staff Committee meeting considered various issues including the fact that some clubs wanted FFE&VTS Community Programme funding support but were unwilling to surrender "signatory control" on a joint account controlled by a local Management Forum. Amongst clubs with this as an issue were Arsenal and Aston Villa, who both wished to continue to operate their community schemes as part of the internal fabric of the club (and as part of the club's own internal accounts). The issue of the operation of local management forums, in conjunction with local bank accounts (and signatory control of those accounts) and the whole status of locally based Football in the Community schemes was to be discussed at length in future.

Another matter to be raised was the possibility of Community schemes organising FA Emergency First Aid courses, subject to the development of an appropriate pack by **Alan Hodson** (FA Medical Officer) on behalf of the FA. Appropriate training could then be delivered to Community Officers at a series of briefing days across the country to be arranged later.

What also became an issue was that the apparent liaison between FA Regional Directors and the FFE&VTS Community Programme was perhaps not quite as effective as it might have been. Indeed, several misunderstandings about contact with Community Officers had already been reported. FA staff, perhaps because of their willingness to become involved and/or to be supportive, were contacting Community Officers and Area Managers directly without following the agreed procedure of contacting FFE&VTS Community Programme Regional Directors in the first instance. Alarmingly, FA staff had also apparently spoken directly to one Community Officer about the opportunity to earn bonuses, which was not part of the agreement at all! Fortunately, these misunderstandings were resolved at an early stage.

The FFE&VTS Community Programme was represented at a University of Birmingham football conference held at the end of September 1991 when full details about the old, and the new, community 'offer' were passed on to those present. It was generally recognised that the Community Programme having a presence at football-related seminars and conferences was important in terms of raising awareness about the now-national work that was going on.

It should also be recognised that the period between September and December 1991 was especially hectic with interviews taking place at so many professional clubs (as listed in Phases III and IV) who had agreed to work with the FFE&VTS Community Programme.

In accordance with the new business plan's requirements in 'Public Relations', arrangements were made through a local (Greater Manchester based) marketing and advertising agency to look at the possibility of a new logo for the newly amalgamated scheme, together with the introduction of a promotional brochure, quarterly newsletter and video (and appropriate script) to attract potential new sponsors for what would soon become a fully-established national scheme.

Graham Shelley from Manchester-based company, Integrated Marketing and Advertising (IMA), was thorough and professional in preparing all the necessary information relating to the scheme. Indeed, Graham's main idea was not only to create a new logo that represented the whole of the 'football family' but also to create and introduce a 'strap line' for the first time. The first ever strap line that was introduced was '*Football's great… pass it on'*. This slogan was first used on a '*Learn the Football Alphabet'* poster that was printed and circulated across the country in 1992. All club community schemes received 200 posters and 1650 leaflets each to use as they saw fit. The leaflets also contained a £5 discount voucher for any Puma purchases, following meetings set up by Graham with **Andy Rigg** and **Louise English** at Sears.

What was interesting from the poster was the fact that, at the time the poster was printed, telephone lines had still not been set up for community schemes at Cardiff City, Luton Town, Shrewsbury Town (where any sort of office accommodation at the old ground, The Gay Meadow, still couldn't be found!) and Tottenham Hotspur. It was also flagged up that the former non-league clubs Barnet and Colchester United were "not participating" and nor were Grimsby Town, Ipswich Town and Maidstone United at the time the poster was printed. Indeed, Maidstone United resigned from the FL at the start of the 1992/93 season. It is, perhaps, also worth noting that Aldershot had been forced to resign from the FL in March 1992 (their results for the 1991/92 season were expunged). Funding previously made available in support of the Aldershot project was immediately offered to non-league club, Farnborough Town, instead so that largely the same area of the country could still be targeted.

The promotional materials prepared by IMA were then made available to a major potential new sponsor before the turn of the year in the form of a presentation entitled "*Taking Football To The People… Together*". Whilst the details for the initial sponsor targeted were in the end unsuccessful, the details still proved to be worthwhile as a potential new sponsor was to sign up and work closely alongside the newly national scheme within just a few years.

The New Year 1992 saw the following:

- Much closer links were established with the ESFA through their new and popular Chief Executive, **Malcolm Berry.**

- Further technical briefings were organised by the FA for new Community Officers and were held at Manchester City Football Club's Maine Road ground on the 4th February and at Coventry City's Highfield Road ground on the following day (5th February).

- A comprehensive meeting of all new Area Managers (held at Coventry City's Highfield Road ground) in early January ran through all matters in which the Community Programme scheme was involved at the time.

A report from **Kevin Jardine** as FFE&VTS Community Programme Training Officer in February 1992 illustrated that, despite the difficulties experienced in operating Employment Training during 1991/92, new ET contracts were available in conjunction with several TECs, notably with new TECs in the south of the country e.g. Avon (Bristol City and Bristol Rovers), AZTEC (Wimbledon), Central London (Fulham), Dorset (AFC Bournemouth), Essex (Southend United), Hampshire (Aldershot and Portsmouth), Heart of England (Oxford United), Hertfordshire (Watford), Kent (Gillingham), North London (with Barnet and Tottenham Hotspur), South Glamorgan (Cardiff City), South Thames (Millwall), Sussex (Brighton and Hove Albion), Thames Valley (Reading) and West Wales (Swansea).

Exciting as this was, substantial difficulties were found in convincing the clubs to run with the proposed new ET contracts, especially at a time when FFE&VTS Community Programme funding was guaranteed to all newly engaged clubs up to the end of 1993 as a minimum without the necessity for any club to take on ET contracts. As a result of this stance, many of the new TEC offers were simply lost altogether, though AZTEC, Essex, Hertfordshire, Kent and Thames

Valley offers were later confirmed, as were offers for Coventry and Warwickshire (Coventry City), Lincolnshire (Lincoln City), North Derbyshire (Chesterfield) and Wolverhampton (Wolverhampton Wanderers).

In the Spring of 1992 **Brian Taylor** (fresh from his limited management exploits at Halifax Town with **Jim McCalliog**) took over as Community Officer at Bury. This followed the appointment of **Dave Bell** (previously Bury's Officer) as the new Area Manager in the South West Region.

The 1991/92 Final of the National Crime Prevention and Thorn Home Security Six a Side Competition for Under 11-year-old boys and girls took place at Wembley on the 23rd May 1992 prior to the Football League's Division Four Blackpool v Scunthorpe United Play Off match. Key thanks must also be extended at this point to former Football League Secretary, **David Dent,** who was personally so very supportive of the move to allow the Final to be played at Wembley prior to one of the Football League matches played there.

A truly exciting development in May 1992 saw the FFE&VTS take responsibility through the now huge number of fully qualified FA coaches who were Community Officers for the delivery of the FA Preliminary Award courses to Youth Trainees at 62 of the 92 FL clubs. The following preparatory table was put together at the time:

YOUTH TRAINEES AT CLUBS	POSSIBLE LEAD COACH
Blackpool/Preston North End/Wigan Athletic	**Andy Welsh**
Manchester City/Manchester United/Stockport County	**Paul Power & Alex Williams**
Oldham Athletic/Rochdale	**Keith Hicks**
Bolton Wanderers/Bury	**Brian Taylor**
Blackburn Rovers/Burnley	**Pete Devine**
Everton/Liverpool/Tranmere Rovers	**Neil Dewsnip**
Chester City/Wrexham	**Mike Rigg**
Carlisle United	**Dave Wilkes**
Crewe Alexandra/Port Vale/Stoke City	**Ian Miller**
Aston Villa/Birmingham City/West Bromwich Albion	**Dennis Mortimer & Barry Powell**
Walsall/Wolverhampton Wanderers	**Eric McManus**
Bristol City/Bristol Rovers/Cardiff City/Swansea City	**Dave Bell & John Relish**
Exeter City/Plymouth Argyle/Torquay United	**Dave Palmer**
AFC Bournemouth/Portsmouth/Southampton	**Jim Hicks**
Sheffield United/Sheffield Wednesday	**Charlie Williamson**
Barnsley/Doncaster Rovers/Rotherham United	**Colin Walker**
Leicester City/Northampton Town	**Neville Hamilton**
Chesterfield/Lincoln City/Mansfield Town	**Dave Bentley**
Derby County/Nottingham Forest/Notts County	**Alan Young & Mike Raynor**
Bradford City/Leeds United	**Cyril "Ces" Podd**

Grimsby Town/Hull City/Scunthorpe United	**John Davies**
Cambridge United/Peterborough United	**Domenico Genovese**
Scarborough/York City	**Ian Kerr & Gordon Staniforth**
Newcastle United/Sunderland	**Mick Ferguson**
Halifax Town/Huddersfield Town	**Daral Pugh**

In the end, however, only around 50% of those officers listed became involved in the delivery of the courses. That said, and if nothing else, this table underlines how strong the FFE&VTS was becoming, not just in terms of qualifications held by Community Officers, but also in terms of the close links established between the successful YT schemes at the professional clubs and the Football in the Community schemes at the clubs.

An 'update' meeting with **Jean Evans** in mid-May 1992 revealed the extent of the "roll out" of *Learning Through Football* across the country. Dates had been set up to outline details of the new opportunity with local teachers with new clubs, having now become firmly established at 11 clubs.

It was widely recognised, however, that as Community Officers were increasingly under pressure to raise funds within three years, the role of co-ordinating *Learning Through Football* was falling on others, e.g. retired teachers or current teachers where funding had been made available to support them (e.g. at Manchester City where work undertaken by qualified teacher, **Lois Gyves,** proved to be extremely successful).

Indeed, in certain areas, the successful implementation of *Learning Through Football* was almost entirely due to the involvement of people (often qualified teachers) rather than the Community Officers themselves, e.g. some of the leading lights included **Ros Watson** in Norwich (where she worked very closely with Community Officer **Peter Mendham** but essentially delivered *Learning Through Football* on her own) and in Blackburn where ex-player **Terry Gennoe** had taken responsibility for running the scheme alongside **Pete Devine**. Terry Gennoe was born in Shrewsbury and enjoyed a lengthy career in the game as a goalkeeper for several league clubs including Bury, Halifax Town, Southampton and Crystal Palace (on loan) before spending a highly successful nine years with Blackburn Rovers where he made a total of just under 300 league appearances.

Birmingham City Council, through **Rick Bailey,** had offered separate funding aimed at supporting the appointment of a separate officer to deliver the scheme across Birmingham. By the time of the next meeting in August, it was noted that an additional 11 new clubs had expressed an interest in working with Jean to deliver the new project, including several clubs in the South.

Club officials had so far responded positively, though some were concerned about the lack of a room that could be used as a classroom. It was agreed that quarterly 'update' meetings would be held. The next review meeting took place at the start of the 1992/3 season in August.

The end of the 1991/2 season saw changes once again: **Paul Curtis** was appointed as Youth Team Coach at Northampton Town (he left in June 1992). As a result, **Russell Lewis**, replaced Paul as the club's Community Officer in mid-July. Born in Blaengwynfi near Port Talbot in South Wales, Russell's playing career had begun when he made his debut for Swindon Town in 1976. He played for the Robins for a total of seven years but in 1983 he moved to Northampton Town where he played up to 1986.

A key supporter of Russell over years to come was to be Director **Brian Lomax** (who went on to become a key and influential figure with the Supporters Direct[10] operation in later years).

---

10. *Supporters Direct was set up to help supporters gain influence in the running and ownership of their Football Club and to establish Supporters Trusts on a local basis. Over many years, Supporters Direct has been able to play a key part in helping supporters to raise monies to purchase and develop many community*

Dennis Mortimer accepted a coaching position within the club at West Bromwich Albion in July 1992. Dennis went on to have an extremely successful career in coaching including spells working for the PFA and for the FA in later years. His replacement as Community Officer at West Bromwich Albion was former player **John Trewick** who took up his new duties in August 1992. John, however, was also to leave a year later to become one of the club's Youth Team coaches. As a player, John had begun his career with West Bromwich Albion where he spent six seasons before later moves to Newcastle United, Oxford United (initially on loan), Birmingham City and Hartlepool United.

Neil Dewsnip submitted his resignation from the position of Community Officer at Everton and left in August 1992. His replacement was **Ted Sutton** who started his new job in mid-November 1992.

Also leaving in August was **Daral Pugh** who left the newly combined Huddersfield Town/ Huddersfield Council scheme to take up a new post as Football Development Officer with Wakefield Metropolitan Borough Council. His replacement the following month was to be popular ex-player **Mark Lillis**. Mark had made a huge impression as a player with his first club, Huddersfield Town, between 1978 and 1984 before a big money move to Manchester City. He then went on to play for Derby County, Aston Villa, Scunthorpe United and Stockport County.

Terry Pashley also vacated his Community Officer post after a short spell as Burnley's Community Officer, having accepted a youth team coaching position at the club in July. This was merely another example of where the Community Officer position encouraged former players to develop their knowledge, experience and qualifications in order to put them in a better position to move on in their coaching careers. Terry's replacement, who came with the support of a great deal of encouragement from the always positive and supportive Burnley Chairman, **Frank Teasdale**, and Club Secretary, **Mark Blackbourne**, was former long-serving Scunthorpe United centre back **Bob Oates** who took up his new duties in September 1992. Leeds born, Bob spent most of his playing career with Scunthorpe United, making over 300 appearances for the club over eight seasons. He moved to Rochdale in 1983 where he finished his career in 1984. With years of experience managing sports centres following the end of his playing days, Bob was well-qualified to take on this new role.

Peter Cunningham resigned from his post as Community Officer at Wigan Athletic in July 1992 and was replaced on a temporary basis by the very capable **Dale Hinks** (a name for the future) until a full-time successor was found. **Frankie Bunn** was eventually appointed to the job at Wigan in October 1992. Born in Birmingham, Frankie began his playing career as an apprentice with Luton Town before becoming a full professional, making just under 60 appearances between 1980 and 1985. He then joined Hull City before, arguably, his most successful goals per game spell as a player at Oldham Athletic between 1987 and 1990. Indeed, he once scored six goals in a League Cup tie for Latics at Boundary Park against Scarborough. In later years, Frankie would enjoy several coaching roles at clubs and, indeed, he was briefly Manager of Oldham Athletic following his appointment in 2018.

Bob and Frankie attended a formal Officer induction in October 1992. Both officers were to make significant contributions to the success of their respective Community operations at Burnley and Wigan Athletic.

The next quarterly Staff Committee meeting in June 1992 confirmed how well things were going, with an expected 100 community schemes forecast to be up and running, in conjunction with several other organisations (i.e. not just FL clubs), before the end of the year.

In addition, it was agreed that a sub-committee should be formed to look at the single issue of the creation of the criteria necessary to support a new 'Capital Fund' aimed at allocating community grants towards community accessible facilities at the professional clubs. Indeed, the FA were keen to utilise the expertise of **Michael Appleby**, who was then in charge of the FA's Hard Play Fund, and he was duly invited to attend the first meeting of the sub-group held at the end of June 1992.

owned clubs.

In the end, the meeting agreed to recommend to the main committee that grants should be made available on the following basis:

- A maximum of £50,000 to be available for full size all-weather pitches (though the preference was for such monies to be put towards fencing and/or floodlighting rather than towards the actual playing surface).

- A maximum of £7,500 to be available towards a classroom/learning centre.

- Amounts to be agreed (depending on the costs) towards minibuses and changing rooms/accommodation in support of full size or 5-a-side all-weather pitches.

All the above would be subject to a minimum of 80% football use together with a guarantee of the club's intention to continue to work with FFE&VTS in supporting their local community scheme. **Bryan Hamilton** (Chief Executive of Wigan Athletic) was also invited to attend the meeting in order to make a short presentation about the importance of the addition of community facilities for the club at their then ground at Springfield Park.

Further FA technical briefings were also arranged and held in September 1992.

The 1992/93 season kicked off with 22 former FL Division One clubs in the new PL and the remaining 70 FL clubs playing across three Divisions.

Staff Committee meetings continued on a quarterly basis with further meetings held in September (at the PFA) and in December 1992 (at the FA). In addition, Staff Sub-Committee meetings aimed at looking at possible funding support for community capital facilities were also held. These meetings were arranged and held just before each Staff Committee meeting so that any recommendations could then be endorsed by the full Staff Committee.

The September Sub-Committee meeting noted that application forms were being printed and would be made available to clubs (with a suitably worded accompanying letter) in order to allow them to apply for funding towards specific community facilities. FFE&VTS Community Programme Regional Directors would be instructed to visit clubs once completed applications had been received so that they could make their own recommendations. The FA requested that their own Regional Directors be allowed to attend visits if possible and, in the end, it was agreed that representatives of *any* of the partner organisations could attend the site visits if they so wished.

Of interest at the time was the fact that several non-league clubs, including Aylesbury United, Basingstoke, Cheltenham Town (then a non-league club), Chorley, Curzon Ashton, Grays Athletic, Halesowen, Hendon, Kettering, Macclesfield Town (also then a non-league club), Netherfield, Sittingbourne, Southport, Slough Town, Stevenage Borough, Woking and Wycombe Wanderers (also then a non-league club), had expressed an interest in applying for capital funding from the FFE&VTS. Despite supportive site visits from FFE&VTS Community Programme Regional Directors at some of these clubs (around November 1992), their applications would, in the end, be turned down as it was later agreed that it would be right and proper for only clubs partnering with the FFE&VTS to be able to apply.

Grants were later approved for several clubs including: Barnsley, Crewe Alexandra, Walsall, Yeovil Town and York City. Grants of £50,000 were awarded to Walsall and to Yeovil in support of the building of full-size all-weather pitches adjacent to their grounds. Grants of £7,500 each were awarded to Crewe Alexandra and York City, supporting the costs of building classrooms at their respective grounds at Gresty Road and Bootham Crescent.

A true gentleman by the name of **Chris Thayne** contacted **Gordon Taylor** in the autumn of 1992 to confirm that his late father, a former player himself by the name of **Billy Thayne**, had left him a silver trophy that he wanted to donate to the PFA for them to use as necessary. Following further conversations, the Billy Thayne Trophy was designated as the new Schools 6-a-side competition trophy. The cup would be presented to the winning school captain each year in much the same way as the FA Cup was presented to the winning captain at Wembley each year. The trophy was popularly received and used in all finals of the Schools Under 11's six-a-side competition up to and including the Final at the end of the 2004/2005 season.

The launch of a new scheme aimed at providing Football League (FL) clubs (the offer was not extended to PL clubs) with tools and materials from Jewsons also saw talks held with representatives of Jewsons and the Sponsorship Workshop (**Jo Chapman** in particular) in the hope that this new deal could complement other grant schemes including the FFE&VTS Capital scheme (especially in relation to the creation of classrooms at clubs). Though this initiative lasted only a few years, it is worth recording how important the grants were in terms of building even only small facilities at grounds.

The FFE&VTS Community Programme were represented at a meeting of the Jewson's Spectator Improvement Grant Scheme held in March 1993, which saw Jewson's grants awarded to 10 clubs as follows:

CLUB	FACILITIES PROVIDED FOR
Blackpool	The provision of a canopy/toilets for away supporters/catering facilities in the South and East paddocks at Bloomfield Road.
Cambridge United	The provision of new seating in Block B of the main stand and an upgrading of the ladies' toilets also in the main stand.
Chesterfield	Grant support for new toilets under the main stand and the conversion of an outhouse into a classroom/learning centre.
Hull City	Support for a Classroom/Learning Centre at Boothferry Park.
Luton Town	Grant support in the form of materials for converting a store into a children's / family room / refreshment area.
Mansfield Town	Support for the provision of seating in the family area (Bishop Street Stand) plus, the provision of glass/perspex sheeting at each end of the stand.
Oxford United	Providing for the extension of a kiosk in the away section of the ground and the removal of the former wooden kiosk plus work on the toilets accessible from the London Road terrace at the Manor Ground.
Peterborough United	Support for the erection of seating on a previous standing area of the London Road terrace.
Reading	Support for a sheltered area for disabled people plus the creation of a family room at their Elm Park ground.
Southend United	Support for the building/improvement of toilets in the East Stand at Roots Hall (already grant supported by a grant awarded by the Football Trust).

Jewsons were also generous enough to come up with their own Awards scheme and the first recipients were as follows:

FL AWARD	DIVISION 1	DIVISION 2	DIVISION 3
EXCELLENCE	Brentford	Huddersfield Town	Walsall
PROGRESS	Notts County	AFC Bournemouth	Crewe Alexandra
DISABILITY	Wolverhampton Wanderers	Leyton Orient	Lincoln City

The Overall Winners were Brentford – who won £25,000 as their reward.

For the record, later Jewsons Family Football Awards Winners were:

FL AWARD	DIVISION 1	DIVISION 2	DIVISION 3
EXCELLENCE	Bristol City	Leyton Orient	Walsall
PROGRESS	Leicester City	Bristol Rovers	Bury
DISABILITY	Middlesbrough	Plymouth Argyle	Lincoln City

The overall winners were Walsall.

Further meetings were held with representatives of Jewsons over the next few years and amongst further grant awards made to clubs were the following:

CLUB	FACILITIES PROVIDED FOR
BLACKPOOL	The refurbishment of the club's training ground at Squires Gate, plus an extension to the facilities there.
BRENTFORD	Multi-purpose room to be used on match days and as a community office/classroom during the week.
CAMBRIDGE UNITED	Replacement of wooden 'plank' seating by plastic seats and the building of a purpose-built enclosure for people with disabilities.
LEYTON ORIENT	The erection of a toilet for people with disabilities plus the extension of the enclosure for people with disabilities.
PORTSMOUTH	The refurbishment of toilets at the ground.
TORQUAY UNITED	Support for a new stand/building centre (including new toilets).
WYCOMBE WANDERERS	The extension of a children's room to include a creche/classroom and toilets (from what was a store room).

Sadly, September 1992 saw a young community assistant, **Sean Fowler**, pass away. Sean had made a key contribution to the success of the Doncaster Rovers Community scheme and it was noteworthy that several community officers attended his funeral.

The full Staff Committee meeting, also held in late September, noted the following:

- The merger of the Norwich City and Norfolk CFA schemes, which was approved.
- It was noted that Sunderland and Durham CFA wished to establish/maintain totally separate community schemes.
- Possible schemes at non-league clubs Barrow (in conjunction with Lancashire CFA) and Kidderminster Harriers (in conjunction with Birmingham CFA) would not be supported by their local CFAs.
- The FFE&VTS were happy to be targeted with staging a certain number of FA Preliminary coaching courses per year.
- Market research should be undertaken into the work of the scheme (to be further considered at the next meeting).
- The Football Trust paper to be tabled had been approved by the full board of the FFE&VTS.

Things seemed to be settling down by the time of the December Staff Committee meeting in that all the football bodies were becoming increasingly focussed on attempting to support the scheme to become all that people wanted it to be. The FA representatives could also see for themselves the commitment shown by the FFE&VTS in striving to support the FA across a few different areas. Good examples of this were the establishment of FA First Aid/medical courses across the country; the distribution of FA fun-week packs to all Community Officers and the encouragement given to Community Officers to attend Soccer Star Workshop events.

Also discussed at the meeting in December was a short assessment of those Community projects at clubs that were deemed to be "at risk" of not becoming "financially self-supporting" by December 1993. Various solutions and ideas were put forward to help ensure that all club community projects were given the best possible chance to enable them to achieve the necessary levels of income to ensure sustainability by the end of December 1993. The targeted figure for all local community schemes was estimated to be (approximately) the equivalent of at least nine months of operation at current financial levels. The move towards greater autonomy for local Management Forums responsible for the operation and running of local Community Schemes was also acknowledged at the meeting.

Up to the end of 1990, local Football in the Community schemes had always been about engaging people, with little or no emphasis on the generation of income. Indeed, early scheme guidelines set out in the 1980s recommended that no money (income) should be dealt with at any time. However, once Football Trust funding (and the newly agreed criteria) kicked in, it became a key target for all community schemes to aim to be financially self-supporting. Whilst this was a fundamental change to the way in which things had been done up to that point, it was clearly essential for future sustainability, especially given the sometimes precarious nature of potential future Government funding for future programmes both for adults and for young people.

From a good governance perspective, it was also recognised that proper books of account would need to be maintained by all local community schemes in order, not only to ensure financial propriety, but also to ensure appropriate protection for Community Officers in the way in which they undertook their business.

In relation to separate books of account for local community schemes, The FFE&VTS Community Programme cleverly planned for the books at a huge number of local football in the Community scheme to be 'audited' by an accountant based in Sheffield, South Yorkshire. **Nigel Sharpe** was thorough and effective in all his work and the audits that he completed for a huge number of community projects up and down the country meant that worthwhile local club-based accounts were kept on record over the years and long before community projects were developed into charitable organisations.

As a result, Community Officers across the whole country invented all sorts of new fund-raising ideas, many of which are still evident and in place today – e.g. school holiday soccer camps or fun courses and after schools coaching sessions. One of the senior managers of the scheme in the early days, **Kevin Glendon**, also came up with the wonderful idea of staging children's birthday parties at football grounds, often with a favourite player also in attendance. This was a dream come true for many children, of course, and a key income generator over many years for many football clubs.

The move towards generating income led to the need for further consideration of the status of community schemes to be defined as separate entities.

The December meeting noted possible interest from two major national organisations in sponsoring the FFE&VTS Community Programme in professional football and it was agreed that discussions should proceed with them with a view to establishing such a deal if possible.

As already noted, it was also agreed that appropriate market research should be commissioned ideally through the University of Leicester if possible. All the football bodies were asked to submit their ideas/observations/suggestions so that a full proposal could be properly considered at the next Staff Committee meeting.

Some concern had been expressed in the Autumn of 1992 about the low Employment Training (ET) recruitment levels at clubs, to the extent that it was agreed that the constitutions to be adopted at local level by clubs were to include a section confirming the club's support for government programmes contracted with the FFE&VTS. To underline this concern, a total of 19 Club Officers were also contacted about their present low recruitment levels. It was also agreed that clubs should be made aware of the 'Learning Through Football' programme and confirm any interest they may have in delivering the programme.

Training Officer **Kevin Jardine**, flagged up the fact that ET was to be replaced by "Training for Work" (TFW). The new programme would be more based around 'output related funding' which could represent as much as around 40-50% (and even higher in one or two areas) of total contracted income. TFW would also be much more flexible than ET. Indeed, it was designed to be tailored to suit individual needs, even though it was still aimed at long-term unemployed adults by helping them find jobs and improving work related skills through a mix of training, job-specific training, work preparation and work on community projects. Priority attention in TFW was to be given to people who had been unemployed for 12 months or more, and to people aged 18-25.

Kevin worked particularly hard to attempt to encourage new Club Officers to consider the possible benefits of supporting a TFW contract. The overall picture, however, was becoming increasingly complicated, especially as in certain TEC areas it was clear that TFW contracts would not be available (and in some areas new 'Employment Action' contracts that had been heavily reduced would be available instead. For reference, "Employment Action" was simply an updated version of "Employment Training"). Detailed below is a full summary of contracts for the contract year 1992/3 which illustrates the complexity of a very varied situation:

TRAINING AND ENTERPRISE COUNCIL	CLUB-BASED COMMUNITY SCHEMES	CONTRACTED PLACES (ROUNDED UP)
BARNSLEY AND DONCASTER	Barnsley, Doncaster Rovers	18
LANCASHIRE AREA WEST (LAWTEC)	Blackpool, Preston North End	12
EAST LANCASHIRE (ELTEC) *	Blackburn Rovers, Burnley	15
BRADFORD & DISTRICT	Bradford City	9
NORTH DERBYSHIRE	Chesterfield	8
SOUTH & EAST CHESHIRE	Crewe Alexandra	5
CUMBRIA	Carlisle United	3
DURHAM	Darlington	6
KENT	Gillingham	8
CALDERDALE & KIRKLEES *	Halifax Town, Huddersfield Town	13
HUMBERSIDE	Hull City, Scunthorpe United	18
TEESSIDE *	Hartlepool United, Middlesbrough	10
LEICESTER	Leicester City	9
LINCOLNSHIRE *	Lincoln City	10
LEEDS	Leeds United	6
MANCHESTER	Manchester City	9
NORTH NOTTINGHAM	Mansfield Town	2

GREATER NOTTINGHAM	Nottingham Forest and Notts County	11
NORTHAMPTONSHIRE	Northampton Town	8
TYNESIDE	Newcastle United	4
OLDHAM	Oldham Athletic	9
GREATER PETERBOROUGH	Peterborough United	7
ROCHDALE	Rochdale	8
THAMES VALLEY	Reading	2
ROTHERHAM	Rotherham United	8
STOCKPORT/HIGH PEAK	Stockport County	4
SHEFFIELD	Sheffield United, Sheffield Wednesday	12
WEARSIDE	Sunderland	8
ESSEX	Southend United	7
WALSALL	Walsall	5
SANDWELL	West Bromwich Albion	6
HERTFORDSHIRE	Watford	6
AZTEC *	Wimbledon	4
WOLVERHAMPTON	Wolverhampton Wanderers	9
COVENTRY/WARWICK	Coventry City	9
BOLTON/BURY	Bolton Wanderers, Bury	12
CEWTEC	Chester City, Tranmere Rovers	12
NORTH EAST WALES	Wrexham	2

Denotes 'Employment Action' places available.

Whilst, on the face of it, this table illustrates a healthy picture, the truth was that funding was increasingly dependent on the achievement of NVQs at levels I and II (i.e. output related funding) and not purely on recruitment levels as had been the case previously. In addition, not all TFW projects were reaching the necessary NVQ targets. It was also clear that income from TFW was now greatly reduced. Indeed, the budget for the year April 1993 to March 1994 saw expected gross income (including output related funding) reduce to just over £370,000 (where £500,000 had been budgeted in the 1991–1993 Business Plan).

Moving into the 1993/4 contracts, there were also substantial changes to the above table with several reductions to the above details, but with the following additions as outlined below:

AVON	Bristol City, Bristol Rovers	6
ESSEX	Colchester United	2
NORTH LONDON	Tottenham Hotspur	3

METROTEC	Wigan Athletic	7
CENTRAL LONDON	Fulham	2
SOUTH GLAMORGAN	Cardiff City	2

TECs were also becoming increasingly likely to reject claims for successful job outcomes (e.g. in the absence of proof/further information) and for NVQ achievement if no evidence was available.

It was also agreed that local Management Forums should reach agreement on supporting local telephone costs (this was eventually agreed and introduced effective from January 1995) together with other costs such as Life Assurance cover for Community Officers (at local level) and insurance costs (e.g. Personal Accident cover for children attending holiday courses, theft etc.) that had been previously been paid (and arranged) by the FFE&VTS Community Programme centrally, so that these costs could properly be passed on to local community projects if agreed. This coincided with a review of all FFE&VTS costs aimed at ensuring that the budget for the three-year Football Trust funded programme balanced.

All these points combined to illustrate how it was necessary to move, as swiftly as possible, towards local community projects being run, operated and supervised by local Management Forums rather than by the FFE&VTS as had been the case up to this point. This would also, of course, take away costs that were previously taken on exclusively by the FF&VTS. This seemed entirely fair, especially as local income, e.g. from holiday courses, was now to be exclusively held by local projects and not by the FFE&VTS at all. The setting up of local accounts, of course, also meant that it would be necessary for local 'audits' (or at least checks) on accounts to be undertaken. Given the increasing interest and future discussions to take place soon about the independence of local community projects in the eyes of HM Customs and Excise, it should be noted that this direction towards local management of projects was entirely the right way to go at the time.

By the middle of October 1992, it was noted that the FFE&VTS was connected with 97 organisations:

- 67 clubs where Community Officers were paid via the FFE&VTS Community Programme payroll (62 professional clubs and 5 "others" which were Farnborough Town, Kent CFA, Merthyr Tydfil, Sheffield & Hallamshire CFA and Yeovil Town).

- 22 clubs that were "grant-aided" with payments from the FFE&VTS Community Programme supporting Community Officers at those clubs (Aston Villa, Brentford, Brighton & Hove Albion, Chelsea, Crystal Palace, Fulham, Leyton Orient, Liverpool, Luton Town, Millwall, Norwich City, Nottingham Forest, Oldham Athletic, Oxford United, Plymouth Argyle, Portsmouth, Queens Park Rangers, Sheffield Wednesday, Southampton, Tottenham Hotspur, Tranmere Rovers and West Ham United).

- 2 clubs where Officers were still to be appointed (Cardiff City and Everton, though **Ted Sutton** was appointed soon after at the Goodison Park club).

- 2 clubs who were still to sign agreements with the FFE&VTS Community Programme (Colchester United and Derby County).

- 4 clubs who weren't yet involved but who, it was hoped, would be involved very soon (AFC Bournemouth, Barnet, Grimsby Town and Ipswich Town).

In addition, other projects were due to be considered further with Barrow, Durham CFA, Kidderminster Harriers (and Worcestershire CFA) and Norfolk CFA. Two more projects (with Cornwall CFA and Nottinghamshire CFA) were "on hold".

Delivery of background information for Community Officers relating to the FA's first aid courses also got underway in the Autumn with over 20 southern based officers attending the first briefing held at the JVC Centre at Arsenal's Highbury Stadium. It was agreed that courses should get underway on a local basis at the end of November. The launch of the FA's First Aid programme followed at Liverpool's Anfield ground in October.

It was also at this time that closer links were forged with the National Playing Fields Association (NPFA) via their Chief Executive, **Elsa Davies**, and with the *Daily Express* via **Tony Brett-Young** and **Ian Cole**. Now called "Fields in Trust", the NPFA have, for many years, undertaken valuable work in protecting playing fields up and down the country and in preserving them as playing fields for the use of future generations. This work was often done despite the constant threat of playing fields being converted into housing estates (or lost for other reasons). Indeed, all club Community Officers were asked to help promote the NPFA through their regular match programme articles wherever possible.

A meeting with **John Williams** and **Eric Dunning** from the Sir Norman Chester Centre based at the University of Leicester also triggered the first steps towards undertaking major research into how well the FFE&VTS Community Programme was meeting its objectives (and targets), as requested at the December 1992 Staff Committee meeting. This was aimed at analysing the perception of the general public, and football supporters in particular, in relation to the scheme's work. John confirmed that surveys of officers at, say, 20 clubs plus an in-depth look at between 4 and 6 club community schemes (across the divisions) should provide enough information for the Board of FFE&VTS as to how things were progressing.

To take things forward, a copy of the Business Plan was despatched to John together with details of the start dates and appointment of Community Officers, plus statistical information as being provided by Community Officers at the time.

Possible clubs to be considered in advance of the work to be undertaken were noted to be:

* Leicester City (local to the Sir Norman Chester for Football Research).

* Burnley and/or Bury in the North West.

* Sheffield United and/or Sheffield Wednesday in Yorkshire.

* Swansea City in the South West.

Based on the FA's push, it was stressed that an early report by the end of October 1993 would be welcome.

Richard Finney, together with Bristol City Community Officer **Shaun Parker**, attended a November conference, arranged by the FA, mainly for Local Authority Leisure Officers and Football Development Officers. The conference was aimed at looking exclusively at the development of girls and women's football. Shaun's attendance had been encouraged following some exemplary work undertaken by him on behalf of Bristol City in engaging girls to play football.

Preparatory work also got underway in relation to a formal presentation to be made to the Football Trust to summarise how things were going in relation to the overall achievements of the Community Programme scheme. The presentation would illustrate how things were developing in relation to the 'phasing' outlined in the 1991-1993 Business Plan and how the budget was going (the budget was noted to be well on target, helped and assisted by the fact that many Officers were actually appointed much later than expected thus providing a net saving on wages costs).

It was agreed that **Mickey Burns**, **Roger Reade** and **Graham Shelley** (from Integrated Marketing and Advertising - IMA. IMA is a top Manchester-based marketing and advertising agency who had previously been involved in the scheme's marketing) should attend the presentation event to be held on the 7th December at the Football Trust's offices at Walkden House on Melton Street in London. Pre-event meetings 'fine-tuned' the presentation which, in the end, was particularly well-received by **Richard Faulkner**, **Pat Finney** and their fellow-Directors/Trustees at the Football Trust, especially as it was made clear that the Trust's money had been well spent as an investment into the future of the game and that targets were being met and, indeed, largely surpassed.

The Christmas 1992 meeting of Regional Directors and Area Managers was an upbeat affair concluded by comments from FFE&VTS Chief Executive, **Mickey Burns**, who finished the meeting by wishing everyone a Happy Christmas, with many thanks for a "*remarkable achievement*" from all concerned.

Newcomers to the FFE&VTS back room team during 1992 included **Julian Hayes** (in May). Julian went on to become a key officer within the administrative framework of the PFA Coaching Department in later years. Also, **Adele Scott** replaced **Natalie Coppage** (Amelia's sister) in the administrative support team in November 1992. Another hard worker in the office, **Kay Richardson**, had departed in April 1992. One other absolute 'trooper' who must be mentioned at this stage was **Flo**. Flo was the office cleaning lady who always did such a superb job on behalf of Manchester Executive Cleaners (led by the wonderfully supportive **Andrea French**). Flo eventually left in 1998.

The New Year of 1993 saw the start of the final year of the three-year Business Plan for 1991-1993. The pressure was still on to tidy up various loose-ends relating to would-be new projects such as the proposed Barrow/Lancashire CFA project which representatives of Lancashire CFA felt wouldn't work as they were already operational in the Barrow area through their existing Football Development Officer, **Roy Tunks**, and the area simply wasn't big enough to sustain two officers.

Mickey Burns expertise was called on to assist in resolving several issues:

- The Coventry City Community Scheme which set out to operate on the basis of being grant supported by the FFE&VTS Community Programme from the start of 1993. Former Coventry City Manager, **Gordon Milne**, was to support the development and growth of the project in the new year.

- The Bolton Wanderers Football in the Community scheme which would aim to work with, and eventually to 'absorb', the on-site work being undertaken at the all-weather pitch facility at Burnden Park (behind the old Burnden Stand).

- Wimbledon's Community Scheme which was to be partly funded by the club in order to allow an Assistant to be appointed.

- Issues with Barnet (where the community scheme was 'on hold'), Derby County, Grimsby Town and Ipswich Town (and AFC Bournemouth following the move made by their former Community Officer, **David Armstrong**, to Weymouth FC) where further discussions would be necessary.

Early on in 1993, with the national Community Scheme having reached, at that point, a total of 93 clubs/associations across the whole of England and parts of Wales, a meeting was held with **Peter Bewsey** and **Allyson Pell** as representatives of NCP (National Car Parks) in order to finalise their sponsorship of the now fully national Schools 6-a-side competition (as endorsed by the English Schools FA).

It was noted that it was possible to secure matching investment from a new organisation set up at this time, 'Sportsmatch'', to match on a pound for pound basis any would-be sponsorship investment. An impromptu meeting with **Charles Langhorne**, as arranged through the then Sportsmatch Director **Mike Scott**, was swiftly arranged. It became clear at the meeting that Sportsmatch matching funding was a realistic possibility for any would-be new sponsors. Follow up meetings with the popular Sportsmatch PR guru, **Martin Cannon**, were also successfully held.

The structure of the competition was agreed as follows:

- Initial local competitions at every club, leading to one winning Primary School from each local tournament (93 winning teams).

- 9 area finals including approximately ten local tournament winners, leading to one Area Final's winner in each area (9 winning teams).

- 2 regional finals (one in the North and one in the South) including 4 or 5 Area Finals winners leading to two winners in each region (2 winning teams).

- The Final (played at Wembley before a Football League match to be played at the stadium).

At this early stage in the evolution of the Schools Tournament, it was recognised that there was a clear need for a coordinator of the competition. Step forward **Richard Finney,** who very kindly agreed to take on the additional responsibility for updating the ESFA and NCP. Amongst other issues that Richard agreed to oversee were: agreement with NCP concerning the list of prizes[11] (obviously paid for out of their sponsorship fee) and the circulation of lists of NCP contacts in each town/city to Community Officers so that local contacts could be made. Under Chief Executive, **Malcolm Berry**, the ESFA also pledged ongoing support for the tournament. In future years, the ESFA were keen to support the competition finals and they were always represented at the Finals.

The 1992/93 tournament was run only over a few months, commencing in early 1993, with the Area finals and regional finals (the southern finals were held in Swindon and the northern finals held in Rotherham) all being staged within just a few weeks. The grand final was played at Wembley Stadium in May 1993. In view of the difficulties caused by having such a narrow timetable for delivery, it was agreed that tournaments should be run over the duration of the whole football season in future years. PFA Deputy Chief Executive, **Brendon Batson,** was kind enough to present the trophy and medals to the winners. The success of this first fully national competition was to lead to a rapid growth of the competition over future seasons.

The monthly management meeting of Regional Directors and senior staff held in January 1993 saw a whole host of issues discussed, including the importance of attempting to reach the main target of establishing 100 Community projects, which were to be up and running by the end of the year. It was also clear that things were starting to get busier, especially as more 'partnerships' and an increased number of events were being established. Amongst the items for consideration were:

- The proposed penalty competition to be run at each project in aid of the NPFA and supported/promoted by the *Daily Express.*
- The NCP (National Car Parks) sponsored schools 6-a-side competition to be run at each project.
- The promotion of the FA'S First Aid courses.
- The promotion of the Duke of Edinburgh's Award Scheme.
- Support from Community Officers for the FFE&VTS run FA Preliminary Award courses to be launched around the country.
- The performance of local community schemes in aiming to become financially self-supporting (it should be noted at this point that careful consideration was given at each monthly management meeting to the income-generating activities of all locally based schemes and, in particular, the original 50 clubs from Phases I and II).

By February 1993, FFE&VTS officials were looking into the possibility of a new, reduced management support structure which would cut the costs of the 'overhead' as against the costs of investing in local community schemes. It was agreed that it was right and proper to look at the initial possibility of reducing from the existing 3 Regional Directors and 9 Area Managers to 3 Regional Directors and 6 Area Managers and then, perhaps, even consider a further move towards a total of 6 Managers in six newly defined regions.

In addition, it was stated at the time that there would be no further revenue funding made available by the Football Trust after December 1993. This meant that it was important for the FFE&VTS to remain involved by offering local schemes at least a small contribution towards local running costs. Assuming that national sponsorship arrangements could be introduced by the start of 1994, it was very good news indeed when the PFA announced (at the May 1993 Staff Committee meeting) that they would be happy to invest a contribution of £500,000 per year,

---

11. *Richard Finney said about the many and various prizes given away over the years as part of many of the scheme's organised events: "The activities and ideas we were able to share and develop ensured opportunities for some fantastic prizes became available for sponsors and projects alike."*

for a minimum of four years, to be shared across the 100 community schemes, subject to certain terms and conditions (the PFA also announced that a further £500,000 per annum would be invested in the YT programme in professional football, also through the FFE&VTS). PFA Chief Executive **Gordon Taylor** said:

> *"Our commitment to the Community Programme, and our belief that it shows the way ahead for football, is now further endorsed by our financial commitment of some £2 million over the next four years. This will enable the scheme, and many of our former members, to continue its many and varied activities from coaching soccer schools for youngsters to helping the disabled, unemployed, senior citizens and ethnic minorities."*

By Spring 1993, there had been further changes at club level including the following:

- **Chris Hemming** had resigned from his post as Community Development Officer with Port Vale. **Jim Cooper** took over from Chris and went on to give many years of service to the club.

- **Dave Harper** was appointed at Bristol Rovers.

- **Leigh Barnard** left Swindon Town. **Ivor Gumm** was put in temporary charge pending the club's input into a possible club community scheme re-structure.

- Grimsby Town had re-committed to working with the FFE&VTS in supporting a Community Programme scheme at Blundell Park and former Grimsby player **John Cockerill** was appointed as the club's new Community Officer, subject to passing the FA's Preliminary Award course (which he later secured). Cleethorpes-born, John played for his local club, Grimsby Town, between 1988-1992, having joined them from Stafford Rangers. He was also to be appointed as Caretaker Manager of the club on several occasions during the 1990's.

The March Staff Committee meeting saw a congested agenda of many different items to the extent that the FL representative, **Chris Whalley**, made the point that not enough work was being left to the FFE&VTS to direct and manage as there was far too much detail coming through at Staff Committee level. This was possibly related to the FA's request at the last Sub-Committee meeting for the group to be allowed to "widen the debate" at that level, together with retaining a keen interest in all aspects of what was happening. Controversially, when asked if the FA could provide an assurance for their support for the FFE&VTS Community Programme scheme under the present structure, the FA would not at the time commit to giving such assurances.

In advance of the meeting, the FA had also requested for several items to be included on the agenda for the meeting – i.e. covering a "rescue plan" for struggling schemes, liaison and coordination, the national curriculum, mini-soccer centres, research, medical courses and local constitutions. Representatives of the PFA in attendance at the meeting stated that this was way too much for one meeting and that the FFE&VTS should be left to run the scheme, and then to report on things to the Staff Committee.

In terms of the performance of Community Officers, it was noted that unofficial financial targets (i.e. surplus cash in bank) had been set (certainly for the original 50 clubs) of £9,000 to be met by the 1st March 1993 and £12,000 by the 1st September 1993. It was also clear that most club schemes were on course to meet their targets (with two notable exceptions being schemes where recent circumstances had made it more difficult to hit the informal targets as outlined). In addition, certain clubs were looking to 'underwrite' the financial requirements as it was their view that community work should not be compromised by having to raise funding. Amongst the clubs moving to adopt this stance at this time were Everton and Sheffield Wednesday.

It should also be noted that "switched on" Community Officers were starting to embrace the idea of approaching more and more would-be-partners for funding that would help them achieve their financial targets. Amongst those experiencing success in securing partner support were:

- Blackburn Rovers local sponsorship support from British Aerospace.

- Chesterfield who had Derbyshire Health Authority interested in financially supporting their programme.

- Fulham, Chelsea and Queens Park Rangers who had secured financial support and appropriate input from Fulham and Hammersmith Council.

- Leeds United who had secured sponsorship support from Norweb.

- Bolton Wanderers and Luton Town who had both secured sponsorship support from McDonald's on a local basis.

It was agreed that preparation should begin in earnest in relation to the preparation of a new Business Plan from the 1st January 1994 to the 31st December 1996. Indeed, it was agreed that a draft, initial version of the new Business Plan should be presented at either the next Staff Committee meeting in May, or at the following meeting to be held in September.

Perhaps the most welcome news shared at the meeting, in the strictest of confidence, with all the partners was the announcement of a major national three-year sponsorship deal being "in the pipeline" with Pizza Hut (see Chapter 10). This news was by far the most important matter raised for discussion at the meeting and was particularly well-received by all the football partners.

The May Staff Committee saw the welcome attendance of FFE&VTS Board representatives **Gordon Taylor** and **Mike Foster**. At the meeting, PFA and FL representatives reported that they had noticed that the FA had recently started using the words "Community Programme" in relation to their own work which caused some concern partly in view of the possible confusion that this may bring, but also partly in view of the general public's likely perception. The FA agreed to come up with a suitable, acceptable alternative (which was, in the end, the adoption of the use of the words "Community Development").

Changes at club level continued in the summer of 1993. Former Baggies reserve team goalkeeper **Mark Ashton** was appointed to the job of Community Officer at West Bromwich Albion replacing **John Trewick**. Mark went on in later years to become a successful Chief Executive at several professional clubs including Oxford United and Bristol City.

Colin Walker was approached to become a club Youth Team Coach in the summer of 1993 at Barnsley where he had been successfully occupied as the club's Community Officer. Colin's replacement was former Doncaster Rovers midfield player **Steve Lister**. Steve had played for his home-town club, Doncaster Rovers from 1978 to 1984 before moving to Scunthorpe United. He also played briefly on loan at York City before retiring from the game in the early 1990's.

Another internal appointment was made by Newcastle United when **Jeff Clarke** took up the post of Assistant Physiotherapist at the club. The subsequent vacancy as Community Officer was filled following the very welcome return to the fold of **Ray Hankin**. Ray would go on to give many years of top service to the club in future years. In addition, Ray built a very close working relationship with **Phil McBride**, Study Support Centre Manager at St. James Park. Between the two of them, they established several successful new initiatives including a "Scoring Goals to Success" venture and a BBC Radio Schools Competition.

John McDermott left the role of Community Officer at Watford in order to take up a Youth Development Officer role at the club. Former Watford striker **Jimmy Gilligan** took over from John. Hammersmith-born, Jimmy first began his playing career as an apprentice with Watford in 1981. He later enjoyed spells with Lincoln City (on loan), Grimsby Town, Swindon Town, Newport County (on loan), Cardiff City, Portsmouth and, finally, Swansea City where his career ended in 1991.

By now, plans were underway to draft the Community Programme's next Business Plan which would 'mirror' the term of the new Pizza Hut Sponsorship and cover the period from 1994 to 1996. This linked in with the fact that it was agreed that contact needed to be made with the Chief Executive of the PL, **Rick Parry**, in order to provide more detailed information for him about the work of the FFE&VTS as a whole (and especially the huge recent growth of the

Community Programme).

At this time, developments concerning the Pizza Hut sponsorship arrangements to be introduced at the start of the new 1993/94 football season were becoming increasingly important. Arrangements for the proposed launch event were also being stepped up so that a final date and venue could be agreed. In turn, this meant that discussions with the National Playing Fields Association (NPFA) and the *Daily Express* about a possible penalty competition had to be put "on hold" until the end of the year.

By the start of the 1993/94 season, it was clear that a total of 97 separate projects would be officially underway with FFE&VTS Community Programme support, with a further 3 new schemes possible in conjunction with Barnet, Ipswich Town and newly promoted Wycombe Wanderers (the latter of whom had secured promotion to the Football League at the end of season 1992/93). If the three projects were to get underway, this would bring the total of projects supported to exactly 100 as originally targeted.

A Staff Committee meeting held in August agreed that the constitution of locally-based Community Schemes needed to be further considered, especially as it was felt that there could be a potential liability to Corporation Tax if they were deemed to be profit-making operations and also if it appeared that they were 'trading'.

A follow-up meeting involving solicitor **John Hewison** and **Steve Conway** (from Boardmans Accountants in nearby Altrincham) was held in August 1994, when it was agreed that the Inland Revenue ruling concerning a "test-case" involving Darlington's community scheme should be taken forward. Indeed, given concerns regarding the FFE&VTS "donation" of £6,000 per year to each Community scheme, it was agreed that a suitable letter should be drafted for the comfort of Community Officers at those club schemes operating as independent entities so that they were aware that a final ruling was awaited.

Great interest was expressed in this matter by the chairman and Directors at Colchester United FC, including **Gordon Parker**, **Peter Heard** and **Peter Powell,** and a meeting with them (also in August 1994) confirmed that:

*   Club Community Officer, **Mickey Cook**, would become an employee of the Colchester United Football in the Community Scheme (on the same terms).

*   The local Scheme would be responsible for PAYE and employer's NI, but the FFE&VTS Community Programme would continue to handle wages and wage returns on an "agency" basis at no cost to the club or to the local scheme.

*   The FFE&VTS Community Programme donation of £6,000 per year could be made at any time, but that it made no sense to make the donation if the local scheme was then going to be subject to corporation tax on any surpluses accumulated in their local accounts.

*   The local scheme will be considered as a separate entity for VAT purposes, therefore needing to generate income in excess of £45,000 per annum (the threshold at the time) even before VAT registration was necessary. As turnover at the time was below this threshold, this meant that 17.5% of income did not have to be paid in VAT. In addition, and to provide some perspective, this meant that the 95 Community Schemes collectively could generate up to £4.275 million before VAT registration would be necessary. At this time, this was considered to be a huge benefit.

The new opportunity to secure "pound for pound" matching funding for sponsorship income, introduced into grass roots football via Sportsmatch, was also noted at the meeting (more information about Sportsmatch will follow).

It was widely accepted that each local scheme would accept responsibility for the employment 'rights' of local Community Officers with effect from the 1ˢᵗ January 1994 – i.e. just after the date when the Football Trust funded Business Plan expired and when each local community scheme was deemed to have become independent. This would also allow the FFE&VTS to "donate" monies as necessary to each Community Scheme based on the PFA's proposed new annual contribution to FFE&VTS AND income from the new national sponsorship with Pizza Hut.

FFE&VTS Community Programme Regional Directors and Area Managers were alerted to the necessary process of appraisal for all Community Officers which would facilitate the offer of a local employment contract (and potentially new terms and conditions, including increased salaries where appropriate).

One other idea put forward at the time was for the FFE&VTS to consider employing a part time wages clerk to take responsibility for the ever-growing payroll of 70+ Community schemes on their behalf (the post would quickly become full-time as the scheme continued to grow so swiftly) though this was, in the end, not acted on until the year 2000.

The autumn of 1993 brought with it a comprehensive review of pay scales for all Community Officers. It was felt that, having introduced pay structure guidelines as long ago as November 1990, and having introduced a significant number of new Community Officers into the fold, a full analysis was required. In the end, the review took into consideration such issues as: Community Officers qualifications, performance and attitude, together with other aspects of officer's performance including activity range, attention to office paperwork and financial performance.

At the same time, consideration was given to the 'support unit' of Regional Directors and Area Managers and the support officers working in TFW. One football club director had already suggested that, moving forwards, the scheme appeared to be "top-heavy" and that a reduction in numbers was going to be necessary at some point. This led to further consideration being given to reducing the number of Area Managers from 9 to 6 (initially at least) and, in view of the reduction in income from TFW, for the field officer, **Tommy Spencer**, to be encouraged to move on to another position if possible. Fortunately, with the support of some additional funding from the FFE&VTS Community Programme, Tommy was able to start work alongside **Tony Currie** at Sheffield United where they formed a formidable and enduring partnership and enjoyed huge success working together over many years. Also, around this time, **Dave Bell** agreed to take up the post of Youth Team Coach/Development Officer at Bristol City.

Following discussions about the possible future re-structuring, **Peter Withe** agreed to continue as Area Manager until the end of 1993. This also saw him working alongside the new Community Officer at Birmingham City being his son, **Jason Withe**. Jason's appointment followed a meeting with manager **Terry Cooper** and Chief Executive **Peter Day,** at Birmingham City when this course of action was agreed. Peter (Withe) would eventually be appointed as Youth Team Coach at Aston Villa in August 1994. Jason Withe was once an apprentice footballer with West Bromwich Albion in the late 1980's though he never played for the first team and eventually moved to Finland from the Hawthorns.

In November 1993, **Paul Power** left his post as Area Manager and moved to the PFA. By this time, Paul had begun to undertake a substantial and important piece of work concerning coaching on behalf of the PFA which also involved comparisons with coaching work in other countries.

In relation to the development of 'partnerships', it should be noted that FFE&VTS had established a special partnership with the Divert Trust, whereby grants were to be made available to Community Schemes in support of diversionary activity for young people between the ages of 10-25, especially those in 'at risk' areas. **Valerie Jones** (Assistant Director, The Divert Trust) was particularly supportive as 4/5 club schemes were successful in applying for funding as early as August 1993. This worked well for all concerned, as did links with the Drugs Prevention Scheme (who also made available grants for community schemes).

Generously, the Divert Trust offered FFE&VTS representation on their main Committee to ensure co-ordination of grant support. A meeting involving FFE&VTS Community Programme officials together with **Pat Finney** from the Football Trust, **Valerie Jones** (Divert) and **Gillian Henderson** (Youth Clubs UK) in September 1994 carefully considered the future direction of the Trust in the hope that more young people at risk could be directly supported by community schemes at the professional clubs.

The September Staff Committee meeting took place without any representation from the FL (all their representatives were otherwise engaged). However, grants under the capital/facility fund were endorsed for certain clubs (mainly FL clubs) including: Blackburn Rovers, Bury, Crystal Palace, Hull City, Manchester City and Wolverhampton Wanderers. In view of the grants awarded, it was agreed that the Capital Fund budget of £460,000, as outlined in the Business Plan, should be maintained. This was supported by the award of a further £250,000 by the Football Trust to be released during the term of the new Business Plan.

Confirmatory note was made that the Pizza Hut sponsorship deal had been endorsed by *all* the partners. FL support was expected to be confirmed at their September Board Meeting. Interestingly, it was **Graham Kelly** as Chief Executive of the FA who recognised that a Pizza Hut deal signed in the name of the FFE&VTS (even allowing for the fact that the FA were effectively a 25% stakeholder in the FFE&VTS), couldn't possibly conflict with any of the FA's existing portfolio of sponsorship arrangements as the two companies were quite distinct. This point was also recognised by **Gordon McKeag** (former Chairman of Newcastle United) on behalf of the FL at the FFE&VTS Board Meeting held on 13th September.

At the meeting, the FFE&VTS also confirmed the planned reduction in the Area Managers based on would-be savings to be made in wage costs as part of the new 1994-1996 Business Plan.

In reference to the new Business Plan, it should be noted that meetings of Community Officers were convened around the country during September so that they were all informed of what was to happen next for them. Meetings were held as follows:

Date of Meeting	Venue	Number of Clubs present.	Clubs Present
10th September 1993	Manchester (FFE&VTS)	7	Blackburn Rovers, Blackpool, Bolton Wanderers, Bury, Carlisle United, Preston North End, Wigan Athletic.
13th September 1993	Manchester (FFE&VTS)	12	Burnley, Chester City, Crewe Alexandra, Everton, Liverpool, Manchester City, Manchester United, Oldham Athletic, Rochdale, Stockport County, Tranmere Rovers, Wrexham.
20th September 1993	Rotherham United	9	Barnsley, Chesterfield, Grimsby Town, Hull City, Lincoln City, Rotherham United, Scunthorpe United, Sheffield United, Sheffield Wednesday.
21st September 1993	Tottenham Hotspur	9	Arsenal, Colchester United, Leyton Orient, Millwall, Southend United, Tottenham Hotspur, Watford, West Ham United, Wimbledon.
22nd September 1993	Peterborough United	10	Cambridge United, Leicester City, Luton Town, Mansfield Town, Norfolk CFA, Norwich City, Northampton Town, Nottingham Forest, Notts County, Peterborough United.
24th September 1993	York City	10	Bradford City, Darlington, Halifax Town, Hartlepool United, Leeds United, Middlesbrough, Newcastle United, Scarborough, Sunderland, York City.

27th September 1993	Aston Villa	10	Aston Villa, Birmingham City, Coventry City, Hereford United, Kidderminster Harriers, Port Vale, Shrewsbury Town, Walsall, West Bromwich Albion, Wolverhampton Wanderers.
March 1994*	South West	16	Brighton & Hove Albion, Bristol City, Bristol Rovers, Cardiff City, Exeter City, Merthyr Tydfil, Oxford United, Plymouth Argyle, Portsmouth, Reading, Southampton, Swansea City, Swindon Town, Torquay United, Weymouth/Dorset CFA, Yeovil Town.

*This meeting was held much later – whilst aspects were covered again, most information was passed on directly to Officers by Regional Director **John Relish** in the autumn of 1993*

Apologies for absence were received from Community Officers at 14 Community schemes: Brentford, **Jason Morgan** (Charlton Athletic), **Shaun Gore** (Chelsea), Crystal Palace, **Eric Randerson** (Doncaster Rovers), Durham CFA, **Geoff Noonan** (Farnborough Town), Fulham, Gillingham, **Mark Lillis** (Huddersfield Town), **Darren Hare** (Kent CFA), **Emlyn Brown** (Queens Park Rangers), Sheffield & Hallamshire CFA and **Paul Johnson** (Stoke City).

Clubs not involved at that time were noted to be AFC Bournemouth, Barnet (still 'on hold'), Derby County and Ipswich Town.

Amongst things discussed at the meetings were the following:

- The fact that Community Officers were effectively becoming 'Project Managers' with increased responsibility to run local community schemes as local and separate businesses (protected by having a local constitution in place. FFE&VTS officials were firmly of the opinion that the long-term future of community work would be best protected by local schemes having their own separate accounts).

- In addition to local income generation, local schemes could increasingly look to secure local sponsorship and FFE&VTS personnel would assist in supporting applications to secure pound for pound 'match' funding from Sportsmatch where possible (and where advance notice of possible arrangements could be given).

- The further development of local schemes – e.g. in terms of having their own local sponsorships to support, will facilitate the increase in local marketing and possible production of local branded materials such as videos, newsletters, information packs etc.

- Funding support from FFE&VTS will reduce as Football Trust funding runs out and will consist of £6,000 a year to each local scheme. This contribution would be made up of a combination of PFA funding and national sponsorship (the latter of which would be optional – i.e. local Management Forums could approve their local support for the national deal or not, as necessary). The combination of PFA and Pizza Hut funding would be available and guaranteed for three years between 1994 and 1996.

- It would be in everyone's best interests for local community schemes to have the option to support national events and activities – e.g. the Inter Schools 6-a-side tournament (and sponsors) as appropriate.

- Increased interest from clubs in the income generating potential of local community activities (e.g. soccer schools).

- Efforts would be made to see if additional support could be extended for those local community schemes that were to have received less than a minimum of two years access to the Football Trust funding by the end of December 1993 (in order to assist those schemes to achieve self-sustainability) — see table below.

FOOTBALL CLUB COMMUNITY PROJECT	START DATE
Exeter City, Gillingham	January 1992
Lincoln City	February 1992
Bristol Rovers, Plymouth Argyle, Watford	March 1992
Queens Park Rangers, Reading, Torquay United	May 1992
Portsmouth	June 1992
Crystal Palace (Second Officer)	July 1992
Charlton Athletic, Norwich City	August 1992
Brighton & Hove Albion, Merthyr Tydfil (with Taff Ely Council), Southampton, Yeovil Town	September 1992
Chelsea, Luton Town, Shrewsbury Town, Tottenham Hotspur	October 1992
Cardiff City	December 1992
Colchester United, Grimsby Town, Kidderminster Harriers	January 1993

In the case of community schemes at Colchester United, Grimsby Town and Kidderminster Harriers, it was clear that they had only received Football Trust funding for a period of twelve months only. As a result, it was felt to be fair to offer all three clubs a minimum of a further twelve months funding. In the end, approximately £150,000 in total was put aside (allocated from the budget) in support of these (newer) projects.

FFE&VTS personnel continued to do what they could in terms of supporting all clubs to develop their community programme work. **Michael Knighton**, who was by now Chairman of Carlisle United, gave notice of his intention to "quit" the partnership with FFE&VTS at the end of the year. Fortunately, following a meeting with scheme officials in early November, agreement was reached for the Carlisle United Community Scheme, which was operating particularly well under the stewardship of former player **John Halpin**, to be given a 12 month 'trial' period, which eventually convinced the club to maintain the Scheme in partnership with the FFE&VTS Community Programme in view of the many benefits.

At the same time, some issues were starting to crop up, possibly based around the organisation of the finances of local community schemes (club personnel were becoming increasingly aware of the fact that Community schemes were beginning to generate income which was viewed as a possible 'opportunity' for clubs directly). One unnamed club had even looked to try and sign a cheque for a substantial four figure amount from a local Community Scheme account in the hope of supporting club coffers directly, until it was pointed out to the chairman of the club concerned that this action was actually fraudulent.

Another club chairman had supported an application to Sportsmatch made in the name of their Community Scheme but without any involvement of the FFE&VTS Community Programme (then a 'partner' in that club's local community scheme). The application was for a substantial sum of money and was based around a sponsorship that had already been paid into the football club's own bank account. It took a meeting with the chairman of the club to attempt to unravel what had gone on and to re-assure Sportsmatch that the money would be spent properly through the partnership account. The club's response (or rather that of the chairman who was personally involved) was to threaten to resign from the agreement with the FFE&VTS Community Programme (though that didn't happen in the end!) In this case, club officials were simply reminded of all the benefits of working alongside the FFE&VTS Community Programme (in particular, VAT exemption from income/access to other external funding streams/support from the FFE&VTS both in financial terms and in kind.)

The end of September 1993 brought good and sad news. First the good news in that former Leeds United and Brighton striker, **Terry Connor**, had been appointed as Community Officer at Swindon Town. Leeds-born Terry Connor had an exciting career as a striker initially with his native Leeds United prior to moves to Brighton, Portsmouth, Swansea and Bristol City, not forgetting a brief loan spell with Swansea City where he finished his league career, before moving to then non-league Yeovil Town. Terry also enjoyed huge success as an Assistant Manager/coach later in his career, notably working alongside **Mick McCarthy**.

The sad news, however, concerned the health of Tottenham Hotspur's new Community Officer, **Len Julians**, who had been diagnosed with cancer. Indeed, by the end of November, Len had reached the point where he was on morphine every four hours. FFE&VTS pledged to support Len as fully as possible during what was clearly a distressing and difficult time for him and his family. Sadly, he passed away on the 17th December 1993.

Sad as it was, at least the FFE&VTS were able to assist the family by ensuring the payment of a successful life assurance claim to the family following the establishment of this cover after the death of **Mick Baxter** in 1989. Purely for reference, it is worth mentioning that this payment was kindly facilitated by, the always wonderfully supportive, **Richard Guest** from PFA Financial Management Limited.

In view of the importance of the accounts in terms of confirming the separate status/ existence of Community Schemes, it is worth noting that all FFE&VTS Community Programme Regional Directors and Area Managers were given specific training on this aspect at a management meeting on the 5th November 1993. Amongst issues raised were:

- The importance of the PAYE system and why it needed to be applied for *all* staff (including part time and temporary staff).
- The employment 'status' of Community Officers.
- The importance of cash books being kept up to date and fully reconciled with Bank Statements.
- The importance of maintaining receipts/invoices and stock records (and stock checks) as appropriate.
- The position concerning Corporation Tax and VAT.

Work in other areas continued up to and throughout Christmas. This included the circulation of a Christmas gift of a bottle of whisky to all Community Officers and two bottles for those clubs where there were two officers (or more) in post at 12 clubs (Arsenal, Aston Villa, Brentford, Brighton & Hove Albion, Crystal Palace, Leyton Orient, Manchester City, Middlesbrough, Millwall, Nottingham Forest, Swindon Town and West Ham United).

An approach was also made to the Football League's newest club, Wycombe Wanderers, via **Jim Melvin**, to check on their interest in setting up a Community Scheme.

It was pleasing to note that close links with the PFA continued during 1993/94, as illustrated by the coverage afforded to Community schemes and Community Officers in the PFA's new magazine (*PFA Footballers World*). Features included were articles as follows:

EDITION	FEATURING
July 1993 (Issue Number 1)	Exeter City and Sheffield Wednesday community schemes.

September 1993 (Issue 2)	Community work at Bristol City, Coventry City, Farnborough Town, Huddersfield Town, Leyton Orient, Millwall, Norwich City, Nottingham Forest, Plymouth Argyle, plus a special feature on **Tony Currie**.
November 1993 (Issue 3)	Community schemes at Bristol City, Burnley and Sunderland, plus a special feature on Pizza Hut
January 1994 (Issue 4)	Community work at Aston Villa, Chelsea, Southampton and Watford, plus a special feature on **Tommy Hutchison**.

In addition, local Community schemes agreed to help circulate the magazines (this followed talks with former player, **Mike Trusson**, whose brief was to promote and sell the magazines).

In terms of sponsorship, it had been hoped (back in late 1993) that the new National Scheme Sponsors, Pizza Hut, may be interested in supporting the national schools 6-a-side tournament but this was not to be. However, discussions with **Bryan Blakeman, David Hope** and **Michelle Ingham** of Refuge Assurance proved to be extremely positive, and a commitment to support the competition for a period of three years commencing in 1993/94 was reached. This commitment was particularly important in that it provided a guarantee that the competition could continue. It also provided yet further evidence of the value of a national/united Football in the Community scheme in being able to attract big-name and high-profile sponsors in future. Research into accessing support from Sportsmatch on a 'pound for pound' basis was encouraging in that **Charles Langhorne** (Sportsmatch official) confirmed that this was again entirely possible. In the end, funding of £25,000 per year for each of the three seasons was received from Sportsmatch in support of the tournament.

As a result, the 1993/94 competition sponsored by Refuge and supported by Sportsmatch saw a huge increase in the numbers of Community Schemes supporting the tournament and in the number of Primary Schools (and therefore the number of children) participating. Indeed, it was estimated that around 12,000 children took part in the competition. Not only that, but the increasing popularity of the competition saw many more clubs using their own grounds and/or training grounds to stage their own dedicated local tournaments.

PARTICIPATING COMMUNITY SCHEMES*	PARTICIPATING PRIMARY SCHOOLS
97	1498

*88 professional clubs took part (still not AFC Bournemouth, Barnet, Derby County or Ipswich Town at the time) plus other non-league clubs and/or associations being: Farnborough Town, Kidderminster Harriers, Merthyr Tydfil, Weymouth, Yeovil Town, Durham CFA, Kent CFA, Norfolk CFA and Sheffield & Hallamshire CFA.

The Area Finals were again held across the country and the Regional Finals were held late on in April. The Final itself was played prior to the Football League's Autoglass Trophy Final between Swansea City and Huddersfield Town (won by Swansea on penalties after a 1-1 draw during normal time). The Billy Thayne Cup was again presented to the school competition winners.

What was encouraging about the competition was that each local Community scheme was incentivised to encourage more and more schools to take part in future, as they were paid what was effectively a local 'facility fee' based on the number of schools that took part in each local competition. This facility fee was set at £12.50 per participating school. So, as an example, if a local scheme had 8 schools talking part in their local competition, they would receive a payment of £100 (one hundred pounds).

A "debrief" meeting with Refuge officials held later on in the year (in June 1994) confirmed that they had been very pleased with the first year's competition and that the tournament run over a whole football season should see significant improvement in the numbers competing.

At the same time as resources were reducing within "Training for Work" (TFW), it was noted that it was going to be necessary for the FFE&VTS to develop their own 'quality assurance' systems (on a similar basis to the BS5750 Standard for manufacturing industry, in terms of formalised procedures and necessary documentation, being the 'norm' that most TECs used as a 'standard'). This was a huge undertaking, but also one that Senior Officers were able to develop over a period of a few months. It was noted that the 'standard' would need to include health and safety, equal opportunities, risk assessment procedures etc. Indeed, the FFE&VTS Community Programme 'Quality Assurance Committee' met for the first time in April 1994 and this was swiftly followed by a meeting of the 'Health and Safety and Equal Opportunities Committee'.

By May 1994, all Community Officers were issued with a short 'Quality Management Systems Manual'. In addition, and in support of the initial manual, a detailed 'Operating Procedures Manual' was issued to all Community Officers in December 1994. Without going in to too much detail each Quality Assurance manual included the following:

QUALITY MANAGEMENT SYSTEMS MANUAL	OPERATING PROCEDURES MANUAL - PROCEDURES
Organisation profile and background	Reception and switchboard
Quality Policy	Document control
Contract and management review	Staff selection and induction
Design and document control	Performance appraisal, staff development and training
Purchasing (and approved suppliers)	Investors in People
Inspection and testing	Health & Safety and Equal Opportunities Policies
Control of non-conforming services and corrective action	Contracts and review
Handling, storage, packaging and delivery	Financial procedures including budgetary control, purchase/receipt of goods, payments etc.
Quality system, audit and review	Recruitment, trainee induction and design & delivery of training programmes, payment of expenses etc.
Training and statistical techniques	Outcome and exit procedures and quality system review

Each of these processes and procedures were dated at the time of issue and were subsequently updated year on year, whilst ever contracts were in place with Government and their agencies.

Difficulties, however, continued in "Training for Work" (TFW). Recruitment levels were worryingly low in several areas and Training Officer, **Kevin Jardine**, sought additional assistance from what were already extremely busy Regional Directors and Area Managers to support delivery in some areas. The budget prepared for 1994 also emphasised that income from TFW was forecast to reduce again. Indeed, no more than a maximum of £406,000 (income) was budgeted for and expenditure was forecast to be at least £246,000 against this (i.e. there would be a net surplus of only £160,000). With all of this as the 'backdrop', there was, perhaps, some inevitability that Kevin might consider his work options in the fullness of time. It came as no surprise when he handed in his notice before the end of the year. Whilst this was very disappointing (Kevin had done a great job up to this point), it was, at least in part, understandable given the reduction in income and therefore the perceived reduction in the importance of the TFW programme. Kevin's replacement was former MSC Community Programme Officer, **Gary Naven**. Fortunately for all concerned, Gary (who finally took up his new duties on the 7th February 1994) was able to throw himself into the job almost immediately, coming up with new ideas and solutions to some of the difficulties that were starting to arise, especially concerning the demands of individual TECs.

At the same time, serious discussions were taking place behind the scenes about the need to further reduce the Management support structure which had been highlighted as a weakness as part of a SWOT (Strengths/Weaknesses/Opportunities/Threats) analysis completed at the time. Under consideration was a possible move towards having 6 Regional Directors only, as opposed to 3 Regional Directors *and* 6 Area Managers. These discussions were important as it was clear that the football authorities were still of the view that the management structure was 'top-heavy' and too expensive.

There were other important meetings held prior to the end of 1993 which included:

- A meeting with **Chris Whalley** from the Football League (FL) to investigate the possibility of running a FL Supporters 6-a-side football competition (which would be sponsored by League Sponsors at the time, Endsleigh Insurance. A 'slot' for the Final would be found prior to the Autoglass Final match to be played at the end of the 1993/4 season).

- A meeting with **John Hewison** from George Davies and Co Solicitors to 'firm up' a legally binding agreement to be set up for professional clubs and the FFE&VTS Community Programme which set out the parameters necessary for each local partnership and which would be flexible enough to be amended for those clubs that wished to run their community schemes as internal departments within their clubs. All agreements would have a "termination clause" added which provided for a period of no less than three months' notice to be given in the event of termination by either party.

- A Sub-Committee meeting of the Board of Directors of FFE&VTS held just before Christmas, which proved to be extremely important in that representatives of the FL (notably **John Reames**, Chairman of Lincoln City, and **Ian Stott**, Chairman of Oldham Athletic) and the PL singled out the FA for what they felt to be a lack of support during the three-year Football Trust supported phase of operation. Officials attending the meeting also agreed that the former "Staff Committee" would now become a Sub-Committee of the Board of Directors of the FFE&VTS, with any/all disputes to go to the Board in future. It was pleasing to hear that the structure in place at that time (3 Regional Directors and 6 Area Managers) was at least endorsed for a further 12-month period with a full review of the structure to be undertaken at the end of the 1993/4 season. The newly drafted Business Plan for 1994-1996 was eventually approved at the next Sub-Committee meeting (held in February 1994).

CHAPTER 9 – 1994-1996

INCOME IDENTIFIED in the new Business Plan for 1994-1996 was based largely around the generous support of the PFA (£500,000 per year for each of the three years) and the Pizza Hut sponsorship deal (see Chapter 10) and included, once again, income derived from 'Training for Work'. The Plan also highlighted "Development Opportunities" which, it was felt, the Community Programme scheme could support, such as:

1. The Public Relations (PR) and marketing of the scheme to be stepped up (nationally and locally) – see below.

2. 'Learning Through Football' could be extended to even more clubs.

3. Even more community accessible facilities could be provided.

4. Work with junior (and adult) supporters' clubs could be stimulated even more.

5. Girls and women's football should continue to be encouraged with a view to a much wider expansion. Football for girls was very evident at most local community schemes in the late 1980's and early 1990's. Indeed, an excellent example could be seen at Tranmere Rovers that not only encouraged more involvement from girls and women but also employed two female assistants, **Louise Edwards** and **Shirley Waring**, whose role was to stimulate greater interest amongst girls and women.

Linked in to the first ever national sponsorship arrangements with Pizza Hut, the new opportunities regarding the PR and marketing of the scheme included:

* A higher national profile and scheme identity.

* A scheme slogan (or strap-line) to be adopted in support of the new scheme logo.

* A promotional video to be raised and made widely available.

* The introduction of promotional newsletters highlighting all the good work going on across the country.

Concerning new facilities, it was noted that the following new facilities had been successfully supported out of the FFE&VTS Community Programme Capital Fund (funded by the Football Trust) between 1991-1993:

NUMBER	FACILITIES	CLUBS	GRANT AWARDED
9	Classrooms/Learning centres	Brentford Bury Crewe Alexandra Crystal Palace Hull City Lincoln City Manchester City Wolverhampton Wanderers York City	£7,500 (each club)
3	Minibuses	Lincoln City Tranmere Rovers Wigan Athletic	£9,000 £5,000 £6,000

4	Full size all-weather turf pitches	Walsall Yeovil Town	£50,000 (each club)
4	5-a-side all-weather turf pitch centres/changing rooms	Barnsley Blackburn Rovers Burnley Manchester City	£14,000 £14,000 £20,000 £50,000
		Total	**£385,500**

Following the confirmation of the additional support of a further £250,000 from the Football Trust, additional awards were also made after 1993 as follows: Barnsley (minibus), Birmingham City (classroom), Burnley (minibus, also supported by a local sponsor), Colchester United (soccer centre at Layer Road that opened in June 1995 AND a minibus, also supported by a local sponsor), Hereford United (classroom), Leyton Orient (classroom AND minibus), Manchester City (minibus), Mansfield Town (£14,000 grant re 5-a-side pitches), Merthyr Tydfil (minibus), Millwall (minibus), Northampton Town (classroom), Port Vale (classroom), Scunthorpe United (classroom), Southend United (classroom), Stockport County (classroom), West Bromwich Albion (classroom) and Wrexham (classroom).

Additional criteria noted that:

- 80% use for football of the facility was essential.
- The facility must be supported by a local Football in the Community scheme also backed by the FFE&VTS Community Programme.
- The budget for 1994-96 recognised the reduction in Area Managers from 9 to 6 (which was largely accommodated by "natural wastage', though it also became clear during 1994 that a further reduction in the number of Area Managers was going to become necessary in view of the high costs associated with each post (not just wages but also travel expenses). In the end, a revised (and reduced) budget for 1995 and 1996 was adopted at a Sub Committee meeting held in February 1995 with an eventual consequent revenue saving in excess of £50,000 for each future year.
- The new year of 1994 saw liaison with clubs continuing, with many more clubs now happy to make direct contact with FFE&VTS Community Programme officials to investigate ideas to take things forward. Some examples included:
- **Sheila Marson** (Club Secretary at Queens Park Rangers) re: arrangements to invoice FFE&VTS for the funding support offered to the club on a monthly basis.
- **Mark Blackbourne** (Club Secretary at Burnley) re: the appointment of an assistant to **Bob Oates**, being **Dean Ramsdale** (who would play a key role in driving forwards the Burnley Community scheme in future).
- **Alec King** (Commercial Manager at Sunderland) re: the future employment of their Community Officer (**Mick Ferguson** at the time) and the operation of their scheme in terms of accounts and the TFW programme.
- **Keith Walker** (Secretary at Mansfield Town) re: employing a women's Football Development Officer alongside **Dave Bentley**.
- **Mike Trusson** (AFC Bournemouth) re: the idea of working alongside the FFE&VTS once again (following his prior involvement in editorial as part of the production of the PFA Footballers World magazines).

This new, enthusiastic contact from club officials was all, of course, extremely positive, and welcome! Just as welcome were some of the statistics noted that covered the period from January 1991 through to June 1993 which confirmed the growth of scheme activities, together with the numbers of people involved, as follows:

Area of Involvement	Numbers Involved (January – December 1991 only)	Numbers Involved (January – December 1992 only)	Numbers Involved (January – June 1993 only)
Tours of the Ground	48,647	51,629	26,619
Match Day Visits	54,523	115,260	81,568
Schools (in curriculum time)	191,407	181,993	153,322

TOTAL FIGURES:

Boys/Men involved	283,904	370,476	304,704
Girls/Women involved	144,850	161,085	142,547
Total Numbers Involved	428754	531,561	447251

Newly appointed as Head of Training/Government Programmes, former MSC front man, **Gary Naven** started his new job with a positive approach. His knowledge and experience in overseeing this important aspect of the national scheme's development was seen as crucial going forwards and he was swiftly involved in meetings to consider important issues such as recruitment levels, the issue of trainee travel expenses, the need to move towards having quality assurance systems in place etc. One other matter for Gary's consideration was the issue about whether Community Officers would be better qualified if they secured the then City and Guilds D32 assessor award (then under discussion with **Lorraine Hatton** and **Colin Hendry**). **Julian Hayes** also played a key role in supporting Gary as he got to grips with all these matters.

Following a great deal of hard work, a total of 58 professional clubs were able to support contracts in the "Training for Work" (TFW) contract year for 1993/4. Indeed, an average of 200 trainees were "in post' during this period, reflecting a great deal of credit on the new TFW manager and his team.

An important part of the relationship with Community Officers concerning TFW related to the provision of 'bonus payments' to local community schemes based on successful local outcomes achieved. For the contract year 1993/94, cheques totalling just under £30,000 were paid out to 33 club schemes including West Bromwich Albion (£2,275), Doncaster Rovers (£2,225), Barnsley (£1,562.50), Sunderland (£1,550) and Hartlepool United (£1,500). **Gary Naven** said:

> *"Training for Work represents a vitally important area of work in which we need to retain a continuity and progressive involvement. Training for Work is an opportunity, not just for trainees but also for club projects in helping them to earn funds to secure their long-term future"*

It should be noted at this point that the FFE&VTS Community Programme was also still picking up the 'tab' for local Community scheme telephone bills. As at February 1994 there were several large telephone invoices received relating to club schemes. It was very clear that FFE&VTS could not continue to fund these invoices in the longer term and it was eventually agreed that FFE&VTS Community Programme support would continue up to the end of December 1994 only.

Indeed, from records available, it was clear that in 1994 alone, the FFE&VTS Community Programme had paid telephone invoices worth well in excess of £20,000 on behalf of approximately 35 Community schemes. This simply could not be sustained in the longer term.

From a club perspective, some changes were noted during the first few months of 1994:

- Bradford City had appointed a new chairman, **Geoffrey Richmond**, who had previously been at Scarborough Football Club (where the Club Secretary had also been **Shaun Harvey** who later joined him at Valley Parade).

- The chairman of the club, who had tried to defraud his own club's Community Programme Scheme, left.

- Concern was expressed about the would-be sustainability of the Weymouth/Dorset CFA scheme (and the scheme folded later in the year).

- The Farnborough Town Community Scheme was struggling to become self-financing (though this was possibly partly due to the long-term sickness of the Community Officer).

- Kent CFA were to appoint Community Officer **Darren Hare** as a member of their own staff in March 1994.

- **George Kent** left his post as Community Officer at Exeter City, to be replaced by popular and well-known ex-player **Steve Neville.** Steve was a former player who began his career as an apprentice with Southampton. After making only 5 first team appearances, he moved to Exeter City. He then moved to Sheffield United for one season but returned to Exeter for his second spell with the club in 1982. He then moved to Bristol City in 1984 before re-joining Exeter in 1988. He moved to Australia following his spell as the club's Community Officer career ended and has been coaching Sorrento FC in Western Australia for several years.

- Manchester United were to take on **Dave Ryan** as a member of their staff and they were to operate the scheme as an internal department (taking full responsibility for PAYE, VAT and Corporation Tax liabilities that might arise).

Exciting new plans were also afoot in the South West Region where all Community Officers had committed to supporting a *"Football Festival for People with Learning Difficulties."* A full programme of events for different age groups, plus a Finals Day held in Yeovil in May 1994, was organised and a small amount of funding support had been kindly earmarked by the South West Sports Council. This once again illustrated the keen support of community schemes in this area. In the end over 1,000 youngsters took part in the Festival.

Worth noting too was the fact there was a huge amount of interest amongst Community Officers in attending the PFA 'Player of the Year Awards Ceremony' at the Grosvenor House Hotel in London and that the PFA accommodated them all.

The Community Programme scheme was also represented at the "Grounds for Optimism" conference held at Leicester City FC on 24th March 1994 and at the PFA Management course held at the Daniel Training Centre in Chorley on 31st May 1994 (a course aimed at current professional footballers who were planning to move into management at the end of their playing careers).

A meeting with solicitor **John Hewison** from George Davies Solicitors held on 12th May 1994 led to careful consideration of the operational aspects of the Community Programme scheme, as was the potential vulnerability to tax. John's recommendations at the time (which make particularly interesting reading now) were noted to be as follows:

- FFE&VTS Community Programme income from Pizza Hut is taxable (and subject to VAT) at the FFE&VTS and any monies passed on as donations by the Community Programme should therefore be outside the scope of Corporation Tax.

- Community Officers should be employed by local projects and each project should be registered with the Inland Revenue as an independent entity. Wages and returns to the Inland Revenue could still be handled by FFE&VTS as an 'agency' if required.

- Each local community project should seriously consider moving towards/applying for charitable status.

- In view of the ongoing concern about whether (or not) Community Schemes might be forced by the Inland Revenue to pay Corporation Tax, it should be noted that by the end of 1994 there was a total of 40 club-based Community Projects that had managed their finances on a local basis without having to call on the FFE&VTS Community Programme donation of £6,000. In turn, this meant that £240,000 was put in a "reserve" bank account by the FFE&VTS that would, in turn, generate bank interest for community schemes.

In July, Regional Director, **John Relish**, held a unique "update" meeting of Community Officers from across the South West whereby he managed to guarantee their attendance by combining the (afternoon) meeting with an evening charity football match against local opposition. Indeed, the match itself was a charity fund-raising event which had been promoted as including well known ex-professionals such as *"**Tommy Hutchison** (ex-Coventry City and Scotland), **Terry Connor** (Leeds, Birmingham), **Alan Curtis** (Leeds, Southampton), **Dave Armstrong** (Middlesbrough, Southampton and England)."* This concept for meetings was something that John continued over a period of several years with great success!

The spring/early summer period of 1994 saw further changes:

- **Mick Ferguson** left Sunderland. Mick's departure also coincided with the local TEC deciding to contract directly with the football club in respect of TFW.

- **Tony Evans** (Wolverhampton Wanderers) became a club employee.

- **Gary Gill** left Middlesbrough and was replaced by former Darlington player **Lawrie Pearson.** Wallsend-born Lawrie began his career with Hull City in the mid-1980's, later signing for Bristol City, Port Vale and Darlington before finishing his career with a single substitute appearance at Chesterfield in 1993.

- **Gary Stempel** left Millwall[12]

- **Martyn Spong** left Brentford at the end of April 1994 and his former Assistant, **Lee Doyle,** took over. Lee proved himself to be an extremely capable, hard-working and likeable successor. Indeed, Lee went on to spend many years at the club building the Brentford Community operation into one of the most respected across the country.

- **Gary Hooper** left Luton Town and was replaced by **Colwyn Rowe.** Colwyn was born in Ipswich and was once an apprentice with Colchester United where he made a handful of appearances (and some substitute appearances) for the club.

- Officials representing Weymouth Football Club confirmed that they could not guarantee the future sustainability of the club's community project, with or without the support of Dorset CFA, and chose to resign from the agreement with the FFE&VTS Community Programme. This also meant that appropriate notice, very sadly, had to be given to the club's Community Officer, **Dave Armstrong**. The effective final date for the scheme would be the end of June 1994.

- **Richard Hill** left Reading as Community Officer and was replaced by **Dave Armstrong** (on an initial 3 month 'trial' basis though Dave eventually left Reading at the end of March 1995).

- **Paul France** was brought in as Assistant Community Officer working with **Ces Podd** at Leeds United. Paul was born in Holmfirth and began his playing career as an apprentice with Huddersfield Town before going on to enjoy brief spells at Bristol City and Burnley before moving into non-league football. Paul was to become an extremely popular and very successful Community Officer in his own right in later years.

- **Dave Harper** resigned from his post as Community Officer at Bristol Rovers and was replaced by the well-known and popular ex-player **Terry Connor** (who moved from Swindon Town where he had been an Assistant Community Officer).

---

12. *The departure of **Gary Stempel** from Millwall (back to his native Panama) was a huge blow to officials at the club as he had been such a key figure in helping to make the Millwall Community Scheme such a success over so many years. Discussions with the club concerning replacing Gary took place over several weeks and, in the end, FFE&VTS Area Manager, **Jim Hicks**, agreed to take up the reigns. Even though Jim had made a huge success of his role as an Area Manager, this move was partly supported by the FFE&VTS in view of their recognition that a further reduction in the number of Area Managers by 1995 was going to be neccessary.*

- **Jack Detchon** resigned from his position at Sheffield & Hallamshire CFA at the end of June.

- At this time, it was still clear that Barnet Football Club had not yet been able to embrace the idea of re-establishing their community scheme. However, **Pat Finney** from the Football Trust was generous enough to confirm that the Trust would make available a further sum of £20,000 purely to support the development of this North London-based scheme.

Another exciting link that stood the 'test of time' over years to come was made in 1994 with the National Literacy Trust (NLT) via their Director, **Neil McClelland**. The first promotion launched with the NLT was a very successful poster campaign in which several well-known footballers of the day were photographed reading books to depict how footballers enjoy reading. Neil himself said:

> *"The poster campaign has been far more successful than I had dared hope. We have distributed nearly 40,000 posters to schools, colleges, libraries and prison/detention centres. Very many staff have written to us to say how influential the images have been. Without doubt, we have jointly contributed to literacy improvement in the UK."*

1994 also saw moves made by the FFE&VTS as a whole (i.e. not just the Community Programme scheme) towards securing 'Investors in People' (IIP) status. The IIP standard was awarded by TECs to employing organisations that achieved prescribed standards of training and staff development. The standard was also seen as a quality recognition of organisations that fully believe in, and support, their staff. Part of the requirement was for all management meetings to consider issues under IIP including:

- The commitment to training and the setting of clear objectives.
- The communication of a vision of where the organisation is going and how employees can play their part.
- An assessment of what training and staff development the organisation needs and can afford.
- The involvement of all staff, giving them ownership and partnership in the training process.
- The monitoring of progress, reviewing and renewing proactively.

Various meetings with **Malcolm Seaton** (from an organisation called Logicrite that specialised in supporting organisations in the IIP process) were held over a period of 18 months or so. All the meetings were aimed at identifying clear targets within the Business Plan, including the setting of specific targets for what the organisation was trying to achieve in terms of its business objectives, for example, income generation, adult (and youth) training, numbers of participants etc. A Staff Development Plan was also to be drawn up which would review the training and development needs of all employees, possibly as frequently as every two months. After several meetings with Malcolm, it was agreed that the FFE&VTS as a whole would aim to apply for IIP status in 1995. Various visits and departmental discussions followed and IIP status was finally awarded to the FFE&VTS in December 1995 when the IIP plaque was presented to **Mickey Burns** by **Richard Smith** from Manchester TEC.

Mickey said after the presentation:

> *"The basis of the FFE&VTS success is dependent on its employees and Investors in People fit that criteria completely."*

Richard Smith said:

> *"This demonstrates the company's ability, which I am sure will continue to be reflected in the quality service it offers to its customers."*

By Summer 1994, and with the continuing growth of Community schemes to such an extent that many local Community schemes now had more than one member of staff, it was clear that the FFE&VTS Community Programme role in providing a wage facility for around 70+ locally based community schemes was becoming increasingly important. Not only that, but it was also true to say that the FFE&VTS were assisting club community schemes from a financial (cash flow) point of view by paying out wages and then recovering them from local community schemes in arrears. At the end of June 1994, wages to be reimbursed to FFE&VTS totalled in excess of £665,000. This confirms the significant support offered to local community schemes, especially to those struggling to make ends meet. This aspect of support was to become an increasing burden for the Community Programme centrally, especially as local schemes continued to grow, and as turnover rose.

There were also other issues to deal with. Sunderland Football Club's local contract with their local provider (ELTEC) meant that responsibility for the successful delivery of the local TFW project was entirely down to the club. In itself, this wasn't a difficulty, if the quality of delivery remained. The club were also adamant that they would run their local community scheme in its entirety.

Peterborough United confirmed that they were looking to set up their own 'community scheme' under a club operation called "Posh Soccer". Difficulties had arisen where the operation of Posh Soccer cut directly across the work of Peterborough's community scheme headed up by **Domenico "Dom" Genovese**. By July, the club had submitted their resignation from the partnership agreement with the FFE&VTS Community Programme. This left Community Programme officials with a dilemma as to how to continue to support Domenico. In the end, and fairly swiftly, a meeting was arranged with **Gerry Knowles** and **Peter Mallinger** from Kettering Town who agreed to set up their own, new Community Scheme to be fronted by Domenico (he was, fortunately, a former Kettering Town player) even though, as a temporary measure, he would spend a short period up to the end of the year working with the rapidly expanding Leicester City Community Programme scheme.

The County FA (CFA) operations (notably at Durham, Kent and Sheffield & Hallamshire) appeared to be struggling with low numbers attending activities organised by them. In addition, they appeared to be becoming increasingly removed from mainstream Community Programme support. They were also finding it difficult to support the Pizza Hut sponsorship arrangements as the CFA schemes were very much more 'Football Development' focussed.

An enquiry from **Sean O'Driscoll** at AFC Bournemouth was greeted positively as the club seemed keen to appoint a new Community Officer at the club. As a player, Sean joined Fulham in 1979 and stayed for four seasons before moving to AFC Bournemouth where he spent the next eleven seasons, making over 400 appearances for the club. Sean was also to become an extremely successful club manager in future years.

Gordon Taylor, from the PFA, reported that all professional clubs were now supporting the new "Kick it Out" campaign, with one exception (who shall remain nameless) whose chairman felt that it wasn't necessary for them to become involved. Community Programme officials agreed to investigate further and to see if there were any specific difficulties concerning this club's support for this new and innovative scheme.

Community Officers who secured the FA Advanced "Full" Licence in 1994 included **Terry Connor** (Bristol Rovers), **John Halpin** (Carlisle United), **Chris Walters** (Crewe Alexandra), **Jimmy Gilligan** (Watford) and **Frankie Bunn** (Wigan Athletic). **Steve Lister** (Barnsley) also secured the FA Intermediate Certificate.

Talking of FA Coaching, a meeting with **Robin Russell** from the FA and **Dave Robinson** from the National Coaching Foundation, confirmed that the FA were hoping to offer a "new Preliminary Award" aimed at embracing all units required to secure the NVQ Level II. In order to move to this, however, it was necessary for the FA to secure new "assessors" and that to become an assessor it was necessary to attend an FA course over 9 days. FFE&VTS Community Programme officials agreed to look at who might be suitable for moving forwards on this basis (all assessors were to hold the FA Advanced Licence).

The 1994/5 season got underway with news of Community Officers:

- **Jason Withe** took up the post of Community Officer at Birmingham City.
- **Jo Swift** left Queens Park Rangers.
- **Mark Ashton** left West Bromwich Albion (though he was to return within a short space of time).
- **Mike Rigg** left Wrexham to work with **Jimmy Shoulder** (Head of Coaching at the Welsh FA). Mike's replacement as Community Officer at Wrexham was **Steve Weaver.**

It should also be noted that following the resignations of Weymouth/Dorset CFA and Peterborough United, the FFE&VTS Community Programme was, by now, directly supporting and working with a total of 95 community schemes. Plans were afoot to work with Barnet and with AFC Bournemouth (which would obviously increase this figure) but there was also an increasing possibility that the established CFA schemes might "go their own way".

Sportsmatch officials were in touch with FFE&VTS Community Programme officials at this time, expressing real concern about an application they had received from an unnamed Football Club who had, seemingly, put an application together based around their Community scheme but that was entirely in the name of the football club (i.e. all monies would be paid and handled by the football club). In this particular case, it was somewhat reassuring to understand that Sportsmatch had requested the FFE&VTS Community Programme to become "honest brokers" and to try and convince the club concerned to consider approaching things differently. Without beating around the bush, it is fair to suggest that the club concerned were given an ultimatum as to whether they wanted to continue to work alongside the FFE&VTS *or* to go their own way and risk what might happen with their application.

Alan Young from Notts County reported on a "first" for the scheme. The Right Honourable **John Major** (Prime Minister at the time) wrote to Alan in person commending him on the excellent work being done by the Notts County Community Programme in conjunction with their local Drugs Prevention team. This was also reported on the BBC Nine O'clock News in mid-September! Speaking in his book "*Youngy – The Autobiography of Alan Young*" Alan also praised the support he received from Manager **Neil Warnock** whilst he was Community Officer at the club:

"I can't speak highly enough of Neil Warnock …. he is a smashing guy and would do anything for you"

This is a view, by the way, that is supported by many Community Officers that worked with Neil Warnock over the years. Support from managers at clubs, especially for releasing players to attend community activities, varied from club to club. In the early days, there were some managers who expressly stated that they would *not* support, for example, the development of opportunities for girls and women to play football and certainly not the formation of women's teams. Whilst Community Officers were as tactful and diplomatic as they could be when faced with this sort of opposition, it was clear that the days of those "old school" managers were numbered and that a new generation of increasingly supportive managers was starting to emerge.

Following up on recent meetings with representatives of Refuge Assurance, a further meeting in August 1994 "set the scene" for the new 1994/5 competition when it was agreed that "Fact Packs" would be developed for all participating players (this being a huge undertaking and commitment from Refuge Assurance). The "Fact Pack" included details of the timetable of events (rounds), rules of the competition etc. Registration forms for all competing players would also become available. A new prize framework was also devised which saw a commitment to give generously to participating Primary and Junior Schools.

A successful application was also made to Sportsmatch for further 'match funding' support during the 1994/5 season (i.e. Year 2 of the 3-year deal with Refuge). A huge majority of club schemes confirmed that they would again be taking part in the competition, particularly as it was clear that the tournament would be held over the duration of the full season, allowing local competitions to be held at any time between September and December.

September 1994 saw the publishing of the results of the research survey undertaken by the Sir Norman Chester Centre for Football Research under the supervision of researcher, lecturer and sociologist **John Williams** and supported by **Rogan Taylor**. The report was sub-divided into various sections and some of the key findings and comments were as follows:

SURVEY OF CLUB COMMUNITY OFFICERS

One of the opening comments was: *"The 1991-1993 Business Plan set out a 'new approach' which laid 'greater stress on the promotion of football* per se *rather than on the more general 'welfarist' philosophies which underpinned the earlier phases of the scheme"*

GENERAL COMMENTS

- It was fundamentally the club which had the final say in the appointment of Community Officers at their club (even though the trend was almost always to interview candidates).
- To have no female input on national policy decision making on football community issues seems to us to be a major failing.
- The management team on the national scheme encourage and support officers in their pursuit of relevant qualifications and pay for many courses.
- In relation to induction training, seven out of ten of the sample did feel at least quite well prepared to take up their post, though it was also recognised that there was an urgent need for better general preparation for work in the areas of administration, finance (accounting), management and marketing. A later recommendation was for Community Officers to spend 2-4 weeks working with established officers; to receive more information about administration, finance (accounting), management and marketing; to attend regular training days; to be trained in basic economic/demographic details about their local areas.
- Community project work *does* encourage people to attend more 'live' games.
- Concerning football for girls and women, the involvement of female participants was "one of the very major advances made in some of the best community schemes."
- Club secretaries and players provide the most active support.

THE REPORT'S RECOMMENDATIONS

- Better training for Officers at clubs
- A higher national profile to be established
- Note to be made of the dangers of chasing revenue funding activities as opposed to those that may be necessary
- Two new staff to be appointed in PR and/or in overseeing Commercial activities
- Membership (Management) Forums should be regularly reviewed (at least once a year) for the input of its members. Consideration to be given to other local bodies which could provide ideas and support and to whether the club and the FFE&VTS Community Programme representation is healthy.
- Forum meetings should take place at least every two months and should be properly timetabled with a pre-circulated written agenda.
- Clubs should provide a short, written account of each Management Forum meeting to club Board Meetings for further discussion and feedback to the scheme.
- Club Board Meetings should contain an agenda item concerning the club's community scheme and the Community Scheme should have discussions and/or make a presentation directly to the club Board of Directors at least twice a year.
- A number of Board members should see the scheme in action on a formal basis at least twice a year.
- Clubs should ensure that the scheme is effectively promoted inside the club and through club channels for external promotion.

CONCLUDING COMMENTS

- The general response in the survey regarding work out of the Manchester (FFE&VTS

Community Programme) office, and to its routine support for schemes, was very positive.

-    "Enormous credit should properly go to the FFE&VTS, to the clubs concerned, to other organisations involved in supporting schemes, but particularly to the Community Officers themselves for sustaining an admirable national programme in the light of often extremely difficult financial circumstances. The scheme has made remarkable progress and can demonstrate great success".

-    The future for community schemes at clubs seems both promising and exciting and fraught with potential dangers.

-    Clubs accept that the activities of Community Officers may not produce a quick commercial return but will produce longer term local benefits, both commercial and social, for the clubs and its supporters.

CONCERN

A number of Community Officers were critical of the "new, national agenda" and the apparent move away from traditional community 'engagement: *"it is precisely those who are poor, unemployed and disadvantaged who are losing active contact with clubs as spectators – i.e. the kind of contact a community scheme can help. A healthy and successful national community programme cannot be run solely or largely on a hand to mouth 'commercial basis'. "*

In depth interviews/contact was made with: Bury – Brian Taylor (Community Officer), Terry Robinson (Chairman), Mr Cowan (Headteacher Coney Green High School), Richard Blackstone (parent), Don McKenzie and Kevin Gallagher (formerly trainees), Everton – Ted Sutton (Community Officer), Bill Kenwright (Director), Derek Johnstone (Commercial and Marketing Manager) and Graham Taylor (Senior Probation Officer), Liverpool – Brian Hall (Community and PR Officer), John Williams (Supporters Liaison Officer), Dorothy Woods (Deputy Headteacher, Toxteth Special School) and Bill Bygroves (Coach) Millwall – Gary Stempel (Community Officer).

Further interesting details were noted as a result of the survey of club Community Officers:

•   100% of Senior Community Officers were male (and a majority were former professional footballers)

•   Two thirds of Community Officers have gained relevant qualifications since becoming a Community Officer.

•   Two thirds of Community Officers received appropriate induction training.

•   44% of Community Officers say that their schemes have private (local) sponsorship.

•   20% of Community Officers say that their Management Forums are not very effective.

•   83% of Officers say that the support from FFE&VTS Area Managers is excellent or good.

•   66% of Officers would prefer to work more closely with their local authority.

It should be noted that the results of the research were all shared with Community Officers at regional meetings held before Christmas at Manchester United's Old Trafford ground (Western Region), Barnsley Football Club's Oakwell ground (Eastern Region) and Bristol City's Ashton Gate (South West Region). Following the circulation of the report and its recommendations, it was 'business as usual' approaching Christmas 1994.

The Management Structure was once again put under review. It was agreed that the adult training programme needed the input of a skilled deliverer of NVQs. As a result, Area Manager, **Andy Welsh,** was approached to become "Director/Deliverer of NVQ Coaching Awards" (the title was to be worked on!) on the basis that he would then work closely with Head of Training/ Government Programmes, **Gary Naven,** to ensure the delivery of coaching awards. This was an important and successful move, particularly when the huge increase in NVQ achievement was taken into account.

Another Area Manager, **Gordon Coleman**, also spoke directly to **Mickey Burns** to announce that he was to take up a new post heading up Nottingham Forest's Community Scheme effective from the 5th December.

These changes led to a full and comprehensive review of the allocation of clubs to each Regional Director/Area Manager on the basis that a reduction from nine Area Managers to six senior Managers (comprising 3 x Regional Directors, **Richard Finney**, **Kevin Glendon** and **John Relish** and 3 x Area Managers, **Dick Krzywicki**, **Dave Palmer** and **John Seasman**) could now be facilitated.

The New Year of 1995 saw several meetings aimed at considering new allocations of clubs. As an example, a meeting in the South confirmed that **John Relish** would, in future, oversee South West clubs *plus* Portsmouth, Reading and Southampton. In turn, of course, this meant that John's newly defined region would now cover a massive geographical area! In the South East, **Dave Palmer** would oversee *all* clubs in and around London *plus* those in Essex and Kent.

The importance of access to Sportsmatch funding was becoming much more widely appreciated by Community Officers though it was also apparent that a few unsuccessful applications had been submitted without reference to FFE&VTS Community Programme officials.

It was felt by many that much closer links with national scheme personnel should assist in this regard, so closer links were directly encouraged. Notably, national scheme officials were able to provide reassurances for Sportsmatch officials that their monies invested with particular schemes could be underpinned on the basis that the FFE&VTS Community Programme were partners and signatories on local community scheme bank accounts. This meant that a new approach could be adopted regarding what were unsuccessful applications submitted without the knowledge of the FFE&VTS.

It was quite apparent that FFE&VTS Community Programme officials (especially **Richard Finney** who was dynamically involved at the time) were developing a unique expertise in leading, developing, completing and submitting Sportsmatch applications. In terms of income generation, together with the enhanced community involvement, this was to prove to be a key factor over the next few years. Richard himself, of course, would also play a key role in supporting clubs to submit the required information to Sportsmatch at the end of each local Sportsmatch-supported project (this included the preparation and return of local accounts information relevant to each local project).

One interesting development during autumn of 1994 saw a good example of the scheme working closely with the PFA to support a former player in difficult circumstances. **John Buckley** had an excellent playing career which first began with Celtic as a junior though he made his first senior appearance following a move to Partick Thistle in 1983. He moved south in 1984 when **Billy Bremner** signed him for Doncaster Rovers. He went on to play for Leeds United, Leicester City (on loan), Doncaster Rovers again (on loan this time), Rotherham United and Scunthorpe United before returning to Rotherham where his career was abruptly ended following a serious head injury in 1993. The injury was so serious that it was felt that John would never again play professional football. A year on from the injury, following keen support from Rotherham United to see if they could assist, funding became available from the PFA to support his short-term appointment as **Fraser Foster**'s Assistant working in the local community (John started the job in June 1995). In the longer term, this experience stood John in good stead as he enjoyed several coaching positions in the game in later years, some of which were spent making a huge contribution to the growth of the women's game.

An autumn meeting with **Chris Earle** from the Central Council of Physical Recreation (Chris would later to go on to work for the FA directly) also outlined the process for operating Community Sports Leaders Awards courses (NVQ level 1).

The Football Trust Community Awards Scheme, this time sponsored by Littlewoods, was underway again and was strongly supported by Trust Secretary, **Pat Finney**. This time, it became very clear that many more clubs were considering applying, as they clearly felt that they had a good chance of winning an award. An early New Year meeting considered the fact that there were likely to be more applications than ever before and that the criteria set needed to take account of:

- The wide range of activities.
- The scope of the work undertaken (and the amount of non-football work).
- The involvement of girls and women, people with disabilities.

A meeting of the Assessment Panel (including **Pat Finney** and **Paulette Johnson** (from the Football Trust), **Adrian Cook** (then Assistant Secretary at the PL) **Chris Whalley** (FL), **Mike Appleby** (FA), **Tony Kershaw** (Federation of Supporters Clubs) and **Roger Reade** (FFE&VTS Community Programme) was held in March 1995 to consider a total of 80 applications and to make arrangements for an official Awards Ceremony to be held in May 1995. In the end, short-listed awards winners were selected for the PL and for the FL on a divisional basis. The winners were:

LEAGUE/DIVISION	COMMUNITY AWARD
PL Winners	Manchester City
PL Runners Up	Coventry City
FL Division One Winners	Sunderland
FL Division One Runners Up	Derby County
FL Division Two Winners	Leyton Orient
FL Division Two Runners Up	Huddersfield Town
FL Division Three Joint Winners	Fulham and Walsall
FL Division Three Runners Up	Colchester United

Leyton Orient's Community Scheme won the overall Community award.

Peter Lee (Football Trust Chief Executive) said:

> *"Football can be rightly proud of the close ties that clubs have established with their local communities and the Football Trust is delighted that their Littlewoods Community Award Scheme is recognising all the fine work that has been undertaken."*

Officers moving on at the end of 1994/start of 1995 included:

- Grimsby Town where **Ian Knight** took over from **John Cockerill** (who became the club's Youth Development Officer). Following his apprenticeship with Barnsley, Ian Knight moved to Sheffield Wednesday where he tragically broke a leg whilst playing for Wednesday against Chester City in the FA Cup. He did, however, go on to play for Scunthorpe United (on loan), Grimsby Town and Carlisle United before the end of his playing career in 1992.
- Swindon Town where **Shane Cook** took over from **Jonathan Trigg** (who took up the post of club physiotherapist). Shane was a former Swindon Town youth team goalkeeper.

One more interesting meeting to take place prior to Christmas involved **Jas Bains** and **Raj Patel** (co-authors of the book, *Asians Can't Play Football*) which commented on the huge interest and involvement of the Asian heritage community in football, but which also highlighted that there was clearly a problem in the lack of Asian heritage footballers 'making the grade' as professional footballers.

An end of year summary of wages paid during 1994 revealed that the FFE&VTS had processed wages on behalf of 72 of the 95 community schemes and that the total wages paid out during the year by FFE&VTS on behalf of those local schemes was approximately £1.27 million. This, of course, included the fact that several projects now employed assistant officers. Amongst those newer officers working as assistants were:

- **Shah Pall Rehman** (Bradford City)
- **Richard Wilson** (Bristol City)
- **David Toombs** (Cambridge United)
- **Graham Benham** (Huddersfield Town)
- **Marc Ledingham** (Hull City)
- **Steve Eyre** and **Alison Vaughan** (Manchester City)
- **Graham Moran** (Notts County)
- **Tommy Spencer** and **Colleen Fawdry** (Sheffield United)
- **Brett Bensley** (West Bromwich Albion. Brett, together with colleague **Clint Roberts**, would also take supervisory charge of the Albion Community Scheme for a spell in later years).

Officially noted at the time was the fact that between 70-75% of all (senior) Community Officers were former members of the PFA.

It should also be noted that **Ian "Spider" Mellor** from the PFA's Commercial department continued to be extremely supportive, bringing several commercial possible deals to Community Officers. In early 1995 amongst flexible opportunities that Community Officers could "dip in to" (if they so wished) were arrangements with:

- Arrow (notably footwear).
- Nintendo.
- Umbro (kit, footwear and equipment).
- Haven Holidays (With Ian's support, Haven generously offered several free holidays for Community Schemes, which were offered through projects working specifically with children with special needs or children with disabilities).

In the end, "Spider" was also able to develop a catalogue of football related kit and equipment that was made exclusively accessible for Community Officers. This was seen as particularly supportive as it meant that Community Officers weren't obliged to purchase, for example, footballs from a particular manufacturer, but that, instead, they could select from several few different suppliers based on quality and price from Ian's catalogue.

By the end of January 1995, it was clear that the schemes at Tottenham Hotspur and at Sheffield & Hallamshire CFA were to effectively 'fold'. The Spurs scheme had never really got started and had been put "on hold" following the untimely passing of former Community Officer, **Len Julians**. The Sheffield project had also never really started again after **Jack Detchon** left in 1994. In addition, it had become clear that the largely football-based projects at Durham CFA and at Kent CFA had been isolated from the FFE&VTS and that future working together in the long term was open to question. However, from a positive perspective, it was agreed that every effort should be made to encourage new community schemes at AFC Bournemouth and at Wycombe Wanderers.

The end of the 1994/95 contract year for TFW saw many club projects lean on this provision for support officers. Indeed, several schemes positively excelled both in helping trainees to secure qualifications and in helping them to move into more permanent employment. Amongst those highlighted as "high-flyers" were TFW projects at Barnsley, Blackpool, Doncaster Rovers, Hull City, Manchester City, Oldham Athletic, Rochdale, Scunthorpe United and Wigan Athletic. That said, it was also noted that Head of Training/Government Programmes, **Gary Naven,** had reported that certain areas were likely to withdraw any sort of offer for the new contract year, especially where clubs had been struggling to maintain anything like the necessary recruitment levels and/or required job outcomes (such as occurred at Hartlepool United, Kidderminster

Harriers, Merthyr Tydfil, Northampton Town and Reading. The contract with Northampton Town was also lost as there had been no successful job outcomes for more than two years). Amongst the TECs not renewing contracts were AZTEC, Kent, Northampton, South Glamorgan and Tyneside.

For the contract year 1994/95, bonus cheques which totalled around £23,500 were paid out to 17 club schemes including: Sheffield United (£3427.50), Sheffield Wednesday (£2156.25), Hull City (£1750), Rotherham United (£1724.62) and Rochdale (£1706.25).

Average recruitment levels during the 1994/1995 contract year are detailed in "Appendix III – Table of trainees in post year by year 1994-2002". Amongst those clubs with excellent recruitment levels during the year were projects at Blackpool, Bolton Wanderers, Chesterfield, Hull City, Leeds United, Manchester City, Mansfield Town, Nottingham Forest and West Bromwich Albion.

A total of 48 club projects supported TFW during the 1994/1995 contract year. The average number of trainees in post at any one point in time was lower than it had ever been (despite a healthy number of club schemes still supporting TFW). Indeed, the average had reached the point where alarm bells were ringing about the future of TFW as a key part of the Community Programme initiative. Recruitment levels at certain clubs were low and unsustainable (e.g. at Coventry City, Darlington and Leicester City). Of all clubs involved, only around ten clubs showed anything like the necessary commitment required to ensure TFW could be successful. This presented a real challenge for **Andy Welsh** who undertook his own visits to 20 or so clubs in the summer, based on his interest in understanding the issues faced by Officers.

At club level, the spring of 1995 saw further changes including:

- **Mickey Cook** left Colchester United to take up a local position in Promotions and Marketing (he also became the club's Academy Director at one point). Mickey was replaced by **Steve Bradshaw** (previously an assistant Community Officer at Arsenal).

- **Dave Armstrong** left Reading and was replaced by Yeovil Town's Community Officer, **Chris Whalley** (Yeovil Town resigned from the Scheme at this point).

- **Paul Johnson** left Stoke City and was replaced by **Andy Morgan** (**Adrian Hurst** was also appointed as Assistant Community Officer at the club. Adrian (Adie) would eventually replace Andy at the club and would go on to become a very popular and extremely successful Community Officer at the club).

- **Phil Attfield** left Gillingham.

The 1994/95 Regional Finals of the Schools six-a-side competition followed the Area Finals and were held on the 4th and 5th April. The Final itself was held at Wembley on the 23rd April, once again with the co-operation and support of the Football League, prior to the Auto Windscreens Final match between Birmingham City and Carlisle United (won by Birmingham 1-0). In attendance, alongside representatives of the ESFA, was **Chris Thayne** together with **Nick Cole** and **Paul Adams** from Refuge Assurance.

The 1994/95 competition saw over 1,800 primary and junior schools take part which, of course, reflected great credit on all involved and it was against this backdrop that Refuge confirmed that they would, once again, sponsor the tournament during 1995/96 (with a further possibility of additional pound for pound funding from Sportsmatch becoming available. See Appendix V for details of Competition winners).

Within the South West region, plans were once again afoot to run another Festival, this time being a "*South West Festival for women and girls*". Included in the festival would be separate competitions for girls aged under 11 and under 15, with the finals being held on the 1st October 1995. In addition, a few women's exhibition matches would be held.

FFE&VTS Community Programme officials also found a new talent being that of supporting clubs to develop applications for facilities to the new National Lottery! This followed a successful bid made by the Bury Community Scheme to develop five a side pitches and changing rooms at their Gigg Lane ground which **Mickey Burns** had more or less completed in full on a free 'consultancy' basis for the club. The next club to secure a major grant from the National Lottery, again with the full and active support of the FFE&VTS Community Programme, was Rochdale Football Club, who secured a grant of just over £120,000 towards the total costs of £180,000 of building a five a side pitch and male/female changing rooms at their Spotland ground. The new facilities would include floodlights, rebound walls and separate male and female changing facilities. Burnley's Community Scheme was also successful with an application for capital funding worth approximately £560,000 towards the total costs of building a full leisure complex attached to the gymnasium/sports hall at Turf Moor.

Sad news was received in the Spring of 1995. Former Community Officer, **Mick Heaton**, tragically died in a car crash near Oswaldtwistle in April aged only 48.

Football Trust Secretary, **Pat Finney** (who had done so much to support the FFE&VTS Community Programme *and* locally based Community Schemes for so many years) announced that she would be leaving the Football Trust in May. By the turn of the new century, the decline of the Pools companies led to the Football Trust being replaced by the Football Foundation, with a whole new funding formula.

His Royal Highness (HRH) Prince Charles also visited a Hull City Football in the Community session put on in Gipsyville, Hull led by Community Officer **John Davies** in May. Prince Charles was keen to find out more about the impact of the community led sessions in relation to young people.

It is worth noting that FFE&VTS Community Programme management meetings continued on a monthly basis at this time. Indeed, the meetings became increasingly important as "snapshots" of what had been achieved, where recruitment plans were necessary, what was outstanding and so forth. So, as an example, the June 1995 meeting saw an agenda which included the following headings (and issues in brackets as appropriate):

AGENDA – GENERAL MANAGEMENT MEETING

1.   Apologies for absence.

2.   Minutes from previous meeting.

3.   Matters arising (including club update re: paperwork outstanding e.g.– agreements/ stats reports/wage payments/personal information missing (e.g. CVs)/copies Business Plans and Audited Accounts etc.)

4.   Events Update (e.g. including the Refuge 6-a-side competition, Football League 2000 and the NPFA Penalty competition).

5.   Commercial Update (supporting deals with Pizza Hut, Haven Holidays, Umbro, Sportsmatch etc.)

6.   Adult Training (including contract update, recruitment levels and issues, NVQ achievement, outstanding appraisals etc.)

7.   Club Update (all non-paperwork issues – e.g. Officers leaving/being appointed/clubs with financial difficulties etc.)

8.   Any Other Business (anything else – e.g. Football Trust Community Awards, club capital applications).

In terms of the summer of 1995, a former professional footballer of some note was appointed as an Assistant Community Officer at Southampton when **Stuart Gray** was recruited at the club where he had finished his playing career. Stuart's professional career began at Nottingham Forest and included a loan move to Bolton Wanderers in 1982. He also played at Barnsley, Aston Villa and briefly at Southampton in 1991/92.

Positions within Southampton's community scheme were reversed soon after that as Stuart took over as the senior club Community Officer within a very short space of time and as **Alan Smith** became Assistant Officer.

Other new Assistants who were making positive impressions at their respective clubs included **Michael Cole** at Chelsea, **Ray Scott** at Southend United, **Andy Kilner** at Stockport

County and **Steve Hughes** at Wrexham. Bolton-born, **Andy Kilner** served his apprenticeship with Burnley where he made his league debut in 1986. He then played briefly in non-league football and in Sweden before moving back to England to play for Stockport County, Rochdale (on loan) and Bury. He was to be appointed as Manager of Stockport County in 1999.

With between 65 and 70 club community schemes using the FFE&VTS payroll service around this time, it should be noted that the summer of 1995 was a crucial time for the sensitive issue of who employed the officers to be raised with the clubs. One of the things laid down in the Business Plan was for all locally based Management Forums to understand that they needed to take responsibility for the employment of their local Community Officer(s) with effect from the start of 1994. This had simply not happened in some areas, so meetings were arranged with Regional Directors and Area Managers to ensure that this important matter could be endorsed and recorded at local level.

Also taking things forward in the summer of 1995 were **Doug Fraser** and **Ian Roberts** from Touché Ross (to be renamed Deloitte and Touché in February 1996) and several meetings with them confirmed the complexity of the present situation, given the status of locally established Community schemes (with their own constitutions), the employment status of local Community Officers, the role of the FFE&VTS Community Programme in providing a "wages service" (and the actual payments being made concerning wages, including the reimbursement of wages to the FFE&VTS Community Programme by local schemes) together with the issues of VAT, Corporation Tax and PAYE.

In relation to the potential risk of incurring corporation tax, the Community Programme had already come up with a very simple solution, which was to withhold the FFE&VTS donation of £6,000 per year where necessary, therefore reducing the surplus of local schemes (and therefore the amount on which tax might be deemed to have fallen due).

The meeting with Touché Ross (later Deloitte & Touché) was an important step forward as over the next couple of years several local tax offices would be raising questions concerning these matters. Amongst those clubs affected by local visits were community schemes at Burnley, Coventry City, Crystal Palace, Everton, Port Vale, Queens Park Rangers and Wimbledon.

Also, worth noting at this time, are the total and average turnover figures of those club community schemes (for 1993/94) that were operating on an independent basis:

Region	Total Turnover	Average Turnover
Eastern (from 28 sets of accounts)	£647,892	£23,139
Southern (from 21 sets of accounts)	£773,923	£36,853
Western (from 28 sets of accounts)	£692,857	£24,745
Totals (from 77 sets of accounts)	**£2,114,672**	**£27,463**

Whilst this represented significant progress, it also compares and contrasts with the £125 million turnover for the 98 professional club schemes over twenty years later – i.e.: as at year-end dates ending in 2017 (with a resulting average turnover per scheme of just under £1.3 million. See Appendix I).

The new 1995/96 season got underway with the mood amongst Community Officers still as positive as ever. Indeed, all Community Officers were now "armed" with a minimum of 30 support packs and kit and equipment to give away to local Primary and Junior Schools, which meant that the new school year started particularly optimistically.

Steve Neville confirmed that he would be leaving Exeter City in early September. It was agreed with the club that the Exeter scheme should be temporarily 'mothballed' as it was apparent that there were financial difficulties within the scheme. That said, after only a very short period of inactivity, ex-player **Eamonn Dolan** was appointed as the club's new Community Officer.

A former Republic of Ireland Under 21 international, Eamonn began his playing career as an apprentice with West Ham United where he also turned professional, making his full debut in 1987. After a small number of appearances, he moved to Bristol City (on loan) and Birmingham City before joining Exeter City in 1991. Sadly, illness curtailed his career, forcing his retirement two years later. After huge efforts undertaken by Eamonn, the good news was that he had been very quick to turn things round in swiftly moving towards a much healthier financial position for the club's community scheme. Eamonn was well liked and respected, particularly in Exeter, and Regional Director **John Relish**, was always quick to "sing the praises" of a job particularly well done by Eamonn for Exeter City.

On the advice of the club's Youth Development Officer, **Robbie Stepney** was appointed at Tottenham Hotspur. As a player, Robbie had made over 200 appearances for Aldershot between 1958 and 1964. Soon after Robbie's appointment, however, **Claude Littner** and **John Ireland** at the club confirmed that they were unsure about the present 'state of play' concerning their community operation and that the club was to review the concept of the scheme by the end of the season. This was followed up by a telephone call from PL Secretary **Mike Foster** (who had, by now, left the FL in order to join the PL as Secretary), who wanted to assist as best he could. In March the following year, however, Spurs appointed Robbie as a coach within the club, leaving the Community scheme at the club to effectively, and once again, be put "on hold". Mike, incidentally, also did his level best to try and encourage representatives of Arsenal to reconsider their 'franchise' arrangements across the country. All Mike's efforts were gratefully appreciated at the time.

Former Bristol City player, **Alan Walsh**, took over from **Terry Connor** in early October at Bristol Rovers. Born in Hartlepool, Alan Walsh began his career in his native North East with spells at Middlesbrough and Darlington before moving to Bristol City in 1984. He also had brief spells with Walsall, Huddersfield Town, Shrewsbury Town, Cardiff City and Hartlepool United. He went on to give five years sterling service as Community Officer at Rovers before leaving to take up a coaching post at Bristol City's Academy.

Jimmy Gilligan took over as new Youth Development Officer at Watford, leaving a vacant post at Vicarage Road that was eventually offered to Wimbledon's Assistant Community Officer, **Kirk Wheeler**. In relation to Kirk's appointment, it followed an interview process in which several candidates, including a number of former players, were interviewed.

The Sub-Committee of the FFE&VTS Board met in November 1995 and agreed to support a new Schools Secondary Schools Competition initially for boys to be run by the Football League (FL). The FL at the time were successful in securing Sportsmatch pound for pound match funding for the sponsorship of this competition by Auto Windscreens. In due course, this competition was to change and would become a tournament exclusively for girls aged Under 13. Whilst neither an exclusively boy's competition nor an exclusively girl's competition was ideal at the time, this was at least a small step towards encouraging community schemes to engage more widely with more secondary schools.

The 1995 year-end summary of wages confirmed that the FFE&VTS had paid out wages on behalf of 70 of the 95 community schemes and that the total wages paid out during the year by FFE&VTS on behalf of those local schemes had risen to approximately £1.36 million. This included the fact that several community projects had taken on new assistant officers. Indeed, at this time, approximately 38 of the 70 projects employed Assistant Community Officers. Amongst those in post were:

- **Freddie Hudson** (employed by Arsenal)
- **Warwick Adams**, **Allan Thompson** and **Nigel Macrow** (employed by Aston Villa)
- **Mary Betts** (Barnsley)
- **Nick Jackson-Cooney** (Blackburn Rovers)
- **Dave Lippiatt** (Bristol Rovers)
- **Stephen Downey** (Colchester United)
- **Colin Lodge** and **Colin Walker** (Crystal Palace)
- **Danny Jacquart** (Fulham)

- **Craig White** (Leicester City)
- **Eddie Leach** and **Louis Garvey** (Manchester United)
- **Mark Hemingray** (Mansfield Town. Mark would go on to become Senior Community Officer in his own right at the Field Mill club in later years.)
- **Nigel Wooley** and **Dean Titterton** (Nottingham Forest)
- **Andy Evans** (Queens Park Rangers)
- **Adam Davy** and **Simon Williams** (Walsall)
- **Daniel Parker** (York City)

All of this was very encouraging, of course, as it showed that local community schemes were expanding and taking on more and more work. It should also be noted that the FFE&VTS made arrangements for longer serving Assistant Community Officers to be added to the national Life Assurance scheme.

Purely as a guide, it is worth noting that, as at December 1995, average wages being paid to Community Officers on the FFE&VTS payroll (63% of all Community Officers) were approximately £13,915 per annum (£267 per week) and to Assistant Community Officers £5,977 per annum (£115 per week).

A summary of club Community Schemes turnover during the year 1995 revealed that a total of 72 Schemes turned over a collective total of £2,110,564, meaning that average turnover across those schemes had risen to approximately £29,313 per annum. By the end of the year, it is also worth noting that the FFE&VTS Community Programme was directly supporting 95 community schemes:

- all 20 PL clubs.
- 67 of the 72 FL clubs (not AFC Bournemouth, Derby County, Ipswich Town, Peterborough United and Wycombe Wanderers).
- 8 projects still operating outside the PL and FL which were: Durham CFA, Farnborough Town, Halifax Town, Kent CFA, Kettering Town, Kidderminster Harriers, Norfolk CFA (now merged with the Norwich City Community Scheme) and Merthyr Tydfil (with the support of Taff Ely Council).

FFE&VTS-supported schemes at Sheffield & Hallamshire CFA and at Weymouth and Yeovil Town had now 'folded'. Wycombe Wanderers community scheme was to get underway with the appointment of **Matthew Smith** in September 1996, though his appointment was, in the end, only short-term as he had left by the summer of 1997 and was replaced at that time by the dual appointment of **Nas Bashir** and **Dave Evans**.

The Christmas area meetings of Community Officers also saw a visit from the very popular financial adviser, **Richard Guest** (PFA Financial Management), who urged all Community Officers to ensure that they made adequate pension arrangements for the future.

After huge efforts from both **Gary Naven** and **Andy Welsh**, the good news, as far as Adult Training (including TFW) was concerned, was that recruitment levels were improving at many club schemes (although problems did still exist in a small number of areas). Andy, in particular, had got to grips with the need for the successful delivery of NVQ qualifications at Levels I and II. Course provision in the Western Region had largely been resolved with a few courses only required in the South and Eastern regions to "mop up" course provision for certain trainees who hadn't yet had the opportunity to attend courses. Gary had also worked hard to ensure that appropriate evidence was collated where successful job outcomes had been achieved and to ensure appropriate Quality Assurance systems were in place. Indeed, three TECs (Cumbria, Lancashire Area West (LAWTEC) and Rochdale) confirmed how pleased they were with all the quality assurance work that had been done in recent months.

An early New Year 1996 meeting of senior managers and Regional Directors looked in more detail at the difference between the role of Regional Directors and that of Area Managers. After lengthy discussions, it was agreed that the difference in roles should be maintained if only in the short term.

In February 1996, a further informal meeting was held with **Brian Marwood** (Commercial Executive at the PFA) to consider the national sponsorship of the scheme following three years of successful liaison work with Pizza Hut. Brian's playing career had begun as an apprentice footballer with Hull City, playing in over 150 league games for the Tigers up to 1984 when he signed for Sheffield Wednesday. He went on to play for Arsenal, Sheffield United, Middlesbrough (on loan), Swindon Town and Barnet. He was also capped for England.

Brian fully understood the sponsorship opportunity and was very positive and supportive, taking away from the meeting not only further information about the scheme's work to date (in conjunction with Pizza Hut) but also a lengthy list of potential new sponsors from various industry backgrounds. Brian kindly agreed to put together a suitable presentation for potential sponsors/partners by the middle/end of March.

Discussions also commenced regarding the future operation of the Kent CFA Community Scheme. To be fair to Kent CFA officials (notably CFA Secretary **Keith Masters**), it was very clear by now that what was being delivered in Kent was based around a more traditional football development scheme (with little or no wider 'community' interaction at all). One possibility being considered (given the nature of the good work undertaken by the then Officer, **Darren Hare**) was a possible merger with the Gillingham Community scheme, although this didn't happen in the end.

Also beginning to 'impact' on the scheme were issues arising out of the 1989 Children Act, which aimed to ensure (quite rightly) that children were 'safeguarded', and their welfare promoted amongst all agencies operating with children – e.g. locally based community schemes. Information from solicitors about the key items of the Act affecting Community schemes was kindly prepared for circulation amongst Community Officers by solicitors from George Davies Solicitors in Manchester.

Also, in February 1996, **Paul France** left Leeds United to join Huddersfield Town (also as an Assistant Officer). Paul, of course, not only became a very popular figure and a key Community Officer at the club but he also played a significant part in setting up and operating a unique child friendly play centre in Huddersfield in later years.

Also, that month (and quite "out of the blue"), Regional Director **John Relish** announced that he had been approached by **Len Ashurst** to join him as part of the Management team at Weston-Super-Mare FC (Len was appointed manager, John would become his assistant). This was approved, on condition that his work with Weston wouldn't interfere with his full-time role as a Regional Director.

Interestingly, as the new year of 1996 wore on, it became apparent that, as more and more money was becoming accessible to Community schemes, some of the professional clubs themselves were becoming increasingly envious of the apparent ease by which community schemes were seemingly able to generate income. In turn, this meant that FFE&VTS Community Programme staff were increasingly involved in issues aimed at protecting not only the self-sufficiency of local community schemes but also the integrity of their operations as a genuine partnership between the club and the FFE&VTS Community Programme.

Already challenging were those projects that were operating as internal departments within clubs themselves, but more and more clubs were looking with increasing interest at the apparent accumulation of monies in their community accounts. By the Spring of 1996 it became clear that there were some professional clubs that were either threatening to pull out of the partnership with the FFE&VTS Community Programme or demanding the payment of amounts of money from the community account to be made directly to the football club.

A subsequent Management Meeting agreed that, as it was clear that this was to be an ongoing issue and that, as a small number of clubs appeared unable to understand the longer-term implications of the work of community schemes (nor the self-sufficiency requirements of locally run schemes), it was necessary to consider if any surplus monies (if there even *were* any surplus monies!) could be paid to the club, for example, to purchase tickets for children and young people to attend matches.

What was to be the final year of the three year sponsorship arrangements with Refuge in support of the Schools Under 11's six-a-side competition proved to be particularly successful and the Final match between Oliver Goldsmith School (representing Millwall) and Kingmoor

School (representing Carlisle United) on the 14th April 1996 rightly ended up with honours even after a 2-2 draw at Wembley. **Lucy Paisley** also became the first girl to play in a Final for a schools 6-a-side team, having played for Kingmoor School (see Appendix V for details of Competition winners).

Further changes in the Spring/Summer of 1996 included:

- The Halifax Town project had become unsustainable and efforts were to be made to investigate if alternative employment could be found for **Paddy Roche** (sadly without success in the end). The Halifax Town Community scheme was effectively "wound up" following Paddy's departure.

- **Terry Bainbridge** left Hartlepool United and moved across to the Middlesbrough community scheme on an initial trial basis though, as that didn't work out, Terry eventually left the Community Programme scheme altogether. The Hartlepool United Community scheme was also put on hold whilst the club considered their next steps.

- **Mark Lillis** took up a Youth Team Coaching post at Huddersfield Town in June, leaving former Town player **Paul France** to take on the senior role.

- **Dean Wheatley** left Lincoln City (for a job offer coaching in Singapore) and he was replaced by **Stuart Donnelly.**

- **Colwyn Rowe** left Luton Town. His replacement was **Jeff Vetere** (Jeff would go on to have an interesting career in football, with spells as a Director of Football at some clubs in later years).

- **Dave Bentley** was offered, and accepted, the Youth team/reserve team coaching post at nearby Chesterfield.

- **Peter Mendham** left the Norwich City/Norfolk CFA amalgamated scheme.

- **Dick Pratley** moved to take up a youth team post at Shrewsbury Town (in early July 1996).

- **Neil Mather** left Stockport County in order to take up an Assistant Community Officer's post at Manchester City. His replacement was to be ex-player and County favourite **Andy Kilner** (who commenced his new duties in July 1996, being formally introduced at a meeting of North West based Community Officers held at Tranmere Rovers' Prenton Park ground in September 1996).

- **Alan Curtis** took up the post of Youth Team Coach at Swansea City. He was replaced by former player, **Linden Jones.** Welshman Linden began his playing career as an apprentice with Cardiff City, making his debut in 1979. He stayed with the club until 1983 when he moved to Newport County. He then moved on to Reading in 1987 before moving back to Newport County (by now a non-league club) in 1992.

- **Shane Cook** left Swindon Town and, uniquely, he was replaced by two officers being **Clive Maguire** (a former teacher, coach and social worker) and **Jonathan (Jon) Holloway** (a former Swindon Town apprentice/youth team player). Clive and Jon formed a fantastic partnership and one that stood the test of time, as they remained in post working successfully together for many years thereafter.

In March of 1996, **Jim Fleeting** from the Scottish FA made contact, as he wanted speakers from the Community Scheme to appear at a forthcoming conference of Scottish club-based Community/Development Officers to be held in Largs, Scotland. Deputy Chief Administrator, **Dennis Leman,** and Burnley's **Bob Oates** from Burnley kindly volunteered to attend.

Also, in March, **Mark Holroyd** left the scheme's administrative support unit to be replaced by **Pat Wilkinson** (formally Pat Mallinson, who had taken up her new financial duties effective from the beginning of May 1996). Pat had worked for the inaugural Community scheme set up at Manchester United in 1986.

May 1996 saw a two-and-a-half-hour BBC Radio Five programme, "Inside Edge" look at the issue of the lack of Asian heritage professional footballers. Various interviews formed part and parcel of the programme and the FFE&VTS Community Programme scheme confirmed some of the excellent work that was being undertaken around the country to ensure a fully integrated approach to community engagement. The programme began by referring to the book *Asians Can't Play Football* by **Jas Bains** and **Raj Patel** and finished with some of the examples of work going on at Aston Villa (including the formation of an Asian heritage supporters' club); Blackburn Rovers (in conjunction with the police in an area called Bank Top); Bradford City (football community work); the "Kicking Out" play launched by Leyton Orient and several others. It was an excellent, landmark programme which confirmed that there was much work still to be done in terms of football and community engagement.

The departure of **Kevin Glendon** as Regional Director overseeing the Western Region was confirmed the same month (Kevin took up a managerial position with nearby non-league club Radcliffe Borough FC starting at the end of September). His departure ultimately led to a further reduction in the number of managers operating across England and Wales, together with a change in the defined areas around the country to five regions (rather than six as had been the case). This would also facilitate the move towards having five Regional Directors (and no Area Managers), a point that was to be adopted and approved in the 1997-1999 Business Plan.

The good news at this time, however, was that Burton Biscuits were interested in taking up the national sponsorship arrangements under the brand of "Wagon Wheels". Further positive discussions were held with **Jerry Charter** (Marketing Director) and **Alison Lucas** (Marketing Manager) and with **Brian Roach** and **Ruth Syszkowski** from their agents Harrison Cowley over the next few weeks (see Chapter 12).

June 1996 saw the ten-year anniversary of the Community Programme in Professional Football when a celebratory party was arranged at the Manchester office. Among the invited guests were many people who had contributed to the success of the scheme during the first ten years.

Figures announced at the anniversary get together included:

- 200 people had moved into full time employment thanks to Football in the Community schemes.

- Activities would be provided in 1996 for approximately 1,000,000 people (of which at least 120,000 would be children attending school holiday courses).

- Over £500,000 had been invested into community facilities such as classrooms, all-weather pitches, minibuses etc.

- Nearly 200,000 people had been encouraged to attend football matches (many for the first time ever) as a result of the involvement of Football in the Community schemes.

Glowing tributes were paid by **Roger Reade** to the "pioneers" such as **Dennis Leman** (who had worked so hard for the scheme for the full ten-year period), **Pat Howard** and **Brian Kidd**. Special mention was made of **Mick Baxter** whose memory was represented by the attendance of his wife **Janet** at the party. Wrexham Manager **Brian Flynn** was kind enough to attend, along with **Brian Hall, Keith Hicks, Tommy Hutchison, Kevin Jardine, Ian Johnstone, Gary Pierce, John Platt** and many more. Various other people were mentioned in the tribute, including **Mickey Burns** ("The best boss I have ever had" said Roger Reade at the time), fellow workers, **Julian Hayes, Kay MacMillan, Gary Naven, Tracey Paul, Adele Scott** and **Pat Wilkinson.**

All guests who attended were also presented with a unique print very kindly drawn by **Leon Evans** and assisted by **Sally** from Spiral Gallery, which contained many of the key people who had contributed to the scheme's success.

Celebrations continued at the Annual Sportsmatch Awards Ceremony held on 28th June 1996 in Leeds when the Community Programme in Professional Football was hailed as "*The best Community Scheme of the Year*" in recognition of the distribution of football resource packs (sponsored by Pizza Hut) and kit & equipment (sponsored by Umbro) to Primary and Junior

Schools. Although Pizza Hut were unable to send a representative, Umbro's **Duncan Thompson** together with Scheme Officials received the awards from **Baroness Trumpington** (representing the Department of National Heritage).

Close links with representatives of Sportsmatch were maintained and the staff at the time, including **Emma Platts**, **Catherine Grover** and **Robin Hodkinson** (and, later **Alex Scott-Bayfield**), not forgetting senior officials **Mike Scott** and **Glynne Jenkins**, were a real joy to work alongside. Indeed, Glynne showed particular interest in what football clubs were doing in their local communities and even asked to attend particular events organised by London based club schemes.

An early July senior management team meeting also revealed that the previous monthly General Management Meetings were to become bi-monthly and would be less focussed on written reports (which would all be circulated in advance of the meetings in future) and more focussed on allowing time for discussion. This would also free up more time for Regional Directors to attend local club Management Forums.

Under TFW, recruitment levels for the 1995/96 contract year are detailed in "Appendix III – Table of trainees in post year by year 1994-2002". Amongst those clubs with excellent recruitment levels during the year were projects at Blackpool, Bolton Wanderers, Chesterfield, Hull City, Leeds United, Manchester City, Mansfield Town, Notts County, West Bromwich Albion and Wigan Athletic.

The average number of trainees in post (at any one time) represented not just a reduction in recruitment levels but also a reduction in income flowing into the scheme's national coffers though it should be noted that the figures quoted also included some trainees recruited under the Government's YT programme. It was clear, in certain areas, that no further places would be allocated under TFW, in which case alternative arrangements would be pursued. There was, however, some good news in that there was an upturn in the number of NVQ Level II qualifications being delivered.

Bonuses were again paid to those clubs that had succeeded under TFW in terms of achievements and the top ten performing club schemes in 1995/1996 were noted to be: Bolton Wanderers, Crewe Alexandra, Darlington, Huddersfield Town, Hull City, Leeds United, Middlesbrough, Notts County, Preston North End and West Bromwich Albion. The number of participating club projects during the contract year 1995/1996 increased to 59.

Special praise was made for **Mark Ashton** at West Bromwich Albion and **Ces Podd** at Leeds United for finishing in the top ten best performing club schemes for a third year in succession.

Following successful fund-raising as part of the Testimonial Year for **Cyrille Regis**, the former West Bromwich Albion, Coventry City, Aston Villa and Wolves striker, Cyrille himself was delighted to make monies available in support of the community schemes at all four of his former clubs. Indeed, minibuses were purchased at Aston Villa and at Coventry City, classroom equipment at West Bromwich Albion and kit and equipment at Wolves. As PFA Deputy Chief Executive, **Brendon Batson,** said this was, *"a great gesture by a great professional"*.

The summer of 1996 saw Community Programme officials consider the huge success of the three-year arrangements with Refuge Assurance. Sadly, it was clear that despite the phenomenal success of their sponsorship, Refuge were unable to take forward their sponsorship for a further period into 1996/97, so the search for potential new sponsors began. Fortunately, **Brian Marwood** (PFA Commercial Executive) was 'on the ball' and early discussions with **Miles Stevens-Hoare**, **Kirsty Hosmer** and **Richard Maskell** from Panini were held, which proved to be fruitful as they committed to sponsor the Schools competition for two years starting in 1996/97. The only dilemma related to the possible participation of PL clubs given that there was, at the time, an arrangement in place involving the PL and Panini's rivals, Merlin. In the end, 8 PL clubs chose to participate in the competition, bringing the total of community schemes committed to being involved to a total of 79 clubs (including 3 Non-League clubs and 68 FL clubs).

The new 1996/7 season saw the FFE&VTS Community Programme supporting a total of

91 schemes:

- 17 FA Premier League (PL) clubs (not Arsenal, Derby County or Tottenham Hotspur, though a meeting with Derby County Chief Executive **Keith Loring,** former Brentford Chief Executive, had been positive in September 1995).

- 68 Football League (FL) clubs (not AFC Bournemouth, Hartlepool United (both temporarily), Ipswich Town and Peterborough United. Representatives of Peterborough United approached the Community Programme in August 1996 with a view to re-joining the scheme on the basis that 'Posh Soccer' had not been as successful as they might have hoped. A follow-up meeting with **Chris Turner** in November confirmed that the club wished to work with the FFE&VTS Community Programme once again).

- 4 Non-League clubs (Farnborough Town, Kettering Town, Kidderminster Harriers and Merthyr Tydfil).

- 2 CFAs (Durham and Kent).

The new season got underway at a time when club attention was increasingly being directed towards the employment status of their Community Officers and the legal status of their Community schemes as what were then 'unincorporated associations' (see later).

Community Programme newsletters were now being widely circulated and proved to be extremely popular, particularly amongst football club staff and Directors. Regional Director **John Relish** also very kindly supported much of the editorial preparation of the newsletters, which were made available on a quarterly basis. The newsletters up to this point, of course, had been consistently spreading strong messages about the close working relationship with national sponsors Pizza Hut.

The first Sub-Committee meeting of the Board of Directors took place in August, though there were apologies for absence from several of the senior personnel of the football world. Unable to attend were **Graham Kelly** (FA), **Rick Parry** and **Mike Foster** (PL), **John Reames** (Chairman of Lincoln City and member of the FL Management Committee) and **Brendon Batson** (PFA). That said, the Sub-Committee meetings had settled into something of a pattern with much of the meeting now seeing the Committee responding to update reports being formulated and presented by FFE&VTS Community Programme officers.

Comment was made at the meeting on the increasing number of Community Officers (especially those who were ex-players) who were moving into youth team coaching positions. It was agreed that this was an essential 'pathway' for the game, and one that guaranteed high coaching standards within the bottom tier of the excellence side of the game.

Also discussed in some detail at the meeting was the proposed new Business Plan covering the period 1997-99. The new Plan would include:

- A new national sponsorship arrangement with Wagon Wheels (see Chapter 12).

- A smaller Management structure, thus further reducing the 'overhead' against income in the budget.

- The removal of the maximum salary for Community Officers (although minimum pay levels would be upheld).

- A budget that would support a maximum of 92 projects only.

- Opportunities for expansion and growth which would be thoroughly explored (e.g. external funding on a partnership basis which was becoming increasingly available for specific project work to Community Schemes via such initiatives as the Single Regeneration Budget initiative, City Challenge funding, Safer Cities funding etc.)

The November Sub-Committee meeting was chaired by the Football League's **John Reames** and saw **Mike Foster** attend on behalf of the PL. The meeting confirmed that, following the withdrawal of the Kent CFA withdrawal (see "changes in personnel" below), the FFE&VTS were supporting at the time a total of 90 community schemes, with plans to talk to other

PL and FL clubs currently not being supported. In addition, several amendments to the draft Business Plan for 1997-99 were agreed, as was support for the proposed new three-year national sponsorship with Burtons Gold Medal Biscuits Limited in the name of Wagon Wheels. Noted at the meeting was the significant support of the FA of Wales for the creation of new Football Development Officer positions in Cardiff, Swansea, Gwent and the Vale of Glamorgan in the south of Wales and also further north, where Development Manager, **Jimmy Shoulder,** had also agreed to provide support across Wales to existing Community Officers at Cardiff City, Merthyr Tydfil, Swansea City and Wrexham.

Amongst changes in personnel prior to Christmas were the following:

- **Shaun Parker** left the post of Community Officer at Bristol City to take up a new role within the club's new Marketing Department. Shaun's replacement was the irrepressible **Dave Bell** (who, by this time, had left the club as Youth Team Officer, hence arrangements to re-recruit him were taken with some considerable care). "Belly" (as he was nicknamed) was appointed after interviews held in September 1996.

- **Adrian "Adie" Shaw** took up the position of Youth Team Coach at Chesterfield allowing **George Foster** to take over from Adie as Community Officer. Plymouth-born George was an apprentice with Plymouth Argyle going on to make over 200 league appearances for Argyle before moving to Torquay United (on loan) and Exeter City (also on loan). He then secured a permanent move to Derby County before joining Mansfield Town in 1983 where he made just under 400 appearances over a nine-year period.

- **Mark Ellis** took up the Grimsby Town post of Community Officer in December 1996, taking over from **Ian Knight** who moved to Sheffield Wednesday. Ian took over from

- **Charlie Williamson** who had taken up a post in the club's youth development department. Bradford-born Mark Ellis played for his local club, Bradford City over a nine-year period, before moving to nearby Halifax Town where his career finished in 1991. Mark's tenure as Community Officer, however, was only to be for a few months before he too was replaced by **Julian Winter** (in June 1997). Huddersfield-born Julian was a former player with Huddersfield Town and briefly at Scunthorpe United in the late 1980's. His experience with the Community Programme Scheme would ultimately support his later moves to become a successful Chief Executive of various professional clubs including Watford, Sheffield United and Huddersfield Town.

- **Darren Hare** left the Kent CFA scheme to take up a position with Folkestone College (in August). After discussions with representatives of Kent CFA, it was agreed that the FA would support this project in future. Because there were some debts to clear, the FFE&VTS Community Programme also agreed to continue to offer funding support in 1997 on the basis that this would help to clear most, if not all, of the debts of the local scheme.

- **Emlyn Brown** left the Queens Park Rangers scheme to be replaced by someone who became the successful face of Rangers community activities for many years to come, **Andy Evans.**

- **Adele Scott,** who had worked especially hard to secure a Business and Technology Education Council (BTEC) Higher National Diploma in Business and Finance whilst with the Manchester-based support office, left in October 1996 to take up a new post working with Social Services. Her replacement (after advertising locally via the *Manchester Evening News* for an Administrative Assistant) was **Stephanie Lunn**. Stephanie went on not only to give excellent service to the Community Programme scheme but also to the PFA who she joined in 2007.

A visitor to the office at this time was **John Clubb**, who was researching the impact of community engagement with particular reference to people with disabilities. This research was significant not least for its findings about the limited opportunities for people with disabilities to play sport but also in that John himself was to become a Community Officer himself at Macclesfield Town in the very near future.

In terms of the continuing operation of TFW, Head of Training/Government Programmes, **Gary Naven,** reported in the autumn of 1996 that recruitment levels at some clubs were still causing concern, especially as several club projects fell well below the now minimum requirement of having four trainees in post at each project. Gary also reported on access to Further Education Funding Council (FEFC) in support of certain qualifications which could be accessed via colleges. Although this took some time to resolve, potential funding arrangements were lined up with South Kent College (to cover Southern club schemes), with additional arrangements being explored in the North and Midlands (arrangements were eventually made with Bedford College covering the Midlands and with Kirby College (Middlesbrough) in the North. These were complicated arrangements which included different "load bands" depending on the nature of the funding but which then effectively defined the colleges as "community colleges").

A Senior Management Meeting/two-day get-together in October 1996 saw a comprehensive review of the 1994-96 Business Plan together with initial discussions about the proposed new 1997-99 Business Plan based around the three-year term of the new sponsorship arrangements with Burtons Gold Medal Biscuits in the name of Wagon Wheels. The discussions embraced the idea of developing even more good relationships with external partners and improved service overall.

Those in attendance at the meeting included **Mickey Burns**, **Roger Reade**, **Dennis Leman** and **Gary Naven** plus the two remaining Regional Directors, **Richard Finney** and **John Relish,** together with Area Managers, **Dick Krzywicki**, **Dave Palmer** and **John Seasman**.

The importance of 'Training for Work' (TFW) was re-emphasised in terms of its importance as an 'income-earner' and as an opportunity to bring in expertise into the scheme. New opportunities were also flagged up, as it was increasingly seen that the role of the FFE&VTS Community Programme at this point was to support local community schemes in as many different ways as possible, ideally by accessing external funding (e.g. funding from the National Lottery (capital and revenue funding), Sportsmatch and from the Government's Single Regeneration Budget which had already been accessed with great success by senior managers working for the Community Programme scheme. In addition, the YT programme was seen as a further opportunity for many Community schemes, in that they wanted additional manpower and the possibility of future [trained] employees). The FFE&VTS Community Programme scheme also facilitated central insurance arrangements for all Community schemes (including Employers and Public Liability cover, All risks cover (12 separate claims were successfully submitted by Community Schemes in 1996 alone), Personal Accident cover for children attending courses together with Life Assurance cover for Officers) which was arranged at vastly cheaper rates than club-based schemes could secure locally. Finally, the FFE&VTS Community Programme also facilitated the payment of wages for a huge majority of local community schemes at no cost to them. This was to become of increasing importance as wages and cash flow played much more of a part over the next few years (and as wage turnover grew so swiftly)[13]. The London and South East meeting of Officers was held at the PFA's "Football Football" restaurant in mid-November and, out of interest, former Area Manager and newly appointed Regional Director at the time, **Dave Palmer**, confirmed at the meeting that in the South East area (including London):

- Including all Assistant Officers, there was now a total of around 50 Community Officers employed at club based Community schemes.

- 'Training for Work' had actively encouraged the full-time appointment of up to twelve assistant officers in the region.

- Cash turnover at these schemes was now averaging around £100,000 per annum (meaning that access to external funding, together with the expertise and contacts to be able to secure such funding, was significantly greater than in other regions).

---

13. *All these funding streams and new opportunities were discussed at regional meetings of Community Officers held in November and December 1996.*

Back to the Senior Management Meeting, other issues discussed at length included the following:

- The reduction in managerial support (5 Regional Officers would take the scheme forward as existing Area Managers would be promoted to the position of Regional Director).

- The importance of staging regular club Management Forum meetings (which, in turn, supported the separate status of local community schemes as "unincorporated associations" and therefore their own entitlement to having their own turnover, tax liabilities, employment status etc.) A minimum of four meetings per year (i.e. quarterly meetings) as a minimum was recommended.

- The unique VAT exemption afforded to local club-based schemes under the Value Added Tax Act of 1994 (Group 10, Schedule 9).

- The need for improved administrative support for each local community scheme so that, for example, Business Plans with recognisable targets were adopted on a local basis and bank mandates were clear and explicit for all involved. In addition, local audited accounts (including profit and loss accounts and balance sheets) needed to be adopted on a local basis, with account made of the wages being paid through the FFE&VTS payroll.

- The need for better communication and quicker responses to requests from all involved.

- The importance of reviewing the frequency and effect of management meetings, liaison meetings and working party/group meetings (the latter meetings had been introduced in order to support the national sponsorship arrangements with some considerable success. These meetings saw up to 10 Community Officers from all around the country "co-opted" to represent the views of all Community Officers).

- Central insurance arrangements made by FFE&VTS on behalf of all Community schemes.

- One other thing raised and noted (though not necessarily appreciated at the time by Community Officers) was the importance of ensuring that all Community Officers received regular pay reviews (at least on an annual basis); additional Employer support with contributions towards personal pensions; private medical cover (in case of serious injury or illness) and life assurance. It was felt that such arrangements provided the sort of security and support required for officers even though, at some clubs, regular annual pay increases, usually at least in line with inflation, were not always appreciated as parent club staff didn't always receive rises with the same frequency as Community Officers.

Also noted at the meeting were details of average wages for Officers in 1995 (£13,915 per annum) and average wages expected for 1996 (£14,560 per annum). It was recorded that 66% of Community Projects used the FFE&VTS payroll services and that 41% of schemes now employed at least one Assistant Officer (see table below for more details). Figures for 1996, 1997, 1998 and 1999 are also printed here for comparison purposes.

Year	Average Annual Salaries of Community Officers (on FFE&VTS payroll)	Percentage of Officers paid via the FFE&VTS payroll
1990	£7,326	100% (50 out of 50 projects)
1991	£11,964	88% (56 out of 63 projects)
1992	£12,222	73% (69 out of 94 projects)
1993	£12,712	72% (70 out of 97 projects)
1994	£13,283	70% (66 out of 95 projects)
1995	£13,915	63% (60 out of 95 projects)
1996	£14,560	64% (60 out of 93 projects)

1997	£15,674	73% (66 out of 90 projects)
1998	£17,335	75% (68 out of 90 projects)
1999	£18,584	81% (73 out of 90 projects)

Also, of interest is the number of assistant officers being paid through the FFE&VTS Community Programme payroll (and their average salaries where appropriate) as follows:

Year	Number of Assistant Officers in post	Average Annual Salaries of Assistant Community Officers (on FFE&VTS payroll)
1990	None	-
1991	None	-
1992	None	-
1993	2	£5,850
1994	13	£6,232
1995	25	£6,000
1996	37	£6,300
1997	120	£7,353
1998	172	£8,242
1999	206	£9,517

Meetings with senior club personnel continued into the winter of 1996/97. Newcastle United's **Freddie Fletcher** and **Alec King** (the latter of whom had recently joined Newcastle from local rivals Sunderland) and **Stuart Bagnall** from Hartlepool United were reassured about the benefits of retaining links with the FFE&VTS Community Programme. Also met, and similarly re-assured, was **Norton Lea**, Chairman at Chesterfield.

Another meeting was held with Sunderland Chairman, **Bob Murray**, Marketing Director, **Jim Slater** and Club Secretary, **Mark Blackbourne**, who outlined the club's plans to move to a new stadium at the site of the former Monkwearmouth colliery in Sunderland. Mark himself would take responsibility for becoming the club's liaison with the Community scheme, which was clearly going to play a huge part in supporting the move to the new stadium. It also became clear that the club was aiming to grow the work of their community scheme and that they wanted to recruit an experienced manager to oversee their scheme. Indeed, the club wanted to hear recommendations from the FFE&VTS as to the 'best' community officers around the country. Following discussions which carefully considered a few worthy candidates, Mark confirmed that the club would like to speak to **Bob Oates** (then Burnley's Community Officer, where Mark had been previously employed as Club Secretary).

Bob himself takes up the story:

> "I was obviously flattered to be approached but despite the club making a more than generous offer, I initially turned them down as, frankly, things were going so well at Burnley and there were fantastic opportunities ahead including the development of the 'barn' at Turf Moor that I wanted to play a part in."

Other club meetings at the time included meetings that clarified the status of local community schemes – e.g. at Barnet and Gillingham where club Chairmen **Tony Kleanthous** and **Paul Scally**, respectively, understood and agreed that the many advantages on offer from operating local schemes as unincorporated associations were worth preserving.

A telephone call from **Malcolm Starkey**, popular Club Secretary at Shrewsbury Town, confirmed that the club wished to appoint **Derek Mann** to the role of Community Officer at the club. Derek took up his new duties in December 1996.

Just before Christmas, the FA staged a conference entitled "Asians in Football" which **Richard Finney** attended on behalf of the FFE&VTS Community Programme. This followed immense pressure that had been placed on the FA to be seen to be more active in encouraging increased participation of Asian heritage young people in football. Interestingly enough, the FA have continued to stage 'Asians in Football' conferences and seminars ever since.

Approaching Christmas, the FFE&VTS Community Programme scheme was again recognised by the Institute of Sports Sponsorship who voted the scheme as the best "*Non-televised national sponsorship*" for offering Pizza Hut/Umbro sponsored resource packs and equipment scheme to Primary schools. The presentation was made at the Royal Automobile club in London on the 19th November and **His Royal Highness the Duke of Edinburgh** presented the award in the company of **Ian Sproat**, **Tom Pendry** and athlete **Roger Black** (who was the guest speaker).

At the very end of the year, York City's extremely popular Community Officer, **Gordon Staniforth**, left the club to be replaced by former professional **Paul Olsson**. Born in Hull, Paul's playing career began as an apprentice with his local club, Hull City. He later moved to Exeter City, Scarborough, Hartlepool United and Darlington.

A summary of club Community Schemes turnover during the year 1996 confirmed that a total of 73 Schemes turned over a collective total of £3,103,727 meaning that average turnover across those schemes had risen to approximately £42,516 per annum.

Wages paid through the FFE&VTS payroll in 1996 totalled £1.773 million (already a huge increase on the previous year). A total of 68 Community projects used the FFE&VTS payroll free service in 1996. This included many assistant officers together with a huge and increasing number of casual staff (mainly casual coaches).

CHAPTER 10 – NATIONAL SPONSORS: PIZZA HUT

BY 1993, the FFE&VTS Community Programme was in a strong position to be able to promote the opportunity for a national sponsor to come on board for the first time, having already consulted with IMA, a highly respected marketing and advertising agency based in Manchester. Whilst details of the opportunity were circulated widely (full details were sent to several well-known and football related organisations such as Coca-Cola, Mars, McDonald's etc.), scheme officials were unsure as to whether any potential national sponsors would fully understand the magnitude of the opportunity, let alone consider taking it up.

That said, efforts to meet with agencies representing the biggest potential national sponsors began in earnest at the end of 1992 and were 'stepped up' early in 1993. Not only that but some PR agencies and marketing organisations had expressed interest in taking forward the sponsorship opportunity to potential clients. One such agency, Brian Hewitt Associates, was able to set up a possible opportunity with agents representing Pepsi/Whitbread. Indeed, the first of the meetings with IMP, official agents for the Pepsi/Whitbread owned Pizza Hut in the UK, took place in Knightsbridge in London in January 1993. This important (some would say "ground-breaking") meeting was attended by **Brian Hewitt** himself and others in attendance at the meeting were **Lesley Kerrell** and **John Quarrey** (both from IMP). Also attending was former Sheffield United and England player **Tony Currie** (Community Officer at Sheffield United) and **Roger Reade** representing the Football in the Community scheme.

There then followed several more meetings during the early part of 1993 at which additional IMP representatives attended, notably **Katrina Galt** and **Julius Denny**, so that IMP could understand exactly what the opportunity might bring with it (with obvious links to virtually every professional club in the country. This was important as, at the time, there were 240 Pizza Hut restaurants across the country, many of which were based in the same towns and cities as the professional clubs). Indeed, Katrina spent some time visiting several club schemes so that she could understand and embrace the extent of the opportunity available.

Among matters being taken forward were the preparation of a dedicated resource pack and the idea of local links involving local Pizza Hut restaurants and local football club community schemes.

Also taken forward were ideas of supporting:
- a special offer voucher campaign.
- a regular newsletter.
- a promotional video.
- Letter headed paper to incorporate the Pizza Hut branding.
- Match programme coverage (within any community sections included in programmes. It is worth noting that Arsenal's match programme at the time carried no formal advertising or sponsorship details at all, so the inclusion of the Pizza Hut/Football in the Community logo certainly carried a unique 'value' with it).

In addition, and quite rightly, the idea of a launch event was also discussed in some detail. Finally, the idea of introducing significant Sportsmatch funding was also raised. It was hoped that the maximum available grant (then £75,000) could also be secured to support and develop the proposed national arrangement.

To be fair to Katrina and the team at IMP, they also convinced Pizza Hut to look at investing significantly in addition to the proposed amount to be invested in sponsorship (then £175,000 in year one, £200,000 in year two and £225,000 in year three. These were, of course, huge amounts in those days). Amongst ideas put forward, that Pizza Hut themselves would pay for, were branded umbrellas, tee-shirts, badges, hats and vouchers, plus investment in the design of a new logo and resource 'aide-memoire'. Significantly, Regional Directors and Area Managers were also being asked to come up with additional information that would support the first national sponsorship deal such as:

- Samples of match programme coverage.
- Examples of local press and media (newspaper) coverage.
- Details of programmes of work being operated by Community Officers.
- Information concerning other involvement – e.g. FA First Aid courses, involvement in the national schools' competition (and publicity).
- Details of local Community scheme audited accounts.

By the time of the next meeting with Katrina (in mid-March 1993), it looked as though the deal was on the verge of being finalised, and a more formal agreement was prepared which effectively summarised the key points for all parties. Things being put forward were:

- A fully amalgamated (and brand new) scheme logo – to be used on all literature and branded merchandise.
- A 'slogan' (or 'strapline'). In the end "*Just join in*"[14] was adopted – and included as part of the new logo.
- A bound 'design manual' for all club-based Community Officers.
- A commitment to using PR specialists in connection with the launch of the new deal (the FFE&VTS agreed to introduce the extremely experienced **Philip Lay** to oversee and to enhance the launch).
- Plans and script for the promotional video.
- Support for PR campaigns.
- Opportunities for Pizza Hut representatives to attend high profile events (e.g. the PFA Player of the Year Awards event at Grosvenor House. Representatives of Pizza Hut were invited to attend the 1993 Player of the Year event – held on the 28th March).

The draft contract (to be effective from September 1st, 1993 for a three-year period ending in August 1996) also became available for consideration soon after a further meeting held at Coventry City's Highfield Road ground at the end of April.

Another meeting with **John Quarrey** from IMP in May aimed to finalise the agreement, and to establish the date for the official launch (for *all* Community Officers). Initial ideas suggested that the launch could be held at Wembley (or even Wembley Arena), though, at a July meeting, it was agreed that Arsenal's Highbury Stadium would fit the bill more appropriately as the venue for the launch, which would eventually be held on Thursday October 7th, 1993.

In terms of arrangements on the day, a follow up meeting with **Katrina Galt** and **Suzi Morris** from IMP agreed the following:

- VIP invitation list (including press and media contacts) to be drawn up.
- Arsenal Vice-Chairman **David Dein** to be invited to give the welcome speech.
- **Gordon Taylor** and **Mickey Burns** to provide information about the Community Programme and the importance of the new partnership with Pizza Hut.
- IMP to prepare press packs (containing further information which was to include "A Day in the Life" of a Community Officer).
- After lengthy discussions (including the suggestion that three separate 'launch' events could be held in the North, Midlands and South), it was agreed that *all* Community Officers and *all* Pizza Hut restaurant managers would be invited to attend the launch event at Arsenal (accommodation would be organised for officers travelling from the North).

A follow-up meeting with **Philip Lay** at the end of August 1993 also considered more

---

14. *A short promotional film promoting Pizzahut and the "Just join in" strapline was made based around filming at a match between Sheffield Wednesday and Manchester United filmed at Hillsborough when the crowd were encouraged to repeat the strapline and when former Community Officer and United's then Assistant Manager,* **Brian Kidd***, encouraged United skipper,* **Bryan Robson***, to repeat the strapline as he was leaving the pitch after completing the pre-match warm-up.*

details about the proposed launch. For example, after having considered that a Community Officer should speak at the launch, it was agreed that the high profile of former Manchester City and Everton player **Paul Power**, would probably make him the most suitable candidate and the most confident person to speak to so many people. It was also proposed that there would be separate briefings for Community Officers and for Pizza Hut managers, rather than regional briefings as had been put forward previously. Philip also kindly agreed to contact representatives of the press and media *and* to note details of those who had confirmed their attendance as they were received. Community Programme officials would draft relevant information for the key speech makers.

A final preparatory meeting held on 30th September involving **Philip Lay** and his colleagues, **Frankie Lambert**, **John Quarrey**, **Katrina Galt** and **Les Mears** from IMP, confirmed the arrangements for the sponsorship launch event to be held on 7th October. It was agreed that a separate meeting involving all Community Officers would be held after the main launch event which would share additional information about the sponsorship arrangements that wouldn't have been shared with the press and media.

It should be noted at this point that the application to Sportsmatch for a further £75,000 was also successful, bringing further welcome funding into the proposed "pot".

Pizza Hut Marketing Director **Steve Dunn** said at the launch:

> "Such a worthy initiative as Football in the Community deserves to be brought to more people's attention so we will use all of our outlets across the country to help with this. We will also provide additional support in the shape of training and promotional materials and use our products to reward the children involved."

Prime Minister at the time, **John Major** also said:

> "I am delighted to learn that the Community Programme in Professional Football will continue to expand with the generous sponsorship of Pizza Hut (UK) and that Sportsmatch has also been able to support this sponsorship with a matching award of £75,000. I place great value on the Community Programme and the development of closer links between football clubs and their local communities."

Following the success of the launch, FFE&VTS officials were keen to ensure that a suitable "introductory fee" was paid to Brian Hewitt Associates, and agreement was reached concerning an appropriate amount at a meeting with Brian before the end of October.

A meeting with **Debbie Byrne** (from Pizza Hut) together with staff at IMP including **John Quarrey**, **Les Mears** and **Liz Marcus**, was held soon after the launch and reflected on its success. The meeting also considered what ideas would be worked on in future. It was exciting to note that IMP had plans to run at least 2 national promotional activities up to the summer of 1994, though it was also noted that Pizza Hut had declined the opportunity to directly sponsor and support the Schools 6-a-side tournament going forwards.

Much appreciation was expressed by scheme officials for the significant investment of both Pizza Hut and IMP in supporting the costs of the launch, and the investment by the Community Programme (notably in the costs of travel and accommodation for officers attending the launch) was also noted. Amongst other points recorded were the importance of:

- The production of local Community Scheme letter headed paper (and compliments slips) to incorporate the new logo (including the Pizza Hut logo).
- The production of hats, tee-shirts and badges for use by Community Officers as they saw fit.
- The printing of the first Football in the Community newsletter in early 1994 which would be circulated to clubs/Pizza Hut Managers/press and media and others.
- Additional opportunities for Pizza Hut that they could be interested in supporting including the Schools 6-a-side competition and the proposed National Playing Fields Association (NPFA)/*Daily Express* Penalty Competition.

- The production of Pizza Hut managers' manuals for all Community Officers.

Purely for the record, Stockport County's Community Scheme was the first local Community scheme to secure a local sponsorship deal with McDonald's and, as such, the County scheme became the first scheme unable to support the national Pizza Hut 'deal' on offer.

Liaison meetings with IMP (mainly with **John Quarrey,** but also often with **Debbie Byrne** from Pizza Hut) continued into the New Year and the first promotional newsletter was indeed printed and circulated at the start of 1994. For obvious reasons, the sponsorship arrangements with Pizza Hut, together with the 'match' funding kindly and generously made available by Sportsmatch, were covered in substantial detail in the first newsletter.

In relation to the two major promotional activities, Pizza Hut and IMP were working on 'top tips' (players collectable cards that were eventually to be referred to as Skills Cards) and a big promotion in the *Funday Times*. The Skills cards were successfully developed with some of the top footballers of 1994/5 and became very popular amongst children. Amongst those who agreed to be involved were:

NAME OF PLAYER	CLUB	TOPIC
DAVID SEAMAN	Arsenal	Catching
MATT JACKSON	Everton	Overlapping
STUART PEARCE	Nottingham Forest	Tackling
PAUL MCGRATH	Aston Villa	Covering
MARK WRIGHT	Liverpool	Defensive Heading
GARY MCALLISTER	Leeds United	Passing
CHRIS WADDLE	Sheffield Wednesday	Crossing
PETER BEARDSLEY	Newcastle United	Dribbling
LES FERDINAND	Queens Park Rangers	Heading at Goal
ALAN SHEARER	Blackburn Rovers	Shooting
CHRIS SUTTON	Norwich City	Control
RYAN GIGGS	Manchester United	Running with the ball

These cards proved to be popular, not least as they were only available by visiting Pizza Hut. One of the fascinating issues arising from this was the close bond between all the professional footballers who took part and the PFA (who helped facilitate player support for the Skills Cards). PFA staff were also tremendously supportive in ensuring the cooperation of the top players of the day.

Senior Pizza Hut officials (including Marketing Director **Steve Dunn** and an additional nine Pizza Hut Managers) were also invited to attend the PFA Player of the Year Awards Dinner held in London in April.

One other fantastic promotion organised by Pizza Hut in the summer saw a television advert (featuring the legendary **Pele!**) which showed a football bouncing around the world and which promoted not only the new Skills Cards but also the Football in the Community scheme. This was well-received in the football world by Community Officers and club officials alike. Other promotional initiatives included:

- Free soccer schools for children who collected redeemable vouchers in the local press.

-    A "charity day" aimed at raising money for Help a London child (a charity set up by Capital FM to help disadvantaged young people) and for Whizz Kidz (a charity that provides disabled children with wheelchairs and other mobility equipment) throughout the rest of the country. Indeed, former Area Manager **Gordon Coleman** and current Area Manager **John Seasman** had raised around £20,000 for Whizz Kidz when they took part in the New York Marathon in November 1993.

-    The addition of a "Football Feast" pizza to the national Pizza Hut menu.

-    A "hat trick" promotion supported by tokens given with every football feast pizza served (PL stickers were also given away with football feast pizzas).

By August 1994, **Barry Powell** at Coventry City had managed not only to secure £4,000 in sponsorship support from his local Pizza Hut but also a further £4,000 from Sportsmatch in 'match funding' (i.e. doubling the money) to help develop the club's community activities. Barry was also assisted and worked very closely at the club's community scheme with his wife **Tina**.

It did, however, become clear that following the departure of **Steve Dunn** from Pizza Hut, there was to be a full review and evaluation of Pizza Hut's involvement in all things, including their sponsorship arrangements. This was slightly alarming, if only as it came so early (within the first year of the three-year arrangements). To be fair, it was clear that the 'review' was based entirely around Pizza Hut going through a difficult period (with a downturn in profits at the time) and not about concerns about Community schemes delivering Pizza Hut's requirements. Indeed, it was reported at a July meeting with **John Quarrey** from IMP that virtually all the larger (city-based) club schemes had supported the Pizza Hut promotional "Soccer Days" during July and August (school summer holidays) with some considerable success in terms of numbers attending. 36 club schemes took part with a total of around 3,000 children participating.

At the end of 1994, Deputy Chief Administrator, **Dennis Leman**, was also tasked with the massive undertaking of compiling a central portfolio of all the press and match programme coverage generated by the Community Scheme across the country in support of the Pizza Hut arrangements. This was aimed at helping Pizza Hut to understand the enormity of the coverage. Dennis spent several weeks compiling what, in the end, became a very impressive record of coverage. This also linked in with the findings of the Sir Norman Chester Centre for Football Research who discovered that it was important for the scheme to build a "national corporate identity" and to secure "a higher national profile …. and the need to advertise it nationally."

The New Year 1995 brought with it the news that Pizza Huts' profits had halved during the last six months of 1994, meaning that any extension of the sponsorship was going to be highly unlikely. In addition, a new Chief Executive and Marketing Director had been appointed, and a smaller promotional budget was anticipated. Indeed, there was to be no further budget to produce merchandise or printed certificates.

Whilst this was disappointing news at the time, it was made clear that every effort was still being made to support and to promote Pizza Hut as part of community activity. Indeed, the April-June 1995 newsletter even included a promotional "pull out" which featured several 'best bits' of the work undertaken with Pizza Hut to date.

Further discussions in February 1995, involving **Debbie Byrne** from Pizza Hut and **John Quarrey** and **Fiona Cialis** from IMP, led to the production of a coaching manual 'pack' that would be sponsored by Pizza Hut, with the possible added support of Sportsmatch pound for pound funding. Without Sportsmatch funding it was anticipated that around 1000 schools' coaching packs could be developed *but* with the added support of Sportsmatch, the value-added potential was for a further 2,000-3,000 schools to receive the packs. In addition, packs of kit and equipment provided by Umbro and match-funded by Sportsmatch could also mean that the same number of schools would receive free 'kit-packs' too (Umbro Director **Martin Prothero** had already given his support for this wonderful value-for-money proposal). **Charles Langhorne** and **Gavin Bisdee** at Sportsmatch were especially supportive in relation to these highly innovative proposals.

In relation to the proposals, Community Programme officials approached **Richard Foweather** from Warwick University. Richard was a leading expert in the field of developing curriculum support materials for schools and he was kind enough to develop the contents so that they fitted entirely within the School Curriculum at Key stages I and II including 'sending, receiving and travelling'. The agreed plan was for a draft copy to be raised by April 1995, followed by 4 weeks testing and a possible launch event in June.

This was an exciting development, and one that Pizza Hut bought into almost immediately. Indeed, Pizza Hut's **Debbie Byrne** (who was always enthusiastic and supportive of new ideas) was especially impressed with this two-pronged proposal. Enormous credit must properly go to all those involved in this super development, particularly in bringing it all together especially Pizza Hut, Umbro, Sportsmatch and the Centre for Education and the School Curriculum Industry Partnership (SCIP) section at Warwick University.

After careful consideration, the FA agreed to support the proposals. Given the size of what would be a considerable investment into Primary Schools (estimated to be worth approximately £500,000) on behalf of sport, this was clearly a super idea to take forward. However, a meeting held at the FA's headquarters on Lancaster Gate in London at the end of June saw the FA express the view that they didn't feel "*that it was the role of the Community Programme to develop resource materials for schools.*" The FA also took the opportunity to insist that the pack must include a recommendation for children to play mini soccer together with a statement to the effect that a more thorough guide to the National Curriculum was available from the FA with in-service training also available for teachers from the FA.

Filming for the video took place with the generous support of Middlesbrough Football Club and their Community Officer, **Lawrie Pearson**, and was shot over two days (23rd and 24th May) at Middlesbrough's old ground at Ayresome Park. It involved school children from nearby Pallister Park School together with several Community Officers including **Tony Currie**, **Tommy Hutchison, Ces Podd, Alex Williams** and **Charlie Williamson**. A thoroughly top-class job in filming and putting together the resource packs was done by **Keith** and **Alison Daniell** and the team from The Media Group. Indeed, the resource packs were "state-of-the-art" and included not just a video showing all the routines but also a very detailed resource brochure which contained diagrams and player information plus an introduction from former Liverpool and Scotland striker **Ian St John**, who was also kind enough to endorse the packs with his own professional expertise.

When finally produced, the Pizza Hut coaching packs were entitled "*Finish with a Game*" and included the teacher's support pack together with a bag of equipment for each school which included training bibs, footballs (size 4 for Under 11's) and a set of marker cones in each holdall.

All would be made available to schools (that were already working with Community schemes) totally free of charge and would support the moves to increase PE in schools (the Government had just announced that they were to pump £25 million into schools in order to help promote the playing of more sport in schools). The packs were all made available for distribution to schools with effect from September 1995. September, of course, was ideal as that was when all the schools went back after their summer holiday break.

Richard Finney said:

> "*It was imperative that the children enjoyed playing and during PE lessons they could take part in football drills, with the introduction of skills sessions and games. At the time, the end of Community scheme meetings of officers often saw them putting on their kit and trying out different drills and games to include in their school-based activities*"

A press and media launch was held at Manchester United's Old Trafford ground on 19th September 1995. The event was kindly and ably "hosted" by **Keith Daniell** from the Media Group. In advance of the launch, **John Davies** from the *Times Educational Supplement* (TES) prepared an excellent article that eventually appeared in TES on Friday 22nd September supporting the circulation of the packs.

Distribution arrangements of the support packs via the Community Officers were also made via area meetings arranged at Manchester United (September 7th), Leeds United (September 21st), Walsall (September 28th), Bristol City (October 12th), The Holiday Inn, Leicester (October 26th) and Arsenal (November 2nd). The bags of kit and equipment were kindly forwarded by Umbro directly to clubs (partly in view of the bulk).

Mickey Burns said at the time:

> *"We are absolutely delighted to be playing a significant part in the promotion of sport in primary and junior schools at no cost whatever to the schools. The Football in the Community Scheme has been one of the outstanding successes of the last ten years and has significantly contributed to increased participation in sport in school time. The sponsorship of the resource packs by Pizza Hut and the provision of packs of equipment sponsored by Umbro, both of which are supported by the Government's "Sportsmatch" scheme will help to provide the opportunity for thousands of children to play football at school"*

The reaction from everyone, but particularly from schools, to receiving the packs and bags of equipment was very positive and overwhelming. Letters of appreciation were received from across the entire country. In fact, reports at the time confirmed that the office in Manchester was "besieged" with letters of thanks, together with glowing localised press coverage.

In relation to press (and media) coverage, of course, it would be fair to say that the FFE&VTS Community Programme scheme didn't originally set out with the intention of securing positive coverage (someone once described the Community Programme scheme as being "football's best kept secret"!) but, on a local basis, the positive coverage for the work undertaken by club schemes in their local communities was, firstly, positive and, secondly, welcome!

Indeed, just about the only problem arising out of the circulation of around 4,000 packs was the fact that given the massive demand from other Primary and Junior schools for the packs, it was very clear that demand far exceeded supply.

Sadly, this was to be the last major promotion with Pizza Hut who, by now, had switched their agency (promotional) arrangements from IMP to FKB Carlson (FKB Carlson's main contact became **Andrew Gilruth**). It also became clear that Pizza Hut, despite the huge successes of promotional activities organised during the first couple of years of the sponsorship, were not going to extend their sponsorship arrangements beyond the original term of three years. Other alternative potential sponsorship leads were to be pursued (in the end successfully) by the FFE&VTS Community Programme personnel and their representatives.

In the absence of any commitment from Pizza Hut to extend the sponsorship arrangements, former players **Ian Mellor** and **Brian Marwood** from PFA Enterprises kindly agreed to begin making enquiries for a would-be successor for the national sponsorship. Initially, Ian and Brian set out to try and sign up 4 or 5 larger companies on a "multi-sponsorship' arrangement at a cost of around £60,000 to each organisation, although early interest from one company, being Burton's Gold Medal Biscuits Limited in the name of Wagon Wheels, soon meant that the idea of multi sponsorship wouldn't be necessary.

CHAPTER 11 – 1997-1999

A NEW BUSINESS PLAN covering the three-year period from January 1997 to December 1999 had been adopted by the FFE&VTS Board of Directors prior to the end of 1996. This plan not only looked forward to the future development and growth of Community schemes but it also celebrated the achievements of the previous ten years. The plan also confirmed that support would come in future from 5 Regional Directors (and no Area Managers).

Amongst those areas of "new opportunity" identified in the Plan were:

- More activity involvement/closer involvement with Asian heritage groups
- Expanding the scheme into supporting Secondary Schools
- Support for the building of even more community facilities (based on the successes of the grant scheme from previous years)★
- More activities (including coaching AND competitive matches) for girls and women

★ By the end of 1996, grant support totalling £504,000 had been offered to clubs in support of:

- 3 full size all-weather (artificial) pitches
- 6 small-sided/5-a-side pitches
- 1 Changing room accommodation
- 20 classrooms
- 16 minibuses

The budget for the period from 1997 to 1999 was set as follows:

DETAIL OF EXPENDITURE	AMOUNT	% AGE
Grant aid to club projects	£1,620,000	53%
Management wages (including travel expenses and pension contributions)	£1,134,800	37%
Marketing	£50,000	1.5%
Other costs – offset against TFW income (including course fees, printing, stationery and advertising, phone etc.)	£261,500	8.5%
TOTAL	£3,066,300	100%

Kicking off the New Year in 1997, well-known former player, **Brian Honour,** was appointed at Hartlepool United as the man to get their community scheme "back on track" (the Hartlepool scheme had been "on hold" until Brian's appointment). Brian began his playing career with Darlington, moving to near neighbours Hartlepool United in 1985. He went on become a true club legend, making over 300 league appearances for the club in a ten-year period. Sadly, Brian stayed in post as Community Officer for only a very short period of approximately nine months.

Jason Maguire was appointed at Barnet, his appointment being confirmed at a local Management Forum meeting held on the 9th January 1997 attended by club Chairman, **Tony Kleanthous** and Chief Executive, **Andrew Adie.**

Ex-player **Peter "Charlie" Aitken** was appointed as Senior Community Officer at Gillingham. Cardiff born, Peter (nicknamed "Charlie" after the former long-serving Aston Villa full back of the same name) began his playing career as an apprentice with Bristol Rovers for whom he went on to make more than 230 league matches between 1972 and 1979. He moved to Bristol City in 1980 and towards the end of his career also played briefly for York City and AFC Bournemouth.

The Senior Management Team ("General Management") meeting at the start of February 1997 saw the presentation of a bottle of champagne to the hard-working **Dick Krzywicki** who celebrated his 50th birthday on the 2nd February. Noted at the meeting were the facts that:

-      Community projects at Barnet, Gillingham, Hartlepool United, Shrewsbury Town and Wycombe Wanderers were now underway; Derby County and Peterborough United were ready to get started.

-      There was a total of 19 club projects where the clubs directly employed community officers but where there were joint signatory control arrangements through local community scheme bank accounts.

-      Six clubs administered their community operations as internal operations, grant-aided by the FFE&VTS (Aston Villa, Liverpool, Manchester United, Portsmouth, Southampton and West Ham United).

-      The FFE&VTS Board of Directors had recommended that Community Programme Regional staff should put forward the idea of pay rises of 3.5% for Community Officers for the consideration of forthcoming club forum meetings.

-      "Learning Through Football" was to continue (at this time, discussions with Nationwide Building Society re possible sponsorship support were at a fairly advanced stage) although clubs were increasingly anxious to see local adaptation of the school's resource pack to include their own clubs specifically. Nationwide themselves (via **Julie Brickett**) undertook to complete some research via their agents and specifically through **Colin Jelfs** (from a company called MGA Broadcasting Limited) which revealed that 80% of Community Officers were in favour of a new educational resource pack, ideally that was locally "customised" to their club.

-      Recruitment under TFW was proving to be difficult once again, with difficulties at Bradford City, Bristol City, Kidderminster Harriers, Leicester City, Reading, Rotherham United and Walsall (it should be noted that Head of Training/Government Programmes, **Gary Naven,** was doing his level best to develop new TFW opportunities in the South, AND to develop new YT opportunities for club schemes across the country at this time. Some of these opportunities would become available via existing FFE&VTS contracted arrangements).

-      Quarterly promotional newsletters would continue (and Regional Director **John Relish** would continue to play a key role in their compilation every three months).

A Sub-Committee meeting of the FFE&VTS Board, also held in February, considered some of the issues relating to Arsenal Football Club who, by this time, were running soccer schools on a franchise basis around the country and across much of the South of England.

Also considered were the key points brought up by Management Consultants, Deloitte and Touché, concerning the status of community projects. Meetings with representatives of Deloitte and Touché continued into the early part of 1997, at which point the Board of the FFE&VTS had agreed to fund a research proposal that, it was hoped, would provide answers to all the scenarios that had been put forward and, hopefully, provide a more permanent solution for locally based Community schemes. The frequency of the meetings was much greater in early 1997 when Deloitte also introduced **Heather Crosby** into the discussions.

Neil Watson was also in touch with scheme officials around this time following the takeover of Leyton Orient Football Club by **Barry Hearn**'s "Matchroom" organisation. After lengthy discussions, Neil reported that the Leyton Orient Community scheme was exploring its own separate status away from the club, even reporting that the possibility of the scheme becoming an "industrial provident society" was realistic at one point! This was helpful background that, in the end helped to inform the Deloitte and Touché research proposal.

Indeed, a meeting held in April 1997, which attracted representatives of Leyton Orient FC (notably Chief Executive, **Steve Dawson**), Waltham Forest and Hackney local authorities and the FFE&VTS Community Programme, reached agreement on investigating the possibilities of establishing a company limited by guarantee with charitable status. This was obviously well intentioned and ultimately proved to be the best way forward not only for Leyton Orient's thriving community operation but also as a guide for other community schemes going forwards. The firm taking forward Orient's interest was Watson Burton LLP in Newcastle (**Neil Watson** also kindly agreed to keep George Davies informed of all developments). The Leyton Orient Community Sports Trust was finally registered with the Charity Commission in September 1998.

February 1997 saw **Tommy Hutchison** announce that he was to leave Merthyr Tydfil (where a fair surplus had been built up in the local scheme bank account. As a result, his departure from the club was handled with a great deal of care) at the end of March 1997. Tommy left to become the Vale of Glamorgan's new Football Development Officer (Tommy's popular Assistant, **Tony Avo**, also left).

In addition, during March, **Bob Oates** had been approached for a second time by Sunderland who, this time round, had convinced him to join the club. In turn, the newly-vacated post at Burnley was to be filled by his former assistant, **Dean Ramsdale**. Assisting Dean would be former professional **Anthony Barlow**.

Having done a super job in leading the development of the Notts County Community Programme scheme (especially in relation to the creation of appropriate training and job outcomes for trainees recruited under the 'Training for Work' programme), **Alan Young** also gave up his position in February at Notts County having been offered a youth team coach's post within the club. Alan's replacement was his enthusiastic Assistant, **Graham Moran,** who went on to become one of the most respected, dynamic and knowledgeable Community Officers in the country. Sadly, for Alan, his new coaching job at the club was only to last until April 1998.

The end of February brought with it a proposal put forward to the Board of FFE&VTS as to whether the Community Programme scheme as a national initiative should continue under the auspices of the FFE&VTS, or not. Whilst it wasn't made clear why this had been put forward, it did appear that there was a view that the FFE&VTS still "leaned" towards the PFA for its main support and was still some way from being an organisation that properly and equally represented the views of all the football partners.

FFE&VTS Chief Executive, **Mickey Burns,** suggested to the Board of the FFE&VTS that they should be "custodians" of the good things in the game – i.e. (at the time) the YT programme and the Community Programme in Professional Football. After a lengthy discussion, the views of the various FFE&VTS 'partner organisations' were to be taken forward to the full Board of Directors where all the football organisations would then be able to consider this further.

Issues to be taken forward included the fact that some of the partners felt that:

-    There needed to be a more effective mechanism for all four partner organisations to work together on a more equal footing.

-    There needed to be an independent body with equal voting rights as an effective 'forum' to run the Community Programme scheme as, in their view, *"the existing forum for the direction of the Community Programme, via the Board of the FFE&VTS and the Sub-Committee, has deficiencies in running the scheme and its structure is flawed."*

Gordon Taylor (Chief Executive of the PFA) had unfortunately been delayed and arrived late at the meeting (when there had already been substantial discussion) and confirmed that it hadn't always been the case that there was strong positive support from some of the other partners, which was why the PFA commitment over the long term had been so consistently strong.

Interestingly enough, at this comparatively early stage in the history of the PL, the FL spoke on behalf of both FL AND PL clubs in putting this proposal forward. The view from the two leagues seemed to be that they wanted to "regulate" the Community Programme scheme based on increased "ownership" by League clubs in the two leagues.

Given the importance of this proposal, it was agreed that there should be further discussions involving all four partner organisations at further meetings (held from March through to June).

The March meeting saw **Andy Williamson** and **Chris Whalley** from the FL, **Mike Foster** from the PL, **Robin Russell** from the FA together with **Gordon Taylor** and **John Bramhall** from the PFA in attendance with **Mickey Burns** and **Roger Reade** from the FFE&VTS. Among the "services" being provided by the FFE&VTS Community Programme were noted to be the following:

- Payroll services.
- Business Planning, accounts preparation and advice, meeting minutes (etc.) as part of the regular Management Forum meetings.
- PR/promotional work.
- Access and support to national activities, events and campaigns.
- Networking and cross-fertilisation of ideas/advice and suggestions.
- Access to education and training.
- Access to insurance cover on a reduced rate basis.
- Quality control (Quality Assurance).
- Core funding/discretionary funding.
- Expertise in accessing external funding.

Views noted at the meeting included those of the PL who wanted to know if it had been established if the FFE&VTS was the best vehicle to deliver the Community Programme in Professional Football. The FA's view was that they felt that a dedicated and active forum could be created to oversee this important work, particularly as the FA seemed to feel somewhat 'marginalised' by the current *modus operandi*.

The FL's view was that the FFE&VTS was still seen as integral to the PFA and was therefore not equally representative of all the football bodies. Their view was that the clubs themselves needed to take much greater 'ownership' of what was happening locally. Meanwhile, the PFA felt that if all the football partners contributed an equal sum of money each year, as the PFA did, there could then be a case for equal representation of all the partners which would also underpin the role of the organisation in supporting community schemes.

Discussions went on for some considerable time. If nothing else was achieved at this meeting, at least there was recognition around the table that the FFE&VTS Community Programme staff provided key support and "expertise" for the future development of local community schemes.

A further meeting was held in April when the issue of the FFE&VTS being perceived to be too close to the PFA was again raised. The FL representatives at this meeting expressed their view that, regarding the Sub-Committee of the Board of FFE&VTS, another separate body entirely separate from the FFE&VTS could be established. The PL felt that more commercial opportunities might arise in future given the right framework with equal representation from all the partners in place. (This was an interesting view as, at the time, the three sponsorships in place, at the time with Wagon Wheels, Panini and Smoby Monneret, had all been facilitated through the PFA Commercial Department, led by former PFA Chairman **Brian Marwood**).

In the end, it was agreed that all partners would submit papers on the possibilities of moving forward to the next Board Meeting to be held on the 3rd July 1997.

The role of the FFE&VTS Community Programme in supporting club community schemes continued whilst these discussions were underway. It was, at least, recognised that the FFE&VTS Community Programme continued to do some amazing and ongoing support work.

Several clubs were in touch with senior FFE&VTS staff (Including **Mickey Burns**, **Roger Reade** and **Dennis Leman**) at this time in relation to bid applications to be made to the National Lottery. Amongst the clubs who contacted the FFE&VTS in 1996/1997 were:

- Blackburn Rovers (Club Secretary **Tom Finn**. In later years, Tom would go on to become a Trustee of the Premier League Charitable Fund – and also Chair for a total of five years too)).
- Bradford City (Community Officer **Richard Angus**).

- Bury (Chairman **Terry Robinson**)[15].
- Darlington (**Ken Lavery**).
- Doncaster Rovers (Senior Community Officer, **Eric Randerson**).
- Everton (**Lord Grantchester, Arthur Abercrombie,** Secretary **Michael Dunford** (who scheme officials had previously met whilst he was Secretary at Derby County) plus the club's architects and Chartered Surveyor).
- Gillingham (club Chairman **Paul Scally**).
- Hartlepool United (**Harold Hornsey** and **Stuart Bagnall** together with the club's architect **David Brown**).
- Lincoln City (Chairman **John Reames**).
- Middlesbrough (Director **Jack Ord** re: interest in working with Redcar and Cleveland Borough Council concerning the possible development of a site on Normanby Road in Eston).
- Queens Park Rangers (Community Officer, **Andy Evans,** expressed an interest in the possible development of Hammersmith Park, off South Africa Road near to the club's ground at Loftus Road and in conjunction with Hammersmith and Fulham Council)
- Rochdale (Secretary **Keith Clegg**)[16].
- Tranmere Rovers (General Manager **Janet Ratcliffe**, Director **Tony Adams** and Director/Chairman **Frank Corfe.** Frank held a variety of positions at the club at different times including Chief Executive, and Vice Chairman).
- West Bromwich Albion (Secretary **Dr John Evans** and Director **Clive Stapleton**).
- Wigan Athletic (through **Steve Morgan** and, later, **Phil Williams**).
- Wrexham (Secretary and later Managing Director, **David Rhodes** and Manager **Brian Flynn**).

One point to note at this time was the fact that 2 or 3 clubs were unsuccessful with bid applications made to the National Lottery Sports Fund where they hadn't engaged with FFE&VTS Community Programme personnel prior to submitting their application.

By July, it became clear that the bids being submitted by clubs for National Lottery funding needed to be part of a bigger national plan. As an example, it transpired that Everton, Liverpool *and* Liverpool County FA (CFA) had all submitted separate bids for significant funding aimed at building new community facilities on Merseyside. It was clear that the Football Trust (and later the Football Foundation) was to become the 'clearing house' for future bid applications and that they would play a key role in knitting together an effective national plan.

By April, the community scheme at Merthyr Tydfil FC (in conjunction with Taff Ely Council which was, by now, part of a combined newly defined local authority in Wales being Rhonnda Cynon Taff) had ceased to operate. In addition, the Durham CFA venture had also ceased. This meant that there were, at the time, 89 projects being directly supported by the FFE&VTS Community Programme (17 PL clubs, 69 FL clubs and 3 Non-League clubs).

It was also noted that one or two club schemes were struggling financially and, even at this comparatively early stage (and following the moves to develop income streams), were dependent on the generosity afforded to them by the FFE&VTS to support their local cash flow, in particular by paying wages on their behalf.

Gary Naven's spring report concerning TFW flagged up the issue that several club schemes were still operating with below four trainees in post, notably at Barnsley, Carlisle United, Coventry City, Kidderminster Harriers, Rotherham United, Scunthorpe United, Sheffield Wednesday and Walsall, though, to compensate for this somewhat, schemes in conjunction with TECs at Calderdale and Kirklees, Humberside, Leeds, Greater Notts, South East Cheshire and Teesside were noted as strong performing areas.

---

15. *As already confirmed, the Community Schemes at Bury and Rochdale were amongst the first club community schemes in the country to be successful with bids to the National Lottery (for the development of their respective community facilities at the club grounds at Gigg Lane and at Spotland). Club Directors and staff were extensively involved and very appreciative of the FFE&VTS Community Programme support and involvement in securing access to National Lottery grants.*

It was, however, also clear that some TECs were winding down their involvement in some areas, meaning not only a further reduction in places but also a reduction in income from TFW. Noted were 'run down' arrangements regarding TFW in Southend and Stockport. Gary did, however, report on increasing interest amongst Community Officers in taking on youth trainees (e.g. at Bristol City and Burnley). In the end 12 club schemes requested information about securing places under the YT programme. On a positive note, it was reported that TECs in the South were looking at possible new agreements in conjunction with Barnet (North London TEC), Crystal Palace, Fulham, Brentford, Millwall and QPR via a sub-contract with South Croydon Chamber via SOLOTEC. From a contractual point of view, it also became clear that there were moves afoot to increase targets for jobs well above the targets set for the achievement of NVQs.

In relation to the 1996/7 contract year, the following details were noted:

136 trainees had found jobs (from 163 contracted during the year – i.e. 83%)

173 trainees had secured NVQs (from 181 taken in during the year - i.e. 95%)

These figures compared favourably with previous years as the following table illustrates:

YEAR	1992/3	1993/4	1994/5	1995/6	1996/7
JOBS FOUND	50	46	96	117	136
NVQS SECURED	130	95	81	95	173

It can, of course, be argued that this work, especially the support given to unemployed people to re-train and to move into work, was directly supporting local communities. Whilst the numbers were small, the contribution to local economies was clearly significant. Indeed, there had been 271 starts from a contracted total of 384 (i.e. approximately 70%) and of the top ten performing Community Schemes under TFW in 1996/7, seven were from Yorkshire and Humberside (as were 14 out of the top 20). Needless to say that significant performance-related bonuses were paid to Yorkshire club Schemes in the summer of 1997.

Under TFW, the total amount paid out to Community schemes in respect of bonuses (for qualifications and jobs achieved by trainees) was in excess of £45,000. This, as **Gary Naven** pointed out, represented an excellent year's work and he asked that his thanks be passed on to all involved. It was, however, noted that recruitment was still proving to be challenging across the country.

Recruitment levels for the 1996/1997 contract year are noted in "Appendix III – Table of trainees in post year by year 1994-2002". A reduction in numbers on the previous contract year was noted.

The ideal was noted at this time to still be at least 4 trainees in post at each project. From the list of 52 club schemes that were involved, only 9 had an average number of trainees in post of more than 4. The 9 clubs with excellent recruitment levels during the year were projects at Bolton Wanderers, Burnley, Chesterfield, Huddersfield Town, Hull City, Leeds United, Manchester City, Notts County and West Bromwich Albion.

A further 12% reduction in average numbers of trainees in post since the previous year was noted.

The Panini Six-a-side Competition Southern Regional Finals were played at South Africa Road (near QPR's ground) and the Northern Regional Finals were held at the Aurora (near Rotherham United's ground) on the 9th and 10th April respectively. Both Regional Finals were attended by well-known players. **Simon Barker** (then with Queens Park Rangers) kindly attended the Southern Finals and **Alan Kelly** (then with Sheffield United) visited the Northern Finals. The Final was played at Wembley prior to the Football League Auto Windscreens Shield Final Match between Carlisle United and Colchester United at the end of April 1997. The 1996/97 competition had been so successful that Panini were quick to confirm their support for a second year even though there were still clearly difficulties concerning the participation of PL club community schemes because of the deal involving the PL with Merlin (see Appendix V for details of Competition winners).

Spring 1997 saw the resignation of **Jason Withe** from the Birmingham City Community project. Sadly, he wasn't replaced for some time, partly due to delays in arranging meetings with senior officials at the club at the time. **Jeff Vetere** also left Luton at the beginning of May to be replaced on an initial temporary basis by **Dean Rastrick**. Sadly, Dean also left in July, after only a short time in post. Blackburn Rovers Community Coach (and former goalkeeper) **Terry Gennoe** left to join Newcastle United.

Following the departure of **Neville Hamilton** at the end of January, Leicester City were keen to continue the expansion of their successful and pioneering community scheme and chose to appoint **Mike Trotter** as Community Officer the following month. Born in Hartlepool, Mike was once a youth trainee with Middlesbrough before moving to Doncaster Rovers on loan in 1988. He also had short spells with Darlington, Leicester City and Chesterfield.

The May Sub-Committee Meeting of the Board of FFE&VTS noted that the Deloitte and Touché report (including issues such as legal status/employment status/VAT status etc.) had been commissioned and was now underway. Details would become available by the 1st July 1997.

Ian Roberts and **Doug Fraser** (both of whom knew all about the FFE&VTS Community Programme operation from previous discussions) headed up the Deloitte team that was responsible for writing and presenting the report. An interim report was made available in July, with the final report printed and circulated to the full Board of the FFE&VTS in August. The report considered the fact that there were considered to be three different types of community scheme in operation:

1. 'Standard' projects (jointly operated by clubs with FFE&VTS)
2. 'Hybrid' schemes where the football club employed the Community Officer(s)
3. 'Club' schemes where the club employs the Community Officer(s) and internal (club) accounts are operated

A key step forward, it was recommended, was for projects to become established as non-corporation tax-payers (ideally by the establishment of the projects as charitable trusts). A follow-up meeting with Ian and Doug, plus **Heather Wilkinson**, was arranged in early September 1997 so that an open and informal chat could be held concerning the Report, its recommendations and the responses to it.

Following the early decision to adopt their own 'constitutions', the status of those independent local Football in the Community schemes was confirmed as being that of an "unincorporated association" in the Deloitte and Touché Report. At these schemes, each locally adopted constitution (including 'general rules') included sub-headings such as "Name", "Aims and Objectives", "Definitions", "Constitution", "Management", Control", "Finance", and "Alteration of Rules". Each local Scheme operated under the control of an independent Management Forum (as defined under "Constitution" and "Management" above) and operated its own local bank account (in most cases not connected with the football club's own main banking arrangements).

It was further recommended that one club (in the end Manchester City were chosen as the 'pilot' club) should be approached with a view to agreeing to volunteer to explore the possibility of their community scheme becoming a registered charity (as with Leyton Orient and Millwall). Officials at Manchester City were particularly enthusiastic about the possibility and backed the plan immediately. Indeed, the Manchester City application for charitable status went ahead following agreement reached at a local Management Forum meeting held in January 1998. This was also endorsed and supported by Club Secretary, **Bernard Halford,** on behalf of the club and by staff, **Alex Williams** and **Alison Vaughan**, and by future Trustee, **Des Coffey**. Representatives of George Davies Solicitors (notably partner **John Hewison** and solicitor **Sarah Davidson**) agreed to take forward the application, which would prove to be a useful 'pilot' and a learning tool for the future, given that the possibilities were that up to 92 professional clubs might all eventually look to move their community schemes towards charitable status at some point. (Note: Manchester City's Community Scheme was re-shaped and re-registered with the Charity Commission in December 2010).

By the Autumn of 1997, following the release of the Deloitte & Touché report, clubs were becoming more and more aware of the benefits of operating their community schemes as independent entities. One such club was Coventry City, where Chief Executive **Graham Hover** called a Management Forum meeting that agreed to transfer the employment status of all Community personnel to the local scheme (rather than as was the case with the club) and to ensure separate payroll arrangements (via the FFE&VTS Community Programme service); all of which would become effective from the 1st January 1998.

May also saw the first official meeting with **Gill Prescott** concerning the potential involvement of Macclesfield Town in setting up a Community scheme. This, of course, followed their promotion to the Football League at the end of season 1996/7[16]

Future Community Officer **John Clubb** also attended. It was agreed that the interests of the club should be brought to the attention of the Board of the FFE&VTS and to representatives of Zeneca, who were key local supporters and a sponsor for Macclesfield Town Football Club. In the end, John stepped forward to become the club's first ever Community Officer. The local Council (through Leisure Officer **Tony Riddington**) would also be approached with a view to supporting the proposed new Cheshire-based programme.

Also, in May, were two distinct events at which the FFE&VTS Community Programme was represented. Firstly, the establishment of a formal headstone at a commemorative service for football's first ever black footballer, **Arthur Wharton**, at Edlington Cemetery in Doncaster. The ceremony was attended by several well-known football people. Following the end of a highly successful playing career with Southend and Hull City, a Testimonial match was also successfully staged for **Frankie Banks** at Southend United's Roots Hall (against an "All Stars" team including former Tottenham and England player, **Glenn Hoddle**).

Bearing in mind figures previously quoted for Community schemes for 1993/94, it is worth noting that in early 1997, a rough 'audit' of the completed accounts for a total of 45 projects showed that total turnover, for these schemes only, had reached £2,043,775 (i.e. an average turnover of £45,417 per project – equivalent to a 65% increase in turnover based on the details made available for 1993/4.)

June 1997 saw Community Officer **Brian Taylor** accept a club offer to become Youth Team Coach at Bury Football Club. His replacement, the following month, was a former player known for his tough tackling as a midfield maestro, **Andy Feeley.** Andy was born in Hereford and began his playing career as an apprentice with his local club, Hereford United, making his debut in 1978. Andy then played professionally for Leicester City, Brentford and Bury.

The end of June saw **Richard Angus** leave the Bradford City Community Scheme. Chief Executive at the club, **Shaun Harvey,** was influential in what happened next in that he presented his ideas for the reorganisation of the community scheme to his Board of Directors, who approved the appointment of former players **Gavin Oliver** and **Ron Futcher** as joint Community Officers at the club for an initial six-month period, commencing at the beginning of September.

---

16. *Between 1986 and 2007 it is worth noting that there were several clubs promoted from non-League football that hadn't previously played in the Football League including Cheltenham Town, Macclesfield Town, Morecambe and Wycombe Wanderers, all of whom were approached in order to establish or to support community work at the clubs. Accrington Stanley also joined the League in 2006 as a new club, even though there had been a club of the same name that had folded in the early 1960's. Of the more established and longer-serving Football League clubs, Halifax Town were now playing in a league below the Football League. After 2007, several more clubs joined the Football League that hadn't previously played at this level including Burton Albion, Crawley Town, Fleetwood Town, Forest Green Rovers and Stevenage Borough. These new clubs all joined at the expense of more established Football League clubs such as Aldershot Town, Chester City, Chesterfield, Darlington, Hartlepool United, Hereford United, Stockport County, Torquay United, Wrexham and York City.*

Gavin Oliver began his career as an apprentice with Sheffield Wednesday where opportunities were limited (he also spent time on loan at Tranmere Rovers and Brighton & Hove Albion). He joined Bradford City in 1985 and went on to make over 300 appearances for the Bantams.

Ron Futcher was born in Chester (with twin brother Paul) and made his debut as a striker for his local club Chester City in 1974. He went on to play for several clubs including Luton Town, Manchester City, Barnsley, Oldham Athletic, Bradford City, Port Vale, Burnley and Crewe Alexandra. He also played in Holland with NAC Breda.

For the record, former player, **Ian Juryeff,** took up a post as an Assistant Community Officer at Charlton Athletic in July (though he was destined to move on to Southampton within a matter of only a few months). Ian was a former Southampton apprentice, making only 2 first team appearances with the Saints before moves to IFK Munkfors (Sweden), Mansfield Town (on loan) and Reading (also on loan). Between 1985-9 he played for Leyton Orient where he amassed over 100 league appearances. He then had short spells with several clubs including Ipswich Town (on loan), Halifax Town (twice), Hereford United, Darlington and Scunthorpe United.

A Sub-Committee Meeting of the Board of FFE&VTS meeting saw the co-option of **Peter Leaver** (representing the PL) and **Howard Wilkinson** (representing the FA). That said, neither of them was in the end available to attend the meeting and sent their apologies for absence. **Robin Russell**, on behalf of the FA, confirmed that Howard's remit for the FA had been to produce a national coach education programme and talent development plan which had already been approved by the FA's instructional committee and was to be considered further by the FA's Executive Committee soon. He felt it was important for the FFE&VTS and its Community Programme to support this plan.

The summer of 1997 saw a comprehensive wage review of all Community Officers, partly to check on average wage details; partly to check that inflationary wage rises were indeed being awarded and partly to see if there were any other noticeable trends that could be of further interest. The good news, after a great deal of work looking into wages payable in the summer of 1997, was that Community Officer wages were increasing, more or less in line with inflation and that, as a result, average wages payable were increasing year on year.

Summer 1997 also saw the resignation of **Glyn Jones** as Community Officer at Cardiff City where the club had begun running their own cash-generating soccer schools for children. Glyn's replacement would not be appointed for around twelve months, though the club did make an internal appointment when former Birmingham City Community Officer, **Derek Clydesdale,** renewed acquaintance with former Blues owner **Samesh Kumar** (who had recently moved to take over at Cardiff). Derek was taken on to oversee the clubs increasing community and fan projects.

Having done a great job at Southampton, **Stuart Gray** was appointed as Reserve Team Coach at the club where he would work with **Dave Jones** (Manager). Stuart also stepped up to become first team coach in November 1998 and went on to great things as a Manager/Caretaker Manager with Southampton, Aston Villa, Wolves, Northampton Town, Burnley, Portsmouth, Sheffield Wednesday and Fulham between 2001 and the present day.

Craig Madden was delighted to be offered the Youth Team coaches post at Stockport County in mid-July, leaving vacant the Community Officer's post at Blackpool. Discussions swiftly ensued with Blackpool's Chief Executive, **Jill Bridge**. Jill was one of the "unsung" Chief Executives in football who operated "below the radar" and wasn't particularly interested in securing publicity for herself but who was simply excellent at her job. Jill's approach (supported by Blackpool's popular Community Director, **Chris Muir**) as to how to solve the dilemma of who was to follow in Craig's footsteps was eminently sensible and immediately gained the support of Community Programme representatives. Whilst there were several candidates interested in the vacancy, Jill's recommendations were to ensure that **Derek Spence** was one of the candidates to be interviewed (along with any other suitably qualified candidates) as he was already running his own football courses across Blackpool and the Fylde Coast in opposition to those run by

Blackpool Football Club. **Derek Spence** was a popular ex-player with all his clubs. Belfast-born Derek began his career with Crusaders before moving to England with Oldham Athletic in 1970. He also played for Bury, Blackpool and Southend United in England with additional spells in Greece with Olympiakos and in Hong Kong with HK Rangers. He was also capped for Northern Ireland. Interviews eventually held on the 15th August confirmed that Derek was the ideal candidate to take on the responsibility of running Blackpool's Community scheme.

1996/97 was a time when much more attention was being paid by the world of football to the issue of Safeguarding (although it wasn't directly referred to as 'Safeguarding' in those days, often being referred to under the headline of 'child protection'). The FA were becoming particularly active concerning the fact that the experience of children playing football should always be safe and that they should not be in any way vulnerable to any sort of abuse. How it manifested itself at that time was at interviews where scheme officials were instructed to ask if candidates "*had any police record*". One candidate (who shall remain nameless for obvious reasons) even had the cheek to answer the question with the answer "I've got '*Walking on the Moon*'!" He didn't get the job!

A meeting of South West based Community Officers held at Reading Football Club in July acknowledged the key contributions made by Community Officers who had recently left or were due to leave in the near future: **Tommy Hutchison** left Merthyr Tydfil; **Stuart Gray** left Southampton and **Glyn Jones** left Cardiff City.

Around the same time, former Community Officer, **Gordon Staniforth,** left his position as one of the PFA's Regional Coaches.

July saw **Bob Hussain** appointed as Assistant Community Officer at Reading. In August, **Julian Hayes** left the FFE&VTS Community Programme to become General Manager of the PFA Coaching Department where he would work very closely with newly appointed PFA Coaching Head, former Blackpool and England full back, **Jimmy Armfield**, and ex Community Officer **Andy Welsh**. Jimmy Armfield was born in Denton, Manchester but played his entire career for Blackpool where he retired from playing in 1970. He went on to become a successful manager in his own right with notable spells in charge of Bolton Wanderers and Leeds United. Jimmy sadly passed away on the 22nd January 2018.

Concerning Julian's former post, a total of 11 Interviews were arranged and held between the 31st July and the 7th August. The successful candidate was **Jayne Sherratt** who impressed the interview panel with her positive approach and took up her new duties on the 15th September 1997. Jayne, like the newly-married **Tracey Parkinson** (formerly Tracey Paul), went on to work for the PFA after the demise of the FFE&VTS in 2007.

Also moving on at the beginning of August was **John Seasman,** who left to take up the role of Chief Scout at Tottenham Hotspur Football Club (he later became Chief Scout at Blackburn Rovers). John's departure left a vacancy as Regional Director in the North West area which was filled by former Oldham Athletic full back, **John Hudson**. John had once been employed at Manchester City's highly-rated Community scheme and knew how to "get alongside" people following his more recent work with Greater Manchester Police. John eventually took up his new duties on the 8th September 1997 when a formal induction was arranged for him. One of the key aspects for John to attend to, following the induction, was to change the bank mandates for all 20 club community schemes that were underway in the North West. Out of interest only, of the 20 bank accounts, 8 were with Barclays, 4 were with the National Westminster Bank (Nat West), 4 with the Royal Bank of Scotland, 1 with the Co-op, 1 with Lloyds, 1 with the TSB and 1 with Yorkshire.

A meeting with FA coach, **John Cartwright,** in July proved to be inspirational for Community Programme officers. John, a huge admirer of the scheme's work said at the meeting:

> *"It's a tremendous scheme and the motivation of (Community) Officers is excellent"*

This, of course, gave a huge lift to scheme officials who also recognised from John that many schemes were now becoming part of the football coaching development "pyramid", in which case, it was deemed to be essential to ensure that Officers received more in the way of coach education (including more access to UEFA "B" and "A" Licence courses). The visionary Chief Executive of the FFE&VTS, **Mickey Burns**, recognised that support from the FA in this manner would obviously be very welcome. His plans were for former players to have a greater presence at professional clubs throughout their coaching structures and, indeed, amongst qualified Physiotherapists[17]. The creation of the Community Programme scheme had clearly been successful in creating an extra 'tier' in the structure of clubs at the bottom end (i.e. in encouraging largely opportunities for participation, leading to spotting local talent in many clubs and for encouraging Officers to develop their coaching skills.)

The new 1997/98 season saw the appointment of **Greg Abbott** as Community Officer at Leeds United. Born in Coventry, Greg began his playing career as an apprentice with his local club, Coventry City, moving to Bradford City in September 1982. He played at Valley Parade for 8 years before moves to Halifax Town and Hull City. He made a total of around 400 league appearances during his career.

The August Senior Management Team Meeting (also referred to as the "General Management Meeting") saw a verbal update including the following issues:

-     The FFE&VTS Community Programme was, at the time, still supporting 90 community schemes (Luton Town who had just resigned from the partnership with the FFE&VTS had been replaced by Derby County).

-     Details of the interim report compiled by Deloitte & Touché concerning the status of Community schemes (and their recommendations for the future) were passed on to all present and copies of the report were circulated immediately following the meeting. Their full report was eventually circulated at the October Senior Management Team meeting.

-     The first Smoby Monneret table football competition would go ahead commencing in September 1997. Community schemes would be invited to participate by letter (see Chapter 12)

-     A quarter of the way through the new TFW contract year, NVQ targets were being achieved whilst the target for persons into jobs was also just about on course.

An August meeting with **Kelly Simmons** (then head of women's football at the FA) saw exciting plans for the development of football for women and girls. Specific criteria for Centres of Excellence for girls would be introduced, together with a performance and an excellence structure. A further idea put forward was to examine whether there might be part-time or even full-time coaching opportunities within community schemes for women players at the very top level (i.e. internationals). What was appreciated was the recognition by the FA that the FFE&VTS Community Programme scheme was a significant supporter of the development of the female game. This had previously not been acknowledged despite the huge steps taken by the Community Programme to support and develop the female game at all levels.

The vacant post of Community Officer working alongside **Alan Smith** at Southampton was filled by **Ian Juryeff** (a former player who began his playing career with Southampton in 1980). Ian left the highly successful Charlton Athletic Community Scheme to take up this post at the end of August 1997. Joining Ian at Southampton would be former England Women's team international **Sue Lopez** who was to work alongside Alan and Ian but under the club's overall community 'umbrella'. Sue, of course, had already done so much to promote and to further the cause of female football (including writing an excellent book entitled "*Women on the Ball: A Guide to Women's Football*"), so it was seen as a positive move made by the club to introduce her into the club's community structure.

A later meeting with Sue confirmed that Southampton, as a club, wished to dovetail their plans with those of the FA and to provide a professional club venue for the development and growth of the women's game in the area.

---

17. *Mickey's vision was realised when a number of former players (including* **Dennis Leman**) *commenced a four-year Physiotherapy course at Salford University, representing another step into the unknown that ended up being a huge success.*

Steve Weaver announced that he was to leave the post of Community Officer at Wrexham at the end of August in order to take up a new position at the club, being that of "Schoolboy Development Officer", which would see him working closely with former Community Officers and now the club's management team, **Brian Flynn** and **Kevin Reeves**. **Steve Hughes** took over on a short-term (six-month) temporary contract.

Fraser Foster also agreed to take up the post of Youth Development Officer at Rotherham United in September 1997. Following interviews for the vacant post of Community Officer at Rotherham, ex-player, **Mark Todd**, was appointed. Belfast-born Mark began his career as an apprentice with Manchester United before moving to Sheffield United in 1987 where he made over 60 appearances over the next three years. He later had spells with Wolverhampton Wanderers (on loan), Rotherham United, Scarborough and Mansfield Town. **Adrian Shaw** also left Chesterfield in order to take up a coaching position elsewhere.

A sign of the united spirit amongst all Community Programme personnel was seen in August when Community Programme officials were called on to speak up on behalf of Wigan Athletic Senior Community Officer and ex-Oldham Athletic striker, **Frankie Bunn**, who was in court for a driving offence. Frankie's solicitors called, after the decision to ban him from driving for a short period had been reached, to thank scheme officials for the excellent character references given in court.

September saw the next "round" of area meetings of Community Officers. Amongst those arranged were meetings at:

-       North East and Yorkshire based officers at Leeds United FC on the 16th September when 13 Community Officers attended.

-       East Midlands based officers at Notts County FC on the 18th September when 20 Community Officers attended.

-       South East and London based officers at Queens Park Rangers FC on the 19th September.

-       West Midlands officers at Coventry City FC on the 24th September.

-       North West officers at Blackburn Rovers on the 25th September[18].

-       South West based officers at Southampton also on the 25th September[19].

Issues raised at the meetings included:

-       The new sponsorship arrangements and the planned promotional activities/events including the new Table Football Competition sponsored by Smoby Monneret with Wagon Wheels (see Chapter 12).

-       The 1997/8 Panini 6-a-side competition (to start in October).

-       'Training for Work' bonuses totalling some £22,000 had been paid to those club schemes that were entitled to payments.

-       New training courses for officers were recommended including the St. John Ambulance First Aid course and the FA Child Protection course.

An exciting meeting with representatives of The Prince's Trust (including representatives of a small number of PL clubs: Aston Villa, Liverpool, Manchester United, Newcastle United, Sheffield Wednesday and West Ham United[19]) was also held in September 1997 when it was generally accepted that football club community schemes were well equipped to support Prince's Trust projects aimed at helping people find work (which would, of course, 'dovetail' very well

18. Regional Directors were advised to ensure that any two meetings were not held on the same day in future (as with the North West and South West meetings on the 25th September). This would help to ensure the availability and attendance of all necessary personnel at future meetings.

19. The six clubs were chosen as most of them were not involved with Adult Training schemes at the time. Indeed, only Sheffield Wednesday of the six clubs chosen had any involvement or experience of working with Adult Training schemes. The fact that a meeting was held with representatives of only the six clubs, however, caused a problem for certain clubs at the next meeting when all PL club chairmen were invited. Indeed, one club chairman left the meeting (held in March 1998) when he found out that his club hadn't been invited to attend the inaugural meeting.

with existing Community Programme work). A follow-up meeting was arranged at Old Trafford when all PL Club chairmen/Chief Executives were invited.

A meeting with **Dick Newby** (The Prince's Trust) and **Tom Findley** and **Deborah Lincoln** (from The Princes Trust Marketing Agency, Purple Patch) agreed to a "pilot" initiative involving 7 club community schemes as the first phase of their proposals (bearing in mind that their target audience was largely for unemployed people). The 7 clubs chosen were Arsenal, Aston Villa, Liverpool, Manchester United, Newcastle United, Sheffield Wednesday and West Ham United. A meeting of senior representatives of these clubs was held at St James's Palace in March 1998 when details of the 'dove-tailing' with opportunities for the longer term unemployed were discussed.

A further meeting was held with **David Richards** and **Paul Weston**, representatives of The Federation of Stadium Communities (FSC), an organisation based in the Potteries that encourages local people to actively engage in dialogue with their local clubs, especially in deprived areas. The Federation at the time had exciting plans to step up their involvement in supporting local community groups and extended an invitation to the FFE&VTS Community Programme to give a short speech at their national conference at the end of September. It was certainly believed that there was merit in bringing club community schemes and local community groups together. Regular liaison meetings were to be held with the FSC over the next seven or eight years not only with David and Paul, but also with new Chief Executive, **Judy Crabbe,** (who was appointed in 2004) and **Chris Lawley**. Help was even offered to the FSC to assist with their interviews for a new post in the West Midlands in early 2005.

At Community Officer level, **John Halpin** agreed to accept an offer to become Carlisle United's Youth team coach effective from the middle of September. John had been extremely successful as Community Officer at the club and had earned the opportunity after doing such a good job engaging with the local community. Club Chairman, **Michael Knighton,** confirmed the appointment of **Paul Devlin** as John's successor, and he would be assisted by **Ron Smith**. The Carlisle Chairman also announced at this time that the club were intending to take the scheme "in-house" and that they would work in future without the support of the FFE&VTS Community Programme.

Rochdale AFC held the opening of their new East Stand on October 7th, prior to a match against Bolton Wanderers. Significantly, the East Stand housed changing rooms for the club's new five-a-side pitch together with new offices for the club's community officers.

The October Senior Management Meeting was the first attended by newly appointed Regional Director, **John Hudson**, and he was duly welcomed by all present. The news of Carlisle United's intentions was shared at the meeting, though it was also noted that meetings with representatives of Derby County and Macclesfield Town (notably with Town Chairman, **Alan Cash**) had gone well and there were high hopes that community schemes would be fully underway there soon.

Plans to stage a formal induction for newly appointed Community Officers were also revealed. The induction would be held on the 4th and 5th November 1997 at the Manchester offices.

Those in attendance from a total of 12 club schemes were:

- **Jason Maguire** and **Paul Aigbogun** (Barnet)
- **Derek Spence** (Blackpool)
- **Dean Ramsdale** and **Anthony Barlow** (Burnley)
- **Andy Feeley** (Bury)
- **Matt Parish** (Charlton Athletic)
- **Kevin Betsy** (Farnborough Town. At the time, Seychelles-born Kevin was also playing non-league football with Woking but, in the end, Kevin left Farnborough's employment in order to sign professional forms for Fulham in 1998 before later moves to AFC Bournemouth (on loan), Hull City (also on loan), Barnsley, Hartlepool United (on loan) and Oldham Athletic.
- **Mike Smith** (Hartlepool United. Mike was a former player with Wimbledon)
- **John Clubb** (Macclesfield Town)

- **Graham Moran** and **Steve Hill** (Notts County)
- **Steve Adams** (Sheffield Wednesday)
- **Steve Hughes** and **Andy Davies** (Wrexham)
- **Nas Bashir** and **Dave Evans** (Wycombe Wanderers. Nas would soon move on to a coaching position at nearby Reading, leaving Dave in sole charge at Wycombe)

The get-together also, of course, provided a terrific 'networking' opportunity and several of those who attended became long-term appointments as Community Officers.

Linked in with 'Training for Work' (which was to focus on the 25+ age group in future) was a further opportunity to develop a new Government-led venture for 18-24-year-olds - the "New Deal" scheme. Details of the new initiative were passed on by **Jane Haywood** to scheme officials which would see a 6-month subsidy for recruited workers (working part-time or full-time), who would also have access to certain training (at up to NVQ Level II) and then be taken on permanently by Employers. This scheme was due to start in January 1998 in 10 "pathfinder" areas, followed by a national launch in April.

On another positive note, income being generated from the Sportsmatch sponsorship "pound for pound matching" scheme was increasing, as were the number of locally based community schemes that were able to secure such funding. Sportsmatch's **Emma Platts** contacted scheme officials to announce plans for a 5ᵗʰ Year Anniversary celebratory event to be held at the end of November at Wembley, that would be generously sponsored by the FA.

Another good example of the diversity of the ever-broadening range of Community Programme work was seen in the staging of the play *Ooh Ah Showab Khan* which several clubs were kindly putting on in their areas, usually in conjunction with their local Race Relations Council. This followed several other super initiatives aimed at combating or raising awareness of discrimination such as the Leyton Orient/Arc Theatre Ensemble *Kicking Out* drama; Charlton Athletic's *Red, White and Black at the Valley* campaign; Brentford's *Equality through Sport* plus others at Exeter City, Manchester City[20], West Bromwich Albion etc. Following hot on the heels of the success of their second play, the Arc Theatre also commissioned a third play in 1999, "*My England*" written by **Clifford Oliver**.

Geoff Noonan also reported that his club, Farnborough Town, had been successful with their application to the National Lottery Fund and that a grant of £103,000 had been awarded towards their proposed new five-a-side facilities (subject, of course, to certain 'match funding' becoming available as outlined in their bid application).

In mid-November, PFA Deputy Chief Executive **Brendon Batson** together with the Community Programme's Chief Administrator were invited to meet the recently appointed Football 'Task Force' at the offices of the Football Trust in order to make a presentation about the work of the Community Programme. Amongst those in attendance at the meeting were members of the Working Group which included **Peter Lee** and **Richard Faulkner** from the Football Trust, Referee **Uriah Rennie**, **Adam Brown** representing Supporters and **John Smith** representing the police, Footballer **Robbie Earle**, Broadcaster **Eleanor Oldroyd** and Businessman **Sir Roland "Tiny" Smith**. Also in attendance was the chairman of the Task Force, **David Mellor** MP plus the three administrators supporting the work of the Task Force, **David Mahoney**, **Susan O'Brien** (who was later to work with the National League community operation) and **Andy Burnham** (later to become an MP and, later, Mayor of Manchester).

The invited guests combined to make a very positive presentation which included the following points about the Community Programme scheme on a national basis:

- There were 300 full time staff and a further 700 'casual' staff in post at the time.
- Healthy activity involvement extended across all age groups, both sexes (with huge new opportunities to play football for girls and women especially) and involved increasing numbers of people with disabilities and minority groups.
- Total involvement was huge with over 300,000 children involved in schools' work

---

20. Manchester City's hosting of Ooh Ah Showab Khan *was undertaken in partnership with Asian Sound Radio and Manchester City Council.*

alone and a further 200,000 people attending professional club matches as a result of their involvement with community programme schemes.

- New funding had been sought and found from sponsors Pizza Hut and Wagon Wheels (and others) and from the PFA.

The Football Task Force (which had been set up in July 1997) completed several reports on seven key aspects of football before it finally concluded its business in December 1999. The seven areas studied were:

- Access to grounds for people with disabilities.
- Football's work in the Community (in addition to the presentation made by Brendon and Roger, fourteen Community Scheme Officers were also 'interviewed' by the Task Force).
- Merchandising policies and procedures.
- Potential conflicts cased as a result of clubs being floated on the Stock Exchange.
- Racism.
- Supporter involvement in running clubs.
- Ticketing policies and procedures.

The reports completed by the Task Force included a report entitled "*Investing in the Community*" (first presented in January 1999) which contained key recommendations including the demand for the PL to donate 5% of future television revenue to "grassroots football". In turn, the PL responded by suggesting that they would 'match' any investment by the Government into football. This led to the creation of the Football Foundation as a worthy successor to the Football Trust.

In terms of clubs, concerns had been expressed at FFE&VTS Board level that Ipswich Town were, even at this late stage, still not working with the FFE&VTS to develop their then limited community involvement. Contact was made with Town Chairman, **David Sheepshanks,** who asked for a meeting to be arranged with Commercial Director, **Paul Clouting**. This was eventually arranged on the 5th September, when details of working with the FFE&VTS were passed on. It took some time for the club to respond after this initial meeting and the club remained outside the 'partnership' arrangements until the autumn of the following year (1998).

Also, in late 1997, Barnsley's Community scheme was involved in meeting with the Advisory, Conciliation and Arbitration Service (ACAS) concerning a complaint from a former member of staff who had fallen out with the then Community Officer, **Steve Lister**. After lengthy discussions with ACAS, an agreement to settle the matter was reached in the end.

In terms of legal action, the Southend United Community Scheme was also involved in litigation against a local sponsor, who had signed a contract worth £5,000 but had refused to pay (notwithstanding the 'consequential loss' of losing Sportsmatch funding once the sponsor hadn't paid). George Davies Solicitors were kindly involved in this matter and the full amount due was eventually secured from the sponsor.

Four regional (Christmas) meetings for Community Officers were held in December:

- Eastern Region at Huddersfield Town on the 10th.
- South West Region at Portsmouth on the 11th.
- South East Region at Fulham on the 12th. Guest at the meeting, **Piarra Powar** from Kick it Out, spoke about the excellent work being undertaken by Community schemes in this area and how even more inclusion work could be established in future.
- Western Region at Everton on the 17th.

Amongst issues raised were the following:

- Opportunities under Adult Training, New Deal AND the YT programme.
- Opportunities to take part in the Panini 6-a-side competition AND the Smoby Monneret Table Football competition.
- Opportunities to take part in new Wagon Wheels activities and events (see Chapter 12) and to support the proposed new Adidas kit and equipment deal[21] if possible.

---

21. *The Adidas sponsorship deal was a huge deal worth £375,000 per annum in total to the FFE&VTS as a whole, with £225,000 of that figure allocated for kit and equipment for Community Programme*

- Opportunities to access Sportsmatch funding if local sponsorship was possible.

The final senior management ("general management") meeting of the year saw all Regional Directors attend a meeting that reviewed things as follows:

Clubs – Macclesfield Town as a club were now working alongside the FFE&VTS Community Programme. News was awaited from Cardiff City and Derby County. A meeting had been held with a representative of Ipswich Town to look at the benefits of working together in future.

Sponsors – The various arrangements with sponsors Wagon Wheels, Panini, Smoby Monneret and Adidas were all available to locally based Community Programme schemes.

Adult and Youth Training – Opportunities existed under Adult Training (for 25+. This was to be re-branded "Work based Training for adults"), New Deal (for 18-24s and rebranded "Work based Training for Young People") AND under the YT programme (for 16-18s). The new separation of Adult Training schemes into two different offers for those above the age of 25 and those below 25 would commence effective from April 1998.

Just before Christmas, **Gary "Dutchy" Holland** left Portsmouth. The end of the year 1997 saw a summary of club Community Schemes turnover reveal that, during the year 1997, a total of 76 Schemes turned over a collective total of £3,912,459 meaning that average turnover across those schemes had risen to approximately £51,480 per annum. Total weekly wages paid through the FFE&VTS payroll in 1997 had risen to £1,921,265. In addition, separate monthly paid wages for the year totalled £209,396. This meant that a total of £2,130,661 was paid out via the FFE&VTS payroll service. A total of 73 club-based Community projects used the FFE&VTS payroll free service during 1997 which included an increasing number of workers and casual staff (mainly casual coaches) working alongside senior Community Officers (262 full time weekly paid staff were paid via the payroll during the year). Whilst this was evidently very positive news that the scheme was continuing to expand, it was also clear that any further growth, and the current method of paying wages on behalf of community projects, could lead to cash flow issues for the FFE&VTS Community Programme should any local projects experience cash flow difficulties and be unable to reimburse the FFE&VTS for wages paid on their behalf. Concerns about this issue were to arise on a regular basis over the next 9/10 years. Regional Directors were also alerted to these difficulties at a senior management meeting in April but were largely powerless in some cases as money was simply not available at certain local projects to pay for wages.

The early part of 1998 saw a unique invitation extended to all FFE&VTS staff by the PFA who invited them all (plus partners) to attend a long weekend at Stapleford Park in Leicestershire. Sadly, five community programme staff were unable to attend through other commitments. All 'heads of department' were invited to say a few words about their work and the support given by the PFA which, in the case of the FFE&VTS both as a whole and for its Community Programme scheme, continued to be simply huge. Indeed, in the case of the Community Programme not only was the scheme being funded directly by the PFA at £500,000 per annum at the time, but also the PFA commercial arm was helping to bring in significant sponsorship deals to the scheme worth a total of around £650,000 per annum. As Chief Executive of the PFA, **Gordon Taylor** was keen in his speech to ensure that a positive image/profile was retained, especially as key operations within the PFA were clearly based around being part of the 'service industry' (as he referred to it). In dealing with people, as he stressed, it was important to be professional, polite and pleasant.

These messages were passed on at a Staff Meeting in mid-January when it was once again stressed that links with the PFA remained especially close, and that they needed to remain that

---

schemes. A further amount would also be made available just in case plans to roll out a new secondary school's initiative were realised. The eventual offer was for 3 different packs of clothing and footwear to be made available by Adidas to Community Officers being a "Managers Pack" (worth £286.45); a Full Time Assistant's Pack (worth £143.20) and a Part Timer's Pack (worth £49.90). Footballs and other Adidas equipment (e.g. marker cones, water bottles, bibs etc.) were also to be made available.

way in future.

In the wider world, Leeds United's Operations Manager, **David Spencer**, had made contact to investigate a restructuring of the club's community operations to merge four separate operations into one department under a soon to-be-appointed new Community Scheme Liaison Officer (including the FFE&VTS-supported Community Programme scheme under **Ces Podd**. The other departments included education/classroom work, senior citizens work and supporter liaison).

Members of the Management Forum responsible for overseeing Manchester City's Community scheme met in mid-January to approve the idea of applying to the Charity Commission to become a registered charity (in line with the recommendations of the Deloitte & Touché report).

In view of the extent of the many different commercial deals now in place for the national Community Programme, **Richard Finney** was appointed as Director of Marketing. In recent months, Richard had qualified as a member of the Chartered Institute of Marketing, meaning he was well equipped and suitably qualified to take on this role. Initially, he was kind enough to agree to continue to liaise with certain club officers in Yorkshire and the North East, although the start of the New Year in 1999 saw this club supervision and liaison passed on to Regional Director, **Dick Krzywicki**. Richard said:

> *"Moving from Regional Manager to look after the national sponsorship activities was an opportunity that was too good to miss, Being the link between our sponsors and the projects made sure club schemes and Officers were able to promote the sponsorships in very positive ways."*

Rather than a direct replacement as Regional Director, it was agreed that **John Hudson** would now oversee all the North West clubs in total, and that the new position of 'Regional Director (Midlands)' would be created in due course. The role of the new Officer would be to oversee both the West *and* East Midlands clubs. Interviews for the new Midlands post were held with five pre-selected candidates at the beginning of April and the enthusiastic and ambitious Grimsby Town Community Officer, **Julian Winter**, was appointed. Following Julian's appointment as Midlands Regional Director, **Graham Rodger** was appointed as Community Officer at Blundell Park. He would eventually take up the post in November 1998. As a player, Graham began his career as an apprentice with Wolverhampton Wanderers in 1983 before moves to Coventry City, Luton Town and Grimsby Town, where he spent a total of six seasons.

The Community Forum (what used to be referred to as the "Sub-Committee" working under the Board of Directors of the FFE&VTS) was also reorganised, so that all four football organisations had two members each on the group as follows:

- FA: **Frank Hannah** (Manchester CFA Chairman and member FA Council) and **Robin Russell**.
- PL: **Mike Foster** and **Nigel Pleasants** (Secretary, Leeds United)
- FL: **Andy Williamson** and **Chris Whalley**
- PFA: **Gordon Taylor** and **Brendon Batson**

The recent expansion of the Board of Directors also meant that the table in the FFE&VTS Boardroom had to be rebuilt to accommodate an additional mid-section, thus allowing additional representatives the extra room to attend Board Meetings!

The first Community Forum meeting was held in late January 1998 at the FA's offices at Lancaster Gate in London and the FA's **Frank Hannah**, having been nominated by **Mike Foster** from the PL and seconded by **Chris Whalley** from the FL, was duly appointed as Chairman of the Forum. It should be recorded at this point that Frank became a dedicated, honest, loyal and very fair Chairman of the Community Forum for the next nine years.

Amongst issues raised at this meeting were the following:

- Carlisle United's resignation from the agreement to work with the FFE&VTS Community Programme was noted.

- Concern was expressed, once again, regarding Arsenal's franchised holiday courses around the UK. It was understood that, to date, the club hadn't responded to approaches made by the PL.
- Steps were being taken to appoint new Community Officers at Birmingham City and at Cardiff City. It was also hoped that recent discussions with representatives of Ipswich Town would lead to the club considering the possibility of committing to work alongside the FFE&VTS Community Programme in future.
- Details of sponsorship involvement with Wagon Wheels, Adidas, Panini and Smoby Monneret were all noted. In addition, details of the re-structuring to create the new position of Marketing Director (aimed at supporting the various new sponsors) with 5 Regional Director posts covering the North West, the North East, the Midlands, the South West and the South East were noted and approved.
- Approaches needed to be made to 20 clubs whose Community scheme workers were employed via club payrolls so that they were informed of the recommendations of the Deloitte & Touché Report.
- The preparation of a Community Programme Annual Report for 1997 was approved[22].

The accounts figures (not including depreciation) included in the reports were (1998 and 1999 figures also shown for reference and for comparison purposes):

INCOME YEAR	1997	1998	1999
Grants from TECs	£200,144	£190,534	£220,078
Wagon Wheels Sponsorship	£225,000	£250,000	£250,000
Umbro Sponsorship	£12,000		
Adidas Sponsorship		£275,000	£375,000
DfEE grant (resource packs)		£8,750	£12,650
Panini/Adidas Predator Sponsorship	£25,000	£25,000	£50,000
Smoby Monneret Sponsorship			£15,000
Sportsmatch		£50,000	
PFA Donation	£500,000	£500,000	£500,000
Club Projects (wages) CONTRA	£2,103,077	£2,982,289	£4,075,938
Bank Interest	£6,606	£590	£3,025
Sundry	£4,221		£5,728
Total	£3,076,048	£4,282,164	£5,507,419

22. *Whilst the Community Programme in Professional Football remained an essential department (and therefore only part) of the FFE&VTS overall, it is interesting to note that a great deal of hard work was undertaken in early 1998 to produce the first set of separate printed reports and accounts covering the calendar year of 1997 (printed accounts were eventually produced in 1997, 1998 and in 1999). The thinking behind this was partly based around projecting the image of a more "independent" scheme and partly around the increasing turnover of the scheme (just under £4 million in 1997). The accounts information contained in each of these reports were checked by* **Mike Birch** *and* **Gary Wood** *from auditors Humphreys, Bower and Gothard.*

EXPENDITURE YEAR	1997	1998	1999
Club Projects (wages) CONTRA	£2,103,077	£2,982,289	£4,075,938
Grant Donations to club projects	£522,000	£534,000	£540,000
Course Fees	£27,276	£19,118	£40,729
Bonuses Payable to trainees	£2,500	£28,876	£20,087
Club project Incentives	£39,820	£8,750	£5,790
Expenditure re National sponsorship			£3,199
Expenditure re Adidas sponsorship		£228,091	£228,730
Expenditure re Umbro packs	£12,000		
Expenditure re Panini/Adidas	£25,002	£25,072	£58,461
Expenditure re Smoby Monneret			£15,369
Expenditure re Wagon Wheels	£9,795	£10,321	£12,933
Wages Regional Directors etc.	£301,553	£333,392	£369,473
Office & Insurance	£14,483	£17,349	£18,148
Interest Payable		£9,678	£10,354
Printing, Stationery, Advertising	£6,747	£5,153	£5,623
Telephone & Postage	£8,549	£10,343	£12,118
Travel Expenses	£68,998	£76,888	£104,749
Sundry	£268	£769	
Rent, Rates, Light & Heat	£4,201	£3,960	£2,975
Accountancy	£4,906	£2,350	£2,350
Legal & Professional	£10,095	£10,347	£10,876
Total	£3,161,270	£4,306,746	£5,537,903

Included in the 1997 Report and Accounts were:

- Photos of all thirteen FFE&VTS Community Programme support staff in post at the time.

- A Report from the FFE&VTS Chief Executive.

- A Report from the FFE&VTS Community Programme Chief Administrator (including references to the various sponsors working with the FFE&VTS Community Programme).

- A Financial Report from the Accountants (including an Income and Expenditure Account and Balance Sheet).

Early 1998 also saw the first meeting with representatives of the National Society for the Prevention of Cruelty to Children (NSPCC) with Senior Manager, **Peter Hambly,** and colleagues. This was effectively the start of much greater support from across the football world, particularly when the massively successful "Full Stop" campaign was launched by the NSPCC in 1999 (and would run for a ten-year period). It was felt that close links with the NSPCC, especially to ensure liaison in any specific child protection issues in future, should be maintained.

Over the next two years, close work with **Elspeth Gilfillan**, **Clare Haynes**, **James Owen** and **Ellie Katsourides** from the NSPCC led to the whole of the 'football family' supporting the Full Stop campaign and great credit should properly be extended to them for all their patient and hard work.

Indeed, **Adam Crozier** (then with Saatchi & Saatchi and later to become Chief Executive of the FA) was also involved in these early discussions. The advantages of working closely with the NSPCC were clear for all to see within a few years. Not only would there be clearer ground rules concerning child protection issues but there would also be much improved offers from within football for children, whether they were involved at Academies or in community activity. In a poll at the end of the 1998/99 season, it became clear too that the vast majority of clubs bought in to the idea of working more closely with the NSPCC. Indeed, well over two thirds of clubs kindly allocated space in their match programmes to promote the NSPCC "Full Stop" campaign.

The excellent Director from Sportsmatch, **Mike Scott**, announced his retirement in February 1998 (and a suitable gift was purchased for him by the FFE&VTS Community Programme). Mike's replacement was another Mike… **Mike Reynolds**, and he was also to become a keen supporter of the FFE&VTS Community Programme.

In line with **Gordon Taylor**'s original hopes for the Community Programme in the mid 1980's, scheme officials were doing their best to keep in touch with MPs and parliamentary advisors. Meetings in early 1998 included those with **Tony Banks** MP (Minister of Sport) and **Glyn Ford** MEP. Both meetings were aimed at ensuring that they were fully aware of the excellent community work going on not only in their local constituencies but also on a national basis.

A further meeting with the FA about the female game was held in February. Essentially, there was to be a launch held in April of the 20 Centres of Excellence across the country for girls, together with a "World Class" performance structure, which Football in the Community Officers could involve themselves in if they so wished.

As far as clubs were concerned in early 1998:

\- Middlesbrough held the opening of their new educational facilities/community classrooms at their new Riverside Stadium led by their Director of Community, former international referee, **George Courtney**.

\- Stockport County offered Community Officer **Andy Kilner** the opportunity to become the club's Youth Development Officer on an initial five-year contract (he would eventually become manager at the club).

\- Popular Community Officer at Leeds United, **Ces Podd**, had been approached to take up a 'secondment' (potentially of between two and five months) starting in March working as a Football Development Officer/Coach on the islands of St Kitts and Nevis in the Caribbean (where he was born). Assistant Community Officer **Greg Abbott** took charge in his absence. Interestingly enough, soon after his return to the UK, Ces was offered work in St Kitts and Nevis on a permanent basis. This was an offer he decided to accept effective from the end of June following a few weeks working in his old role at Elland Road. A meeting with **Peter Jenkins** from the St Kitts and Nevis FA in August 1998 confirmed these arrangements.

\- **Peter "Charlie" Aitken** left Gillingham. Despite further contact with chairman **Paul Scally** about the benefits of continuing to work alongside the FFE&VTS Community Programme, the club went on to appoint their own club Community Officer.

March 1998 saw a first meeting with **Alison Lockwood** and **David Carley** from the Department for Education and Employment (DfEE) aimed initially at evaluating the success of the *"Playing for Success"* initiative and to consider what study support initiatives were already underway in conjunction with clubs. Following the completion of a suitable 'mapping' exercise, a template was to be prepared which would identify what was achievable and how it was to become more accessible. As this was considered to be an important extension to clubs existing involvement in the community, it was also agreed that **Dennis Leman** would take responsibility not only for raising a report about what was underway but also for future liaison with the DfEE.

Indeed, Dennis, kindly, also chaired a 'Working Group' set up by the DfEE that included **Des Coffey**, **Sue Atkinson**, **Jean Evans**, **Tarun Kapur** and **Sally Champion**, all individuals who were more directly involved in the delivery of curriculum based educational work.

The next 'round' of regional meetings of Community Officers also commenced in March with meetings at Leeds United (North East and Yorkshire), Leicester City (Midlands) and at Burnley (North West). Of interest were presentations made by FA women's regional officers (**Julie Lewis** and **Donna McIvor**) about the growth of the game for girls and women. The FA, who had recognised the enormous part played by Community schemes in encouraging increased participation amongst girls, confirmed that:

- There were 40 million women playing football worldwide.

- New centres of excellence were to be established (with particular target groups being under 12's, under 14's and under 16's).

- 2 coaching centres were to be established in each CFA area.

- The Sports Council were to be a key partner in connection with 'World Class' schemes based on performance, potential and starts.

- Funding would become available (largely to Local Authorities) to support the growth of the game for female players.

April saw the remaining regional meetings held at Coventry City (West Midlands), Swindon Town (South West) and at Charlton Athletic (South East and London). Guests attending these meetings included **Ros Potts** from the FA (about female football as outlined above) and **Tom Findley** and **Peggy Walters** representing the Princes Trust who made short presentations at each meeting about the work of the Trust.

A great deal of time, of course, was also taken up by discussions at the regional meetings about the various sponsorships now in place on a national basis (i.e. especially Wagon Wheels, Panini, Smoby Monneret and Adidas). Head of Training/Government Programmes, **Gary Naven,** also provided much more information for Officers about the New Deal arrangements.

In March, news was received that popular Community Officer at Crystal Palace, **Nicky Johns**, had been involved in a serious car accident, sustaining serious neck and back injuries which caused continued pain in the future. Despite the seriousness of his injuries, he was able to return to work where he continued to do a great job for many years.

The situation concerning clubs was outlined at a General Management (Senior Management Team) Meeting held in April 1998:

- Projects at Birmingham City and Cardiff City were still "on hold" (though this was to change at Birmingham City the following month when **Dean Holtham** was appointed as the club's Community Officer). Welshman Dean began his playing career as an apprentice at Cardiff City before moving to Swansea City and, later, Newport County making a handful of appearances with both clubs.

- There were no further developments to report concerning possible projects at Derby County or Gillingham. At Derby, however, **Richard Clifford** and **Mike Umphray** had arranged a round-the-table meeting also involving representatives from Derby City Council and local sponsors to be held at the end of the month. The local 'sponsors' included Kennings, the Midlands Co-Op and McDonalds who were ready to invest in the proposed new community initiative at Derby so hopes were high that a community scheme would be underway soon.

- There had been no further response from Ipswich Town.

- Representatives of Tottenham Hotspur had requested a meeting to discuss the possibility of re-establishing a Community Scheme at the club (supported by the recently appointed Academy Director at the club, **Colin Murphy**).

These details were also circulated at the May Community Forum meeting held in Manchester and attended by **Andy Williamson** and **Chris Whalley** from the FL and by **Robin Russell** and **Frank Hannah** from the FA.

At the end of April, **Roger Reade** was pleased to be approached by the FA to join a 'Working Party' aimed at considering the proposed new 'Charter Mark' standard for clubs and children's coaching courses. The 'Charter Mark', of course, was the original name given to what became the highly successful 'Charter Standard' programme for clubs and leagues. Amongst those people involved from the FA were Council members **Maurice Armstrong**, **Alan Clarke**, **Peter Hough**, **Jim Kenyon**, **Keith Masters**, **Mick Parry**, **John Waterall** and **David Worsfold**. Further Working Party meetings were also held throughout 1998, 1999 and into the year 2000. Community Programme interest at this time centred around the possibility of a 'standard' or quality mark for holiday courses up and down the country, although the FA's main focus was based around the provision of a quality 'standard' for grass roots football clubs.

Because of the deal involving the PL with Merlin, which continued into the new season 1997/8, the Panini Six-a-side Competition, in the end, saw a total of 73 club projects (including 5 PL clubs) take part.

The 1997/8 Competition saw the Regional Finals again staged at South Africa Road (Southern Finals) and at Rotherham United's Millmoor ground (Northern Finals) with the Final again played at Wembley prior to the Auto Windscreens Shield Final match between Grimsby Town and AFC Bournemouth (won by Grimsby by 2-1) thanks to the support of the Football League.

The first ever Smoby Monneret Table Football Competition took place in season 1997/8 at the PFA's London restaurant, "Football Football" when **David Beckham** presented the prizes and trophies to all the participants (see Appendix V for details of Competition winners).

Regarding the Six-a-side competition, the Summer of 1998 saw Panini confirm, somewhat reluctantly, that they were not to continue their sponsorship of the Schools Competition. However, working practices with Adidas at this time were so strong that Adidas representatives readily agreed to sponsor the tournament for the next two years in the name of their now popular Predator football boots (as worn by **David Beckham**).

Former Charlton Athletic striker **Garry Nelson** had, by this time, taken over from **Brian Marwood** as PFA Commercial Executive and sponsorship 'liaison' officer. Born in Braintree, Garry had experienced a super playing career which began with Southend United before later moves to Swindon Town, Plymouth Argyle, Brighton & Hove Albion, Notts County (on loan), Charlton Athletic and, finally, Torquay United. Garry also, of course, wrote two best-selling books about his time as a footballer.

Responsibility fell on Garry to finalise the agreement with Adidas on behalf of the FFE&VTS Community Programme. Adidas at the time were also keen to explore the idea of establishing a new Secondary School's competition exclusively for girls (eventually agreed at Under 13's level) …. with a super first prize of a trip to the USA for the winners. Aided by the personal support of **Richard Finney**, an application for match funding from Sportsmatch was also made. This new competition effectively took over where the FL's tournament left off.

The end of the 1997/8 football season saw former Welsh international **Jeremy Charles** appointed to work alongside **Linden Jones**, Community Officer at Swansea City. Linden did a fantastic job over many years with the Swans.

Jeremy Charles was a former Swansea City apprentice who went on to make over 220 league appearances for the Swans before later moves to Queens Park Rangers and Oxford United. He also played for the Welsh Under 21's team. Jeremy worked with Linden for a short spell in community work before later being appointed as Swansea's Director of Youth Development.

Also moving on was **Mark Ashton** who had been appointed as Marketing Manager at West Bromwich Albion at the end of the season.

The June General Management Meeting of the senior management team was the first to be attended by new Regional Director **Julian Winter** and saw a comprehensive 'update' from **Gary Naven** about Adult and Youth Training, the New Deal (including the two separate options available being "employed" or "education and training" and the necessary administration and paperwork to support either option) and NVQs. In addition, several Community Officers continued to stay loyal to the Adult Training programme by working hard to ensure positive recruitment levels and access to further training continued at their clubs. By now, Gary's job title had changed to "Head of Adult and Youth Training".

Average recruitment levels under TFW (plus YT programme places) for 1997/1998 are detailed in "Appendix III – Table of trainees in post year by year 1994-2002". [23] Amongst those clubs with higher than average recruitment levels during the year were projects at Burnley, Crewe Alexandra, Leeds United, Manchester City, Notts County, Sheffield United, Stoke City, West Bromwich Albion and Wigan Athletic.

The 1997/1998 contract year also saw a reduction in participating club projects from 52 to 49. It was also reported that **Frankie Bunn** had been appointed as a Youth Team coach working within the new Academy at Manchester City alongside Manager **Joe Royle**, thus leaving vacant the position of Community Officer at Wigan Athletic.

Also appointed as a Youth Team coach, this time at Bradford City, was former Manchester City striker **Ron Futcher**. This left **Gavin Oliver** in sole charge as Community Officer at Valley Parade. Gavin himself was eventually to move on in the Spring of 1999 when he was replaced by **Ian Ormondroyd**. Ian's playing career began with his local club, Bradford City, in 1985 before moves to Oldham Athletic (on loan), Aston Villa, Derby County, Leicester City and Hull City (on loan). He returned to Valley Parade for the 1995/6 season, ending his career with further moves to Oldham Athletic and Scunthorpe United.

Noted at the meeting too, following the appointment of **George Foster** at the FL, was the fact that **Nicky Law** had been appointed as new Community Officer at Chesterfield. A former apprentice with Arsenal, Nicky went on to enjoy a lengthy career with several clubs including Barnsley, Blackpool, Plymouth Argyle and Notts County. He went briefly on loan to Scarborough before being transferred to Rotherham United, Chesterfield and, finally, Hereford United.

Former Middlesbrough/Hartlepool United player **Keith Nobbs** was appointed as Hartlepool United's new Community Officer following the departure of **Mike Smith**. Born in Bishop Auckland, Keith Nobbs had been an apprentice footballer with Middlesbrough (making a single league appearance) before joining Halifax Town in 1982. He then moved to Hartlepool United in 1985 where he played for seven years, making over 270 league appearances.

A June meeting with **Graham Mackrell** (Club Secretary) and **Dave Richards** (Club Chairman, later to become Chairman of the PL) at Sheffield Wednesday outlined an appropriate way forward for the club's community operation. Up to this point, the club had chosen to operate their community scheme as a non-fund-raising department within the club.

Following Halifax Town's promotion to the FL from the Football Conference (now the National League), the club were very keen to explore whether they could re-commence work with the FFE&VTS Community Programme once again. A July 1998 meeting with Club Secretary, **Hilary Molyneux-Horrocks,** went very well and arrangements to work with the club were to re-commence in the very near future. Hilary would prove to be equally as supportive when, as **Hilary Molyneux-Dearden**, she became Club Secretary at Rochdale.

The 1998/9 season kicked off with a meeting involving FFE&VTS Community Programme officials and **David Spencer** and **Nigel Pleasants** (Club Secretary) at Leeds United where it was made clear that, following the departure of former Community Officer **Ces Podd**, the club were keen to "grow their business" of community engagement and to develop a closer link with their new Academy. Future meetings would set out a new framework or structure for the club whereby the Community operation at the club (to be entitled "*Community United*") whilst maintaining its own separate identity, would essentially fall under the club's "umbrella" scheme by becoming only part of the club's total ambitions for young people. The club were also clear

---

23. *Figures noted included the numbers of Youth trainees in post equivalent to approximately 6.3 trainees in post per week.*

that a new, more experienced 'Community Officer' would be required to oversee the umbrella scheme in due course. Curriculum Vitaes (CVs) for some experienced Community Officers were passed on to the club for their further consideration. Amongst the CVs passed on was one for **Mick Ferguson** who had, of course, done such a marvellous job setting up and supervising Sunderland's Community operation since its inception. Indeed, Mick was interviewed for the job in mid-August and (following a re-interview) accepted a significant offer from the club to take over in October. It was also agreed that **Greg Abbott** would continue in the role of Assistant Community Officer. In the end, **Emma Stanford** took overall control of all the club's community operations when she was appointed as Community Affairs Manager.

Following the departure of **Bill Prendergast** as Manager of Crewe Alexandra's Soccer & Community Association based at Shavington, Club Secretary **Gill Palin** confirmed that the club, led by Chairman **John Bowler**, were hoping that **Chris Walters** would be able to consider taking on the dual role of being Community Officer and managing the Shavington centre. This was a proposal that was openly welcomed by FFE&VTS Community Programme personnel, particularly as Chris had proved to be an excellent Community Scheme organiser and supervisor. This also involved the necessity to consider details of a possible merger of the then two legally separate operations. Long-serving trustee for the Soccer & Community Association (a charity that was first set up in 1987), **Harry Bamford**, was also involved in these discussions and supported the moves for the FFE&VTS Community Programme to present a plan to the Association's trustees outlining the terms of a possible merger of the two organisations (the Soccer Centre had already been set up as a Charity).

The start of the season also saw the appointment of **Anne-Marie Clark** as Community Affairs Manager at Crystal Palace.

Other meetings included follow-up meetings with **Neil McClelland** from the National Literacy Trust (NLT) whereby the 'Reading is Fundamental' scheme organised by the Trust would be promoted by community schemes across the country. Neil also kindly agreed to meet representatives of sponsors Wagon Wheels and their agents Harrison Cowley to announce plans for the "Year of Reading" (to run during the 1998/9 football season and to include a month of 'sports reading' in March 1999) and to explain more about his hopes for even more partnership working.

Another meeting saw **Malcolm Bradshaw** and **Bob Jackson** from Alliance Publishing announce how they could support community schemes by printing regular (usually annual) hand-books at no cost to the schemes by arranging for local advertising support aimed at covering the print costs. It also became clear that several Community Officers had already reached agreement with Alliance to produce these handbooks at local level.

After only around 18 months in post, **Jason Maguire** left the Barnet Community Scheme at the end of August. The vacant post was advertised locally during August and led to the appointment of **Gary Karsa** as Community Officer, with **Mark Tyrell** as his Assistant. Gary was to go on to hold various coaching positions at professional clubs in future.

Bristol City, led by **David Burnside**, chose to resign from working alongside the FFE&VTS Community Programme to focus more on their Academy, and to embrace their existing school's community programme work within their Academy programme.

Coventry City moved to appoint former players **David Busst** and **Lloyd McGrath** as Assistant Community Officers alongside **Claire Maslen** and **Gerald Murphy**.

David Busst was born in Birmingham and joined Coventry City from Moor Green Rovers in 1992. His promising career as a central defender was sadly ended following a serious injury sustained in 1995. David would go on to become a long-serving Head of Community following his appointment in 2003.

Born in Birmingham, **Lloyd McGrath** began his career as an apprentice with Coventry City for whom he played in the 1987 FA Cup Final. He played for Coventry for a total of ten years before a brief spell with Portsmouth.

Steve Rogers stepped down from his role as Community Officer at Plymouth Argyle. His replacement (admittedly after a gap of some six months or more) was former Argyle legend and goalkeeper **Geoff Crudgington**.

A new appointment was made at Wigan Athletic where former player, **Jason Beckford,** became the club's latest Community Officer when he commenced his new duties on the 3rd August. Brother of Manchester City's **Darren Beckford**, Jason played for several clubs during his career including City (where his playing career began as an apprentice), Blackburn Rovers (on loan), Port Vale (also on loan), Birmingham City, Bury (on loan), Stoke City, Millwall and Northampton Town where he made one single substitute appearance before finishing his playing career.

The first General Management (Senior Management Team) Meeting of the new season held at the start of August identified that around 24 Community projects at local level owed a collective sum of approximately £135,000 for the reimbursement of wages already paid out by the FFE&VTS Community Programme up to the end of June. This underlined the cash flow difficulties that were to become an increasing problem for FFE&VTS Community Programme personnel to deal with over the next few years. Indeed, some club project personnel even went so far as to assume that support for their cash flow inadequacies was 'part and parcel' of the service provided by the FFE&VTS Community Programme to clubs! In addition, it had become clear that Regional Directors were being drawn into the management of club project cash flows, and that they were spending more and more time supporting local Community Officers to develop systems that reconciled monies owing against money in the bank.

Also identified at the meeting was the fact that Regional Directors were, understandably, becoming increasingly busy supporting the rapid expansion of local community schemes. As a result, communications between Regional Directors and the Manchester support office were, on occasion, becoming less frequent, though it was agreed that it had been useful for this important issue had been identified at the senior management meeting.

Also discussed were the essential steps necessary to undergo the Investors in People re-assessment in November/December. **Clive Cheetham**, from the FFE&VTS, took the lead in ensuring that the necessary portfolio of evidence was available in good time, ideally by the end of September. Key, of course, was what happened to staff to help them improve their own work performance and therefore the performance of the business operation. As part of the re-assessment, certain club schemes would have to go through an "external inspection".

A positive meeting with **Paul Clouting**, Ipswich Town's Marketing and Commercial Manager, was held in mid-September and it was hoped that the club would, at long last, give serious consideration to the idea of establishing a separate local community operation in the name of the club.

The Annual Sportsmatch Awards evening was held in October 1998 at Twickenham and attended by several senior FFE&VTS Community Programme and club officials and Community Officers including **Lee Doyle** (Brentford), **Steve Ford** (Brighton and Hove Albion), **Jason Morgan** and **Matt Parish** (Charlton Athletic), **Steve Bradshaw** and **Steve Downey** (Colchester United), **Jeff Hawkins** and **Anne-Marie Clark** (Crystal Palace), **Gary Mulcahey** (Fulham), **Stuart Donnelly** (Lincoln City), **Andy Morgan** (Stoke City), **Kirk Wheeler** and **Rob Smith** (Watford) and **Jim Lowther** and **Kieron Wicks** (Wimbledon).

The Community Forum met again at the end of October at the FA's Lancaster Gate offices. In attendance were **Mike Foster** and **Nigel Pleasants** representing the PL; **Frank Hannah** and **Robin Russell** from the FA; **Andy Williamson** from the FL; and **Mickey Burns**, **Roger Reade** and **Dennis Leman** from the FFE&VTS. The main item (discussed at length) was the unanimous concern of all four 'football family' parties about Bristol City's proposed absorption of their previously successful Community Scheme into their Academy operation. This was believed to be short-sighted and likely to prove to be a bad move in the longer term. The meeting also noted the proposed re-organisation of community schemes at Leeds United and Crewe Alexandra, together with new appointments including **Lee Turnbull** at Halifax Town (newly promoted to the FL) and **Mitch Cook** at Scarborough.

Stockton-born **Lee Turnbull** had been a popular figure as a player at all his clubs having begun his career as an apprentice with Middlesbrough before later moves to Aston Villa,

Doncaster Rovers, Chesterfield, Doncaster Rovers (again), Wycombe Wanderers, Scunthorpe United and Darlington.

Mitch Cook was born in Scarborough and went on to play for several Northern clubs including Darlington, Middlesbrough, Scarborough, Halifax Town, Scarborough (again – this time on loan), Darlington, Blackpool and Hartlepool United before a further brief return to Scarborough in 1995.

The very good news about the Community Forum at this stage was that, under the excellent chairmanship of Manchester FA's **Frank Hannah**, the FFE&VTS 'partners' at meetings had settled into being collectively supportive of the Community Programme nationwide operation. This general support had been encouraged by all the respective Chief Executive Officers at the partner organisations, including **Rick Parry** at the PL (though he was to leave the PL in June 1997 in order to take up the position of Chief Executive at Liverpool Football Club).

Head of Adult and Youth Training, **Gary Naven,** continued to apply himself to the increasingly complicated nature of adult training work. Indeed, his report to the Senior Management Team Meeting in October now included separate reports on the New Deal 'Employed Option' and the "Education and Training Option'. The latter of the two reports also included details of which TECs were offering contracts to work with the FFE&VTS Community Programme and also noted that Gary was attempting to broaden horizons by working on new areas of the country including Wales and the South of England, even though overall numbers under Adult Training had very clearly and substantially reduced over the contract year 1997/8.

Tommy Wheeldon was appointed at Exeter City as **Eamonn Dolan**'s replacement after Eamonn's appointment as Youth Team Coach at the club (Eamonn sadly passed away in June 2016). Tommy was a former professional footballer who made a small number of appearances for Torquay United in 1981 and 1985.

After lengthy consideration, **Iain Leckie** had agreed to take up the position of Youth Team coach at Darlington Football Club. Replacing Iain as Community Officer would be former Darlington player **Kevan Smith**. Kevan began his playing career with Darlington before later moves to Rotherham United, Coventry City and York City. He returned to Darlington in 1989/90 and spent two more seasons with the club before moving on again to Hereford United initially on loan. He then moved to Sliema in Malta.

A survey of London-based Community Officer salaries undertaken at the end of 1998 confirmed that wages payable to London officers varied between £22,000 per annum up to a "top" wage then being paid of £30,000 per annum.

Also, for interest only, annual statistical information recorded at the time included the following:

- 1 million people were involved in scheme activities and/or events each year with approximately 30% female involvement. 900,000 of these were children and/or young people.

- 130,000 children attended school holiday courses every year

- 200,000 people attended football matches each year as a result of community scheme activities (the vast majority of whom were first-time attendees). This huge figure was obviously achieved as a direct result of the generosity of clubs in making tickets available for Community Officers use.

- Former Area Manager and Bristol City Community Officer, **Dave Bell,** was appointed as Cardiff City's new Community Officer at the end of November. He was to work with **Derek Clydesdale** who had been brought to the club by owner **Samesh Kumar**. Sadly, Dave was, in the end, only in post for under a year.

- The next 'round' of meetings exclusively for Community Officers took place in December 1998 as follows:

- 18 North East and Yorkshire Officers met at Middlesbrough Football Club on the 1st December.

- 19 Midlands Officers attended a meeting at Coventry City Football Club held on the 10th December.

- 19 South East Community Officers met up at Ashdown Forest Hotel in East Grinstead on the 11th December.

- 13 South West Community Officers met at Hereford United Football Club on the 15th December.

- 19 North West Community Officers met at Blackburn Rovers Football Club on the 16th December.

The various meetings were also attended by representatives of Burtons Biscuits (**Duncan Knight** and/or **Polly Moorsom** from Harrison Cowley) and by representatives from Adidas (**Clive Evans**, **Mally Leigh** and/or **Mark Leigh** – see Chapter 12). Also noted at the meetings was an increasing appreciation by directors of football clubs of the huge benefits of their own community operations.

Strong views were expressed by FFE&VTS Community Programme officials at all these meetings that the newly-established 'excellence' based Academies at clubs should be kept totally separate from participation-based club Community Schemes (although there could, and hopefully would, be areas of 'overlap'). Academy rules had created complications concerning young players travel whereas club Community schemes had established a clear understanding regarding which areas each club would be able to operate in to ensure that no duplication occurred. In London, for example, each local borough was 'allocated' to particular local clubs (irrespective of size or stature).

Wages for Community Schemes increased again in 1998. This, of course, represented huge expansion and growth at the time. Indeed, weekly wages paid out by the FFE&VTS Community Programme covering the six-month period from January to June 1998 totalled over £1,178,836, representing a simply huge increase from previous years. For the period from July to December 1998, total wages paid out on behalf of approximately 74[24] community projects reached £1,360,362 making a grand total for the year of £2,539,198. In addition, monthly wages were paid out to casual/monthly paid community staff to the value of £574,268 (£293,276 for January to June and £280,992 for July to December), making a grand total of £3,113,466 for the year.

The largest local schemes paid through the FFE&VTS Community Programme payroll at this time included Newcastle United and Sunderland in the North East, Manchester City and Stockport County in the North West, Coventry City and Nottingham Forest in the Midlands, Charlton Athletic, Fulham and Millwall in the London area and Bristol Rovers in the South West.

For 1998, collective turnover totalled £5,155,336 for 76 schemes, thus working out at an average turnover of £67,833 per scheme. The range at the time extended from the lowest (£9,500) to the largest (£305,000). More than 15 schemes had turnover in excess of £100,000 for the year.

The first few weeks of any New Year, including those of 1999, always brought with them huge efforts to reconcile the wages paid on behalf of locally-based Community scheme by the FFE&VTS Community Programme AND the challenge of ensuring prompt reimbursement of any amounts outstanding in respect of wages. This was a major undertaking and one that became

---

24. *A total of 18 club Community Schemes were also grant supported in 1998; all of them took responsibility for the payment of wages and PAYE (Aston Villa, Blackburn Rovers, Brentford, Brighton & Hove Albion, Chelsea, Everton, Gillingham, Leyton Orient, Lincoln City, Liverpool, Manchester United, Oxford United, Queens Park Rangers, Sheffield Wednesday, Southampton, West Ham United, Wimbledon and Wolverhampton Wanderers. During 1999, and following advice from HM Customs and Excise, agreement was reached with three clubs to move their community scheme payroll to the FFE&VTS Community Programme being Blackburn Rovers, Everton and Gillingham).*

increasingly labour-intensive as each new year of growth passed by. 1999 also brought with it a sensible idea for those club projects whose wages were being paid through the FFE&VTS payroll. Most clubs were to put in place standing orders with regular monthly payments being made to the FFE&VTS Community Programme. This was to assist what was becoming a cash flow issue for the FFE&VTS Community Programme (the scheme's bank account had gone overdrawn for the first time at the end of 1998 due to increasing payments of wages on behalf of club projects). 36 club schemes had set up appropriate standing orders by the end of August 1999 (though a further 37 separate club schemes were still to make similar arrangements at that time).

Moves towards charitable status continued as Sunderland AFC took up their interest in the idea. A meeting held with Sunderland AFC Financial Controller, **Peter Walker**, in early 1999 confirmed the huge success of the club's community operation *and* the additional fact that the community scheme at the club was now running a lottery at the club! Peter was concerned enough to want to ensure that the scheme set up proper (not-for-profit) accounts. In addition, club Director, **David Stonehouse**, was anxious to ensure that the club's community scheme was protected by being "ring fenced" and separated from the club at the earliest opportunity. Deloitte and Touché sent a representative, **Ian Roberts**, to the meeting to advise the club further on the possibilities and benefits of charitable status. After a lengthy and particularly worthwhile meeting, it was agreed that Sunderland would move their community scheme towards charitable status as soon as possible (eventually registered with the Charity Commission in August 2001).

In addition, the introduction of the National Minimum Wage Act 1998, which first introduced the national minimum wage in April 1999 (the hourly rate then was £3.60 per hour), was noted. Senior Staff member, **Pat Wilkinson,** produced a specific report which highlighted those Community Officers (mainly Assistant Officers to be fair) who would be affected and those clubs 'at risk' of breaching the law by paying below the minimum level so that they could take appropriate action as necessary.

As local schemes grew, so did potential legal problems and issues. As an example, January 1999 saw a complaint of racism levelled against a Community Officer in the South by an Assistant Community Officer. Fortunately, **Sarah Davidson,** from George Davies Solicitors, became involved in this complaint at an early stage, helping to facilitate an agreed settlement in due course.

Several London club schemes were also working with the Single Regeneration Budget funded project, though this was extremely cumbersome and complicated, notwithstanding the huge amount of bureaucracy also involved. Certainly, Regional Director **Dave Palmer** already had his hands full at this time in overseeing and supporting the fast-developing London based club schemes without adding to his ever-growing workload. Particular thanks and a great deal of credit must also properly go to **Ophelia Soares** from the Thames Gateway Youth Football Project, who looked after the Single Regeneration Budget (SRB) 3 project funds for four London community schemes at this time (Charlton Athletic, Leyton Orient, Millwall and West Ham United) and to **Graham Dodkins** who, in the end, oversaw developments at all four projects. The Thames Gateway Youth Football Project was described by Minister of Sport, **Tony Banks**, as:

> *"An excellent example of how sport can be a driving force in motivating young people and uniting individuals and their communities. It is exactly the kind of project that this government wishes to encourage."*

Work undertaken included: coaching programmes on housing estates, closer work with local Probation Services (and young offenders), truancy programmes etc.

A preliminary meeting with **Andy Hanson** from the British Council proved to be an interesting get-together, and one that would lead to the FFE&VTS Community Programme being invited to make a presentation to other European countries in Strasbourg later in the year.

News at the clubs included the fact that, at the end of February, **John Kerr** had been appointed as Chester City's new Centre of Excellence Director. Former Chester City and Queens

Park Rangers player **Brian Croft** took over as Community Officer from John. Brian had already gained some useful experience in community work during a short spell at Stockport County prior to taking up the post at Chester. Brian was a former professional footballer who began his career as an apprentice with his local club, Chester City, where he had two successful long-term spells. He also played briefly for Cambridge United, Queens Park Rangers, Shrewsbury Town (on loan), Blackpool, Torquay United and Stockport County before moving to non-league Southport.

A very positive meeting was held in mid-February with Ipswich Town Chairman **David Sheepshanks**, **Paul Clouting** and, later, **David Brooks** who was overseeing the club's community remit at the time. The club acknowledged that they hadn't been aware of all the benefits of working alongside the FFE&VTS Community Programme operation, particularly in accessing DfEE support and in securing access to additional funding. It was agreed that all details would be communicated to the club's full Board of Directors, who duly endorsed the proposals.

A meeting with **Keith Lamb** (Middlesbrough FC Chief Executive), **Alan Bage** and **George Courtney** (Community Scheme Chief Executive) led to ideas being discussed about taking forward the club's interest in developing the proposed "*Middlesbrough FC Community Centre*" at nearby Eston. Possible partners included Grangetown SRB, Redcar and Cleveland Council and the Tees Valley Development Corporation. If things were to develop, the centre would continue to be run as a registered charity (first registered in 1996), and the club's Football in the Community operation would be 'merged' with the existing Trust. The proposed chairman of the new Trust would be club Director **George Cook**. Further meetings also revealed the club's plans to set up an overarching 'umbrella' scheme (not dissimilar to the Leeds United umbrella scheme) which would bring together the club's Community Programme scheme, the Community Centre at Eston AND the Willie Maddren Centre (including several classrooms) in the East Stand at the Riverside ground which had been opened in February 1998. These were exciting plans that were immediately welcomed and endorsed by the FFE&VTS Community Programme. The agreed target date of the 1st January 2000 for the 'merger' was also agreed. Unbeknown to FFE&VTS Community Programme officials, however, the club's plans to reorganise its community affairs also led to the unfortunate redundancy of **Lawrie Pearson,** who had done such a good job for the club up to this point.

A meeting with popular ex-Wolves striker **John Richards** at Wolverhampton Wanderers also confirmed that, despite the advantages of operating their community scheme as a charitable organisation (the club confirmed they were aware of the benefits), they nonetheless wanted to continue operating their community scheme (under the watchful eye of Community Officer, **Tony Evans**) as an internal department within the club. FFE&VTS officials confirmed that this was fine, though it was suggested that the situation should be reviewed if, at any point, the club discovered that they were missing out on potential access to potential sources of external funding.

Some of the bigger club schemes were 'spreading their wings' by operating courses for children in other areas well away from their own locality. The latest clubs at this time to operate in other neighbourhoods were Everton who had set up an 'Everton Community Development Scheme' in the Sterling area of Scotland (something that had been picked up by the Scottish FA) and Leeds United who had pledged to operate across other areas of West Yorkshire. The FFE&VTS Community Programme always assisted where such "boundary disputes" arose, and where it was necessary to define "local areas" for clubs where two or more clubs were in close proximity.

Contact kindly made by **Peter Cates** from the PL led to a greater awareness of the increasing importance and emphasis being placed on child protection. As a result, all senior staff were duly issued with a document raised by the National Coaching Foundation Child Protection so that they could familiarise themselves with this important topic. Officials at the PL had gone to some considerable trouble to prepare appropriate documentation concerning child protection for the use of their Academies. The next Senior Management Team meeting (attended by all 5 Regional Directors) highlighted the main forms of abuse, the importance of clubs adopting a Child Protection Policy and Procedures (and of having a named person heading up Child Protection within each club).

The first Community Forum meeting of the New Year of 1999 saw all the 'football family' represented and agreeing to work together in preparing a response to the Football Task Force report 'Investing in the Community' via the FFE&VTS Community Programme. Interestingly enough, PFA Chief Executive, **Gordon Taylor,** confirmed the PFA's strong support for the Task Force recommendation that player involvement become a specific objective of club-run community operations and of the PFA publishing details of player community visits. Indeed, in future years the PFA Community Department, led by **John Hudson,** was to further develop strategies for ensuring the co-operation of managers (and management teams) in supporting player appearances in the local community at local clubs. In addition, comprehensive statistics concerning player appearances and examples of 'good practice' would be developed and printed for circulation to the outside world.

One other recommendation supported by the PFA was for a regular annual community awards scheme to be established on a similar basis to the former Football Trust Community Awards Scheme, thus recognising and promoting good practice.

The Community Forum agreed to set up a sub-committee in order to prepare a response to the initial draft Task Force report (to be sent to Minister of Sport, **Tony Banks MP**, when completed). Needless to say that the sub-committee strongly supported both of the PFA's recommendations.

In addition, at the Community Forum meeting, it was noted that **Dennis Leman** would be aiming to present a report on education schemes in football for the further consideration of all the partners.

Spring 1999 meetings of Officers were held as follows:
-    March 24th – North East and Yorkshire Officers at Leeds United.
-    March 26th – East Midlands Officers at Leicester City[25].
-    March 31st – North West Officers at Burnley.
-    April 2nd – West Midlands Officers at Coventry City[26].
-    April 22nd – South West Officers at Swindon Town.
-    April 23rd – South East and London Officers at Charlton Athletic.

An April 1999 meeting with **Alison Lockwood** and **David Carley** from the DfEE saw the presentation of the comprehensive report prepared by **Dennis Leman** which included the fact that 9 PL and 12 FL clubs employed teachers to deliver either 'Playing for Success' or similar curriculum-based programmes. A new generic resource pack was to be developed and include sections on:
-    The football match.
-    The players.
-    Football as a Business.
-    Fans/Supporters.
-    The stadium.
-    The World.

The DfEE were hopeful that this (as yet un-named) new venture could be launched by September (possibly in Westminster and possibly attended by a senior MP). Six clubs, who were already involved in the 'Playing for Success' initiative, had been selected as potential pilot scheme clubs (Bolton Wanderers, Leeds United, Newcastle United, Sheffield Wednesday, West Ham United and Wolverhampton Wanderers). The launch eventually went ahead at Manchester United's Old Trafford ground on the 14th April 2000.

The operation of the various employment schemes across the country was reviewed in the summer and average figures regarding recruitment under Adult Training including 'New Deal' and Youth Trainee places for 1998/1999 are detailed in "Appendix III – Table of trainees in

25. *Future meetings of Midlands based officers would be combined so that officers from the East and West Midlands attended the same meeting.*

post year by year 1994-2002"[26]. Amongst the clubs with higher than average recruitment levels during the year were projects at Huddersfield Town, Notts County, Sheffield United and West Bromwich Albion.

The actual number of participating club projects remained at 49, though lower numbers of trainees in post across New Deal, Adult and Youth Training were again evident.

One of the most dynamic and forward-looking Community Officers of the 1990's was **Neil Watson**, Senior Officer at the Leyton Orient Community Sports Trust. Neil was constantly in touch with FFE&VTS Community Programme officials about the rapid developments taking place at Brisbane Road and the proposed move for the Trust towards charitable status (the Trust had been registered as a charity in September 1998). Not only that, but Neil was keen to establish an appropriate working relationship between the Trust and Leyton Orient Football Club (then under the ownership of **Barry Hearn,** the well-known sporting promoter who was primarily responsible for snooker's success since the 1970's). Indeed, when the club announced plans to build a new South Stand (off Buckingham Road), Neil was quick to recognise that he would be happy to re-site the Trust in offices under the stand and to pay the club what was felt to be an appropriate rent for the use of the offices (later fixed at around £8,000 per annum, a colossal amount for community schemes in those days, and an action that breached the agreement between clubs and the FFE&VTS whereby clubs were to provide office accommodation for their community schemes free of charge. It is understood that the proposed 'charge' was later withdrawn pending agreement about an appropriate 'contra' deal).

Admirably, Neil also led the way for sports clubs (especially football clubs) to play an increased part in social interventions in their local communities and the FFE&VTS Community Programme was more than happy to assist him in this where appropriate.

Neil moved on to become Director within the Positive Futures programme in 2002 and, some years on from that, he was appointed as Director and Head of Programmes at Substance, an organisation that gives organisations the framework, tools and insight needed to increase the understanding and impact of their own work. Neil's very able Assistant, **Grant Cornwell**, took over as Head of the Leyton Orient Community Sports Trust.

The Final of the Predator Community Cup for under 11's was held at Wembley on April 18th, 1999 prior to the Auto Windscreens Shield Match between Millwall and Wigan Athletic (won by Wigan by 1-0).

The inaugural Predator Community Cup Competition for Under 13's girls saw Collegiate High School from Blackpool win the first ever all girls tournament.

The 1998/9 Smoby Monneret (second) Championship, held at Wembley, saw former Crystal Palace and Sheffield Wednesday striker, **Mark Bright**, present the trophy and medals (see Appendix V for details of Competition winners).

Figures for participation in the three national competitions operated during season 1998/9 were most encouraging as follows:

Predator Community Cup Competition for Primary/Junior School boys and girls in the Under 11 age group:

    78 Community Schemes

    1825 teams

    £13,100 paid to club schemes

Predator Community Cup Competition for Secondary School girls in the Under 13 age group:

77 Community Schemes

703 teams

£5,900 paid to club schemes

Smoby Monneret Table Football Championship in association with Wagon Wheels:

---

26. *The figures included the numbers of Youth trainees in post equivalent to approximately 11.25 trainees per week (an increase on the previous year). The figures also saw a specific drop in TFW trainees in post from 87 per week at the start of the contract year to approximately 27 by the end of the year..*

84 Community Schemes

6,793 participants

£3,425 paid to club schemes

The end of April 1999 saw the annual PFA 'Player of the Year' Awards Evening at the Grosvenor House Hotel in London. Attending as guests of the FFE&VTS Community Programme were **Mike Reynolds, Simon Scott** and **Charles Reynolds** (Sportsmatch), **Adrian Mayes** and **David Yarr** (Smoby Monneret). A full table for ten representatives of Burtons Biscuits (Wagon Wheels) and their agents Harrison Cowley was also booked (the ten representatives included **Paul Chmielewski, Duncan Knight, Adrian Sharpe** and **Alan Twigg**). Of particular interest in the Professional Football Annual produced for the Awards Evening was a quote for the future about Football's work in the community and the "utopia" it was looking for:

> *"Utopia (would be) a community-based scheme with sporting, social and educational. Programmes operating at most clubs. And if Football in the Community can obtain the necessary resources to fund that dream then society, as well as football, will benefit."*

At the clubs, **Mike Cook** took up the post of Centre of Excellence Director at Cambridge United. Mike's former Assistant **David Toombs** took over as Senior Community Officer/Head of Community.

Perry Suckling joined the Leyton Orient Community Sports Trust team as an Assistant Community Officer. Perry was a well-known former goalkeeper whose career began as an apprentice with Coventry City before later moves to Manchester City, Crystal Palace, West Ham United (on loan), Brentford (also on loan), Watford and Doncaster Rovers. His involvement at Orient lasted some six months or so before he was recruited as a goalkeeping coach by the FA. One highlight for Perry during his short period of employment at Orient, however, was when he met **Her Majesty the Queen** at one of the Orient Community Sport Programme's activities.

Derek Mann left the post of Community Officer at Shrewsbury Town at the end of April 1999 in order to join Wolverhampton Wanderers as a Community coach working alongside **Tony Evans**.

Barry Gordine was appointed as Reading's new Community Officer. As a player, Barry had joined Sheffield United from non-league Gravesend & Northfleet in 1968. Whilst he didn't play for the Blades first team, he did move to Oldham Athletic later that year, making over 80 league appearances over a three-year period.

A two-day induction at the Manchester office was arranged for recently appointed Community Officers on the 19th and 20th May. In attendance were **Ian Ormondroyd** (Bradford City), **Brian Croft** (Chester City), **Kevan Smith** (Darlington), **Geoff Crudgington** (Plymouth Argyle) and **Barry Gordine** (Reading).

In something of an end-of-season reshuffle, **Rick Passmoor** left Scunthorpe United to become **Mick Ferguson**'s Assistant at Leeds United. The vacant position he left behind at Scunthorpe went to **Lee Turnbull** who moved from his post as Community Officer at Halifax Town. This suited Lee who had been commuting to Halifax from his home in Doncaster. Both Rick and Lee became top class Community Officers in the longer term in view of their hard work, dedication and enthusiasm.

The summer of 1999 saw a comprehensive 'review' of match programme coverage of the Community Programme sponsors which confirmed that there was real "value for money' for any would be sponsors in future. Indeed, not only was the coverage assessed but even the size of the Community Programme logo as it appeared in programmes was measured (ranging from 1.0 cm to 5.0 cm) so that a 'fair value' could be placed on the coverage received during the previous season.

A summer meeting of the Burnley FC Community Programme Management Forum and chaired by club Chairman, **Frank Teasdale,** (with club Chief Executive, **Andy Watson** also in attendance) confirmed that the ever-enthusiastic **Dean Ramsdale** should take on not only responsibility for the operation of the 'outreach' Community Programme but also the operation of the new Leisure Centre at Turf Moor. Dean therefore became "Leisure and Community Manager". Dean's Assistant, the equally capable **Anthony Barlow**, would, at the same time, be promoted to a more senior role taking more responsibility within the Community Programme scheme.

Also, in the summer of 1999, **David Deacon** (Managing Director at Portsmouth FC) approached the scheme to investigate whether Portsmouth Football Club could re-commence working with the FFE&VTS Community Programme.

Steve Lister left his post as Community Officer at Barnsley Football Club in mid-June 1999. His replacement (in the autumn) was former Rotherham United Community Officer and (later) Youth Development Officer, **Fraser Foster**.

New appointments noted in the summer of 1999 included:

- Former footballer, **Tibor Szabo,** at Halifax Town. Tibor made a small number of playing appearances for Bradford City in the 1977/78 season.
- **Brian Williams** at Shrewsbury Town (Brian had previously been the Community Officer at Hereford United).
- **Mike Smith** at Stockport County (Previous Community Officer, **Andy Kilner**, had been appointed as the club's Manager).
- **Mark Ashton** at West Bromwich Albion (in what would be Mark's second spell as the club's Community Officer).

It is also worth noting the names of some of the hard-working Assistant Community Officers who were making positive impressions at their clubs including:

- **Lyn Forster** (Blackpool)
- **Dave Jupp** (Brighton & Hove Albion)
- **Nick Harrison** (Burnley)
- **Dave Ridgeon** (Charlton Athletic)
- **Ben Bartlett** and **Steve Bartlett** (Colchester United)
- **Sarah Newbould** (Doncaster Rovers)
- **Marc Richardson** (Hull City)
- **Chris Hodges** and **Angela White** (Leicester City[27])
- **Fleur Collier** and **Marc Maddocks** (Manchester City)
- **Annette Campbell** and **Lou Waller** (Millwall)
- **George Shipley** (Newcastle United). Though he was born in Newcastle, George began his playing career as an apprentice with Southampton before later moves to Reading (on loan), Lincoln City, Charlton Athletic and Gillingham.
- **Scott Stackman** (Northampton Town). Scott was a former Northampton Town apprentice who made a single substitute appearance for the club.
- **Ian Cosier**, **Dave Wardle** and **Gary Williamson** (Stockport County)
- **Rob Smith** (Watford). Rob would go on to become a long-serving, respected and very capable Head of Community/Community Director at Watford.
- **Clint Roberts** (West Bromwich Albion)

The summer also saw the unveiling of the Walter Tull memorial wall in a garden of remembrance at Northampton Town's new Sixfields Stadium. This followed important work, much of which was undertaken by club Director **Brian Lomax** and **Phil Vasili** (who spent considerable time researching the background of Walter Tull) both of whom were keen to ensure that some form

---

27. *The end of the 1998/9 season saw the Leicester City Community Programme scheme continue its excellent work and its rapid expansion with new sponsors such as Global Self Drive and the local Midland Bank facilitating some of its wider growth. At the same time, the scheme was also successful in expanding its football development work with girls and women.*

of permanent recognition was secured for Tull's contribution as one of the first ever professional footballers of mixed heritage. Walter Tull played for Clapton, Tottenham Hotspur and, of course, Northampton Town (for whom he played between 1911 and 1914). He was killed in action in the First World War in 1918.

Initial discussions about working with the English Federation of Disability Sport (EFDS) with **Tony Fitzsimmons** took place, though it was noted that it was regrettable that there was very little in the way of funding available to support this sort of dedicated work. In addition to discussions with the EFDS, the FFE&VTS Community Programme Scheme was approached by several charitable organisations to see if they could assist. Amongst those approaching the Scheme were 'Strip-4-Shelter', 'Make a Difference Day' (organised by Community Service Volunteers, a volunteering charity), 'Time to Care' (Family Holiday Association) and others.

The 1999/2000 football season got underway as scheme officials learned that **Barry Powell** had been offered a three-year contract managing the club at Aberystwyth Town Football Club in Wales and that he was going to accept their offer, thus leaving the post of Community Officer at Coventry City available. In the end, **Martin Tully** was successful in becoming the club's next Community Officer.

Darren Hare (previously employed through the Scheme at Kent CFA) also took up the post of Community Officer at Gillingham.

After only a short time in post, Manchester-born **Jason Beckford** left the Wigan Scheme to become a Community coach at the club where he had started his playing career in 1987, Manchester City. His replacement was **Bill Collier,** who had already proved to be very popular indeed with club officials.

Good news was received from **Brian Croft** at Chester City who confirmed that he had secured new, significant support on a local basis from the Duke of Westminster which would help guarantee the future of the Community Scheme at the club in the longer term.

Following contact from **Arthur Heywood** at newly promoted Cheltenham Town, it was agreed to set up a meeting aimed at discussing the possibility of the club setting up a new community scheme in partnership with the FFE&VTS Community Programme.

September also saw **Alan Green** interview **Roger Reade** about the Community Programme scheme on Radio 5 Live (an interview that was kindly arranged by **Adnan Nawaz**). This opportunity was much appreciated, and one that Alan himself said that he enjoyed as he had previously been unaware of the full extent of the work being undertaken by clubs in their local communities. One story mentioned during the interview related to the rise of **Kevin Kilbane** (now a BBC Commentator on football) who played for St Gregory's School in Preston in the Community Programme schools 6-a-side tournament as a 10 year-old boy back in 1987 and who went on to enjoy a successful playing career with, amongst others, Preston North End, Everton and the Republic of Ireland.

The end of September saw a visit from the dynamic **Jim Roddy** and his colleague **Kevin Frael** from Derry City Football Club. Jim and his colleagues at the club played a major role over the next few years in ensuring that the club embraced the whole community of Derry/Londonderry.

Wolves Community Officer **Tony Evans** announced that he had been successful in accessing a significant amount of money to support new proposals in Wolverhampton to combat teenage pregnancy in the city area, as part of a partnership arrangement which had been formally launched by **Tessa Jowell** (then Minister of Health).

The FA also confirmed that they were to launch their Charter Mark (quality standard) for Schools and for Holiday courses in October 1999 (although this was later re-named the "Charter Standard" award).

The first Regional meetings of the new football season for Community Officers were held in the Autumn of 1999 as follows:

- South West meeting at Bristol Rovers Football Club on the 9th September (a total of 9 clubs were represented at the meeting though there were no officers attending from Cardiff City or Hereford United).

- South East meeting at the Ashdown Forest Hotel in East Grinstead (near Crawley) on the 17th September.

- North West meeting at Burnley Football Club on the 22nd September (a total of 18 clubs were represented including **Nicola Murphy** (representing Blackburn Rovers), **Alan Johnson** and **Ted Sutton** (from Everton), **Eddie Leach** (representing Manchester United) and **Bill Collier** (newly appointed Community Officer at Wigan Athletic).

- 18 clubs were represented at the North East and Yorkshire meeting held at Grimsby Town Football Club on the 29th September, including newly appointed Officers **Tibor Szabo** (Halifax Town) and **Lee Turnbull** (Scunthorpe United).

- Midlands meeting at Stoke City Football Club on the 1st October when 15 club Community Schemes were represented (Aston Villa were represented by FOUR Officers being **Ron Wylie**, **Warwick Adams**, **Nigel Macrow** and **Allan Thomason**!

Noted at the meetings was the fact that the Scheme now employed around 400 community officers on a full-time basis, with an additional 1,500 part-time and/or casual workers. A topic of debate at the meetings were the Football Task Force recommendations which prompted much discussion amongst Community Officers, especially where they had experienced difficulties securing the support of players from within their first team squads for community activities.

Contact from **Gary Mulcahey** at Fulham confirmed that the club intended to make all of the 18 women involved in playing for Fulham's women's team fully professional. Whilst Gary's enquiry was referred to the PFA (so that possible membership of the PFA could be considered for the players), it is worth recording that this was a real "red-letter day" for the further and continuing growth and development of women's football.

The 1999 Sportsmatch Awards Ceremony, with guest of honour **Kate Hoey MP** (then Minister of Sport), was held on the 11th November at Lords Cricket Ground and was attended by all FFE&VTS Community Programme senior officers and Regional Directors. **Gordon Taylor** (PFA), **Mickey Burns** (FFE&VTS) and **Clive Evans** from Adidas were also in attendance. Mickey received a special award from Kate for the FFE&VTS Community Programme's enormous contribution to grass roots sport.

A November meeting with **Andrew McAteer** from the Irish FA proved to be more than worthwhile. Indeed, it was rewarding to know that, in addition to the Scottish FA and the Welsh FA now looking long and hard at the way the Community Programme operated, the Irish FA were also aware and interested enough to make notes of how the scheme's success had been achieved.

Dennis Leman was kind enough to arrange a further two-day induction for newly appointed Community Officers also in November. In attendance were **Fraser Foster** (Barnsley), **David Toombs** (Cambridge United), **Darren Hare** (Gillingham) and **Bill Collier** (Wigan Athletic).

Around 130 people from all over Europe attended the "*Harnessing the Potential*" conference held in Strasburg between the 21st and the 23rd November organised by the British Council. **Dennis Leman** and **Roger Reade** attended and gave a short presentation about the work of the FFE&VTS Community Programme scheme to date. The presentation was communicated to all those present via interpreters and received a particularly positive response.

Summarising at the end of the presentation the following statement was made:

> "*Football can be a powerful force for good, especially in motivating and inspiring young people and in uniting individuals and their communities. In time, the true worth of football may become more fully appreciated especially as it is quite clear that football can change peoples' lives for the better.*"

Trips abroad were few and far between, though, the same year, **Richard Finney** kindly agreed to represent the FFE&VTS Community Programme and to make a presentation about the FFE&VTS Community Programme's work, alongside several officials from the FA, on a short trip to Lagos, Nigeria as part of the FA International Development Programme.

Towards the end of the year, **Mike Trotter** left Leicester City. Replacing Mike was one of his very able assistants, **Craig White**.

Ipswich Town also indicated that they would like to work with the FFE&VTS Community Programme by confirming that their lead Community Officer would be **David Brooks** (who had been overseeing community matters at the club). Later Community Officers included **Carolyn Shaw** and **Trevor Cox**.

The Christmas regional meetings of all Community Officers took place in December (with opportunities to socialise after the meetings!) as follows:

- 8th December: Midlands Group at Notts County FC.
- 9th December: South East Group at Charlton Athletic FC.
- 10th December: North East Group: Leeds United FC.
- 15th December: North West Group: Norbreck Castle Hotel, Blackpool.
- 16th December: South East Group: Swansea City FC.

A great deal of work was increasingly being undertaken by Regional Directors in ensuring that local club Community schemes had their own sets of independent accounts produced each year. For the first time, it was possible to analyse separate and printed accounts at least 70 local community schemes with year-end dates in 1998 (approximately 18 clubs still maintained their accounts as internal departments within their respective clubs at this time).

For 1999, turnover at 79 locally based Community schemes reached £6,798,447 – i.e. an average of £86,056 per project. The largest turnovers were reported at Chelsea, Leyton Orient and Sunderland whose turnover was in excess of £300,000. The smallest turnovers at the time were reported at schemes at Chester City, Darlington, Doncaster Rovers, Hereford United, Kettering Town, Lincoln City, Mansfield Town, Scarborough and Scunthorpe United.

It should also be noted from the FFE&VTS Community Programme payroll that wages paid out on behalf of local community schemes increased massively again from 1998 to 1999. This, once again, represented huge further growth on the previous year. Indeed, weekly wages paid out by the FFE&VTS Community Programme covering the six-month period from January to June 1999 totalled £1,538,103 and for July to December 1999, £1,795,996, thus representing a further massive increase. So, for the period from January to December 1999, total weekly wages paid out on behalf of the 79 community projects reached a grand total for the full year of £3,334,099. In addition, separately paid monthly wages totalled £530,747 for the period January to June and £492,087 for July to December. Total monthly wages for the year therefore reached £1,022,834. The grand total of wages paid during the year was therefore a mammoth £4,356,933.

All in all, and thirteen and a half years since the scheme had been founded, all was looking good concerning the future growth and operation of the Community Programme in Professional Football as the new millennium approached....

CHAPTER 12
NATIONAL SPONSORS: WAGON WHEELS

THE PIZZA HUT NATIONAL SPONSORSHIP arrangements had been formally concluded at the end of August 1996. However, a meeting with **Jerry Charter** and **Alison Lucas** from Burtons Gold Medal Biscuits and with **Brian Roach** and **Ruth Syszkowski** from their agents, Harrison Cowley, at the end of May 1996 saw real interest in the sponsorship opportunity pursued. What seemed to be of special interest were the promotional opportunities that had been put together with Pizza Hut including the grand launch, the use of the Skills Cards (and the strong support of the top players), the Pizza Hut 'Soccer Days', television advertising, the resource and kit packs issued to primary and junior schools together with the full range of coverage afforded via match programmes, certificates, letter headed paper, newsletters etc. At this point, it is also worth recording the significant hard work undertaken by **Brian Marwood** in talking not only to Harrison Cowley but also to Burton's Gold Medal Biscuits. Brian set out to deliver a top-class successor to Pizza Hut, and he was to achieve this when the deal with Burtons was signed off.

From Burton's perspective at the time, their total turnover then was around £200 million per annum with Wagon Wheels being their 'flagship' seller. One of the ideas they came up with, following the meeting, was to invest their overall television advertising budget into the sponsorship that would exclusively promote the Wagon Wheels brand. One thing was made clear from the outset, led by Jerry and Alison, Burtons were very keen indeed on developing the idea of becoming exclusive national sponsors. Indeed, a 'follow-up' meeting within a week with **Brian Roach**, confirmed the interest and took things forward to the next stage.

The draft contract was carefully considered at a meeting held in August and additional points were noted as follows:

- Burton's Gold Medal Biscuits wanted the guarantee of a total of six key activities to be incorporated in the agreement (and added as an Appendix to the contract). Ideas put forward included a young journalist/football broadcaster of the year competition; a Mother's Day competition (both to commence in early 1997); more card collections (similar to the Pizza Hut Skills Cards) the first of which should be launched officially in Spring 1997; a Team Kit design competition (to be launched in May 1997); a wrapper collection and reward scheme (to be launched in the autumn of 1997) together with the provision of 'free product' to all local community schemes at holiday courses.

- An internal launch event (and, later, a separate external national launch event) would be supported and was to be followed up by six separate area meetings before the end of 1996.

- The Pizza Hut contract terminated on 30th September 1996, leaving a clear three-month period for all Pizza Hut branding[28] to be removed up and down the country before ensuring that the new Burtons Biscuits branding would appear at the start of 1997.

- Regular liaison meetings would be held that would also involve representatives of Burtons' agents Harrison Cowley.

Until the interest from Burtons became concrete, other presentations, following work commissioned via **Keith and Alison Daniell** from the Media Group, continued to be made to

---

28. *Pizza Hut branding was noted to be included on mugs, clipboards, brass plaques, resource packs, letter headed paper (various national and local designs), compliments slips, personal cards, footballs, equipment packs, match programmes, application forms, certificates, tee-shirts, pin badges, enamel badges, newsletters etc.*

well-known organisations and potential sponsors. These included videos, folders and newsletters, all of which had been circulated/made available to all would-be community scheme friendly potential sponsors since the spring of 1995.

In mentioning The Media Group, their involvement was not only welcome and timely but also extremely important in terms of raising the Scheme's general awareness and understanding of the importance of positive press, media and public relations. In particular, increasing press and media coverage for the scheme, plus managing occasional complaints, meant that FFE&VTS Community Programme senior managers, to a certain extent at least, leant on the professional expertise provided by The Media Group. Indeed, The Media Group's involvement was to extend to cover media training for senior managers, the production of much more professionally produced news magazines together with all their existing added-value involvement in launch and other events, the preparation of the excellent resource packs etc.

Managing Director of The Media Group, **Keith Daniell**, said:

> *"Like most people involved in the Football in the Community Scheme, I firmly believed in the project. I've always loved football and at last football was organising itself in putting something back. Although it was clearly a time when the politics of football were so incredibly divisive, clubs were clearly onside with supporting their community schemes. Not only that but people were doing their level best to support the broader development of the Scheme's work. For us, it was a real pleasure to provide support in a comparatively new aspect in what was a thoroughly enjoyable time for us all. Plus, and this shouldn't be underestimated, everyone was supportive – certainly in my experience. I don't think we ever got pushed back: not by the big-name players, the managers or the media."*

Keith, Alison and everyone at The Media Group really pulled together to provide essential support that would stand the Scheme in good stead for future growth.

Burton's also undertook considerable research into the opportunities that might become available, even setting up a formal 'site visit' to Old Trafford at the end of October 1996, coincidentally also the time when the contract was signed. The agreement was for three years between 1ˢᵗ January 1997 and the 31ˢᵗ December 1999 and was worth a cash total of £750,000 (£250,000 per year) plus added investment in the various events/activities coordinated over the term of the agreement. As already discussed, the agreement also recognised the appointment of Harrison Cowley as Burton Biscuits' agents.

Burtons were extremely supportive in developing three separate sets of collectable cards (given away with packs of Wagon Wheels) with one set of cards developed during each of the three years:

- Skills Cards featuring **Alan Shearer** (goalscoring), **Niall Quinn** (heading), **Colin Hendry** (tackling), **Georgi Kinkladze** (dribbling), **Lee Sharpe** (wing play), **David James** (goalkeeping), **Gareth Southgate** (sweeping), **Pat Nevin** (crossing), **Matthew Le Tissier** (passing), **Andy Hinchcliffe** (corner kicks), **Gary McAllister** (free kicks) and **Julian Dicks** (penalty kicks). It should also be noted that a framed set of the cards was presented to each player as a thank you for their support (although two players managed to drop and smash their sets, so they requested new framed versions, which were duly provided!)

- England World Cup 'Dream Team' cards featuring **Gordon Banks**, **Gary Neville**, **Stuart Pearce**, **Sol Campbell**, **Gareth Southgate** (again), **Paul Ince**, **David Beckham**, **Bryan Robson**, **Alan Shearer** (again), **Geoff Hurst**, **Bobby Charlton** and **Bobby Moore**.

- 'Super Striker' cards featuring **Gianfranco Zola**, **Robbie Fowler**, **Dion Dublin**, **Teddy Sheringham**, **Emile Heskey**, **Darren Huckerby**, **Danny Cadamarteri**, **John Hartson**, **Duncan Ferguson**, **Steve Bull**, **Kevin Phillips** and **Chris Sutton**.

By November 1996, a draft contract had been prepared, shared and further discussed not only with representatives of Burtons Biscuits but also with the full FFE&VTS Board of Trustees/Directors.

One thing that was noticeable was the proactive stance adopted by Burtons Biscuits staff, especially **Jerry Charter**, **Alison Lucas** and **Richelle Flanagan**.

Discussions in November also agreed to adopt the Football in the Community logo, duly underlined with the Wagon Wheels logo. Wagon Wheels certificates, banners, plastic logos (for classrooms at clubs), "empty belly" posters, baseball caps, sweatshirts and even lunch boxes adorned with suitable promotional panels were all ordered with the new logo. In addition, **Richard Finney** agreed to supply the necessary wording for the first collection of Skills cards. Everything was looking very positive indeed at this point.

That is, of course, apart from the Wagon Wheels certificates which contained a red and blue alternative striped background. Inevitably, these certificates were very well received by Community Officers across the country and especially at Crystal Palace (whose colours have traditionally been red and blue, and often stripes), but not so well received by many of Palace's neighbour clubs, notably their near neighbours and 'rivals' Charlton Athletic and Wimbledon! Suffice to say that a new design for the certificates <u>without</u> the red and blue stripes was adopted almost immediately!

It was also agreed that the external (national) launch would be held on the 16th January 1997 at Stamford Bridge, home of Chelsea Football Club, and that a 'working party' meeting of Community Officers would be established at the end of January (the first having been held in September 1996 following the suggestions put forward by Wagon Wheels/Harrison Cowley).

Meanwhile, the internal launch event was held at Manchester United's Old Trafford on the 11th December 1996 when **Roger Reade** and **Alison Lucas** addressed several Community Officers plus representatives of Burtons Gold Medal Biscuits. Both confirmed at the meeting how genuinely excited they were with what lay ahead.

As agreed, 1997 saw the introduction of the first of the six "activities" being the Mother's Day and Young Journalist competitions with terrific support from local Community Officers who were also genuinely excited with the new pro-active arrangements underway with Wagon Wheels.

An exciting meeting with representatives of *Shoot* magazine (including editor **Dave Smith**), that had been set up by Harrison Cowley, promised a great deal in terms of 'partnership' working, though for various reasons, more longer-term arrangements were not in the end possible (partly due to a "re-structuring" at the magazine publishers). In addition, at the same meeting, Wagon Wheels representatives confirmed that they were to be present at the "Match of the Day – Live" event to be held at the start of April. Here again, the key point to note is that it was terrific that the sponsors were being so positively proactive.

The idea of a 'Working Party' of Community Officers was a great success, with at least seven meetings staged before the start of September 1997. Amongst those Community Officers who attended these meetings were: **Ian Knight** (Grimsby Town/Sheffield Wednesday), **Jim Hicks** (Millwall), **Barry Powell** (Coventry City), **Mike Cook** (Cambridge United), **Andy Kilner** (Stockport County), **Bob Oates** (Sunderland), **Chris Whalley** (Reading), **Dave Ryan** (Manchester United), **Kirk Wheeler** (Watford), **Lee Doyle** (Brentford), **Gordon Staniforth** (York City), **Emlyn Brown** (Queens Park Rangers), **Alan Young** and, later, **Graham Moran** (both from Notts County).

The March meeting agreed to consider the various promotional activities undertaken, with some useful points put forward and agreed. As an example, **Barry Powell** (Community Officer at Coventry City) suggested that the 'Design a Kit' competition[29] should be restricted to Primary and Junior Schools only in view of the difficulties of approaching secondary schools. Barry also expressed his delight at just how proactive Wagon Wheels were already. He said that he was already very busy indeed supporting the various events put forward by the national sponsors! It was also noted that the first in the Wagon Wheels series of skills cards were to be launched at the forthcoming 'Match of the Day Live' event at the NEC in Birmingham between the 3rd-6th April.

---

29. *There were three winners in the 'Design a Kit' competition, one of whom, Steven Stewart, came from Aberdeen! The other winners were Stephen Jennings (from Birmingham) and Tom Gill (from Leicester).*

Jim Hicks (Millwall's Senior Community Officer) also suggested that the excellent lunch boxes provided by Wagon Wheels should only be issued to primary school children as they weren't really appropriate for older children (e.g. of secondary school age).

One other benefit for locally based Community Officers (and the local community!) was the excellent access to 'free product' – i.e. Wagon Wheels biscuits which were generously distributed to club based Community schemes throughout the duration of the sponsorship.

As March moved into April, the PFA also considered the fact that Marketing Manager, **Alison Lucas,** had expressed an interest in attending the PFA Player of the Year Awards Dinner to be held on April 13th. Historically, the Dinner had always been men-only. On this occasion, her request was turned down, but it would be nice to think that this issue being brought to the fore led to the realisation by the PFA hierarchy, within only a few years, that it was essential for the PFA to be seen to be encouraging the attendance of women at the Dinner.

Spring 1997 also saw a deal done via a promotional agency run by **Mary Foster-Berry** to establish a table football competition sponsored by French toy makers Smoby Monneret which, it was felt, local community schemes could establish in areas where they had previously experienced difficulties in engaging with particular groups. The key benefit for locally based community schemes was the fact that each scheme would receive a football table worth several hundred pounds! Meetings with Mary and her colleague, **Patrick Harrison**, were always positive and certainly helped to take things forward smoothly to local Community Officers.

After the success in negotiating separate sponsorship deals with Burtons Gold Medal Biscuits, Panini and Smoby Monneret, sincere thanks were expressed to former PFA Commercial Executive, **Brian Marwood** (who had by now joined Nike UK) and to his replacement at the PFA, **Garry Nelson**.

At the same time, **Paul Power**, who, by now, was working for the PFA coaching department, indicated that he was to join Manchester City in a coaching capacity. He was to take up a new role within the club's Academy and left the PFA on the 30th May.

A meeting in June looked at the various activities that were being developed by Wagon Wheels (backed by their agents, Harrison Cowley) and the FFE&VTS Community Programme. New ideas were plentiful and one idea that was to get off the ground was the idea of a "Prime Minister's press gang" (later to be re-titled "Prime-Minister's Young Journalist Competition"). This would involve a competition for children to come up with the best questions to be posed to the Prime Minister (should they have the chance to meet him). Amazingly, this idea not only went forward but it also saw eight lucky children have the chance to travel to Number 10 Downing Street to meet Prime Minister, **Tony Blair**. Whilst the opportunity was not to present itself until sometime much later in 1999, the huge amount of work undertaken by **Kate Garvey** in the Prime-Minister's office must also be acknowledged.

As far as the arrangements with Wagon Wheels, everything seemed to be going particularly well. Invariably when things are going so well, something happens to disrupt things! In July, **Jerry Charter** (who had driven forward the Wagon Wheels sponsorship with huge enthusiasm and commitment up to this point) announced that he was to leave[30]. FFE&VTS Community Programme officials at first feared the worst, especially given a similar experience a few years earlier when **Steve Dunn** had left Pizza Hut. That said, staff at Wagon Wheels seemingly remained positive and, at a July liaison meeting, were even noted to be looking at plans for a World Cup collection of skills cards to be put together in 1998 (to coincide with the next World Cup to be held in France).

Ian Mellor (also working with the PFA's commercial arm) announced in July that, following lengthy discussions with representatives of Adidas and Nike, separate and substantial offers had been made by both companies to supply kit and equipment to community schemes. It was noted that the Board were to consider both offers in due course but that a possible start date for the

---

30. It was later discovered that **Jerry Charter** was to move to Topps who, at the time, were producing collections of soccer cards.

new arrangements could be as soon as the 1ˢᵗ January 1998. This obviously represented still more good news (even though it was acknowledged at an early stage that not all clubs would be able to support either arrangement in view of their own local kit/equipment arrangements). The offer made by Adidas would also embrace support for the YT programme run by the FFE&VTS (the deal was subject to a minimum of 75% of all club projects supporting the Adidas deal overall. The following year, once the deal with Adidas was in place, the actual percentage was recorded at 76% of clubs taking up the Adidas deal).

August 1997 saw the first meeting following the departure of **Jerry Charter** from Burtons Gold Medal Biscuits. This meant that this was an extremely important meeting which could define the future relationship for the sponsorship deal. Attending were representatives of Burtons, Harrison Cowley and the FFE&VTS Community Programme. Amongst those attending on behalf of Harrison Cowley were **Nichola Cain** and **Polly Moorsom**. Special tribute was paid at the meeting to Deputy Chief Administrator, **Dennis Leman,** who had worked exceptionally hard ("behind the scenes" as it were) to ensure that all necessary information requested by Wagon Wheels was properly collated and put together, often despite there being real difficulties amongst certain Community Officers in preparing information requested.

Issues reviewed at the meeting included:

-    The Smoby Monneret Table Football Competition for 1997/8. Burtons were to review their decision as to whether to support the competition (or not) given that the community/ Wagon Wheels logo would be widely promoted as part of this new activity. In the end it was agreed that the competition would be run in the name "*Smoby Monneret Table Football Championship in association with Wagon Wheels.*"

-    Audit of publicity. This was something that Burtons had expressed interest in on the basis that they could then try and gauge the impact of their sponsorship, though the actual "mechanics" as to how it would be measured hadn't been finalised. Amongst measures to be considered were: the frequency, size and use of the joint logo; coverage in the press, media and match programmes; photographs, application and other forms; promotional leaflets and brochures; other materials such as footballs, tee-shirts, bibs etc. Burton's initial attempts at quantifying these aspects were based around a points system which, in truth, didn't really do justice to the coverage received. After lengthy discussions, it was agreed to check and finalise the first six-month summary, at which point further discussions could be held.

-    Plans for the World Cup cards in 1998 were well on track and support had been confirmed from all the former England players who were to be involved (cheques regarding donations to charities selected by each former player had also been prepared). It was noted that the skills cards promotion in 1997 had led to a significant increase in brand share for Wagon Wheels (up to 10% in one month) given the popularity of the cards.

-    Other issues included attention to the proposed football "fun books" (28 page booklets full of facts, figures, quizzes and competitions); the 'Design-a-Kit competition; the sport sponsorship deal with Adidas (which would enhance the Wagon Wheels arrangements and contribute to raising brand awareness) and holiday courses (including arrangements for Burtons staff to visit certain courses); the now annual Mother's Day competitions and the Prime Minister Young Journalist/"Question Time" competition.

Following up on this meeting, and with the support of **Alison Lucas** and **Rachael Allison** from Burtons (both of whom had been very supportive and positive indeed), it was agreed that a formal letter would be sent to all Community Officers seeking their support in promoting the agreed new activities. Feedback from a meeting with **Brian Roach** in November 1997 confirmed that the fun books had been particularly successful and very popular amongst young people. A further review meeting in November looked at the many different projects that were underway at the time and the visits by Burtons Biscuits personnel, firstly, to view certain holiday courses and, secondly, to attend several meetings of Officers.

In relation to the Smoby Monneret Table Football Competition for 1997/8, it was agreed to stage the Final in April 1998 at the PFA's London restaurant, "Football Football". England player, **David Beckham**, attended the first finals when he was kind enough to present the prizes and trophies to all the participants. The winner of the first ever Table Football Competition was **Martin Hiley** (who had won the local tournament run by Southampton Football Club) and the main prize was for him and his father to attend an England match at the World Cup Finals in France in the summer.

Thanks to the extensive involvement of the PFA Commercial team, other commercial opportunities also presented themselves. As an example, meetings were held with **Simon Sheard** and **Ian Marsh** from Pontins and, understanding the arrangements with Wagon Wheels, a suitable offer was made which would allow locally based community schemes to offer holidays as prizes within their local communities.

The start of 1998 saw Burtons' representatives respond positively to the appointment of **Richard Finney** as the Scheme's first Marketing Director. He would now become the pivot around which the sponsorship would operate, becoming the sole point of liaison for Burtons, Harrison Cowley and for other sponsors too. Given the increasing shift in the importance of ensuring that all sponsors were fully catered for, this was a significant and positive change in the scheme's structure that went down well with all sponsors.

The next 'Working Party' meeting of Community Officers was held at Coventry City's Highfield Road ground in March. Community Officers in attendance were: **Dean Ramsdale** (Burnley), **Mike Cook** (Cambridge United), **Graham Moran** (Notts County), **Julian Winter** (Grimsby Town), **Dave Ryan** (Manchester United), **Andy Kilner** (Stockport County), **Barry Powell** (Coventry City) and **Kirk Wheeler** (Watford). Particular focus was given to the various and numerous activities being promoted by Wagon Wheels. There was also a lengthy discussion about the possibility of making an inflatable target on behalf of the sponsors which could be used at every community scheme. This led to the Wagon Wheels inflatable "target ring" becoming very popular around the country (The target ring was launched in the press and media by **Kevin Phillips** from Sunderland).

Adidas, meanwhile, were very pleased with their new sponsorship arrangements and confirmed an invitation to ALL Community Officers to attend a 'grand' seminar at their main office in Hazel Grove in Stockport, Cheshire at the end of June. A separate press 'launch' was held in London in September. In addition, certain representatives of the PFA and FFE&VTS (including the Community Programme scheme) had been invited by Adidas to Paris to view their proposed new 4 v 4 tournament at the start of June.

A July 1998 meeting with representatives of Wagon Wheels and Harrison Cowley was the first meeting attended by **Duncan Knight** (representing Wagon Wheels) and the hard-working **Alan Twigg** who, by now, had replaced **Brian Roach** as Managing Director of Harrison Cowley. A busy agenda looked at the huge number of many and varied initiatives that were underway at the time. Amongst the many issues discussed, in addition to those identified at the previous meeting, were:

- The availability of complimentary tickets for Wagon Wheels with the kind support of PL clubs themselves.
- The continuing availability of 'product' (Wagon Wheels biscuits) as giveaways for people attending courses.
- Feedback from the successful Working Party group of Community Officers.
- The production of Wagon Wheels inflatable target rings (which were to be 'trialled' soon[31]) and arrangements to support a more formal 'launch' event at Chelsea Football Club in early 1999.

In April 1999, FFE&VTS Community Programme officials were contacted by Huddersfield

---

31. *The first inflatable target ring was 'trialled' at a UEFA "B" course held at Manchester City's (then) training ground at Platt Lane in Manchester in the autumn where, memorably, former Northern Ireland striker and now Blackpool's Community Officer, **Derek Spence**, fired the ball straight into the ring from about 18 yards away with his first kick! It then took at least another twenty minutes for anyone else to perform the same feat!*

Town's busy and popular Community Officer, **Paul France,** who commented that he hadn't received any Wagon Wheels 'product' (biscuits) for more than six months, to the extent that he had spent a fortune buying Wagon Wheels to give away to huge numbers of children attending his holiday courses!

By October, **Paul Chmielewski** had taken over from **Jerry Charter** at Burtons and, to be fair to him, he had been extremely understanding and supportive of an arrangement that he had inherited. That said, it was becoming clear that an extension to the Burton Biscuits (Wagon Wheels) 'deal' was unlikely despite the compilation of a healthy portfolio of activities and events which worked to everyone's advantage at the time.

In early June, as anticipated, the FFE&VTS Community Programme received confirmation from Burtons (Wagon Wheels) that they were not to renew their national sponsorship when it ran out at the end of 1999. Despite this, people from the FFE&VTS Community Programme and Wagon Wheels collaborated to ensure that the eight winners of the young journalist competition got the chance to meet the Prime Minister (**Tony Blair**) at number 10 Downing Street in early October. This was a fantastic occasion and one that the eight lucky winners embraced and enjoyed to the full.

Armed with this knowledge, a meeting of the 'Working Party' was held at Birmingham City's St. Andrews ground in October when the possibilities of new sponsors and what might (and might not!) be deliverable by any new sponsors. As several Community Officers had moved on since the last meeting, those attending included several new Officers:

- **Fraser Foster** (Barnsley), **Dean Holtham** (Birmingham City), **Derek Spence** (Blackpool), **Gary Mulcahey** (Fulham), **Jamie Houchen** (Norwich City/Norfolk CFA), **Peter Rhoades-Brown** (Oxford United), **Lee Turnbull** (Scunthorpe United) and **Clive Maguire** (Swindon Town). Also attending were Working Party regulars **Dean Ramsdale** (Burnley) and **Graham Moran** (Notts County). Fellow-established members of the group, **Lee Doyle** (Brentford) and **Kirk Wheeler** (Watford) were unavailable.

Amongst several excellent ideas put forward were the following:

- The introduction of a 'contingency/development fund' (which could, amongst other ideas, be set up to assist those projects struggling in either, or both, financial or cash flow terms).
- The importance of any new sponsors having appropriate credibility.
- The introduction of a Community Player of the Year award.

Plans to find a replacement national sponsor (underway since the summer of 1999) were, in the end, to prove successful part way into the first year of the new millennium.

CHAPTER 13 – INTO THE NEW MILLENNIUM - 2000-2003

THE VERY GOOD NEWS at the start of the year 2000 was that none of the computers or IT equipment used by the FFE&VTS Community Programme were in any way affected by the "millennium bug" that many so-called experts had forecast would have an impact! Instead it was back to work as normal on Tuesday the 4th January 2000 after the Bank Holiday break for all Community Officers.

From a Business Plan point of view, an interim Business Plan was adopted covering the period from January to December 2000 mainly because of the short-term lack of a high-profile national sponsor.

The budget for the year saw expenditure set as follows:

DETAIL OF EXPENDITURE	AMOUNT	% AGE
Grant aid to club projects	£540,000	39%
Management wages (including travel expenses and pension contributions)	£467,500	34%
Marketing (sponsorship support)	£280,000	20.5%
Other costs – offset against TFW income (including course fees, printing, stationery and advertising, phone etc.)	£87,500	6.5%
TOTAL	£1,375,000	100%

Alan Smith (popular Southampton Community Officer) continued to be off work with serious illness at the start of the year (having been ill for some time and having also endured several operations). The good wishes of all at FFE&VTS were properly extended to him for a speedy recovery.

To accommodate the further expansion of community schemes, more and more interest was being shown by Officers in how to access external funding. An example of this was seen at a meeting at Manchester City's old ground at Maine Road when a New Opportunities Fund meeting was held. Several community officers were able to attend, as did **Brendon Batson** (PFA Deputy Chief Executive) who generously provided full details for all Community Officers about how to access grants from the Millennium Awards for All programme.

The first General Management (Senior Management Team) Meeting of the new millennium was held at the beginning of February and reviewed the progress made to date. With the inclusion of newly promoted Cheltenham Town (who replaced relegated Scarborough in the FL at the end of the 1998/9 season), there were now a total of 90 clubs whose community schemes were being supported by the FFE&VTS Community Programme.

Slightly alarmed by falling numbers, Head of Adult and Youth Training, **Gary Naven**, arranged a seminar at Leeds United FC for Community Officers whose adult and youth training numbers had reduced since the previous year. Around 20 Community Officers attended the meeting on the 18th February when reminders were made of how support for the FFE&VTS Community Programme adult and youth training programmes could end up with the payment of sizeable bonuses for these club schemes.

It was noted that **David Blunkett MP** had kindly given up some of his free time to visit a match at Stockport County's Edgeley Park ground at the beginning of February (when County played Charlton Athletic), so that more information about the club's new learning centre could be shared with him. The Learning Centre was formally opened that month.

Also, in February, **Tibor Szabo** resigned from his post as Community Officer at Halifax Town and **Kevin Stonehouse** took over. Born in Bishop Auckland, Kevin began his career with Blackburn Rovers before moves to Huddersfield Town, Blackpool, Darlington, Carlisle United (on loan) and finally Rochdale. Kevin, however, didn't stay long as Community Officer at the Shay and moved to Darlington where he became a popular Community Officer. He very sadly passed away in July 2019.

Billy Legg took over as Halifax Town Community Officer in the Autumn of 2000. Born in Bradford, Billy's career began as an apprentice with Huddersfield Town where he made just under 60 league appearances between 1964 and 1968.

New appointments at other clubs included:

- **Derek Brazil** (Cardiff City). Dublin born, Derek began his career with Manchester United before loan moves to Oldham Athletic and Swansea City, then making a permanent move to Cardiff City where he played between 1992 and 1995.

- **Adriano Girolami** (Hereford United)

- **Mark Morris** (Wrexham). Chester-born, Mark played in goal for Wrexham for eight seasons following completion of a spell at the club as a youth trainee.

Given the ever-increasing importance being attached to Child Protection, a meeting was held with the excellent **Tony Pickerin** at Lilleshall where Tony was kind enough to share as much information as he could about the new Child Protection Policy prepared by the FA (and the importance of football's links with the NSPCC). The FFE&VTS Community Programme proposed that all local schemes should be issued with manuals with appropriate procedures relative to the overall Policy. Tony confirmed that he was looking to recruit around 60+ Child Protection tutors to help with the delivery of the proposed three-hour Child Protection training courses around the country. It was agreed that close liaison would be necessary to take things forward.

A Child Protection 'Steering' or 'Working' Group was also to be established and would involve people such as **Jenny Myers** (NSPCC), **Jeff Davis** (Disability Manager at the FA), **Sue Law** (FA), **Peter Cates** (PL), **Richard Hodgson** (FL), a representative of the FFE&VTS, **Alan Hodson** (FA) and several CFA representatives including **Sue Hough** and **Jim Kenyon**, plus Tony Pickerin himself. The first meeting of the Steering Group was held in mid-February 2000, with several more to follow throughout the year. **Sue Law** and **Lucy Faulkner** were appointed as co-ordinators (on a 'job share' basis initially).

Developments in employment law and the increasing occurrence of litigation involving staff who had left community schemes within the last twelve months or so led to the excellent idea of the creation of an 'Employment Seminar' for all management staff eventually arranged on the 7th March. Senior Partner **John Hewison** and solicitor **Gary Tobin** from George Davies & Co Solicitors presented the seminar as it was becoming more and more apparent that litigation was going to increase in future as far as persons leaving community schemes were concerned, and especially as schemes were growing so swiftly. It was also confirmed that employees reserved the right to go to employment tribunals, which were often extremely unpredictable. Amongst the main issues discussed were:

- The Working Time Regulations (1998).
- Ill Health Dismissals.
- The Dismissal Procedure.
- Redundancy (and procedures).

The seminar proved to be well worthwhile and successful in raising awareness amongst senior managers of all these issues.

Developments in relation to Child Protection were reported at the February Community

Forum quarterly meeting (again chaired by **Frank Hannah**) when some interesting statistics were also presented covering the period between 1993-1998:

Total numbers of people involved in community activities across all club community schemes:

	1993	1994	1995	1996	1997	1998
Total	803,725	796,215	795,069	907,244	951,526	1,001,449

Included in these figures were the following numbers:

	1993	1994	1995	1996	1997	1998
Holiday Courses	95,598	108,347	114,234	124,315	139,610	147,537
After Schools Sessions	37,792	38,376	47,322	69,133	73,353	84,242

The month of March saw comprehensive and full day "appraisals" with each individual Regional Director, which also provided the opportunity for a two-way conversation about the future and about all the various outstanding issues to attend to in their own regions. In terms of wages arrangements, it should be noted that thanks primarily to massive efforts by all the Regional Directors, Standing Orders were in place with *all* club based Community schemes by the end of the year 1999. This had the effect of considerably easing what had become an increasing strain on the FFE&VTS Community Programme 'cash flow' arrangements. Indeed, standing orders to the value of approximately £175,000 per month were in place by the end of the year (increasing to £200,000 by the end of December 2000). This was helpful but, even with Standing Orders in place to the tune of around £2.1 million per year, arrangements were still woefully short of the £4.0 million+ required to fully cover the costs of Community Scheme wages.

At the clubs, **Darren Hare** left the Gillingham Community Scheme at the end of March and his replacement was **Steve Lovell** (who was destined to become the club's Manager some years later). Swansea-born, Steve Lovell began his playing career as an apprentice at Crystal Palace where he played until 1982. He then went briefly on loan to Stockport County before a permanent move to Millwall. Following a brief loan with Swansea City, Steve joined Gillingham where he made over 200 league appearances up to 1992. He finished his career with AFC Bournemouth.

Club Community Officer, **Nicky Law** was appointed Caretaker Manager at Chesterfield FC in mid-April which created a difficulty as his role as Community Officer was effectively put "on hold" pending clarification of his future! Eventually (i.e. once the situation concerning Nicky's appointment as full time Manager had been confirmed), **Andy Morris**, took over as Community Officer effective from Monday the 26th June. Born in Sheffield, Andy make a handful of substitute appearances for his first club, Rotherham United, before moving to Chesterfield where he made a name for himself, scoring 56 goals in266 league appearances. At the end of his playing career, he had short spells with Exeter City (on loan) and Rochdale.

Around the same time, **Dave Bentley** left Mansfield Town to join Chesterfield as Youth Team Coach leading to the appointment of **John Gannon**, as Community Officer at Field Mill. John's career as a footballer began with his local club, Wimbledon, as an apprentice in the mid-1980's. After a loan spell with Crewe Alexandra, he then moved to Sheffield United where he played for seven seasons before short spells with Middlesbrough (on loan) and Oldham Athletic.

Manchester United, led by the dynamic **Neil Bradburn**, launched their own Study Support

Centre at Old Trafford on the 14th April 2000 at a grand event attended by **David Blunkett MP** and by **Sir Michael Bichard** the latter of whom was the Permanent Secretary at the DfEE.

The PFA 'Player of the Year' Awards Evening took place on the 30th April 2000 and guests invited to attend by the FFE&VTS Community Programme included **Dave Ward** and **Vince Lucas** representing Railtrack, **Mike Reynolds** and **Glynne Jenkins** representing Sportsmatch and **John Hughes** and **Adrian Mayes** representing Smoby Monneret.

As far as the various national competitions were concerned, the Southern Regional Finals of the 1999/2000 Predator Community Cup 6-a-side competition took place at Loftus Road (home of Queens Park Rangers FC) and the Northern Finals took place at Rotherham United FC's Millmoor Ground. The Final swiftly followed at Wembley on the 16th April 2000 prior to the Auto Windscreens Shield Match between Bristol City and Stoke City (won by Stoke by 2-1).

Brentford FC and Rotherham United FC were kind enough to stage the Regional Finals of the Predator Community Cup Competition for Under 13's Girls when Nunthorpe School (representing Middlesbrough) and Cator Park School (representing Crystal Palace) won through to reach the Final.

The Final of the 1999/2000 Smoby Monneret Table Football Championship in association with Wagon Wheels was played at the Millennium Dome (now the 02) on the 11th April when former Wimbledon goalkeeper, **Neil Sullivan,** took time out to present the trophy and medals (see Appendix V for details of Competition winners).

The 1999/2000 competitions were equally as successful as the previous year with slight increases in the numbers in all three competitions as follows:

Predator Community Cup Competition for Primary/Junior School boys and girls in the Under 11 age group:
  82 Community Schemes
  2,116 teams
  £14,900 paid to club schemes

Predator Community Cup Competition[32] for Secondary School girls in the Under 13 age group:
  77 Community Schemes
  846 teams
  £7,050 paid to club schemes

Smoby Monneret Table Football Championship in association with Wagon Wheels:
  81 Community Schemes
  7,549 participants
  £3,250 paid to club schemes

Promoted to the Football League at the end of the 1999/2000 season in May was Kidderminster Harriers FC, and it was great to see the club's Community Officer, **Nick Griffiths**, so pleased to become part of the Football League, following the club's exclusive non-league history up to that point!

May 2000 also saw a further induction arranged for newly appointed Community Officers at the FFE&VTS Community Programme Manchester office. This was necessary as there had been so many new appointments within the previous six months or so. Those that attended were **Derek Brazil** (Cardiff City), **Mike Cook** (Cheltenham Town. Mike had recently left Cambridge United), **Steve Lovell** (Gillingham), **Kevin Stonehouse** (Halifax Town), **Adriano Girolami** (Hereford United), **Craig White** (Leicester City) and **Mark Morris** (Wrexham). All were welcomed to the office, which was interestingly referred to as the "nerve centre" and the

---

32. The Final of the Predator Community Cup Competition for Under 13's girls, that was due to be played at Wembley in May, was postponed at short notice due to heavy rain as it was felt that the Wembley pitch would be damaged by going ahead with the game. Despite the inconvenience and upset caused to all involved, the Final was eventually replayed at Wembley at the end of August.

home of 'Football in the Community'!

The induction get-togethers proved to be an important catalyst for building and/or maintaining the phenomenal closeness, friendship and positive relationships that existed between Community Officers dating back to day one of the scheme's existence in 1986.

Talking specifically about the number of former players involved as Community Officers, **Richard Finney** said:

> *"The camaraderie between the Officers sometimes had to be seen to be believed. Always willing to help and share with each other, football had given them team spirit and they knew the value of sharing good practice, of giving advice and of asking for advice"*

Regional Director, **John Relish**, backed this up with a good example of this very special bond:

> *"**Frankie Prince** (Torquay United's Community Officer) had sadly broken his leg and there was real doubt as to whether the Torquay scheme could become self-sufficient. So, after a quick meeting, **Tommy Hutchison**, **Alan Curtis**, **Peter Rhoades-Brown** and myself organised some holiday courses in Torquay which were promoted on the back of the ex-players well-known names and which raised additional, significant funding for Frankie's account. This was symptomatic of the way in which we all rallied round to help each other, and underlined the fantastic camaraderie that we had in place at the time."*

There were, of course, many former players who become involved in community scheme work who were never actually senior Community Officers in their own right. Amongst them were **Steve Walters** (at Crewe Alexandra), **Neil Woods** (Grimsby Town), **Malcolm Shotton** (Leeds United) and **Graham Bell** (Oldham Athletic) to name but four at the time.

Steve Walters was born in Plymouth and came through the ranks at Crewe Alexandra where he had been a youth trainee. He made 135 league appearances for Crewe Alexandra and was also recognised by England Schools and England Youth.

Born in Goole, **Neil Woods** began his playing career as an apprentice at Doncaster Rovers in 1982, before moves to Ipswich Town, Glasgow Rangers, Bradford City and Grimsby Town. He also spent short loan spells at Wigan Athletic, Scunthorpe United and Mansfield Town before transferring to York City in 1998 where he finished his career.

Malcolm Shotton was born in Newcastle and began his playing career as an apprentice at Leicester City though he made his name as a defender with Oxford United, with whom he played between 1980 and 1987, making over 260 league appearances. He also later played for Portsmouth, Huddersfield Town, Barnsley (twice) and Hull City before moving to Ayr United.

Born in Middleton, Manchester, **Graham Bell** played for Oldham Athletic between 1974 and 1978 before moves to Preston North End, Huddersfield Town (on loan), Carlisle United, Bolton Wanderers and Tranmere Rovers. He made over 400 league appearances in total during his career.

Even at this stage, mention was made of the importance of being able to access external sources of funding such as Sportsmatch, the New Opportunities Fund, Single Regeneration Budget funding, Coalfields Regeneration Budget funding and, of course, from local sponsorship deals, and in accessing the FFE&VTS Community Programme adult and YT programmes as a form of securing alternative manpower resourcing.

In relation to adult and youth training, the operation of the various employment schemes continued into the new millennium and whilst it was clear that figures under the TFW programme had reduced considerably, trainee numbers under 'New Deal' and under the YT programme still largely held up.

Total recruitment figures for the contract year 1999/2000 are detailed in "Appendix III –

Table of trainees in post year by year 1994-2002" [33].

Amongst those clubs with excellent recruitment levels during the year were projects at Bolton Wanderers, Huddersfield Town, Manchester City, Middlesbrough, Port Vale, Sheffield United, Stoke City and West Bromwich Albion.

The actual number of club projects participating in Adult and YT programmes in 1999/2000 remained at 49 during the contract year.

The 16th May saw the next quarterly Community Forum take place when the FA's Head of Football Development, **Kelly Simmons,** together with representatives of the PL, **Kathryn Robinson** and **Ali O'Dowd**, were welcomed to their first meetings. Amongst issues noted and/ or reported at the meeting were:

- The situation concerning the possible partnership (sponsorship) with Railtrack.

- The importance of establishing support from the 'football family' for the NSPCC.

- An update concerning the FA's involvement in driving forward the Child Protection "agenda" under the leadership of **Tony Pickerin.**

- The development of the DfEE resource materials (nearing completion at the time).

- The distinction to be drawn between the operation of Academies and Community schemes at clubs (the agreed wording in the minutes of the meeting was: *"It was agreed that the distinction between the operation of Football in the Community projects and the operation of Centres of Excellence or Academies should be maintained, especially in view of the taxable benefits and financial advantages afforded to Football in the Community projects"*).

Also, at the August 2000 meeting, Community Forum members were alerted to the fact that an Interim (one-year) Business Plan would be put together for the year 2000 and that a more comprehensive Business Plan, including the proposed new partnership arrangements, would then be raised effective for 2001-2003.

As already considered, the FFE&VTS Community Programme agreed that, as the payment of wages on both a weekly and monthly basis was becoming such a huge and regular task, it was appropriate to recruit a "wages clerk". Wages of around £12,000-£12,500 were initially suggested. The post was finally advertised late on in the year 2000 as a "Payroll Administrator" position, and interviews were eventually held in mid-December. Former Manchester City Assistant Secretary, **Ian Niven**, accepted an offer to take up the position, taking up his new post effective from the 22nd January 2001. Ian was an absolute delight to work with and was always positive and supportive, proving to be a more than capable administrator in a role that became increasingly busy as the years went by.

The PFA also took the decision to sponsor the DfEE 'resource pack' to the tune of approximately £17,500. The resource packs were to be called *"Learning FC"* and would be made available before the end of the year 2000. When the packs finally did become available, scheme officials were delighted to receive a call from **Peter Cates** from the PL in which he confirmed that, in his view, 'Learning FC' was simply "superb".

Leeds United were busy building their new Academy and former Community Officers **Brian Kidd** and **Andy Welsh** were amongst the people approached to join the club and to contribute towards its new Academy at Thorp Arch, near Wetherby.

Another former player and Community Coach, Ormskirk-based, **Alan Kershaw**, took up his post as an Assistant Community Officer working alongside **Ted Sutton** at Everton Football Club on the 1st June.

33. *The figures include the numbers of youth trainees in post equivalent to approximately 12.33 trainees per month (an increase on the previous year). Additionally, TFW trainees in post averaged 29.07 per month with approximately 70.17 trainees in post under New Deal and others.*

The end of June 2000 saw the first new Football Foundation Community and Education Panel meeting take place. Amongst those in attendance were **Gordon Taylor** (in the chair), **Tom Pendry** and **Peter Lee** plus **Susan O'Brien** and **Bob Booker** (formerly of the Football Trust), **Neil Watson** (Leyton Orient Community Sports Trust), **Monica Hartland** (Supporters Clubs), **Terry Brown** (Chairman of West Ham United) and **Roger Reade** (the latter as an Observer, from the FFE&VTS Community Programme). The FA's Director of the National Game would also join the Panel on his/her appointment. In the end, **Steve Parkin** was appointed to this post. Steve's early hopes were:

"to have an awareness of what is in place and to enhance what is already there".

Terry Brown was a huge admirer of the Football in the Community scheme, with a first-hand knowledge of the work of the successful West Ham United in the Community Scheme headed up by **Roger Morgan**. Terry was a pleasure to work alongside, as was his Personal Assistant/Secretary, **Alison Lovett**, who was also particularly positive and supportive during this time. Meetings with Terry and Alison towards the end of 2001 were convened to carefully consider the benefits of charitable status, though this was not to go ahead until the end of the 2005/6 season.

Another gentleman who was a real pleasure to work alongside was **David Rowland** who supported the scheme with the supply of various items of football memorabilia over a period of several years around this time. Indeed, David personally discovered some West Ham United memorabilia which FFE&VTS Community Programme officials were delighted to pass on to Terry and Alison at the club.

Although there were no meetings of Community Officers planned for the summer of 2000, Regional Director, **Dick Krzywicki**, did arrange for two update meetings to be held at Hull City FC on the 9th June and at Darlington FC on the 23rd June. These two meetings preceded a national get-together (seminar) of all Community Officers, including an overnight stay at the Britannia Country House Hotel in Didsbury, Manchester, which was greatly enjoyed by all who attended!

July 2000 saw the formal departure of **Pete Devine** from Blackburn Rovers following receipt of his resignation letter of the 7th July. **Anthony Barlow** moved across from Burnley to neighbouring Blackburn Rovers to take up the vacant position of Community Officer the following month.

It was noted that the recommendations of the Community and Education Panel would go to the main Board of the new Football Foundation to be 'signed off'' and authorised. Several applications were considered at the June meeting (including 18 applications from Community schemes worth just under £80,000). Other applications were also considered from independent organisations, including the ARC Theatre and the National Association of Disabled Supporters. Panel meetings were to be held every two months throughout the year in future. Notable from this meeting was the fact that early approval was given to the concept of supporting Football in the Community Scheme legal costs incurred in moving towards charitable status.

The official launch of the Football Foundation was to be held on the 25th July 2000 at 10, Downing Street. In addition, a new *"Head of Community and Education"* position was advertised and an appointment made by the Football Foundation before the end of the year. In the end, following the creation of a short-list of 5 (and later 6) people and by the time of the October Panel meeting, **Mandy Ayres** had been appointed to this important post.

One person to make a huge impression on Community schemes was **Glenn Keeley** from the English Federation of Disability Sport (EFDS). Glenn was a former professional himself having once been an apprentice with Ipswich Town. He went on to play for several league clubs including Newcastle United, Blackburn Rovers, Everton (on loan), Oldham Athletic, Colchester United (on loan) and Bolton Wanderers where his career ended in 1988.

Glenn's early input to the scheme meant that the EFDS would become a key player in the future of community schemes in the longer term (he also attended a senior management team

prior to the FL LDV Vans Final won by Blackpool who beat Cambridge United 4-1. VIP guests at the Final were **Andrew Franklin** from Railtrack and **Chris Thayne**.

The Adidas Community Cup for girls aged under 13 Regional Finals for the North were played at Barnsley's Academy (at Oakwell) and, for the South, at the South Africa Road all-weather pitch adjacent to Queens Park Rangers ground (Loftus Road). The Final was played at Selhurst Park, home of Crystal Palace FC on the 6th May 2002 when the guests presenting the trophy and medals were **Mark Risley** from Adidas and **Marieanne Spacey** (Arsenal and England).

The Smoby Monneret Table Football Competition Finals for 2001/2 was played on the 18th April 2002. Once again, Anfield, home of Liverpool FC staged the Finals and former Liverpool and England full back, **Phil Neal**, was kind enough to present the trophy and medals (see Appendix V for details of Competition winners).

A summary of the participating numbers for all three competitions is shown below:
-    Railtrack "Play Safe" Community Cup Competition for Primary/Junior School boys and girls in the Under 11 age group:
89 Community Schemes
2,799 teams
£19,500 paid to club schemes
-    Adidas Community Cup Competition for Secondary School girls in the Under 13 age group:
82 Community Schemes
1,134 teams
£9,000 paid to club schemes
-    Smoby Monneret Table Football Championship in association with Wagon Wheels:
88 Community Schemes
10,462 participants
£6,300 paid to club schemes
Recruitment figures of trainees under adult and youth training held up reasonably well via 'New Deal' and the YT programme. Total figures for the contract year 2001/2002 are detailed in "Appendix III – Table of trainees in post year by year 1994-2002" [38].

Amongst those clubs with excellent recruitment levels during the year were projects at Huddersfield Town, Stoke City and West Bromwich Albion.

The number of club projects participating in Adult and YT programmes in 2001/2002 increased to 54 during the contract year.

The Community Programme Scheme was well represented at the "Playing for Success" conference held at the end of May 2002 at the Hanover Hotel in Hinckley, Leicestershire when the famous quote of **Nelson Mandela** was widely promoted and circulated:

> *"Sport has the power to change the world, the power to inspire, the power to unite people in a way little else can. It speaks to people in a language they understand. Sport can create hope where there was once only despair. It is an instrument for peace even more powerful than governments. It breaks down racial barriers. It laughs in the face of all kinds of discrimination. The heroes sport creates are examples of this power. They are valiant not only on the playing field but also in the community, spreading hope and inspiration to the world."*

A meeting for Midlands-based Community Officers was held in early May at Notts County FC. Further meetings were held for North West based Community Officers in Chester later in

---

38. *These figures include the numbers of youth trainees in post which increased significantly during the year to an average of approximately 59.58 trainees in post per month. 'New Deal' trainees in post averaged 29.25 per month with approximately 13.17 trainees in post under other arrangements.*

May where a morning meeting was followed by a group visit to Chester Races. A Regional meeting for Yorkshire/North East Community Officers was held at Hull City in June saw a morning meeting followed by a game of golf for all those who were interested.

Interviews held in May 2002 saw the short-term appointment of **Kate Regan** as a support administrator at the FFE&VTS Community Programme Manchester office for a period of 6 months only. Kate had recently been successful in securing a Bachelor of Arts (BA) in business management and was anxious to secure some business experience before considering further the possibility of going to America in 2003. Kate's appointment was welcomed by all concerned and she made a huge contribution to solving the problem of the ever-increasing workload of the Manchester office at the time.

In June 2002, led by the journalist **David Conn** and supported by **Chris Green**, the BBC's Five Live channel broadcast a popular, if sometimes controversial, programme called "*On the Line*" and decided to focus one of their programmes exclusively on "Football in the Community" schemes up and down the country (some of the more worthy programmes were later featured in print in the books "Football Confidential" and "Football Confidential 2"). The conclusion that was reached was that, whilst it was true to say that Community Programme schemes were thriving, prospering and doing excellent work all around the UK, none of this super work was being directly funded by the professional clubs themselves.

What is forgotten here, however, is the very fact that the establishment of community schemes at clubs by the FFE&VTS Community Programme had been based entirely around them not having to fund the schemes in the first place. It was also fair to suggest that this wasn't really 'news' in 2002. Community schemes had been fully funded by the Government's Community Programme Scheme ever since they were first set up in 1986!

In 2002, community programme schemes at clubs were still developing (despite offering a comprehensive range of activities literally "from the cradle to the grave"). Available resources were, at that time, still extremely limited. This limited access to funding had a clear knock-on effect on available training, funding for schemes and, indeed, on wages. As the years went by, and as available funding began increasing, so better training, increased resourcing and higher salaries for community officers all 'kicked in' leading to a point where schemes had the expertise necessary to fulfil the demands of genuine community scheme work.

David Conn (respected writer for *The Guardian*) also took this debate further in his excellent book *The Beautiful Game? Searching for the Soul of Football* in a chapter appropriately entitled "A Positive Future". Amongst those people interviewed directly by David was **Roger Reade**.

June 2002 saw approaches made to **Roger Levermore** (University of Liverpool) and to **Rick Fenoglio** (Manchester Metropolitan University) to look at the possibility of undertaking further comprehensive national research into the Football in the Community Scheme.

The summer of 2002 also witnessed developments at clubs including:

-    Some community staff at Leeds United FC were, sadly, made redundant as club funding previously made available to underpin the club's Community Scheme was withdrawn. The impact on the club and its community scheme over the next twelve months was, of course, more than significant and even the club's Operations Manager, **David Spencer**, had left the club by Spring the following year.

-    Port Vale benefitted from huge support from Pop Star, **Robbie Williams,** when a grant of approximately £20,000 was issued to the club's Community Scheme (Robbie Williams is a life-long supporter of Port Vale FC).

-    PFA Deputy Chief Executive **Brendon Batson** left the PFA to join West Bromwich Albion as Managing Director at the club.

-    The move of Wimbledon Football Club (including its Community Scheme, and Community Officer **Kieron Wicks)** to Milton Keynes became reality.

Also arranging visits to view certain Community Schemes in the summer of 2002 were the newly appointed members of the Independent Football Commission (IFC). Leading the Group was **Dr Chris Gamble,** who was an absolute joy to work alongside whilst ever the IFC were involved in reporting on the key issues of the time in football.

A General Management Meeting (senior management team) at the end of June reflected on the fact that some Community schemes simply didn't have the financial capacity to meet their wage demands, leaving FFE&VTS Community Programme personnel to consider whether the 'credit' facility afforded to these schemes was actually not healthy for the schemes concerned. In other words, if they were to survive in future, would they be able to survive without the FFE&VTS Community Programme?

The FFE&VTS Community Programme was also invited to send a representative to deliver a keynote speech to the "Ability Counts" conference held at Leeds United's Elland Road ground at the end of June. Scheme officials praised the EFDS under **Tony Fitzsimmons** and **Glenn Keeley** for the massive progress they had made in ensuring appropriate opportunities had been established for people with disabilities across a broad spectrum. The hope was also expressed that, in the fullness of time, all Community schemes would have the resources and commitment to employ a Football Development Officer with a specific commitment to working with people with disabilities.

The last event of the summer prior to the start of the 2002/2003 season saw members of the Community Forum gather for their usual quarterly meeting at the start of August. The main items on the agenda for the meeting were, firstly, a presentation made by representatives of KPMG concerning the set-up of their proposed model re research and, secondly, discussion regarding the proposed research work. After a round-the-table discussion, it was felt that the Manchester Metropolitan University proposal should be taken forward and recommended to the Board for adoption. A meeting soon followed in mid-September with **Rick Fenoglio** and **Brendon McGuire** regarding the timing and arrangements for the (comprehensive) research to be undertaken (see Chapter 15).

September 2002 saw another meeting of the FA's Child Protection Working Party and it was acknowledged that considerable progress had been made, especially by **Tony Pickerin**. Amongst the successes to date were:

- Research undertaken by **Celia Brackenridge**.
- Initial conference successfully staged/further conference held on the 1st October 2001 at Derby County FC.
- Policy and Procedures in place and reviewed.
- Best Practice Guidelines produced.
- 260 tutors in place (115 accredited already).

Staff at the PFA and at the FFE&VTS all wore soccer shirts in support of the Strip-4-Shelter day on the 20th September and a suitable donation was then made to support the charity, Shelter.

The disappointing news of September 2002 was that **Alan Jones** had resigned from his post as Club Secretary/Director of Birmingham City FC. Alan had been extremely supportive of all community developments at the club and had proved himself to be an excellent administrator and a terrific point of liaison.

At this point, it is also worth mentioning how well clubs had reacted to taking more responsibility, and even 'ownership', of the operation of their respective local community schemes by encouraging the interest of at least one Director on the club's main board. These people were passionate about their club and wanted nothing but the best for their club's community involvement during the late 1990's and early 2000's and included: **Tony Adams** (Tranmere Rovers), **Bryan Bodek** (Manchester City), **Ron Craig** (Bristol Rovers), **David Deacon** (Portsmouth), **John Howard** (Cambridge United), **Keith Humphreys** (Stoke City), **Geoffrey King** (Southend United), **Brian Lee** (Wycombe Wanderers), **Richard Matthewman** (Blackburn Rovers) and **Michael Rains** (Stockport County).

Several club chairmen were also extremely supportive during this period including: **Ivor Beeks** (Wycombe Wanderers), **Alan Cash** (Macclesfield Town), **Peter Coates** (Stoke City), **Bill Kenwright** (Everton), **Frank Teasdale** (Burnley). Also noteworthy were **John Reames** (Lincoln City) and **Ian Stott** (Oldham Athletic) who were two more club chairmen with particular interest in their own club community operations, partly encouraged, no doubt, as a result of being the FL's representatives on the FFE&VTS Board of Directors/Trustees.

The PL were beginning to develop their own community activities and, as part of this, a "Community Briefing Day" was arranged at their offices on the 26th September for PL Community Officers only.

A fascinating visit took place in early October when **Greg Swann** and **Michael Milhouse** from one of Australia's biggest professional Australian Rules football clubs, Collingwood, visited to consider the impact of 'Football in the Community' schemes on behalf of the professional clubs across England and Wales.

At the same time, Regional Director **Dave Palmer** and around 20 South East Community Officers and their Assistants enjoyed a three-day break in mid-October to Ireland with a focus on best practice, team building and also including a visit to a race meeting at the Curragh and a round of golf at Portmarnock Golf Course.

Following the discussions with **Joe Roach** (Head of Youth) and encouraged by **Sean O'Driscoll** (now Manager) at AFC Bournemouth, **Steve Cuss** took up the new post of Community Officer at AFC Bournemouth.

At the end of October, a meeting took place at Blackpool FC involving several interested parties, including the club's Community Director **Chris Muir** (formerly a Director at Manchester City who was always very supportive of Blackpool's community work, having joined the Board at Bloomfield Road). Also attending were **Joel Lavery** and **Matt Hilton** from Blackpool Borough Council (Matt would, in later years, become Fleetwood Town's Community Officer), **Mike Taplin** from Blackpool Connexions and **Janet Finn** representing Inclusion projects at Lancashire Connexions. Connexions aim was "*to enable all young people to realise their full potential*" (especially 13-19-year olds). Blackpool and the Fylde College also became involved following the first meeting. This was a positive meeting that brought together various partners with the potential to become a solid partnership with a view to making a difference in the Blackpool area.

George Davies Solicitors of Manchester had been instrumentally involved in preparing clubs to move towards charitable status, and also in considering the huge demands being placed on them (especially the considerable number of club schemes seeking advice as to the legal process necessary to become a registered charity). However, to assist in the increasing demand, Watson Burton LLP in Newcastle also contacted club community schemes in October 2002 to offer their professional services. Indeed, Watson Burton were to develop a comprehensive binder full of relevant information for Football in the Community schemes interested in moving towards securing charitable status. Great credit must go to **John Devine** (then an Associate of Watson Burton LLP) for devising this helpful and informative pack full of all the necessary information needed. Included in the packs were:

- Copy of the Certificate of Incorporation of a Private Limited Company.
- Copy of the Memorandum and Articles of Association.
- Copy of the form APP 1 being the registration application form (application form for registration as a charity) – plus any additional information such as a copy of the organisation's Child Protection Policy.
- Copy of the form DEC 1 being the declaration by charity trustees.
- Supplementary documentation including copies of promotional literature, press and media coverage, information about particular projects undertaken etc.

In addition, Watson Burton also offered a draft copy of the necessary minutes required in order to transfer assets and any undertaking of the existing local Community Programme scheme into the newly established charitable organisation (together with a transfer of undertaking agreement).

The Sportsmatch Annual Awards ceremony successfully went ahead at Twickenham on the 5th November 2002 and was attended by several senior Community Programme personnel.

By the end of the year, the huge research work being undertaken by Manchester Metropolitan University was well underway (detailed questionnaires were sent to all Community Officers in November/December). In addition, the KPMG work on the new five-year Business Plan had been virtually completed (the Board of the FFE&VTS had accepted the final plan at their

September Board Meeting). Effectively there would be 4 new "Programme Advisory Groups" (PAGs) including one specifically to oversee the work of Football in the Community, which would replace the former Community Forum.

KPMG also identified so-called "core" areas of work-support offered by the FFE&VTS Community Programme to club schemes including access to training and development, marketing (and access to sponsorships), payroll and cash flow, central insurance PLUS access to national events and tournaments. The "thrust" of the KPMG work was for the Board to become more "strategic" with less focus on the detail.

The end of the year also saw **Clive Maguire** and **Jon Holloway** at Swindon Town's Community Scheme recognised by the FA for their work in the field of social inclusion.

In terms of adult and youth training, **Gary Naven** reported to the November General Management Meeting that adult training contracts were likely to be "wound down", but that there were now 55 club schemes involved in supporting the YT programme. The growth in the number of participating clubs was great news that was duly welcomed by all concerned.

Following interviews held in mid-November for the newly created full-time post of Payroll Administrator, Manchester United supporter, **Lynn Leonard,** was appointed with effect from the 2nd December 2002. Lynn very quickly became a vitally important member of the Manchester office team, especially given the continuing huge growth of local Community Schemes payrolls.

The Christmas "round" of Community Officers went ahead as usual with meetings as follows:

27th November 2002	North East and Yorkshire Community Officers
29th November 2002	Midlands Community Officers
5th December 2002	North West Community Officers
10th December 2002	South West Community Officers
11th December 2002	South East Community Officers

Attending several of these meetings was **Darran Bowles** from the Princes Trust who was kind enough to present more information about the Trust's work and their hopes to work alongside Community schemes in future. Darren, of course, became a very positive force for good in building links between Community Schemes and the Princes Trust (as did **Jamie Roberts** following his later appointment).

Weekly wages paid out by the FFE&VTS Community Programme covering the six-month period from January to June 2002 totalled over £2,455,711. For July to December, wages totalled £2,726,514. This meant that for the 12-month period from January to December 2002, total wages paid out on behalf of all community projects (plus the Thames Gateway scheme operating at four London clubs) reached a grand total for the full year of £5,182,225. Added to this was the now increasing number of club schemes with casual/part-time staff that were being paid on a monthly basis, worth £2,016,413 for the period January to June 2002 and a further £1,377,035 for the period July-December 2002, making a total of £3,393,448 for the year. The grand total turnover for the year via the FFE&VTS payroll of wages therefore reached the huge sum total of £8,575,673.

A rough "spot-check" on numbers being paid through the FFE&VTS Community Programme payroll at the end of the year, revealed that around 460 staff (at 80 club schemes) were being paid on a weekly basis with a further 2,115 on the monthly paid payroll. These were, of course, simply incredible numbers.

A summary of club Community Schemes turnover during 2002 (finally completed in 2003) revealed that a total of 79 Schemes turned over a collective total of £12,299,517 meaning that average turnover across those schemes had risen to approximately £155,690 per annum. This, of course, represented further huge growth from the previous year. It also, however, became clear at this time that even now one or two club schemes were still financially "at risk" not least as they had low turnover and little, if any, 'surpluses' to bring forward.

Based on information secured from the FFE&VTS Community Programme payroll for the year 2002, average wages for senior Community Officers rose to approximately £22,167 per annum (based on the actual wages paid to 75 different club based Community Officers). In addition, average wages for Assistant Officers reached around £12,089 per annum based on the salaries of over 260 Assistants paid through the FFE&VTS Community Programme payroll (not including approximately 80 Youth Trainees).

The regional analysis of average wages paid in different regions showed that in the North West and North East regions, the average wage paid to (senior) Community Officers in 2002 was approximately £21,590 per annum. In the Midlands and South West, the average was slightly lower at around £20,620 per annum. In the South East (where the annual turnover of local Community schemes was significantly higher than anywhere else in the country), the average was still around £26,900 per annum.

When considering that all Community schemes eventually became charitable organisations, it is worth noting at this time that approximately 17 Football in the Community Schemes had either moved towards, or had already been awarded, charitable status by the Charities Commission at this time.

Amongst well-known Assistant Officers appointed at Community Schemes around this time were:

-    **Vince Overson** (at Burnley). Born in Kettering, Vince began his career as an apprentice at Burnley where he played for six seasons. He then moved to Birmingham City and Stoke City before returning to Turf Moor for a brief spell in 1996. He also played briefly on loan at Shrewsbury Town.

-    **Paul Newman** (at Derby County).

-    **Gary Childs** (at Grimsby Town). Gary was born in Birmingham and played much of his football in the West Midlands with West Bromwich Albion (where he began his playing career as an apprentice), Walsall and Birmingham City before moving to Grimsby Town in 1989. Assisting Gary would be **Matthew Franklin**.

-    Ex-Norwich City player **Jeremy Goss** (at Norwich City). Jeremy made over 150 league appearances for the Canaries between 1983 and 1995.

The New Year 2003 started with news that club scheme wage debts owing to as at December 2002 to the FFE&VTS Community Programme had risen to over £800,000. This meant that the future payment of wages on behalf of local community schemes would, once again, have to be carefully re-considered.

John Gannon confirmed that he had been offered the Assistant Manager's job at Mansfield Town where he had, of course, been extremely successful as Community Officer up to this point.

Graham Moran, from Notts County's Community Scheme, made a super presentation at the Football Foundation's 17th Community and Education Panel Meeting in January 2003 which concerned their successful "Heading for Goal" project. Essentially the project aimed to work with Secondary Schools on "pre-exclusion" work across the city of Nottingham so that everyone concerned had an achievable programme set for them on an individual basis. The project was extremely successful and was based around the club having access to its own dedicated education 'centre' at the club's Meadow Lane ground for the use of the young people involved. Indeed, **HRH Prince Edward** also visited Meadow Lane in April 2004 to view the project for himself. Further meetings of the Foundation's Community and Education Panel were held in March, May, July, September and November 2003.

Keith Daniell from the Media Group became even more of a key contributor to the scheme's ongoing success in 2003 as he not only took over the design and print of the successful "Football in the Community News" newsletter but also laid on some appropriate media training for senior officers from the FFE&VTS Community Programme. His "handy hints" when involved in press/media interviews were especially useful. Keith also agreed to prepare notes for the possible adoption of a 'communications strategy', which would need to be recommended to the Board by the new (Community) Programme Advisory Group (PAG).

The first ever Community-based PAG Meeting took place on the 4th February 2003 and was attended by **Frank Hannah** and **Kelly Simmons** from the FA; **Cathy Long** and **Emma Stanford** representing the PL; **Gary Linke** and **Pat Brown** from the FL; and **Simone Pound** from the PFA. Also attending were **Mickey Burns**, **Roger Reade**, **Dennis Leman** and **Julie Moran** from the FFE&VTS (Julie had recently been appointed as 'in-house' FFE&VTS Accountant/Financial Controller). **Frank Hannah** was elected to the position of Chair. It was an interesting meeting not least as it was agreed that the Football in the Community Scheme's aims and objectives should be reviewed. It was also agreed that **Keith Daniell** should be invited to attend the next PAG meeting so that he could present his recommendations regarding the adoption of the proposed new communications strategy. (In the end, Keith plus **David Leatt** and **Andrew James** attended the next meeting in May on behalf of the Media Group). Meetings of the Community Programme Advisory Group were to be held on a quarterly basis and further meetings took place in May, August and November 2003.

A review meeting with **Rick Fenoglio** and **Brendon McGuire** from Manchester Metropolitan University noted that the first draft of the research would become available by around September 2003, with the final report available around October 2003 (sadly, the Report itself didn't eventually go to print until early in 2004). Amongst items to be covered, notably in the questionnaires to Community Officers and to Football Governing Body officials including **Mike Foster** (PL), **Andy Williamson** (FL), **Robin Russell** (FA) and **Gordon Taylor** (PFA) and **Peter Lee** (Football Foundation), were:

-   A valuation of the benefits in finance, the game and in the wider community.
-   A brief look at other community "schemes" around Europe and the rest of the world.
-   Sections re the FFE&VTS, clubs and Management Forums, the Scheme and the future.

The final research report is commented on in more detail in Chapter 15.

A meeting of the newly established 'National Football Partnership' brought together several key people from the FA, English Schools FA, Football Foundation, Youth Sport Trust and Sport England in March 2003. The new-found importance of the FFE&VTS Community Programme meant that an invitation was also extended to send a representative to this meeting. Noted at the meeting was the establishment of County Sports Partnerships and the reduction of Community Sports Coaches working for Sports Coaching UK. The work of Connexions was also noted (it was generally felt that 'splashing money around' wasn't working particularly well) and it was felt that a 'mapping exercise' should be undertaken noting the input of the Home Office Positive Futures Scheme (**Neil Watson**), the DfES (**Alison Lockwood**), Connexions (**Jane Haywood**), the Youth Justice Board (**Sarah Blaquiere**) and local football in the community projects. (A positive meeting involving Football in the Community officials and Sarah Blaquiere at the end of February had openly talked of the benefits of community engagement with young people using football as the means of engagement. In the end, the PL was able to negotiate an arrangement with Sarah to establish 'pilot' schemes with three club community schemes being Everton, Charlton Athletic and Southampton).

Nigel Hargreaves from the FA also spoke about the shocking state of facilities across the country and the total costs of restoring them which, even in 2003, was estimated to be as high as £2 billion. A "Facility Development Plan" was to be produced. Quarterly meetings of this group were also to be established.

April 2003 saw the first discussions about a possible new Business Plan which would cover the period from mid-year 2003 to mid-year 2005 and include a full review of the Business Plan covering the previous three years.

An April 2003 meeting with representatives of Boston United was well-received and led to agreement being reached between the club and the FFE&VTS Community Programme to establish community links. Attending on behalf of the club were **John Blackwell**, **David Pickett** and **Jan McLucas** (Jan ran the club's Study Support Centre).

April also saw a process of recruitment start at the PFA whereby they were looking to appoint a senior coach to work alongside **Jimmy Armfield** as Head of Coaching at the PFA.

In the end, and despite his obvious love of his work at the Millwall Community Sports Scheme, **Jim Hicks** accepted the position, taking up his new duties in the summer (a suitable 'leaving do' was arranged for Jim in mid July 2003). At this time, **Loo Brackpool** took on the role as Millwall's Head of Community.

During the adult and YT programme contract year 2002/3, recruitment of young assistants was predominantly via YT with only a very small number of trainees recruited under New Deal. This meant that figures recorded for the year were significantly different to those recorded previously. Total figures for the contract year 2002/2003 are detailed in "Appendix III – Table of trainees in post year by year 2002-2007" [39].

Amongst those clubs with excellent recruitment levels during the year were projects at Blackburn Rovers, Bolton Wanderers, Burnley, Huddersfield Town, Hull City, Nottingham Forest, Sheffield United and West Bromwich Albion.

The number of club projects participating in Adult and YT programmes in 2002/2003 increased to 63 during the contract year.

The 1st May 2003 saw the annual 'Playing for Success' conference successfully staged at Hinckley in Leicestershire, with one notable presentation made by a 'team' of officers including **Lee Turnbull** from Scunthorpe United and **Angeline Mather** from North Lincolnshire Council about their new Study Support work at Scunthorpe United entitled "*Study United FC*" and which embraced out of school hours learning for local school children (including 14-19-year-olds at risk of disaffection with school/learning).

Of interest around this time were figures being bandied about including the facts that:

-   Playing for Success was now in operation at 58 study support centres.
-   An average of 19 or 20 schools were involved at each centre each year.
-   An average of 16 or 17 children per school were attending each centre (leading to between 17600 and 19700 children being supported each year overall).

By May 2003, new club interest in working with the FFE&VTS Community Programme was once again expressed extended by Carlisle United, Leyton Orient and Portsmouth.

The proposed new Business Plan was presented in draft form at the May Community Advisory Group meeting and received the support of all the partners.

Another important meeting took place in May when FFE&VTS Chief Executive **Mickey Burns** and Financial Controller **Julie Moran** met with senior Community Programme officials to review the "debt management" arrangements for the scheme which were causing increasing concern (particularly as schemes continued to grow so swiftly). It had become clear that local Football in the Community schemes Direct Debit and/or Standing Order arrangements were simply not covering anything like the full amount of wages paid out by the FFE&VTS Community Programme.

By the end of June 2003, monies received by Standing Order/Direct Debit had risen to approximately £300,000 per month, though this was still a long, LONG way short of the total amount of wages being paid out by the FFE&VTS Community Programme from its own reserves on behalf of approximately 80 local Football in the Community Schemes.

In addition, approximately 10 Football in the Community schemes were struggling in financial terms at the time to the extent that they were unable to pay the full amount of their wage's debts to the FFE&VTS. [40]

It was agreed that it was essential to review direct debit/standing order arrangements and to identify those community schemes that were struggling in financial terms. It was also suggested

---

39. *These figures include the number of youth trainees in post which increased significantly once again during the year to an average of approximately 112.08 trainees in post per month. In turn, 'New Deal' trainees in post averaged 16.82 per month*

40. *At the end of June 2003, five club community schemes alone owed the FFE&VTS Community Programme a total of £213,463 which, it seemed, they were not in a position to be able to pay.*

that a cost per scheme should be calculated so that the 'wages bureau' that was effectively in place and costing FFE&VTS directly, could then aim to become self-sufficient.

Match programme coverage during the 2002/3 season was assessed once again and the following clubs were selected as those with the best community coverage:

2002/3	Winners	Runners Up
PL	Sunderland	Fulham Southampton
FL Division One	Sheffield Wednesday Stoke City	Burnley
FL Division Two	Port Vale	Bristol City Notts County
FL Division Three	Doncaster Rovers	Cambridge United

A Summer Board Meeting of the FFE&VTS recommended that the FFE&VTS role in supporting club community schemes did not include "bankrolling" community schemes and urged that **Julie Moran** look at establishing a more robust system of debt management. It was also recommended that all Regional Managers be approached to ensure that 'debt management' was incorporated as part of their job descriptions (Regional Managers found this to be extremely disappointing as they felt that their role should be to be more proactive in generating access to new sums of external funding rather than to 'police' local accounts information).

Soon after this, Julie left her position to move into a more senior accounting post. Her replacement was **Simon Tuley**. Simon, like Julie, was very experienced and proved to be an excellent appointment as Financial Controller who joined the FFE&VTS at a very difficult time. Indeed, Simon's early work included bringing all the FFE&VTS accounts fully up-to-date, plus offering some great ideas that would help modernise financial systems.

At the clubs, **Mike Spinks** left his post as General Manager/Secretary at Barnsley FC. Mike had been extremely supportive throughout the formative years of the club's community scheme and was to be greatly missed. Mike it was who had first reported on takings through the club shop having doubled when the club started opening the shop on weekdays for children to visit after they had been on community scheme-organised ground tours at Oakwell. Excellent support was forthcoming in the near future, however, when **Gordon Shepherd** took over as chairman at the club and gave **Wayne Bullimore** sterling support in his role as Community Officer at the club.

Lawrie Pearson made a very welcome return to the community officers "fold" by taking up the vacant post of Community Officer at Carlisle United at the end of June.

Also, in the summer, Gillingham's Community Officer, **Steve Lovell**, took up the job of Manager of Hastings FC.

Domenico Genovese took up the post of Manager at Kettering Town FC.

Around the same time, **Kirk Wheeler** left Watford, though he was eventually to be appointed as Community Officer at Aldershot Town Football Club the following year.

Further successful meetings were held with representatives of Boston United and Peterborough United, and both clubs committed to working with the FFE&VTS Community Programme. Indeed, **Nick Reeson** was soon appointed as Boston United's Community Officer.

A National Football Partnership Meeting held in July, and chaired by the FA's **Ros Potts**, reflected on the fact that 26 CFAs now had their own Football Development Managers. FA Head, **Steve Parkin**, put forward his hope that the partnership meetings would:

"avoid duplication, maximise funding opportunities and provide a co-ordinated approach to football and facility developments".

Also calling into the office in July was **Jane Standring** from the Scheme's stationery suppliers. Jane had been a loyal and long-term provider of stationery for the national scheme over many years.

Moving into the new 2003/4 season, it is worth noting that the FFE&VTS Community Programme was then working with a total of 89 of the 92 PL/FL clubs. The exceptions were Arsenal (who continued to operate franchises in other club areas), Leyton Orient and Yeovil Town (though it was hoped that a meeting with Yeovil Club Chairman, **John Fry,** to take things forward could be arranged in the near future).

In addition, 7 Conference (now National League) level clubs (Barnet, Exeter City, Halifax Town, Hereford United, Kettering Town, Scarborough and Shrewsbury Town) were being supported. A total of 25 clubs had by now moved to establish their community schemes as registered charities.

In September 2003, FFE&VTS Community Programme officials made a successful presentation about the opportunities that professional football could afford socially excluded groups at the Football and Social Inclusion conference held in London.

A Football Foundation Community and Education Panel meeting also held in September 2003, saw separate applications for funding submitted by the Rotherham United Community Scheme and by Rotherham Council. Supporting the recommendations of the recent Bassam Report, the Panel unanimously agreed that they would only support an application in Rotherham if the club, the club's Community Scheme AND the local Council collaborated in true 'partnership'. In the end, the parties agreed to work together to consider formulating a single bid for the town.

Everton re-launched their Community Scheme as a registered charity at Goodison Park at the end of September. The Everton community scheme, of course, would go on to become one of the most successful and well-respected community schemes in the country over the next 10-15 years.

The situation concerning Wimbledon Football Club's future also overlapped into the operation of the club's Community Scheme. Contacts leading the move to establish MK Dons Football Club were **Pete Winkelman** and **Mike Dove**. It was agreed by the FFE&VTS to work with MK Dons FC on the basis that they were a brand-new club.

September 2003 also saw **David Busst** become Coventry City's Senior Community Officer/Manager. David was a former Coventry City player who was popular in the city and whose professional career had been so sadly taken away from him after a serious injury whilst playing against Manchester United at Old Trafford in 1996.

Also developing at this time were links with **Wasim Khan** from the Professional Cricketers Association (PCA). Wasim's hopes were based on the idea that the PCA might become involved in community work in much the same way as the PFA.

Revealed in October was the fact that the Football Foundation had awarded grants worth £2,786,598 to 48 club based Community Schemes in connection with 62 separate projects. The spread of the awards was:

North West £493,157	11 club schemes
North East £164,120	5 club schemes
Midlands £734,454	11 club schemes
South West £441,164	10 club schemes
South East £953,703	11 club schemes

This represented terrific support from the recently-formed Football Foundation. It also underlined the success of the locally based Community schemes who, as separate organisations, successfully passed the 'fit and proper' organisation exercise.

The 9th October 2003 saw a further meeting arranged by the PL in London where invitations to attend were sent to Community Officers from PL clubs only so that they could be briefed about PL projects.

Meetings with club officials were, of course, held on an on-going basis, but one interesting meeting took place in November 2003 involving Vice Chairman **Geoffrey King** and club Secretary **Helen Giles** at Southend United when the benefits of charitable status were closely examined. After much discussion, it was agreed that this represented the right way for the Southend United scheme to go and the Southend United Community and Educational Trust was duly registered with the Charity Commission the following year.

The November (Community) Programme Advisory Group (PAG) meeting went ahead as planned when the idea of adopting a national communications strategy by the FFE&VTS Community Programme was discussed. In the end, the Strategy was approved for a short-term period of around six months – i.e. up to April 2004 only. Concern was also expressed about the nomination of member club-based representatives to sit on the Advisory Group.

Another interesting meeting that went ahead on the 1st December 2003 involved **Shaun Harvey**, Chief Executive at Bradford City. What he was keen to work on was the appointment of a Cohesion Officer within the club's community remit whose role would embrace work with the local community (especially the local Asian heritage community) and link up work with Kick It Out, the Commission for Racial Equality and the local Equality Unit.

Other meetings held in December 2003 saw Scheme officials meet again with **Dr Chris Gamble** from the Independent Football Commission whose work now extended to checking on the perception of the Football in the Community scheme which seemed at the time to be viewed purely as a 'coaching scheme' (and no more). In contrast to this view, and by coincidence, at around the same time, Community Scheme officials met with **Francisco Baeza** and **Chris Kemp** from Buckinghamshire Chilterns University (later Bucks New University) to explore further the idea of Community schemes taking forward Foundation degree opportunities for local young people using community schemes as the potential 'deliverer'.

One of the comparatively minor issues attended to by the FFE&VTS Community Programme was the small matter of ensuring appropriate insurance on behalf of the many Community Schemes every year. Insurance cover included the provision of arranging Combined Liability Insurance (Employers and Employees) for Non-League clubs, All Risks insurance, Personal Accident cover re school children attending holiday courses/other activities and Life Assurance cover for at all clubs. In total in 2003 approximately £20,000 worth of cover was arranged via **Bill Garside** from Windsor Insurance. In later years, the Scheme was also grateful to **Ian Birtwistle** for continuing to arrange this unique cover.

Weekly wages paid out by the FFE&VTS Community Programme covering the six-month period from January to June 2003 totalled £3,048,850. For the period between July and December 2003 £3,083,098 was paid out. So, for the 12-month period from January to December 2003, total weekly wages paid out on behalf of 85 community projects (plus the Thames Gateway scheme operating at four London clubs) reached a grand total for the full year of £6,131,948. Added to this were those club schemes (now numbering 71 clubs in total) with casual/part-time staff that were being paid on a monthly basis, worth £2,738,478 for the period January to June 2003 and a further £1,850,357 for the period July-December 2003 making a total of £4,588,835 for the year. Incredibly, this meant that the grand total of wages paid via the FFE&VTS had reached a total of £10,720,783 for the year. This continuing rapid growth was simply staggering!

Information secured from the FFE&VTS Community Programme payroll for the year 2003 confirmed that average wages for senior Community Officers rose once again to approximately £23,418 per annum (based on the wages paid to 75 different club based Community Officers). In addition, average wages for Assistant Officers reached around £12,641 per annum based on the salaries of over 400 Assistants paid through the FFE&VTS Community Programme payroll (not including Youth Trainees).

The regional analysis of average wages paid in different regions showed that in the North West and North East regions, the average wages paid to (senior) Community Officers in 2003 was approximately £22,984 (previous year £21,590) per annum. In the Midlands and South West, the average was slightly lower at around £21,570 (previous year £20,620) per annum. In the South East, the average reached £31,789 (previous year £26,900) per annum.

A summary of club Community Schemes turnover during the year 2003 (completed in the summer of 2004) revealed that turnover at 79 local community schemes reached a collective total of £15,105,950 (at the community schemes that operated on a local basis) meaning that average turnover across those schemes rose significantly to more than £191,000 per annum.

The largest turnovers (over £300,000 for the year) were reported at Brighton & Hove Albion (£314,115), Burnley (£560,301), Charlton Athletic (£746,216), Chelsea (£476,613), Colchester United (£591,894), Leeds United (£474,546), Middlesbrough (£742,210), Millwall (£322,842), Newcastle United (£405,311), Norwich City (£632,222), Notts County (£338,473), Southampton (£453,407), Sunderland (£648,414), West Bromwich Albion (£357,582) and Wycombe Wanderers (£361,004).

Purely for reference, it was noted that the lowest turnovers (i.e. at the time below £50,000) were reported at schemes operating at Barnet, Halifax Town, Hartlepool United, Kettering Town, Mansfield Town, Scarborough, Torquay United and York City.

Details of average wages across the Leagues were:

PL average Officer wages	£32,358 (previous year £31,148)
FL average Officer wages	£22,636 (previous year £21,135)
Non- League Club average Officer wages	£17,826 (previous year £16,588)

CHAPTER 14
NATIONAL SPONSORS: RAILTRACK

THE THIRTEENTH BIRTHDAY of the Community Programme in Professional Football on the 16th June 1999 saw a round-the-table meeting with representatives of sales promotion agency, Brewer Blackler, held in London. Brewer Blackler represented a major breakfast cereal who were interested in the national sponsorship, having seen for themselves the success of the Wagon Wheels deal. By complete coincidence, a second major breakfast cereal company also showed interest in the sponsorship opportunity at this time.

Within a few months and towards the end of September 1999, there was an interesting local sponsorship launch event involving Railtrack and the Charlton Athletic Community Scheme. Worth a local total of £60,000 (plus Sportsmatch pound for pound matching funding), this was an effort by Railtrack to try and raise local awareness of the huge issue of trespass and vandalism near railway lines in the South of London. Flagged up and promoted by the senior Community Officer at Charlton, **Jason Morgan**, this swiftly became an opportunity for further discussion about the opportunity to become national sponsors of the scheme. Discussions with several agencies, and direct discussions with several other big-name organisations, took place towards the end of 1999 and, indeed, during the early part of the year 2000, concerning the national sponsorship of the FFE&VTS Community Programme scheme.

A meeting was also kindly arranged by the PFA's **Garry Nelson** with representatives of Railtrack (including **Vince Lucas** and **Dave Ward**) which would follow on from the local launch of their new sponsorship of the Charlton Athletic FC Community Scheme. Indeed, the meeting was arranged at the Valley prior to Charlton Athletic's home game against Grimsby Town on the 22nd March 2000. A follow-up meeting in April also secured the commitment of Railtrack towards working with the FFE&VTS Community Programme as a 'partner' (rather than as a 'sponsor'). Key to their plans was the idea of a co-ordinated national effort across the country towards reducing trespass and vandalism (especially amongst 9-15-year-olds) by promoting a national *"stay safe"* message aimed at *"keeping kids safe"*.

After reaching agreement on a three-year partnership arrangement (commencing in September 2000 and finishing in August 2003), plans were then put in place for the national launch which, quite appropriately, was held at Charlton Athletic's Valley ground. In attendance were **David Dent** (Football League Secretary), **Gordon Taylor** (Chief Executive, the PFA), **Mickey Burns** (FFE&VTS Chief Executive) and **Gerald Corbett** (Chief Executive, Railtrack). Commenting at the time, Railtrack's Commercial Manager, **Vince Lucas**, said:

> *"Everyone connected with Railtrack is deeply concerned about the number of children killed or seriously injured whilst trespassing on the railway, and if, through our new association with the national Football in the Community Scheme, we can avoid the death or injury of just one child, then it will all be worthwhile"*

The figures produced at the launch were staggering. In 1999 there were over 17,000 reported acts of trespass and/or vandalism. The Football in the Community Scheme would promote the new scheme logo and new strapline "Stay safe, play safe".

The deal with Railtrack was worth £350,000 per year (x three years) plus £50,000 for each year of the three-year sponsorship term to cover sponsorship of the Under 11's school competition (in other words, the whole deal was worth a minimum of £1.2 million in total). The new logo and strap line then appeared on all literature, promotional information and in match programmes too.

A meeting with representatives of Adidas and Sportsmatch also considered the concept of Community schemes becoming involved in delivering a "*Want to Play*" day in August 2000. This predominantly football activity would be arranged for approximately 5,000 children around the country. It was hoped that children from deprived backgrounds could be encouraged to attend. The Adidas investment of £50,000, was in the end, 'matched' by a Sportsmatch award of a further £50,000 and a total of 81 Community schemes took part (those that were unable to take part were clubs whose kit was provided by other manufacturers – i.e. Aston Villa, Bolton Wanderers, Chelsea, Everton, Ipswich Town, Leeds United, Liverpool, Manchester United and West Ham United). It's also worth noting that the cash summary, once all "Want to Play" days had been completed, showed that the vast majority of monies paid out went either to club schemes as "facility fees" and to cover the costs of gifts given to participating children.

The 'Working Party' of Community Officers met at Leicester City FC in April 2001. In attendance were: **Fraser Foster** and **Lee Turnbull** (representing Yorkshire and the North East), **Dean Ramsdale** (North West), **Dean Holtham** and **Graham Moran** (Midlands), **Peter Rhoades-Brown** and **Clive Maguire** (South East). Apologies for absence were received from **Derek Spence** (Blackpool/North West), **Lee Doyle** (Brentford/South East) and **Kirk Wheeler** (Watford/South East). The role of the Working Party was also clarified to be (simply!) a consultation group that would meet on an informal basis from time to time, particularly with a focus on sponsors and sponsor-related activity.

The majority of Community Officers were happy with the new arrangements with Railtrack, especially so as the previous PR/activity involvement with Wagon Wheels had proved in the end to be so demanding.

The Working Party also discussed the impact of the TOP Sport programme (a more general PE and Sport support programme for schools), and, suffice to say that, whilst responses were reasonably positive, virtually all Community Officers felt that a football-driven delivery would be better received in schools.

Also noted at the meeting was the fact that a "contingency fund" of some £25,000 had been established following the adoption of this suggestion from a previous 'Working Party' meeting.

The first 'chunk' of this contingency fund was used in offering funding of £6,000 to the Luton Town Community Scheme as the 91st scheme to be supported by the FFE&VTS Community Programme.

A 'follow-up' Working Party meeting was held at Leicester City Football Club in September. One of the key things noted at this meeting was the move towards Community schemes looking to set up projects working broadly within the field of 'social inclusion'. In particular, it was highlighted that this was the direction that Sportsmatch appeared to be moving. Also noted, following the rejection of the Schools bid by the Football Foundation, was the fact that all ten members of the Working Party represented only FL clubs – i.e. PL clubs weren't represented at all. It was unanimously agreed that this needed to be attended to!

Noted in April was the generosity of Railtrack who had, by now, become not only partners of the FFE&VTS Community Programme but also local supporters of community schemes at Barnsley, Birmingham City, Bristol Rovers, Charlton Athletic, Coventry City, Crewe Alexandra, Leicester City, Notts County, Watford, West Ham United and Wycombe Wanderers.

A September meeting with Adidas officials confirmed that the sponsorship arrangements were working out well for all concerned. As a rough-check at the time it was noted that:

-   73 professional clubs supported the Adidas deal in full.

-   10 professional clubs supported the equipment aspect of the deal only (Blackburn Rovers, Bolton Wanderers, Derby County, Huddersfield Town, Ipswich Town, Manchester City, Millwall, Sheffield Wednesday, West Bromwich Albion and West Ham United).

-   9 professional clubs were unable to support any aspect of the deal in view of existing club kit deals (Aston Villa, Chelsea, Everton, Leeds United, Liverpool, Manchester United and West Ham United).

Things were going well with Railtrack throughout 2001, until news broke completely 'out of the blue' that Railtrack had gone into administration! The good news, however, was that things were to continue almost unaffected as sponsorship monies had been properly paid to the FFE&VTS and Railtrack officials were to continue to liaise with Scheme officials as though they weren't in administration anyway. **Danielle Gillett** represented the Railtrack interest from this point onwards.

Links with Coca Cola through the dynamic **Chris Masterson** were also developed during 2001 as the development of a football themed lesson plan/learning aid was taken forward. Several Club Community Schemes ended up better off with the local sponsorship support of Coca Cola.

Into 2002, the first Working Party meeting of the New Year saw the group meet at Leicester City FC at the end of February. Following **Fraser Foster**'s appointment as a Regional Director, **Paul France** (Community Officer at Huddersfield Town) was appointed to join the Group …. with representatives of PL clubs to join for the second meeting of the year.

Railtrack, by now effectively under "new management", changed their strapline to "Safety is our goal" and linked this to the promotion of their new player 'Safety' cards and a "Design a Safety Poster" competition. **Richard Finney** explained the background to the Poster Competition:

> *"Prizes for the five regional winners of the Railtrack Design a Safety Poster Competition were to have their posters displayed in every railway station in their area of the country. In addition, as part of the prize structure, there was a Raleigh bicycle made available for each of the 90 local winners."*

In September 2002, after two years of the initial three-year deal, Railtrack had an option to extend their sponsorship for a further period of two years. Given the circumstances, however, it was accepted by Scheme officials that this option may not be taken up. **Danielle Gillett** kindly agreed to take this up with Network Rail officials. In the end, and as expected, this was to no avail and what had clearly been a successful sponsorship for both parties would come to an end.

A further Working Party met in September 2002. This time there were representatives from two PL clubs invited to attend being **Jason Morgan** from Charlton Athletic (though he was unable to attend this meeting) and **Dean Holtham**, already a member but now representing a PL Club following Birmingham City's promotion to the PL.

The meeting listened to details of the research work now underway with Manchester Metropolitan University (see Chapter 15) and was favourably received. Also well received were the new development areas including:

- The success of the YT programme across so many club schemes which also provided a welcome additional resource.

- New Opportunities Funding which had been received by a huge number of club schemes. It was strongly felt that the FFE&VTS Community Programme should become more involved in developing the expertise necessary to "tap in" to new external funding where available.

- The move into tackling social exclusion using football as the vehicle to help tackle this important issue.

The next Working Party Meeting was held at Watford Football Club on the 6th March 2003. Moves into new areas of operation including education, health and inclusion were noted and fully understood. Other ideas that arose out of the meeting included:

- Funding for training of Community Officers; opportunities for distance learning and workshops in specific areas such as employment law, health & safety and finance. (Employment law workshops were kindly arranged by **John Hewison** and **Alan Lewis** from George Davies Solicitors following the presentation of this idea. The seminars were eventually held in Leeds, Birmingham and Wycombe in June and July 2003. Indeed, 25 clubs were represented at the first seminar held at Leeds United FC. Health and Safety workshops were also arranged in May and June 2004 in Leeds, Stoke and Southampton).

- The adoption of a national 'communications strategy' (with The Media Group) with an intention to provide much greater circulation of community activities and increased awareness of the scheme's work to the outside world.

- The importance of moving away from purely football activities, especially in moving to adopt and to deliver more work in the field of social inclusion.

In relation to the 2002/3 competitions, the Railtrack "Play Safe" Regional Finals were played at Rotherham United on the 11th March (Northern Finals) and the Southern Finals played at South Africa Road (near Queens Park Rangers FC) on the 12th March 2003. The Final itself was played at Cardiff's Millennium Stadium prior to the Leyland DAF Vans (LDV Vans) Trophy Final won by Bristol City (who beat Carlisle United 2-0). The trophy and medals were presented by **Paul Denton** from Network Rail and **Chris Thayne**. What was an excellent game was again refereed by **Billy Margetts**.

The Adidas Girls Competition saw regional finals held at Barnsley Football Club on the 8th April and Motspur Park (Fulham FC Training ground) on the 10th April 2003. The Final was played at Crystal Palace's Selhurst Park ground on the 5th April prior to the FA Women's FA Cup Final when the FA's **Kelly Simmons**, was kind enough to attend and to present the trophy and medals.

Brandon Daniels (representing Port Vale) won the last ever (2002/3) Smoby Monneret Table Football Championship held in the Billy Bremner Suite at Leeds United's Elland Road ground on the 27th March when Leeds players **Jason Wilcox** and **Nick Barmby** were kind enough to assist Smoby's **Adrian Mayes** to present the trophy and medals (see Appendix V for details of Competition winners).

A summary of participating numbers in all three competitions is as follows:

- Railtrack "Play Safe" Community Cup Competition for Primary/Junior School boys and girls in the Under 11 age group:

88 Community Schemes

2,916 teams

£20,380 paid to club schemes

- Adidas Community Cup Competition for Secondary School girls in the Under 13 age group:

84 Community Schemes

1,224 teams

£9,460 paid to club schemes

- Smoby Monneret Table Football Championship in association with Wagon Wheels:

83 Community Schemes

7,730 participants

£5,775 paid to club schemes

Summer 2003 brought with it a review and valuation of Sportsmatch monies received by local Football in the Community schemes during the first ten years of operation of Sportsmatch.

The details revealed were simply incredible and underlined the importance of the role of the FFE&VCTS Community Programme scheme in supporting bid applications from local projects.

In summary, within the ten-year period, 84 Football in the Community projects received a total of just under £3 million (£2,887,000) – i.e. an average of just under £35,000 per project. It was also clear that several community schemes had become well aware of the opportunity to enhance and develop local sponsorship funding by securing significant grant awards from Sportsmatch over the years. Indeed, the top ten 'Sportsmatch' community scheme beneficiaries were noted to be:

Club Community Scheme	Amount Received
Sunderland	£118,000
Burnley	£102,000
Notts County	£102,000
Derby County	£97,000
Manchester City	£97,000
Everton	£95,000
Leeds United	£95,000
Charlton Athletic	£76,000
Watford	£73,000
Aston Villa	£66,000
Huddersfield Town	£66,000

With Railtrack's sponsorship due to end in September 2003, work was well underway, during the early part of 2003, to look at alternative possibilities. In particular, meetings were held with two key agencies one of which was called Eurolink, led by **Darren McKimm**. Positive meetings with Darren, and with representatives of Kellogg's Frosties took place during the autumn of 2003.

Amongst the many discussions with agencies during the term of the Railtrack partnership, was a series of ongoing meetings with representatives of a large agency representing one of the biggest sponsors of grass-roots football. In the end, what was formulated was a plan based on extending the remit of the Community Programme scheme into in-schools activity AND after-schools' sessions at Secondary Schools, although the bid application in the end covered both Primary <u>and</u> Secondary Schools in England and Wales at key stage III (i.e. for 11-14-year olds only). The plan was for the sponsors money to be used as "match funding" for an application for significant additional funding (of up to £1 million) to the newly established Football Foundation[41] so that a national initiative could be launched that would represent a further expansion of the FFE&VTS Community Programme support operation.

Added into the equation was the apparent willingness of Adidas (at an early stage in the discussions) to become involved and to provide the necessary equipment for schools that would be required. This, of course, meant that the proposals, if approved and fully formulated, would be a HUGE deal! The would-be-partnership was lauded as:

"arguably the biggest single grassroots scheme in the world."

Other ideas put forward included:

---

41. *The Football Foundation was football's new charitable organisation that would effectively replace the Football Trust. The Football Trust had been funded by the Pools Companies (Littlewoods, Vernons and Zetters), and funding was drying up at this time following the Government's approval to introduce a National Lottery in 1994. The newly formed Football Foundation, however, was backed by the new commitment of the PL to invest substantial amounts of its increasing television deals into grass roots/community work, subject to receiving matching investment from The FA and from Government. One of the Football Task Force recommendations had been, of course, for the PL to invest more significantly into community work.*

- The development of an attractive website aimed at 11-14-year olds with regular features and offers including match tickets.
- Card collections.
- Standardisation of match programme coverage (something that the Football Foundation have enjoyed across all match programmes for many years).
- A school attendance incentive scheme.
- Closer links with junior supporters' clubs.
- A "Good Practice" manual.

The bid was eventually finalised in early 2001 and went forward with the apparent support of football's governing bodies. However, a March 2001 meeting with the Football Foundation's new Head of Community and Education, **Mandy Ayres**, identified several points which could count against the bid. For example:

- £1 million was a sizeable amount from within the Community and Education Panel's annual budget of around £8 million, especially as it would relate to only one project (the counter-argument to this was that 92 community schemes would be supporting and delivering the proposed venture).
- Account didn't appear to have been taken of the differing 'needs' of all the Schools that would be involved (although part of the proposal was for the support to be 'tailored' around each school's needs).
- School work was not a priority for the Community and Education Panel.
- In Mandy's experience, "top down" schemes didn't work.
- The likelihood was that if the national scheme was successful then local Football in the Community schemes might be prevented from applying for funding for their own localised projects.

Despite these potential issues, consideration of the bid application by the Community and Education Panel went ahead as planned. The initial outcome was for a follow-up meeting with representatives of the FA. After this, the bid was recommended to the Board of the Football Foundation by the Community & Education Panel (the Board met on the 13th June 2001 though, in the end, further consideration was deferred until the 22nd August).

After careful consideration (and an initial 'deferment'), and despite the following points:

- The investment of 15 months careful research and planning and lengthy consultation with all relevant parties and with Primary and Secondary schools.
- The potential inward investment of approximately £1.5 million into the coffers of football's grass roots.
- The clear success of the Football Trust in supporting the 'pump priming' model in the early 1990's when the injection of £4 million not only created pathways towards self-sufficiency but was also viewed as an extremely successful longer-term investment.
- The bid application represented a "roll-out" of Community scheme involvement at schools where there was no existing contact or provision – i.e. a minimum of a further 4,000 schools were expected to become involved.
- The support of the vast majority of 92 'parent' football clubs (only one or two clubs had raised any sort of issues with the proposals).
- The potential significant creation of at least 90+ new jobs/employment opportunities.

the bid was turned down. Head of Community and Education, **Mandy Ayres**, was kind enough to make contact following the meeting in August 2001 to confirm that the application had been unsuccessful. Some you win, some you lose!

Of great interest following the decision of the Board of Trustees of the Football Foundation, **Mandy Ayres** confirmed, at a meeting of Community Programme officials held on the 3rd September 2002, that she *"would like to think that £2 million per annum (of the Community and Education Panel budget) would go to local Football in the Community schemes"*.

The six-monthly Working Party Meeting of Community Officers held at Notts County

FC in November 2003 saw new ideas put forward, once again, and the main message noted was that money was becoming increasingly available to support Community Schemes in the field of social inclusion work (notwithstanding that there was felt to be an 'expertise gap' amongst Officers themselves in accessing funding and in working with new partners able to deliver in this field that needed to be filled). One of the ideas put forward was the potential appointment of an 'ambassador' not just at each club scheme but also on a national basis. Although it was felt that it was still a little early to push this idea, other topics included:

- The staging of a national conference for Community Officers with keynote speakers.
- The appointment of at least one Strategic/Fund-Raising Officer.
- The appointment of an additional Regional Director (in the Midlands), bringing the total number of support managers "in the field" up to six.

CHAPTER 15 –
"RESOURCES AND OPPORTUNITIES" RESEARCH BY MANCHESTER METROPOLITAN UNIVERSITY

THE RESEARCH UNDERTAKEN BY Manchester Metropolitan University (Department of Exercise and Sport Science, Football Development Unit) was eventually printed early on in 2004 and represented only the second major piece of research into the scheme's operation (the first having been concluded in 1994). The very detailed work was undertaken over a thirteen-month period between October 2002 and October 2003. The overall aim of the research was to examine in detail the state of 'Football in the Community' as a national programme, its evolution and the challenges and opportunities confronting it at the time.

The key questions posed by the researchers were:
1.   What is the current state of the Football in the Community programme?
2.   How has the programme evolved over the last decade?
3.   What are the challenges and opportunities that now confront the programme or are likely to confront it in the near future?

Amongst the work undertaken by Manchester Metropolitan University was:
-   The circulation and return of highly detailed and comprehensive questionnaires to 92 senior Community Officers (85 were returned – i.e. 92%). Incidentally, these questionnaires were 38 pages long!
-   Face to face, semi structured, individual and focus group, interviews with 16[42] club-based Community Schemes (larger schemes).
-   Detailed interviews with three pre-selected Community Officers at 'high quality' club schemes which had undergone significant changes.
-   Website analysis.
-   In-depth interviews with certain senior club officials (at a total of 14 clubs).
-   In-depth semi-structured interviews with Regional Directors and with senior officials (including the Chief Executive of the FFE&VTS).

The printed research report was, in the end, circulated to a wide variety of people though, in truth, the full scale of the possible impact of the research findings and its recommendations were somehow lost by the time the results were printed. That said, the research recommendations were very clear and were based on comprehensive and thorough research as follows:
-   The provision of regional (specialist) Funding Officers to assist Senior Officers in the preparation of financial bids (ideally in each region) following the noted success of **Peter Kay** at the FA.
-   Appropriate training and advice to be made available for Community Officers, particularly in the field of financial advice, to support the issue of "financial pressures" (being their main concern – see below).

---

42. The 16 clubs selected were selected on a geographical basis and included:
- North West: Blackburn Rovers, Burnley, Crewe Alexandra, Liverpool,
- North East and Yorkshire: Sunderland, - Midlands: Birmingham City, Notts County, Stoke City, Wolverhampton Wanderers
- South West: Bristol City, Hereford United
- South East: Charlton Athletic, Colchester United, Millwall, Southend United, West Ham United

- An increase in the number of Regional Directors serving local schemes (the research had revealed strong evidence that the rapid rate of growth of local community schemes was outstripping the resources of the Scheme's infrastructure and that the staffing level was *"inadequate to meet the needs of a growing number of schemes"*).

- More comprehensive training (and workshops) in specific areas for all community-based personnel (e.g. in employment law, personnel management skills, financial planning) and a structured mechanism to determine future training needs (another concern expressed by Community Officers related to "staffing/employment related difficulties" – see below). Other training needs included considerations regarding health and safety, equal opportunities and child protection.

- Increased evaluation of national (and local) marketing strategies including the staging of a national conference on a regular basis.

- The creation of better (internal and external) communication mechanisms for sharing of best practice (including more regional and more regular meetings).

- Arrangements to maximise communication across the 'key agencies' – i.e. Football's governing bodies (facilitating the views of all the agencies involved).

- Investigations into the idea of 'kitemarking'/rating the quality of local schemes especially where there is a *"high quality of provision"*.

- Improvement in website coverage/provision with more emphasis and investment in ICT resources and training specifically (this would help with another concern of Community Officers being "mounting paperwork" – see below).

- The creation of links and accessing of new information from emerging sports team Community Programmes and organisations around the world such as the Sports Philanthropy Project in the United States. (It was felt that more information about how this project operated could be helpful as a lead to the sort of role that the FFE&VTS Community Programme could play in future).

- Greater opportunities for career development within Community schemes/the national framework of 'Football in the Community'.

Comparisons were made with the in-depth review work undertaken in 1994. Also considered were the responses of the FFE&VTS to the recommendations of that report over the nine years since the original report had been prepared. As an example, it was noted and reported that the vast majority of clubs were considerably more "community-minded" and that "community responsibilities" were being taken on board by Chief Executives, Managers and by senior officials (including Directors).

The research showed that 98.8% of Community Officers were found to be looking for help with financial bids and with building partnerships. In addition, the research had recommended the appointment of several funding/partnership/strategic officers. Schemes were much less dependent on the national programme (FFE&VTS) support and the Report made the interesting conclusion that:

> *"a further movement towards greater scheme financial independence seems the obvious way forward"*

The Report made it clear that many schemes were *"making very substantial contributions to community life in England and Wales"* and were *"operating at a greatly enhanced level; of provision"*. At the same time, it was clear that there was *"an admirably strong degree of loyalty to the national programme among Senior Officers with the vast majority of officers greatly valuing the role played by the Support Office"*, even though many Officers felt at the time that *"the support office has been unable to keep pace with the rapid growth that has occurred in some schemes"*.

In terms of activities, the four main activities identified by Senior Officers as "core business" were still:

- in-school programmes (48%)
- after school programmes (45%)

- holiday courses (45%)
- soccer schools (20%)

Other activities identified included: Saturday Clubs (16%), football for girls and women (15%), match day activities (14%), education 12%, opportunities for people with disabilities (9%), in school curriculum coaching (8%), social inclusion work (8%), penalty competitions (7%), birthday parties (6%), and community courses (6%).

Developing schemes beyond the 'core', however, was apparent at many local schemes and a variety of *"important social needs"* were being met including work with girls and women, people with disabilities, minority ethnic groups etc. It was also acknowledged that the range of scheme activities were becoming increasingly numerous and varied.

Many Community Officers felt that club officials appreciated the positive impact of a healthy community scheme much more than when the previous research had been undertaken in 1994. Indeed, it was apparent that senior club officials (Chief Executive Officers and Chairmen) confirmed *"the more central positioning of schemes within their clubs' overall operations."*

The three main areas of great concern for Senior Officers were confirmed as:
- Financial pressures (88% of Senior Officers[43])
- Mounting paperwork (62%)
- Staffing/employment related difficulties (47%)

Broader comment was made following feedback from all the constituent partners of the Scheme including the Football Foundation, the FA, the PL, the FL and the PFA. One suggestion put forward was for the FFE&VTS Scheme itself to take the lead in *"developing stronger relationships with all of its football partners"*.

Contact was made with the Sports Philanthropy Project (SPP) in the United States of America (USA) where many club schemes are linked together through the work of the SPP. Some notable differences when compared with the Community Programme included:
- A secure web-site for 'members' of the SPP.
- The sharing of best practice and ideas via an annual conference.
- The creation of "Community Enhancement Plans" [44]

The membership idea worked particularly well in that membership in the USA had grown significantly over the period since the Project had been first established. Members were unanimous in expressing the view that they found consistent value in the services provided by the membership body.

Rick Fenoglio said:

> *"We attempted to find a model elsewhere in the world to shed light on the contents of the national programme. In the States, the SPP had been in operation for a number of years and had a mission to coordinate and lead the various programmes in place across sports clubs. The diversity of American programmes and sports was not that dissimilar to the range of sports programmes being delivered by Football in the Community. Unsurprisingly, the issues faced by American communities are largely the same as in the United Kingdom."*

---

43. 88% of Senior Officers saw the writing of (financial) bids for additional funding as part of their overall job responsibility.

44. Community Enhancement Plans are extensive reviews of the mission, objectives, structure, operations, staffing, implementation strategies and community partnerships of sports club community programmes. In other words, they are very similar in content to Business and/or Development Plans. The Community Enhancement Plans are confidential reports, together with recommendations, which represent a plan for maximising the local scheme's effectiveness and its impact on the local community. Indeed, work relating to the preparation of 'Community Enhancement Plans' is not dissimilar to that undertaken in work relating to a 'Strategic Review'.

It is worth mentioning at this point that one of the recommendations of the Report was for links to be fostered with the community operations of professional sports teams in America. As such, researcher, **Rick Fenoglio,** was to lead a 'delegation' of four people on a 'fact-finding' tour to Boston, USA in January 1995 to meet with Greg Johnson from the USA-based 'Sports Philanthropy Project' (see Chapter 18).

Another interesting point to come out of the research revealed that the induction programme for newly appointed Community Officers was now *"superior to that which was in place at the time of the last research point in 1994"*.

Another aspect of the research was its conclusion that *"Football in the Community now stands on the cusp of a new and exciting era in its development"*. This was true in so many ways, though it was clear that the growth of the PL, together with the need to plough more and more monies into grass-roots football, and its increased 'ownership' of its member club community work, meant that it was likely that any new and exciting era may proceed with the separate involvement of the PL and the FL.

Concerns were expressed by senior officials about keeping pace with the growth of local community schemes and efforts to be *"all things to all people"* which was becoming increasingly difficult at that time given the move into matters relating to disadvantage, social exclusion and health not to mention existing work that was growing and developing, especially in relation to education. One of the senior officials stated that when asked if Football in the Community was at a crossroads he said:

> *"I don't think we are at a crossroads. I think we are at a junction of lot of roads… even a thousand roads. Each local scheme individually can go down any one of these roads and they can even go down a lot of roads together at the same time. We need to encourage the schemes on whatever road(s) they decide to travel down."*

Another senior Manager, when asked about keeping pace with the rapidly broadening range and diversity of local scheme stated:

> *"If you look at charities up and down the country, they've all got fundraising managers. They've all got people who are involved daily with the bidding process and with building partnerships. They know how to write the bids and they know when the bids have to be in. We're not reacting quickly enough to the demand that's coming from (Senior) Officers".*

Rick Fenoglio commented further:

> *"As researchers we were proud that we had shed a light on a programme that does immeasurable good in the community."*

Brendon McGuire added:

> *"Looking back on our research report now, I am confident that we asked the right questions, at that moment in time, to establish where 'Football in the Community' was positioned and where it might possibly go next in terms of development. I remember feeling full of admiration for much of the work that was being undertaken in clubs. This involved seeing talented young community staff doing sterling work in their club communities and also more established figures (including some very high-profile ex-players) putting good things back into the game. Sometimes it was humbling to witness this. As researchers we were left feeling that 'Football in the Community' lived up to its reputation as being "football's best kept secret" and that communities were significantly strengthened by its impact"*

Footnote: The research revealed that:

- the percentage of former professional footballers who were acting as "Senior Officers" reduced from 67.9% in 1994 to 61.8% in 2003.
- 100% of Senior Officers at the time of the research in 2003 were male.
- Over 50% of Senior Officers had been in post for more than five years.
- 31% of Senior Officers stated that their schemes were operating as registered charities in 2003.

CHAPTER 16 – 2004 - 2005

THE START OF THE NEW YEAR in 2004 arguably marked the start of the change in the way community 'business' was to be conducted in future partly as a result of the greater involvement and increased investment of the PL. At the same time, there was an apparent reduction in expectations from the FFE&VTS Community Programme as a support organisation. Several different factors all combined to impact on what had been the smooth running of the organisation up to this point not least the increasing involvement of the PL in community developments which may well have been kick-started by the sponsorship, interest and funding support of Barclaycard.

Also, in early 2004, **Mickey Burns** departed as Chief Executive. Mick had been a top-class Chief Executive Officer, creative, hard-working, innovative, honest and extremely loyal to his staff, and his departure was met with overwhelming sadness by all the FFE&VTS staff. A statement released at the time simply said:

"Mick has resigned and given his reasons to the Directors of the Society"

After many meetings and much to-ing and fro-ing, the Board of the FFE&VTS eventually agreed to re-structure the FFE&VTS so that the three separate areas of operation would be overseen by **Simon Tuley** (finance), **Pat Lally** (education and scholarships/apprenticeships) and **Roger Reade** (Community Programme). London-born Pat was a former player who had begun his playing career as an apprentice with Millwall before moving to York City in 1971. He then played for Swansea City, Aldershot (on loan) and Doncaster Rovers.

Pat Lally's appointment was especially important at this time following the Government's proposed move to encourage agencies to move towards adopting the "Modern Apprenticeships" programme. 'Modern Apprenticeships' targeted 16-17-year-olds and provided a training route to address skill needs, outlining the training to be provided and the qualification(s) to be obtained. Sadly, this was only a short-term arrangement as it was made clear that new football body organisations (soon to be established) would deliver the former scholarships programme on behalf of the PL and the FL. Once these arrangements had been concluded, this would leave the FFE&VTS with the Community Programme as the only operational part of the organisation. (In the end, former Chief Executive of Huddersfield Town, **Alan Sykes**, took over this important work at a newly established organisation called "League Football Education" that would run programmes at FL clubs with the support of the PFA. At the time, the PL were also exploring the possible establishment of their own operation. 'Premier League Learning' would become established to operate this support operation for PL clubs).

A new chairman of the FFE&VTS was appointed being **Professor John Goodman CBE** (who had taken over from **Professor Sir John Wood** following Professor Sir John's retirement) and he outlined at a Board of Trustees meeting that it was likely that the two Leagues might become more involved in supporting their own member clubs work in their local communities, particularly in relation to commercial deals (such as the existing Barclaycard sponsorship of the PL). As a result, the Board of the FFE&VTS agreed to endorse the view that no new contracts (be they sponsorship arrangements or otherwise) be agreed without Board consideration and approval. Indeed, the first such agreement to be taken to the Board was the proposed new Community Programme sponsorship deal with Kellogg's Frosties (see Chapter 17)

Ten years of existence was celebrated in style by 'Kick it Out' with a champagne reception at the Great Eastern Hotel in London on the 21st January.

Tragic news followed in February 2004 when it was revealed that one of Wrexham's popular Community Coaches, **Danny Forooghian**, died after a car crash in which he had been a passenger. Danny was aged 18.

There was yet more sad news in March as former Manchester City and Blackpool Community Director **Chris Muir** passed away in a Blackpool hospice. Manchester City Secretary, **Bernard Halford,** said:

"Chris was a lovely man who made a huge contribution to football"

The funeral was held at the White Church in Lytham St Anne's on the 1st April 2004.

It was "business as usual" as work continued in early March 2004 when a two-day induction was arranged in the Manchester office for 13 newly appointed Community Officers: **Steve Cuss** (AFC Bournemouth), **Wayne Bullimore** (Barnsley), **Stuart Jacobs** (Cambridge United), **David Busst** (Coventry City), **Simon Carnall** (Derby County), **Jamie Vittles** (Exeter City), **Gary Childs** (Grimsby Town), **Stuart Smith** (Luton Town), **Mark Hemingray** (Mansfield Town), **Mark Rivers** (Reading), **Gregg Broughton** (Rushden & Diamonds), **Adie Hurst** (Stoke City) and **Darren Oldroyd** (Wimbledon. Darren would also move on to MK Dons as Community Officer in due course). Having been in charge since 2002, **Duncan Riddle** adopted the new title of "Senior Community Officer" at Aston Villa (later becoming "Head of Community" in 2006). At the same time, **Paul Hardyman** was appointed as Senior Community Officer at Portsmouth. Portsmouth-born, Paul played for his local club between 1983 and 1988 following a move from non-league Waterlooville. He later moved to Sunderland, Bristol Rovers, Wycombe Wanderers and Barnet.

Another royal visit went ahead on the 27th April when **His Royal Highness (HRH) Prince Edward** visited Notts County's Community Scheme to view for himself the excellent work being undertaken at Meadow Lane. The same day, Watford launched the Watford Community Trust as a registered charity.

The 2003/4 Competitions saw Regional Finals of the new Kellogg's Frosties Cup played at Rotherham United on the 10th March (Northern Finals) and at Swindon Town on the 11th March 2004 (Southern Finals). The Final was played at the Cardiff Millennium Stadium on the 21st March prior to the LDV Vans Final (in which Blackpool beat Southend United by 2-0). The match was refereed by **Billy Margetts** and the presentation of the trophy and medals was made by **Peter Harrison** and **Gavin Bowyer** (Brand Managers for Kellogg's Frosties) and **Chris Thayne**... together with **Tony the Tiger** from Kellogg's!

The Adidas Girls Under 13's Competition saw the regional finals held at Scunthorpe United Football Club on the 20th April (Northern Finals) and the Southern Finals held at Wycombe Wanderers Football Club on the 22nd April 2004. The Final was eventually played at Villa Park on Saturday the 8th May after the original match (due to be played at Wembley) had been called off due to the state of the Wembley pitch after heavy rain. Refereeing the match for the first time was Hertfordshire CFA referee and self-confessed sports fan, **Nigel Rothband**.

Participating numbers in both competitions were as follows:
-    The Kellogg's Frosties Competition for Primary/Junior School boys and girls in the Under 11 age group:
92 Community Schemes
3,032 teams
£19,708 paid to club schemes
-    Adidas Community Cup Competition for Secondary School girls in the Under 13 age group:
83 Community Schemes
1,307 teams
£8,495 paid to club schemes[45]

---

45. *The Smoby Monneret Table Football Competition did not continue into the 2003/4 season.*

At a meeting of the Community Advisory Group held in May, it was agreed that no more support would be offered for any new commercial arrangements in the name of the FFE&VTS Community Programme (especially as 'commercial' arrangements with new community partners were developing elsewhere). Indeed, it was requested that a paper be raised based on the idea of eliminating the commercial involvement with sponsors so that the Leagues themselves could develop their own community partnerships and then, perhaps, consider the possibility of considering 'bankrolling' the FFE&VTS Community Programme scheme.

The Group also agreed not to support any extension to the 'Communications Strategy' work with the Media Group which had been so successful up to this point, partly as the PL had started building closer links with *Match of the Day* (who were to include a short-filmed feature on different community initiatives based at PL clubs), *Shoot* magazine and with national newspapers all aimed at raising the profile about PL club work in their local communities. Indeed, this was undoubtedly a major step forward in raising awareness of the good work of PL club-based community schemes.

May saw the appointment of former West Bromwich Albion Community Manager **Mark Ashton** as Chief Executive at Watford Football Club. This reflected great credit on Mark and the work he had undertaken up to this point and all at the FFE&VTS Community Programme sent their best wishes to Mark in his new role.

The now annual 'Playing for Success' conference went ahead at the end of May. Guest speaker, **Dave Richards** (Chairman of the PL) enthused about club involvement in the community and reflected on the work of the Football Foundation, Playing for Success and the Princes Trust all of whom, he rightly felt, were "*at the heart of all of it*".

During the adult/youth training contract year 2003/4, recruitment of young assistants had become almost exclusively via the YT programme. Figures recorded for the contract year 2003/2004 are detailed in "Appendix III – Table of trainees in post year by year 2002-2007" ★[46]. Amongst those clubs with excellent recruitment levels during the year were projects at Colchester United, Huddersfield Town, Hull City, Nottingham Forest, Notts County and Stoke City.

The number of club projects participating in Adult and YT programmes in 2003/2004 increased to 66 during the contract year. Much credit for this increase was properly due to **Gary Naven**, in particular for all his hard work in spreading the message of the YT programme opportunity amongst so many new club schemes (especially in the South of England).

Match programme coverage during the 2003/4 season was assessed once again and the following clubs were selected as being those with the best community coverage:

2003/4	Winners	Runners Up (various)
PL	Newcastle United	Blackburn Rovers, Everton, Fulham, Leicester City, Manchester City, Wolverhampton Wanderers
FL Division One	Stoke City	Burnley, Cardiff City, Ipswich Town, Millwall, West Bromwich Albion, West Ham United

46. These figures include the numbers of Youth trainees in post which averaged approximately 127.50 trainees in post per month. In turn, 'New Deal' trainees in post reduced further to 3.24 per month.

FL Division Two	Colchester United	Brighton & Hove Albion, Notts County, Port Vale, Sheffield Wednesday, Stockport County
FL Division Three	Doncaster Rovers	Bristol Rovers, Cambridge United, Huddersfield Town, Hull City

In June 2004, Head of Adult and Youth Training, **Gary Naven,** announced that he was to leave after ten and a half years' service in order to take up a position within his own family business (which followed on from the sad death of his father at the beginning of the year). Gary had done a super job heading up adult and youth training, and he had almost single-handedly guided schemes to take up opportunities where contracts could be negotiated and where change was necessary.

Also leaving at the end of June to join the PFA was **Pat Wilkinson** who had worked so hard since her appointment in 1996. **Lynn Leonard** stepped up to take over from Pat. Pat had been absolutely brilliant in all aspects of her administrative and accountancy work for the Scheme. Sadly, Pat passed away in September 2019.

Given that commercial/sponsorships were to reduce, Gary's departure presented an opportunity to re-deploy **Richard Finney** from his post as Marketing Manager so that he took over from Gary as Training Officer. This also allowed for further consideration to use the monies saved to appoint a dedicated Funding Officer. This was taken forward and approved by the Board leading to interviews being arranged for short-listed candidates on the 5th August.

Yet more tragic news followed that Swansea City's Assistant Community Officer, **Neil Jenkins**, had died in a car accident on the 4th June along with his fiancée. This came as devastating news to their families but also to many people within the FFE&VTS Community Programme, not least Regional Director **John Relish** who had been a keen supporter of the growth and development of Swansea City's community scheme.

Good news was received in June when **Kirk Wheeler** (who had left Watford the previous year) confirmed that he was to become the new Community Officer at non-League Aldershot Town commencing on the 2nd August (then an independent and local community scheme).

In view of the departure of Community Officer **Domenico Genovese** to pastures new, the decision was made to 'wind up' the Kettering Town FC Community Project at the end of June 2004.

By the end of June 2004, a summary of monies showed that Community Schemes owed in excess of £800,000 to the FFE&VTS Community Programme in respect of wages (noting too that the total amount of wages processed via the FFE&VTS Community Programme payroll during the previous twelve months had been well in excess of £10 million). Whilst much of this debt was short-term (i.e. the majority of community schemes could pay the amounts owing in respect of wages), some of the debt had accumulated despite efforts to improve the 'debt management' processes within the organisation. In turn, this underlined the fact that the monthly Direct Debit/Standing arrangements were inadequate.

In July 2004, Assistant Community Officer at Southend United, **Ray Scott** sadly passed away. Ray had done some sterling work for a few years as Assistant to Senior Officer, **Frankie Banks**. Ray's funeral was held on the 19th July. Tragically, the day before (18th July), one of Tranmere Rovers popular community coaches, **Samir Bencheikh**, lost his life in a car crash. Samir had been a passenger in a car driven by his friend, footballer Alex Cole. Samir was 18.

In view of the reduction in income to arise as sponsorship income reduced, it was clear that a new budget needed to be prepared for the FFE&VTS Community Programme. Consequently, in an effort to come up with a balanced budget, work started in the summer investigating whether possible financial savings and/or staff reductions could be made. One consideration being taken forward was yet another reduction in the number of Regional Directors from 5 to 4 (instead of an increase in the number of Regional Directors from 5 to 6 as had been recommended in the Manchester Metropolitan University Research – see Chapter 15).

Another consideration put forward was to consider reducing the financial contributions being made by the FFE&VTS Community Programme to non-League clubs. This would also include a new policy in that newly relegated clubs from the Football League (FL) would only be guaranteed funding for twelve months following their relegation. Meanwhile, FL Board approval for the FFE&VTS Community Programme to continue to support FL club community schemes (subject to PFA funding continuing) was secured irrespective of what was to happen in relation to PL clubs.

The interviews for the position of Funding Officer were held on the 5th August 2004 and three experienced candidates were interviewed. In the end, after lengthy discussion, the post and a two-year contract was offered to **Angeline Mather,** whose prior experience at North Lincolnshire Council and in working with the Scunthorpe United Community Scheme tipped the balance in her favour. The position was certainly full of pressure from minute one in that the Scheme could not afford for the position not to be successful straight away, meaning that Angeline had to *"hit the ground running"* as they say! Her start date was set as the 4th October 2004.

This was a huge gamble by Scheme officials, even though it did provide further evidence of work done by the FFE&VTS Community Programme in positively responding to the recommendations of the Manchester Metropolitan University Research Report.

Angeline's appointment coincided with some successful work done, ironically, in generating new funding from the "Aim Higher" programme by **Rob Halsall** from Manchester Metropolitan University. Rob managed to put together approximately 25 local bid-applications on behalf of locally based Community Schemes which offered extra support for Key Stage 4 attainment for pupils working out of school hours (Years 9/10). The 25 community schemes came from all round the country (North West x 5; North East x 5; Midlands x 6; South West x 2 and South East x 7).

Karen Duggan was the Aim Higher National Project Manager.

A conference entitled "Raising achievements and aspirations through football" for successful club schemes would eventually be arranged in March 2006 at Derby County Football Club. Former Chief Executive of the Youth Sport Trust and Chair of UK Sport (and now Head of Female Football at the FA), **Sue Campbell**, spoke at the conference about her own hopes to create an environment in which young people could be responsible for their own destinies by creating a process of "engage, enrich and empower".

.By Autumn 2004, scheme Regional Directors were spending time, quite properly, attending an increasing number of Trustee meetings at those clubs that had become registered charities in their own right (it was estimated that approximately 24 schemes had been registered with the Charity Commission and a further 8 schemes had started moving towards securing charitable status by September 2004, being 10 PL clubs and 22 FL clubs).

Autumn 2004 saw Sunderland AFC decide to make up to nine of their senior community scheme staff redundant. The key senior figure affected by this was senior Community Officer, **Bob Oates**, who had done a simply outstanding job in building up the work of the club in their local community. It later became known that the club had also chosen to cancel all summer holiday courses and to refund all monies to would-be participants. In addition, the club had taken over signatory control of the community scheme bank account.

Meetings with Community Officers were arranged in the autumn of 2004 in the five regions as follows:

4th October 2004 - Notts County FC (Midlands Community Officers)

6th October 2004 - Bristol Rovers FC (South West based Community Officers)

12th October 2004 - Liverpool FC (North West Community Officers)

18th October 2004 - Charlton Athletic FC (for Community Officers in the South East)

4th November 2004 Leeds United FC (Yorkshire and North East Community Officers)

The meetings allowed full 'updates' on developments at the FFE&VTS so that all Community Officers were aware of what had gone on, and what the future held for them. **Angeline Mather** herself also attended and confirmed that there were some "quick wins" that she was to explore early on. She also outlined that she would be working hand in glove with officers to explore other potential funders. Angeline announced that her hopes included the organisation of some funding awareness workshops on a regional basis. It was recognised at the time that a fair and relevant system of charging 'commission' on any new monies secured by Angeline would need to be developed (it was noted that one particular independent North West based money-raising agency charged up to 60% commission on any new monies raised for organisations. Yes - 60%!!).

Also, in October, the FA staged a Charter Standard Holiday Course conference at which the FFE&VTS Community Programme was given a platform to talk about how Charter Standard would improve holiday course provision, particularly in terms of quality and safety & enjoyment for children attending.

With support from **Kate Egford** (Senior Development Manager at Sport England), a meeting was also set up on the 5th October to consider Sport England's introduction of a "Whole Sport Plan" that would unite the requirements of all bodies within one sport – i.e. football, led by **Sir Trevor Brooking CBE** (Trevor had been a legendary midfield player with West Ham United, his only club, between 1966 and 1983, making over 500 league appearances for the club during his playing career. He was also an England international with 47 full caps. He was knighted in 2004).

The meeting attracted representatives of the English Schools FA, the Football Foundation, the FFE&VTS Community Programme Scheme and the PFA. After much discussion, it became clear that the proposed 'Whole Sport Plan' represented a marvellous opportunity for football. The "bottom line" was that football had until November 1st to submit a football bid-application (news of the outcome would be confirmed by January 2005). Amongst matters to be included were PE and school sport, Further Education, Girls Centres of Excellence, boys, people with disabilities, coaches, facilities and even the wider agendas of health, crime and disorder. Further meetings were proposed at the end of October and in January 2005. Kate was also kind enough to set up a later meeting to consider support for the staging of the Women's European Championships to be held in 2005.

The Sportsmatch Annual Awards event for 2004 was held at Twickenham, home of England rugby union, when the Football in the Community's adidas sponsored "Supernova Goal Striker Challenge" came second in the youth category. Fulham's Community scheme won the Ethnic Minority Sports Category for their initiative with sponsors Western Union.

Plans were also underway to provide a surprise party for **Dennis Leman** who was to celebrate his 50th birthday at the start of December 2004. **Ian "Spider" Mellor** was kind enough to contact several former playing colleagues on the basis that they could attend, unbeknown to Dennis of course! In the end, amongst those who attended were Janet Baxter (newly-married and now Mrs **Janet Baxter-Bennett**), former team-mates **Frank Carrodus**, **Brian Hornsby**, **George McBeth** and **Paul Power** plus Community Officers **Mick Ferguson**, **Brian Hall**, **Dean Holtham**, **Mike Smith** and **Stuart Smith**.

Weekly wages paid out by the FFE&VTS Community Programme covering the six-month period from January to June 2004 totalled £3,096,531. For the period between July and December 2004, a further £3,109,192 was paid out. Therefore, for the 12-month period from January to December 2004, total weekly wages paid out on behalf of 85 community projects (plus the Thames Gateway scheme operating at four London clubs) reached a grand total for the full year of £6,205,723. Added to this was the amount of club schemes with casual/part-time staff that were being paid on a monthly basis, which was worth £2,550,760 for the period January to June 2004 and a further £2,366,100 for the period July-December 2004 making a total of £4,916,860 for the year. As such, the grand total for wages paid out via the FFE&VTS payroll reached the staggering total of £11,122,583.

From a statistical point of view, in 2004 the FFE&VTS Community Programme payroll for the year 2004 suggested that average wages for senior Community Officers rose once again to approximately £24,977 per annum (based on the wages paid to 78 different club based Community Officers). In addition, average wages for Assistant Officers reached around £13,184 per annum based on the salaries of more than 400 Assistants paid through the FFE&VTS Community Programme payroll (this figure did not include Youth Trainees).

The regional analysis of average wages paid in different regions showed that in the North West and North East regions, the average wages paid to (senior) Community Officers in 2004 was approximately £24,104 (previous year £22,984) per annum. In the Midlands and South West, the average was slightly lower at around £23,546 (previous year £21,570) per annum. In the South East, the average reached £33,332 (previous year £31,789) per annum.

A summary of club Community Schemes turnover during the year 2004 (completed in the spring/summer of 2005) revealed that turnover at 70 local community schemes reached a collective total of £16,703,700 (at the community schemes that operated on a local basis) meaning that average turnover across those schemes had risen again to approximately £238,624 per annum.

By now, things were starting to happen in various ways. The South East clubs began looking at whether an additional local (regionally based) charity (overseen by some sort of regional "Board") could be set up with a view to driving access to new sources of funding and new projects.

Led by Bolton Wanderers dynamic Community Officer, **Geoff Lomax**, and encouraged by the FFE&VTS Community Programme, a 'syndicate' of North West club schemes was also coming together to investigate establishing a local marketing group, an increased number of 'networking' meetings and a strategic programme at each North West club so that a 'bigger picture' of opportunity could be developed for the region.

In addition, the FFE&VTS Board had requested that a "Strategic Review" of the organisation be produced so that the work being undertaken by the FFE&VTS Community Programme could be properly evaluated. Various informal meetings of staff and Regional Directors followed leading to a draft paper being made available before Christmas.

The Strategic Review paper was also put together following lengthy discussions with representatives of the FA (**Kelly Simmons**), the PL (**Emma Joussemet,** previously **Emma Stanford**), the FL (**Andy Williamson, Michael Tattersall** and **Robin Gibson**), the PFA (**Richard Jobson**) and all staff of the FFE&VTS Community Programme. One thing that was apparent was the acceptance of the concept of all commercial/sponsorship arrangements going exclusively to the respective Leagues to take forward.

The presentation to the Board of Directors/Trustees took place on the 16th February 2005.

Key aspects of the "Strategic Review" were:

- The declaration of a new vision *"to maximise the potential of Football in the Community schemes to have a significant impact on the health, social development and well-being of their local communities"*.

- The importance of all parties understanding that worthwhile partnerships were key to growth and expansion *"for genuine community and club benefit"*.

- How key it was for all local Football in the Community schemes to have the support of a 'support agency' to help bridge the gap between clubs and local community groups/ associations. In addition, the support agency working in partnership with local clubs allowed continued access to external funding AND the unique exception from having to pay VAT on income.

- The fact that local schemes were now being developed so that 'core' activities such as schools work/holiday courses and match day activities were being added to with worthwhile work allied to <u>education</u> (classrooms at grounds/Playing for Success and the delivery of "Learning

FC"); health and social inclusion (including crime and disorder/support for the PAT 10 Report re more jobs, less crime, improved educational attainment etc.)

- Moving forward, in order to continue to promote "best practice", annual national conferences should be arranged; the national competitions should be preserved as a focal point for local activity; more funding Officers would help the local schemes to develop even more quickly (particularly in the field of partnership working).

- The move away from long-term support for non-league club-based schemes (which it was felt should become the role of those particular Leagues).

This was all backed up at the time by the fact that "4 out of every 5 people believe that football clubs have an important contribution to make to their local community".

The response from the FA, the FL and the PFA was overwhelmingly for the 'support agency' to continue with its current role and for all 'commercial properties' to go to the partner organisations. The Board also agreed that the FFE&VTS should be encouraged to apply for funding from the Football Foundation in support of the proposed Regional Funding Officers.

At the time, it was noted that the FFE&VTS Community Programme support extended to all PL clubs with the exception of Arsenal; to all FL clubs with the exception of Chester City, Leyton Orient, Peterborough United and Yeovil Town. In addition, a new exception was Sunderland where the club's community coaching involvement had now disappeared. In relation to Sunderland, **Lesley Spuhler** (who had originally been recruited by ex-Community Officer, **Bob Oates**) was to take over as Community Director (she was listed as Director of the SAFC Foundation in the FL's 2006/7 Handbook). Indeed, as Sunderland's Head of Community, Lesley was later to be awarded an OBE in the New Year Honours List in December 2015 for her community work and for her services to charities in the North East.

In addition, support was still being offered to 6 Non-League clubs that were mainly former FL clubs.

Before the end of the year, it was noted that:
- **Brett Whaley** had been appointed at Boston United
- **Billy Legg** was to leave his post as Community Officer at Halifax Town
- **Fraser Foster** left his position as Regional Director in the Midlands in order to take up the post of Community Director at West Bromwich Albion. Former Sunderland Head of Community, **Bob Oates**, was kind enough to agree to take over from Fraser on a temporary basis for the period January to March 2005 only initially (pending the Board's response to the 'Strategic Review' document once it had been completed).

2005 saw further internal meetings aimed at making the final alterations to the "Strategic Review" document. In addition, a meeting with **Peter Lee**, Chief Executive of the Football Foundation (and former Chief Executive of the Football Trust) was arranged prior to the end of January. Peter's views were rather that the FFE&VTS Community Programme and the Football Foundation should work more closely together and ultimately come together. Also seen for their own further thoughts on the "Strategic Review" were **Gordon Taylor** (PFA), **Darren Bernstein** (FL) and **Alex Horne** and **Sir Trevor Brooking CBE** (FA). The Strategic Review followed on and adopted the recommendations of the "Resources and Opportunities" research undertaken by Manchester Metropolitan University and was presented to the Board on the 16th February 2005 (see Chapter 15).

Angeline Mather looked forward to the staging of two workshops (one in the north at Leeds United FC and one in the south at Oxford United FC) following her first success in generating total funding of £13,000 for the Blackpool Community Scheme.

Lawrie Pearson resigned from his position at Carlisle United and moved to Gretna Green FC.

Links with Portsmouth's growing community operation were developing thanks to much better communication and closer liaison with **Rosie Francis**, by now the club's senior Community Officer who was working with ex-Pompey player **Paul Hardyman**.

John Hudson was approached by **Gordon Taylor** at the PFA with a view to leading the PFA's proposed new community department as Liaison Executive/Community Affairs Manager. John left the FFE&VTS Community Programme with grateful thanks for all his hard work over the previous 8 years and with everyone's best wishes for the future.

Initially, approval was given for the FFE&VTS Community Programme to advertise John's former position as Regional Director in the North West on a permanent basis in the Guardian newspaper (the advert was placed in March 2005 and five candidates were selected for interview on the 6th April). A Board Meeting held on the 12th April, however, agreed that the scheme should continue only with the support of four Regional Directors (not five) up to the end of June. This did, however, mean that **Bob Oates** could continue his good work as a Regional Director on a temporary basis for a further period of just under three months up to the end of June.

Because of the forecast budget deficit, checks were also undertaken on whether FFE&VTS Community Programme support could be further reduced to only three regional directors. The 3 Regional Directors would each take charge of working alongside 24 clubs each. In turn, this meant that **Richard Finney**, **Dennis Leman** and **Roger Reade** would have to take responsibility for supporting approximately 24 club schemes between them. This was to be a key part in the 'downsizing' of the FFE&VTS Community Programme. At the time it was also noted that responsibilities for overseeing the 18 PL club schemes were shared between **Dick Krzywicki** (Newcastle United), **Dennis Leman** (Aston Villa, Birmingham City, Bolton Wanderers, Everton, Liverpool, Manchester United and Wigan Athletic), **Dave Palmer** (Charlton Athletic, Chelsea, Fulham, Tottenham Hotspur and West Ham United), **Roger Reade** (Manchester City and Middlesbrough) and **John Relish** (Birmingham City, Portsmouth and West Bromwich Albion).

With the budget such as it was (and with a forecast shortfall in the current year budget of around £250,000), it was also agreed, as a 'cost-cutting' exercise, that two members of the current administrative staff of four should be made redundant. **Gareth Dando** (then at George Davies Solicitors) was kind enough to offer sound advice as to how the necessary process and selection procedure (using a "Redundancy Selection Matrix") would normally work. This was obviously an extremely uncomfortable and difficult time for all at the FFE&VTS Community Programme. Fortunately, the two staff selected, **Tracey Parkinson** and **Jayne Sherratt**, were taken on by the PFA in administrative roles. At least this meant that what could have been an otherwise painful process became somewhat less painful in the end for Tracey and Jayne. Even Flo the cleaner was cut back to working only three days per week rather than five.

This left the FFE&VTS Community Programme short of the real resources necessary to continue. Indeed, only eleven members of staff remained: 1 Training Manager and 1 Assistant (**Richard Finney** and **Steph Lunn**); 3 Regional Directors (**Dick Krzywicki**, **Dave Palmer** and **John Relish**);

1 Funding Manager (**Angeline Mather**); 2 Wages/Accountancy staff (**Lynn Leonard** and **Ian Niven**);

1 Personal Assistant/Secretary (**Kay McKechnie**, previously MacMillan) plus 2 Senior Administrators (**Roger Reade** and **Dennis Leman**). Loosely, these departments were defined as "Training", "Payroll/Accounts", "Funding", "Field Support" and "General". All departments would now be expected to "break even". This meant that "Payroll/Accounts" needed to raise approximately £50,000 per annum and, similarly, "Funding" had to raise £40,000 as a minimum. These expectations were, of course, extremely optimistic.

Meanwhile, Accountant **Simon Tuley** was also checking out the possibility of 'hiring' a payroll bureau to undertake the payroll on behalf of club schemes. One estimated cost came in at between £65,000-£70,000 as a cost for one year. In addition, Simon also began the search for new (cheaper) office premises. Manchester City's new ground at 'Sport City' was one possibility being taken forward at this time.

Life went on as liaison and/or "update" meetings took place at many clubs (e.g. Barnet, Coventry City, Grimsby Town, Leyton Orient and Newcastle United) and several of these were either based around possible moves towards charitable status[47] or around possible reductions in scheme budgets.

Regarding competitions run during the 2004/5 season: The Regional Finals of the Kellogg's Frosties Cup were played at Scunthorpe United on the 15th March 2005 and at Wycombe Wanderers on the 16th March 2005 and the Final was played at the Cardiff Millennium Stadium on the 10th April prior to the LDV Vans Final (in which Wrexham beat Southend United by 2-0). Refereeing the Final match again was **Nigel Rothband** (from Hertfordshire CFA). The Kellogg's Frosties Cup and medals were presented by **Gavin Bowyer** (Brand Manager – Kellogg's Frosties) together with **Chris Thayne**.

The 2004/5 Girls Under 13s Regional Finals were played on 13th April 2005 at Rotherham United FC (Northern Finals) and on the 18th April at Queens Park Rangers FC (Southern Finals). The Final was played at West Ham United's Upton Park ground when the trophy and medals were again kindly presented by FA Head of National Football Development, **Kelly Simmons** (see Appendix V for details of Competition winners).

Details of participating schools were as follows:

-       The Kellogg's Frosties Competition for Primary/Junior School boys and girls in the Under 11 age group:

92 Community Schemes

2,954 teams

£19,201 paid to club schemes

-       Adidas Community Cup Competition for Secondary School girls in the Under 13 age group:

83 Community Schemes

1,287 teams

£8,365 paid to club schemes

At the clubs:

-       After a meeting with Barnet's **Tony Kleanthous** (Chairman), it was agreed that **Janet Matthewson** be appointed to oversee the club's community affairs. This was a terrific appointment at the time, especially given Janet's previous experience in office management and in construction/health and safety work.

-       **John Halpin** returned to take up the role of Community Officer at Carlisle United after a short spell as Youth Team Coach at the club, replacing **Paul Devlin**.

-       **Brian Croft** left Macclesfield Town to be replaced by a new two-man team. Joint Community Officers, **Paul McGuire** and **Ian Cosier**, were appointed in good time for the start of the new season.

-       **Geoff Crudgington** took up the position of goalkeeping coach at Plymouth Argyle, leaving **Mark Rivers** to move from Reading in order to take up the post of Community Officer at the club.

-       Following Mark's move to the South West, **Lee Herron** took up the post of Senior Community Officer at Reading.

The month of May saw two conferences held. The first was organised by the FA and was entitled "The Power of Football". It was held at Tottenham Hotspur FC on the 23rd May. Several awards were presented to Community Schemes including:

-       FA National Football Development Award for Health – Manchester City
-       FA National Football Development Award for Education – Notts County
-       FA National Football Development Award for Disability - Everton

Chairman of the FA Development Committee, **Ray Berridge** and **Sir Trevor Brooking CBE** (FA Director, Football Development) presented the awards to **Tom Flower** (Manchester City), **Graham Moran** (Notts County) and **Dave Connor** (Everton).

---

47. *It should be noted that, at this time, grants were still available from the Football Foundation towards the legal costs incurred by local Community Schemes in moving towards charitable status.*

The second conference was the annual 'Playing for Success' conference this time held in Stratford on Avon on the 26th and 27th May.

Match programme coverage during the 2004/5 season saw the following clubs selected as those with the best community coverage:

2004/5	Winners	Runners Up (various)
PL	Charlton Athletic	Fulham, West Bromwich Albion
FL Division One	Stoke City	Ipswich Town, Wolverhampton Wanderers
FL Division Two	Doncaster Rovers	Brentford, Port Vale,
FL Division Three	Notts County	Rushden & Diamonds

2004/2005 was almost exclusively a youth training contract year (places under "Modern Apprentices" were first allocated during the contract year) and figures recorded for the contract year are detailed in "Appendix III – Table of trainees in post year by year 2002-2007" [48].

Amongst those clubs with excellent recruitment levels during the year were projects at Blackburn Rovers, Bolton Wanderers, Huddersfield Town, Norwich City, Notts County, Stoke City, Walsall and Wolverhampton Wanderers.

The total number of club projects confirmed as participating in the YT programme during the contract year 2004/2005 was 67.

As more and more community schemes moved to become registered charities, so the role of FFE&VTS Community Programme managers moved towards becoming trustees of the charities.

The strategic management of these schemes also changed as the management and operation of the charities became the full responsibility of the charity boards. No longer would the FFE&VTS Community Programme be responsible for health and safety, employment legislation, the preparation of accounts and risk assessments etc. The role of supporting Community Officers, however, continued very much as before.

At the same time, FFE&VTS Chairman **Professor John Goodman CBE** warned against staging further Community Programme Advisory Group meetings. Instead, his preference was for meetings to be held with the individual partner organisations so that their individual requirements/concerns could be attended to. Detailed reports, however, were still requested by the Board of Trustees.

Meetings held in July included useful meetings with **Dave Roberts** and **Paul Kenton** at Lincoln City (re payment of wages outstanding. Paul himself would eventually oversee the community operation at Sincil Bank for a short spell in later years) and with **Lorraine Rogers** at Tranmere Rovers. Also held in July was a meeting with **Francisco Baeza** from Buckinghamshire Chilterns University. Francisco was a dynamic leader in education, and he came up with several ideas to take forward for further consideration about how football could engage students.

July 2005 also saw **Simon Tuley** leave the FFE&VTS, representing a further blow to the FFE&VTS Community Programme. Simon did a super job, supporting and overseeing the re-structuring, bringing the accounts fully up-to-date and introducing an appropriate budget that

---

48. *These figures include the numbers of youth trainees in post which averaged approximately 97.66 trainees in post per month and modern apprentices (and others) which averaged 48.61 trainees per month ('Modern Apprenticeships' would ultimately completely replace the YT programme).*

allowed for easy cross-checking on financial information. Looking to the future, it was noted that the new organisation, "League Football Education", were to appoint their own accountant to replace the role previously adopted by Simon. Meanwhile, **Tad Detko** (FL) and **Darren Wilson** (PFA) kindly decided to take forward plans to appoint a possible replacement for Simon (working on a part-time basis only) within the FFE&VTS framework. Interviews were held in September and **Jane McIntosh** was appointed to the position of 'Financial Controller'.

Manchester-born **Darren Wilson** was a former youth trainee with Manchester City before playing briefly for local club Bury where he made 30 appearances in 1991.

Also, in July, **Grant Cornwell**, Assistant Community Officer alongside **Neil Watson** at the Leyton Orient Community Sports Trust, was awarded the MBE in recognition of his work with young people during 16 years working with Orient's community scheme. Grant went on to become a successful Chief Executive of the Tottenham Hotspur Foundation and, much later, Chief Executive of the Hampshire and Isle of Wight Community Foundation in April 2018.

Conversations were also taking place at this time with **Lisa Hayes** from George Davies Solicitors in Manchester about the possibility of taking over the editorial of the quarterly newsletter though, in the end, and under pressure from the partners (who wanted to take more and more responsibility for work undertaken by clubs in the community), the decision was made to discontinue the previously popular quarterly newsletters after the final (summer 2005) edition had been produced so these conversations were not taken forward.

The new 2005/2006 season saw a presentation to representatives of Sportsmatch at which it was noted that grants to support Community Schemes since 1993 (and up to September 2005) had reached an incredible £4.4 million. It was very clear that the support of Sportsmatch had helped local club-based community schemes to thrive, and to develop into the areas of health, education and social inclusion. The Sportsmatch Awards Evening was also noted to be taking place at Manchester City's City of Manchester Stadium (soon to be renamed the Etihad Stadium) on the 17th November 2005.

A report to the FFE&VTS Board Meeting in September confirmed that FFE&VTS Community Programme support continued to 18 PL clubs (not Arsenal or Sunderland), 69 FL clubs (not Chester City, Peterborough United or Yeovil Town) and to 6 non-league clubs (Cambridge United, Exeter City, Hereford United, Kidderminster Harriers, Scarborough and York City. The Kettering Town project had been "wound up" at this point). Staff morale was also noted to be remarkably good.

The PL staged two separate 'Community contacts' meetings for PL Community Officers (alongside the Department of Health) at Manchester City (for northern based Community Officers) and at Arsenal (for southern based Officers) in September 2005. Some "best practice" examples were given where Community Officers were already working with local health authorities and Primary Care Trusts (PCTs). Details of the new 'Barclays Spaces for Sport' initiative were also passed on and it was noted that Barclays had plans to deliver 21 'flagship' projects by 2007.

The FL and the FFE&VTS Community Programme joined forces to meet with the North West Regional Development Agency at the end of October 2005.

Through **Elspeth Gilfillan**, from the NPFA, an invitation to meet with **HRH (His Royal Highness) the Duke of Edinburgh** was arranged in London at the start of December 2005, and he was genuinely interested in what Football in the Community was all about.

The PL established a meeting with representatives of the Metropolitan Police which was to lead to the creation in the longer term of the then "Kickz" project (later to be renamed "Kicks"). Three "pilot" club schemes were selected to begin with being Brentford, Fulham and Tottenham Hotspur. It soon became apparent that significant funding was to become available for PL and FL club schemes to become involved in this super new initiative.

Indeed, it is worth noting that at the time it was clear that the PL were becoming increasingly busy in the field of 'community' with positive links developing with various potential community 'partners'. The PL also staged a 'parliamentary reception' that was attended by 100+ Members of Parliament.

At the same time, the FL (who had already launched their own version of the Schools Under 11's 6-a-side competition sponsored by British Telecommunications (BT) for FL club schemes that would replace the 6-a-side competition previously run by the FFE&VTS Community Programme for PL, FL and certain Non-League clubs) announced that they were to organise their own conference for Community Officers and also stage their own Community Awards event. In addition, the FL were looking into printing their own promotional magazine (as were the PFA at the time).

A report entitled "Football and its Communities" (produced by **Adam Brown, Tim Crabbe** and **Gavin Mellor** at Manchester Metropolitan University) was produced at this time and provoked various interesting responses from the football authorities.

A staff meeting prior to Christmas 2005 saw the remaining members of the FFE&VTS Community Programme praised not only for their loyalty and dignity but also for managing to maintain a professional and positive attitude during a really challenging year.

Richard Finney and **Stephanie Lunn** were starting to get to grips with the new 'Modern Apprenticeships' programme at club-based community schemes. The payroll service operated so well by **Lynn Leonard** and **Ian Niven** still maintained 75 club schemes using the 'service' (which turned over approximately £11.5 million in 2005 – see below). Positive first steps had been taken by **Angeline Mather**, and Regional Directors (**Dick Krzywicki, Dave Palmer** and **John Relish**) and Managers (especially **Dennis Leman**) had all reacted very well to what seemed to be ever-increasing workloads including support for more community schemes (Regional Directors were now overseeing 24 club schemes each; Dennis Leman himself oversaw 12 clubs schemes).

Weekly wages paid out by the FFE&VTS Community Programme covering the six-month period from January to June 2005 totalled £3,223,679. For the period between July and December 2005 £3,055,820 was paid out. So, for the 12-month period from January to December 2003, total wages paid out on behalf of 85 community projects therefore reached a grand total for the full year of £6,279,499.

Added to this were the club schemes with casual/part-time staff that were being paid on a monthly basis, worth £2,298,789 for the period January to June 2005 and a further £2,946,096 for the period July to December 2005 making a total of £5,244,885 for the year. This meant that the grand total of wages paid out via the FFE&VTS payroll reached £11,524,284 for the whole year.

A summary of club Community Schemes turnover during 2005 revealed that a total of 70 Schemes turned over a collective total of £17,240,945 meaning that average turnover across those schemes had risen to approximately £246,299 per annum.

In 2005, the FFE&VTS Community Programme payroll for the year suggested that average wages for senior Community Officers rose once again to approximately £26,564 per annum (based on the wages paid to 74 different club based Community Officers). In addition, average wages for Assistant Officers reached around £14,012 per annum based on the salaries of approximately 400 permanent Assistants paid through the FFE&VTS Community Programme payroll (this figure did not include youth trainees/modern apprentices or casual coaching staff).

The regional analysis of average wages paid in different regions showed that in the North West and North East regions, the average wages paid to (senior) Community Officers in 2005 was approximately £25,600 (previous year £24,104) per annum. In the Midlands and South West, the average was slightly lower at around £25,038 (previous year £23,546) per annum. In the South East, the average was £33,332 (previous year £35,585) per annum.

CHAPTER 17
NATIONAL SPONSORS KELLOGG'S FROSTIES

A NEW SPONSORSHIP AGREEMENT was established with Kellogg's Frosties covering the period from the 1st January 2004 to the 30th June 2005 worth a total of £350,000 over a year and a half. Also agreed was the fact that Kellogg's Frosties would sponsor the Primary and Junior Schools 6-a-side competition in seasons 2003/4 and 2004/5. Although the term of the agreement covered only 18 months, there were high hopes, at the time the deal was struck, that this could be extended further if required.

In essence, the agreement confirmed that Kellogg's Frosties would become a business partner of the Community Programme, and a title sponsor of the Under 11's 6-a-side competition for two seasons. In addition, Kellogg's Frosties would also become title sponsor of all holiday courses at Easter and during the February and October half term holidays. The deal also allowed for the FFE&VTS Community scheme to seek alternative partners (up to a maximum of three) who were not competitors. It also allowed Kellogg's staff to have access to tickets to attend PL and FL matches.

The two 6-a-side competitions (played during the 2003/4 and the 2004/5 seasons were hugely successful. The first tournament, in 2003/4, saw over 3,000 school teams and 92 local, club-based Football in the Community schemes take part. Kellogg's Frosties were especially pleased when the Final was played at the Cardiff Millennium Stadium on the 21st March prior to the LDV Final. The presentation of the trophy and medals was made by **Peter Harrison** and **Gavin Bowyer** (Brand Managers for Kellogg's Frosties) together with **Tony the Tiger** from Kellogg's!

The second tournament, in season 2004/5, saw just under 3,000 school teams (and, once again, 92 club -based community schemes) participate. Once again, the trophy and medals were presented following the Final by **Gavin Bowyer** (Brand Manager, Kellogg's Frosties) which was again played at the Cardiff Millennium Stadium on the 10th April prior to the LDV Final (Wembley Stadium was being re-built at this time).

All in all, the arrangements with Kellogg's worked very well (boosted by regular appearances of **Tony the Tiger**!) except for the fact that in real sponsorship terms, eighteen months was probably not a long enough time for the two organisations to be working together.

The Kellogg's arrangements came to a natural close at the end of the 2004/5 football season on the 30th June 2005.

CHAPTER 18 – 2006 - 2007

THE START OF THE NEW YEAR 2006 saw **Dennis Leman**, **John Hudson** and **Roger Reade**, accompanied by **Rick Fenoglio** (from Manchester Metropolitan University), given the chance to visit **Greg Johnson**, Head of the USA's "Sports Philanthropy Project" based in Boston, Massachusetts. The visit proved to be extremely informative and beneficial. Indeed, it was especially useful in flagging up a possible way forward for the FFE&VTS Community Programme should the Trustees of the FFE&VTS choose to support this in future. Greg was kind enough to identify examples of best practice including work undertaken with clubs such as the Green Bay Packers, the New York Jets, the St Louis Cardinals, the St Louis Rams, the Tampa Bay Buccaneers and many others. This meeting followed the recent publication of the MMU Research Report which had featured the work of the Sports Philanthropy Project.

The first Board Meeting of the New Year (at the end of January) saw several pressing issues raised and discussed. Items included in the report were:

- Positive and hopeful meetings had been held with representatives of Peterborough United (where **Luke Weston** had been appointed by the club as Head of Community) and Yeovil Town.

- Approximately 20 club schemes had moved from weekly to monthly payment methods for their permanent and casual staff

- The new budget would 'balance' if PFA payments were maintained[49] (**Alex Horne** from the FA put forward a proposal that a new 3-year Business Plan covering July 2006 to June 2009 for the Community Scheme should be adopted, possibly via a brand-new charitable organisation, though this proposal was not in the end supported. Indeed, although a draft Business Plan was prepared covering the period from July 2005 to June 2006, it was, in the end, never formally presented to the Board).

- Financial controls needed strengthening. In particular, standing orders covering the full amount of wages would be necessary. Any club schemes struggling to meet their financial commitments would be dealt with as a matter of urgency. Wage debts had risen to over £900,000 as at the end of the year.

February saw Blackpool's popular Community Officers, **Lyn** and **Derek Spence**, meet with Prime Minister, **Tony Blair**, to discuss their involvement in the local community. In his book *From the Troubles to the Tower*, Derek admitted that he enjoyed the responsibility of looking after the Prime Minister that day - even though he was a bit nervous. As he described:

> *"In fact, I was beyond nervous: I was bloody terrified!"*

Led by **Darren Bernstein** at the FL, plans to stage the first ever FL community conference got underway. The Millennium Stadium in Cardiff was to 'host' the conference to be held in May. The conference would host individual 'workshops' and a "marketplace" for all Officers to visit whilst they were present.

The FL also hosted a first meeting to consider judging the 'Community Club of the Year' awards. The awards were presented at a Football League Awards evening held on the 5th March

---

49. *The PFA annual contribution had increased to £940,000 per year following the decision to withdraw all possible commercial income to the FFE&VTS Community Programme.*

at the London Hilton Hotel.

An informal meeting of senior staff held in mid–March 2006 saw management staff agree that the move towards becoming more like the USA's Sports Philanthropy Project (and becoming involved in "community enhancement" plans) was appropriate for the FFE&VTS Community Programme. The idea of having regional strategic and fund-raising officers arose once again. Also discussed was the idea of dropping specific support (including financial support) for non-league club schemes.

In terms of the clubs, former Regional Director **Julian Winter** was appointed as Head of Watford's Community Foundation where he would work closely with another former Community Officer, **Mark Ashton** (now Chief Executive of the club). In time, Julian would go on to become Chief Executive of the Football Club himself.

An interesting March meeting took place with Community Officers, **Alan Sefton** and **Freddie Hudson**, from Arsenal in that they agreed to consider undertaking a "mini-audit" of all their current partnerships including all work with operators in other PL and FL club areas.

Also, in March, **Andy Ruffler** (from Chamberlink) made contact in relation to the renewal of the Investors in People (IIP) award. The renewal process commenced in June and, to be fair to Andy, he did everything he could to help the much-changed organisation to attain its renewal goal. In the end "retained recognition" status was awarded to the organisation, though it was clear that there was more work to be done in order to meet the necessary criteria.

Exceptionally close links were being forged with the FL through **Andy Williamson** and **Michael Tattersall** at this time. Both Officers understood the impact that the 'downsizing' had created. In relation to the Schools tournaments, the FL revamped them slightly by offering an inter schools under 11's tournament for boys and girls for all of their clubs in each of their three divisions, leading to the playing of a 'grand final' before each of the relevant divisional Play Off Finals at the end of the season. If nothing else, this created more opportunities for children to experience of playing on the hallowed turf at Wembley! The FL were also, of course, absolutely delighted to have the control brought about by owning all sponsorship/commercial rights. A meeting with Andy and Michael in late March also outlined plans for the proposed national conference to be held in Cardiff in May. **Roger Reade** was invited to deliver the opening speech[50].

The workshops to be delivered were to be as follows:

Club Scheme	Topic
Brentford	"Structure and Development" (having just secured charitable trust status in January 2006)
Burnley	"Football and multi-sport/on-site provision" (combining leisure centre work with outreach work)
Notts County	"Working with Local Authorities" (and many other local partners across various health/education/inclusion programmes)

At the end of the conference, the conclusions drawn were summarised as follows:

- Clubs and communities needed to be brought still closer together

- The profile of the community scheme in terms of the 'political agenda' needed to be raised

---

50. *In his speech, Roger outlined and emphasised the new areas of opportunity including health, education and social inclusion work; the importance of developing partnerships and accessing external funding; the close links particularly with the Football League and the PFA and the proposed new vision: "to maximise the potential of community schemes and to have significant impact on the health, social development and well-being of clubs local communities"*

- Lines of communication needed improving

- Possible funding streams (local, regional and national) needed to be investigated and developed

- New training requirements (and resources to support them) needed identifying

- New momentum for the Football League needed to be found in terms of delivery

- A new commitment to the Community Scheme needed to be found

In relation to the 'downsizing', this was particularly noteworthy especially as, at the same time, the Football Foundation were growing their support team. In April for example, the Foundation advertised for both a "Facilities Project Manager" in the East Midlands and East Anglia AND for a "Community Development Manager" in Central London. By June, additional adverts had appeared for "Senior Development Managers" in health and wellbeing, education and life-long learning, equalities, social inclusion.

The contract year 2005/2006 saw the continuation of the YT programme/'Modern Apprenticeships' contract with figures recorded for the contract year detailed in "Appendix III – Table of trainees in post year by year 2002-2007" [51]. Amongst those clubs with excellent recruitment levels during the year were projects at Bolton Wanderers, Burnley, Huddersfield Town, Port Vale, Stoke City and Walsall.

There was a total of 55 club projects participating in Adult and YT programmes in 2005/2006 – i.e. during the contract year.

The numbers of modern apprentices were to reduce yet further over the next contract year following news from Manchester-based **Mary Evans** on behalf of the Learning & Skills Council (LSC) which confirmed that the FFE&VTS Community Programme 'Modern Apprenticeships' contract was to terminate on a "wind down" arrangement from August 2006 whereby the 120 or so young people involved would all be expected to complete their terms of engagement (in the end, by April 2007). There would also be no further recruitment thereafter. A possible link up with League Football Education to sub-contract a small number of modern apprenticeship places was also, sadly (and understandably), ruled out at an early stage.

Financial Controller, **Jane McIntosh**, confirmed that she was to leave at the end of April. Interviews to replace Jane were held in mid-May although the Board decided not to appoint a like for like replacement and, instead, chose to appoint/co-opt **Joanne (Jo) Harding** from Beaver Struthers Accountants. Jo had worked with the PFA and understood the workings of the FFE&VTS. She took up her new duties in early June. Jo's work was to become even more significant over the next few months as the list of monthly debtors (i.e. monies owing by club Community Schemes) regularly reached £800,000 at the end of each month. FFE&VTS Chairman **Professor John Goodman CBE** confirmed that this professional and flexible support was particularly appropriate at this time.

Also leaving after a successful nine week 'placement' was **Rachel Gerrard** who had completed some particularly interesting research on behalf of the Scheme.

From 2005/6 season, the PL and the FL made separate arrangements to stage their own versions of the schools' competitions. Indeed, the FL were able to source a new sponsor for their Under 11's competitions (three separate divisional competitions were held in both tournaments) leading to the birth of the "BT Community Cup". At the same time, the FL were also speaking to a potential new title sponsor for the national FL (only) Community scheme overall.

For the revamped Under 11's (boys and girls) and the Under 13's (girls) Competitions organised by the FL during season 2005/6, participating numbers at 68 FL club schemes were 2281 schools in the Under 11's tournament (£14,826 paid out in 'facility fees') and 1038 schools

---

51. *These figures include the numbers of modern apprentices in post (which averaged approximately 93.9 trainees in post per month) and youth trainees in post (which averaged 33.1 trainees in post per month).*

in the Under 13's competition (£6,747 paid out in facility fees). See Appendix V for details of Competition winners.

By now, of course, it was very clear that the PL and the FL were indeed going to go their own separate ways in terms of community engagement. What was also very clear was that both organisations were making significant strides forward in terms of their own arrangements to promote and support community schemes at their own member clubs (the FL had already secured significant sponsorship support from BT for their competitions and from Puma regarding kit and equipment). This news was also being widely promoted amongst all club-based Community Officers.

Indeed, at a meeting of North West Officers in May 2006, senior officers from the FFE&VTS Community Programme urged Community Officers that their futures were now "up to them. It is now to be about where you and your club want to take things". **Angeline Mather** also flagged up opportunities to access funding – e.g. from Awards for All, Aim Higher (already secured), the Football Foundation (significant grant awards had already been made to many professional club-based community schemes), Sportsmatch, the National Lottery and more.

Following successful conversations with **David Carley** and **Alison Lockwood** (commencing in February), the 'Playing for Success' national conference was again successfully held in Stratford on Avon at the end of May. Amongst several worthwhile workshops held during the conference were those staged by **Pete Bradshaw** from Manchester City; **Paul Thomson** from Arsenal (about the 'Double Club') and **Jan McLucas** from Boston United.

The following month, sad news arrived with the death of former Community Officer **John Kerr** after a heart attack on the 4th June. This was a real tragedy especially given that John had passed away having only just been appointed as Academy Director at Cardiff City at the age of only 46.

The 16th June saw the 20th anniversary of the establishment of the Community Programme in Professional Football, though celebrations were somewhat more muted than had been the case on the 10th anniversary.

The end of June saw the popular **Steve Raynor** leave his post as Community Officer at Bury to take up an exciting post with the rapidly growing Everton Community operation. Steve did a brilliant job in building up Bury's presence in their local community and his move to Everton would see him take up even more responsibility at a much bigger charitable operation.

Shaun Danby was appointed as Community Officer to succeed Steve at Bury. Also, having served for some time as a very capable Assistant Community Officer, **Mike Brennan** took over as the Senior Community Officer at Blackburn Rovers.

At the end of June, a meeting of South West Community Officers was held at Cheltenham Town FC.

The end of June also saw all 'loose-ends' tied up concerning the former Kettering Town Football in the Community scheme which was formally closed down on the 30th June. The FFE&VTS Community Programme were, however, able to offer support and advice about embracing community ventures to another non-league club when meeting with **Colin Taylor** and **Darren Davies** from Oxford City FC the following month.

Of interest at the time, the FFE&VTS Community Programme was noted to have processed wages on behalf of 32 club community schemes that had secured charitable status. Further evidence of the huge expansion of Community schemes across the country is seen in the fact that the total amount of wages processed on behalf of these 32 club schemes during the previous year was £5,650,798 (i.e. an average turnover of £176,587 for the year per individual scheme).

Mike Foster and **Bill Bush** of the PL announced at an early July meeting that it seemed that some community schemes were living a largely "hand to mouth" existence. They were both, of course, absolutely 'spot on'! They both, quite rightly, stated that if there was an expectation to do "stuff of scale" (as they put it), there was a real need to secure sustainable and larger funding in future.

The Board of FFE&VTS made the decision that it was necessary for a percentage 'commission' to be charged by Angeline for any successful bid applications that she may have been involved in on behalf of Community Schemes. It was noted that she had been involved in several successful bid applications to external agencies and to the Football Foundation, though it was generally felt that she shouldn't be involved in bids to the Foundation as that was essentially a 'football family' partner and one that would be willing to support local community schemes in the right circumstances.

In total, however, and as at the end of August 2006, Angeline had been involved in generating approximately £900,000 for 13 different Community schemes (£829,000 from the Football Foundation: £71,000 from other agencies).

September saw "one-to-one' conversations with all FFE&VTS Community Programme personnel.

Strong views were expressed suggesting that all staff were in favour of moving to a new organisation, even to work with only FL clubs if necessary. Relations between senior Community Programme personnel and FL officers were exceptionally close at this time, with meetings regular and frequent (usually involving Chief Operating Officer **Andy Williamson** and his Deputy, **Michael Tattersall**). Indeed, both Andy and Michael at the time committed to keeping Community Programme staff within any new organisation if possible. Discussions were quite open about the need for 4 new areas of 18 x FL clubs in each area to be overseen/supervised by 4 "area managers".

Also mentioned for the first time was the idea of having "bronze, silver and gold" awards for Community Schemes based on the quality of their local operations. In the end, this was something the FL took forward after all support from the FFE&VTS Community Programme finished.

John Nagle from the FL contacted officers as the League were going ahead with the production of their first promotional newsletter in the autumn of 2006. Included were articles about the 'Kick it Out' week of action; the FL Fans Survey, the Community Cup competitions; "Fans of the Future"; the FL Awards and features on clubs MK Dons, Southend United, Stoke City and Wycombe Wanderers.

Also supporting these plans at the time was FL Marketing Manager **David Malkinson**. David's involvement would extend to the Community Club awards, "Fans of the Future", FL branding and other aspects. Plans for 2006/7 also included the FFE&VTS Community Programme personnel supporting the operation of the two inter-school competitions and a second Community Officers conference.

October 2006 saw Burnley Football Club Chief Executive **Dave Edmundson** consider stepping down from this role at the club in order to take on the role of Chief Executive of the Burnley Leisure Centre and Community Programme charity. Dave was particularly supportive of former Community Manager **Dean Ramsdale** (who had left at the end of July) and he certainly understood the community landscape. In the end, this plan of action was delayed as internal checks on the finances of the community scheme at the club were undertaken (Dave would eventually oversee the Football League's new Community operation set up from October 2007 to October 2011).

Sandra Lewis left the Northampton Town Community Scheme at this time after 10/11 years of loyal service and received the massive thanks of all concerned (not least from her husband **Russell Lewis**!)

The end of October FFE&VTS Board Meeting noted that the FFE&VTS Community Programme continued to support 19 PL clubs (still not Arsenal), 68 FL clubs (not new-to-the FL, Accrington Stanley, Chester City, Sunderland or Yeovil Town) and 7 Non-League clubs (Cambridge United, Exeter City, Kidderminster Harriers, Oxford United, Rushden & Diamonds, Scarborough and York City. It should, however, be noted that a change of ownership at York City led to their resignation from working with the FFE&VTS Community Programme by January 2007). In addition, noted at the meeting was the fact that the PL were, like the FL, to run their own schools' tournaments for their own member clubs.

Following several meetings with club Secretary, **Bernard Halford**, Manchester City confirmed that their match against Fulham in November would recognise and celebrate the 20 years of successful operation of City's Community Programme scheme.

Meetings to discuss possible future operations also took place with **Angela White** at Leicester City's Community scheme and with **Sarah Copley** at Lincoln City's scheme.

By the end of the year (2006) there were over 40 community schemes that had started the move towards securing charitable status (including the 32 that had already become registered with the Charity Commission). This represented real progress. Indeed, the attendance of FFE&VTS Community Programme officials at Trustees meetings all over the country was becoming more and more apparent as part of their day to day duties.

Most, if not all, of the FFE&VTS Community Programme staff at this time were still working as hard and as diligently as ever. Indeed, the Trustees confirmed that they were:

> *"Pleased with the way the function (of the Community Programme) continues professionally".*

Weekly wages paid out by the FFE&VTS Community Programme covering the six-month period from January to June 2006 totalled £2,778,928. For the period between July and December 2006 £2,812,476 was paid out. As a result, the total wages paid out during the 12-month period from January to December 2006 on behalf of 85 community projects therefore reached a grand total for the full year of £5,591,404.

Added to this were those club schemes with casual/part-time staff that were being paid on a monthly basis worth £3,081,003 for the period January to June 2006 and a further £3,567,599 for the period July to December 2006 making a total of £6,648,602 for the year. So, the grand total paid out in wages via the FFE&VTS was an incredible £12,240,006.

A summary of Club Community Schemes turnover during the year 2006 revealed that based on turnover at approximately 60 local community schemes which had reached a collective total of £15,936,780 (at the community schemes that operated on a local basis), average turnover across those schemes had risen again to approximately £265,613 per annum.

By the end of 2006, the FFE&VTS Community Programme payroll for the year illustrated that average wages for senior Community Officers had risen once again to approximately £27,088 per annum (based on the wages paid to 75 different club based Senior Community Officers). In addition, average wages for <u>Senior</u> Assistant Officers reached around £19,700 per annum based on salaries paid through the FFE&VTS Community Programme payroll (this figure did not include modern apprentices or casual coaching staff).

The New Year 2007 kicked off with news of **Mike Reynolds** departure from Sportsmatch. Indications were that Sportsmatch were, like the FFE&VTS Community Programme, likely to go through a period of change following Mike's departure. Plans were already afoot via Southampton's Head of Community, **Mark Abrahams**, to secure a signed Southampton shirt for Mike (a lifetime Saints supporter) as a leaving/"thank-you" gift.

January 2007 brought with it the sad news of the death of former Community Officer **Derek Mann**, as confirmed by **John Howarth** (Secretary of Shrewsbury Town at the time). Derek had been working as Head Football Coach at Telford College of Arts and Technology.

Also, in January, **Gordon Taylor**, Chief Executive of the PFA, launched the PFA's centenary celebrations at a pre-planned ceremony in Manchester's Town Hall when he stated that:

> *"The PFA is today one of the strongest unions in the world with an incredibly loyal membership. It has pioneered football's links with the wider community".*

A sequence of high-profile fund-raising events were to be held by the PFA during 2007 as part of a "One Goal One million" campaign in order to attempt to raise £1 million to help fund a new children's unit at the University Children's Hospital in Manchester.

John Flatters became the FFE&VTS-supported Community Officer at Yeovil Town whose Chairman, **John Fry**, had now confirmed that the club was happy to work alongside the FFE&VTS Community Programme in future, particularly as there were several local partners that he was keen to work with including South Somerset District Council, Yeovil College and Somerset CFA. One early telephone call to the Manchester office from John Flatters suggested that, during his first few days of work, he had managed to save a young boy's life by jumping in a nearby river to save him from drowning!

Roger Reade was invited to stand in for the absent and otherwise engaged Minister of Sport at Colchester United's Celebration Event having seen the huge success of the Colchester United Community Sports Trust as a registered charity over the past five years. Acknowledgement was made to the hard work and endeavour of former Community Officer **Mickey Cook** and of the huge success of the scheme since **Steve Bradshaw** took over. Steve went on to become Chief Executive of Colchester United FC in later years.

Even at this stage, FFE&VTS Community Programme senior staff were keen to support people wherever and whenever they could. **Clive Maguire** from Swindon Town had been in contact about the son of a former player who had contracted cancer, and **Dennis Leman**, **Dave Palmer** and **John Relish** all became actively involved in securing signed Chelsea, Liverpool and Manchester United shirts to help raise funds for the boy concerned.

The six remaining senior officers within the FFE&VTS Community Programme that were still involved in supporting club schemes recognised that it was becoming an almost impossible task to focus on providing appropriate support and that much of the time was now being spent "firefighting" instead of being involved more strategically.

The end of January saw only 53 modern apprentices remaining in post (at 32 club schemes), and they were all due to leave before April 2007.

With the list of monthly club scheme debtors reaching around £900,000 at one point, the Board agreed that it was necessary to "toughen up" the criteria around payment. Whilst this "toughening up" was long overdue, it was the first time that club schemes had been informed that if they weren't able to pay their debts, further payments of wages would be stopped. Three club schemes fell victim to this new rule in February 2007 being the projects at Boston United, Exeter City and Rushden & Diamonds. Other club schemes (notably Lincoln City and Sunderland) also owed significant amounts, to the extent that payment plans were formulated for those projects.

February also saw an approach made to **Rob Heys**, Secretary at Accrington Stanley FC, to investigate their possible interest in community matters following their promotion to the Football League the previous year.

April 2007 saw **Simon Morgan** appointed as "Head of Community" at the PL. Simon had previously been Head of the Fulham Community operation and had done a super job.

Ken Merrett announced his retirement from the role of Secretary at Manchester United in the summer (He had been extremely supportive of the community scheme at Old Trafford). His replacement would be the popular **Ken Ramsden**. **Trish Hurst** had taken over as Chief Executive of United's Foundation, though her stay was comparatively short in the end and **John Shiels** would be appointed to the post the following year (2008).

Also contacting Scheme officials in April was **Thomas McCallion** concerning the visit of a group of people from Derry to view some community schemes which, in turn, would allow them to set up a pilot scheme in conjunction with Derry City FC. **Noel Mooney** on behalf of the FA of Ireland was also in contact seeking more information to support possible developments in Ireland in conjunction with their top ten clubs.

The April Board of Trustees Meeting noted that the most likely event at this stage was for the FL to take over the employment of the Community Programme staff.

April 2007 also saw a formal meeting with **Ann Durrant** from a Macclesfield-based organisation called Media 4 Change who passed on more information about Corporate Social Responsibility (CSR) and how football clubs were starting to look at interpreting CSR for themselves. This was ahead of CSR strategies being prepared at the majority of the big clubs (with the notable exclusion of Chelsea, who produced their first CSR Report for the 2005/6 season. Indeed, this first report managed to include a list of over 125 charities that Chelsea had directly assisted including such wide-ranging organisations as Age Concern, Alzheimer's

Society, Breast Cancer Care, Help a London Child, Mencap, The NSPCC, The Prostate Cancer Foundation and the Teenage Cancer Trust).

The PL and FL again made their own individual and separate arrangements to stage schools competitions in the 2006/7 season and the FL Competitions saw the following involvement: In the Under 11's tournament, 2033 Primary and Junior school teams took part at 67 FL club schemes with £13,214 paid out in "facility fees". The Under 13's girls tournament saw 892 school teams participate at 63 FL club schemes with £5,798 paid out to them as facility fees. Participating numbers were slightly reduced on the previous year (see Appendix V for details of Competition winners).

The FL set up the first of two "Community Working Party" meetings in May, attended by notable club representatives such as **John Bowler** (Chairman, Crewe Alexandra), **Dave Edmundson** (Burnley), **Neil Doncaster** (Norwich City) and **Mark Arthur** (Nottingham Forest). **Andy Williamson** and **Pat Brown** from the FL also attended. Their own objectives (not exclusively concerning community but also in relation to fans) were identified as:

• Generate greater revenue for member clubs

• Create the greater involvement of clubs within their local communities

• Enhance the competitive appeal of the FL to fans

• In terms of what was underway at the time, it was noted that there were 3 main areas of community involvement/engagement:

• Mainstream ("core" activities such as after school coaching and holiday courses)

• Football club centred activity (e.g. tours of the ground, matchday activity, Saturday clubs)

• Education projects (e.g. "Playing for Success")

It was also noted that schemes were moving into areas such as work in crime & disorder, health and social inclusion. The recommendations of the Manchester Metropolitan University Report "Resources and Opportunities" were also noted at the meeting. **Mark Arthur** stated that he was very keen to support the view that all community schemes should move towards charitable status at the first possible opportunity.

By now, it became clear that the FFE&VTS Community Programme would no longer be responsible for supporting community schemes at clubs effective from the 31st July 2007. This meant that new, alternative structures would have to be established and introduced effective from 1st August 2007. In the end, it became clear that the PL would financially support a new FL Trust on the basis that this would be a totally new operation. There would also be a 'solidarity' payment to the FL in support of clubs playing in the FL Championship. It was discussed and agreed that some form of new criteria regarding the possible payment methodology (possibly linked to quality assurance/standards; criteria to be worked out) for club schemes needed to be carefully considered.

By coincidence, the 'Playing For Success' annual conference in Stratford (also held in May), included a workshop presented by **Allison Tripney** from West Bromwich Albion in which she commented in detail on the 'Quality in Study Support' (QISS) framework where there were three 'standards' being the bronze ("emerged"/getting started) level; the silver ("established"/ keeping it going) level; and the gold ("advanced"/aiming for quality) level. The standards could be offered to schools and/or Study Support Centres as a flexible package of training and support. These standards or levels were to be 'mirrored' for FL club community schemes in due course.

Amongst other meetings held in May was a meeting with **Norman Beverley** and **David James** (Chairman and Director) at Stockport County in which it was agreed to move their own local community organisation towards charitable status using the legal expertise of Watson Burton LLP.

Middlesbrough FC also celebrated the opening of their Herlingshaw Education Centre at the Eston Centre. Working closely with Chairman **George Cook** was the energetic **Rob Lake** who would go on to become Head of the West Bromwich Albion Community operation in future.

May 2007 also saw **Frankie Banks** announce his retirement from the post of Head of Community at Southend United. Frankie, who did a superb job over many years for the club, was replaced by **Steve Goodsell**.

The end of the 2006/7 season brought with it, a study of all community coverage in match programmes during the season with the following clubs selected:

2006/7	Winners
PL	Fulham, Watford
FL Division One	Leicester City, Stoke City, West Bromwich Albion
FL Division Two	Doncaster Rovers
FL Division Three	Notts County Stockport County

2006/7 also saw the final "wind-down" arrangements regarding the last of the modern apprentices based at club schemes. Average numbers recorded for the contract year 2006/2007 are detailed in "Appendix III – Table of trainees in post year by year 2002-2007".

The total number of club projects confirmed as participating in the "wind-down" YT programme during the contract year 2006/2007 was only 37.

The June FL community conference held at Leicester City saw 9 separate workshops, all offering a good range and choice for Community Officers in attendance. Keynote speakers were **Andy Williamson** and **Roger Reade**, underlining the fact that at this point in time, the FL and the FFE&VTS Community Programme staff were still close and harbouring the possibility of FFE&VTS personnel being transferred to the proposed new Community organisation/ Trust. Some workshops were presented with information about employment law (delivered by **Debbie Coyne** from George Davies Solicitors), the NLT ('Reading the Game') and accessing external funding/Sportsmatch. Other workshops included 'Fit for Football' and 'Fans of the Future' together with club presentations made, for example, by **Steve Bradshaw** (Colchester United), **Ian Thornton** (Norwich City), **Fraser Foster** and **Allison Tripney** (West Bromwich Albion) and **Steve Ford** (Brighton and Hove Albion whose community scheme had just won the "Community Club of the Year" accolade).

The remaining eleven FFE&VTS Community Programme support staff were to be made redundant.

Roger Reade attended the July Board Meeting to state how dignified, loyal and diligent all the staff had been to date. He also stated how professional they had been, even during the period when it had become obvious that the staff were to be made redundant with no offer to transfer to similar employment.

It also became clear that the Football League were to operate a new 'support' agency that would *not* offer payroll support to community schemes and would not sit on Management Forums or Boards of Trustees supporting local community schemes. Crucially, however, more money would become available in support of local Community Schemes. Indeed, irrespective of whether clubs were members of the PL or the FL, increased funding and more partnership opportunities were going to be made available to all professional club schemes, meaning that their local drives towards increasing and developing their work involvement would be greatly "stepped up". In turn, this was a huge positive for the continued growth and development of

'Football in the Community' schemes at the clubs.

'Work' continued for FFE&VTS staff at this point (to their great credit) and **Janet Preston** was welcomed into the fold by FFE&VTS staff as Community Manager at newly promoted Morecambe FC.

FFE&VTS Community Programme staff as a group continued to be as positively supportive as possible. An example of this was seen in support offered to **Mal Jackson** at Rhyl FC. Mal wanted more information about how he could develop the community side of the club with a view to increasing attendances, interest in the club and sales overall. Former Community Officer **Dave Bell** was also given support in his application to work with the FA of Ireland (in the Cork area). Various club Community Officers were in touch for specific information, which was duly provided. Also going through largely the same experience as FFE&VTS personnel at this time were Sportsmatch officials, who kept in touch and were grateful for employment advice offered. During the period September–November, many of the Community Schemes that had secured charitable status held Trustees meetings which FFE&VTS officials attended, offering all the advice and information required in order for them to continue without FFE&VTS involvement in future. Management Forum meetings were also held for the same reason. Another key issue to be attended to was the requirement for new signatories on bank account mandates to be signed.

Richard Finney confirmed that, following support from the FFE&VTS, further Sportsmatch grant awards had been made to Community Schemes including Blackpool £4,500; Boston United £5,000; Manchester City £10,000; Newcastle United £10,000 and Notts County £32,000.

In terms of moves towards alternative employment, **Dennis Leman** and **Dave Palmer** joined **John Hudson** in the PFA Community Department. **John Relish** joined the new Football League Foundation/Trust as a Regional Manager. In other words, at least three of the eleven staff were able to continue their work in the community. Of the remaining eight staff, four were able to secure jobs elsewhere and four were sadly not immediately able to secure alternative employment but were continuing to investigate other opportunities at the time the redundancy was made effective.

The end of October saw the appointment of a new Burnley FC Community Sports Trust senior officer, with **Lyn Hammond** acting on behalf of the club.

The end of November saw **Mark Todd** move from Rotherham United to take up the post of Community Development Manager at Sheffield United and also saw **Mick King** take over from **Roger Morgan** as Head of West Ham United's successful community operation. Mick had done a great job supporting the 'Asians in Football' scheme working alongside Roger for many years prior to this. Roger himself had chosen to retire at this point.

The winter of 2007/2008 saw the FL set up their own separate community support operations headed up by former Burnley Chief Executive, **Dave Edmundson,** as General Manager of the new Football League Trust/support organisation. Indeed, Dave's spell in charge of the Football League Trust (originally set up to oversee community matters plus the FL Youth Development Programme – though the two areas of operation were separated when **Mike Evans** took over), between the end of 2007 and 2011, saw significant progress made for the 72 community operations based at FL clubs.

Dave's appointment followed a period at Burnley where, by his own admission, he first began to understand the value to a club of an extended and positive involvement in the local community. Indeed, it was under his leadership at Turf Moor that the club were re-branded "*the club for its people*".

Dave's involvement at the FL brought with it confirmation in his own mind that there was, perhaps, still a number of people at senior level within clubs with a lack of understanding about the real benefits of community involvement on behalf of their clubs. Amongst the steps he took to help combat this were the following:

• The development of a new message (with the help of pro-community people such as **Mark Arthur**, **Neil Doncaster**, **Roy Whalley**, **Patrick Nelson** and **Mal Brannigan**). Another source of advice was **Steve Waggett** at Charlton Athletic who Dave felt had created the perfect 'model' for other clubs to follow.

- The lobbying of Members of Parliament in Westminster with a view to securing serious support from central Government.

- The move for all club-based community operations to become registered charities.

- The introduction of monitoring and evaluation via Substance so that the return on investment could be properly calculated.

In addition, **Dave Edmundson** moved to raise awareness of the community work being undertaken by clubs, most notably by working hard to secure appropriate 'slots' at Conferences and Seminars up and down the country. He was also the person who introduced the bronze, silver and gold quality assurance standards for club schemes inspired by the Duke of Edinburgh's Award Scheme that Dave initially introduced at Burnley and then rolled it out to over 25 clubs in the Football League Trust. Before handing over the reins to **Mike Evans**, he also worked closely with **Dame Julia Cleverdon** (Chief Executive of Business in the Community). Julia was a principal adviser to Prime Minister **David Cameron** and a driving force behind the establishment of the NCS programme, which the FL Trust successfully tendered to deliver in 2011 following an application led by **Loo Brackpool**. There is no doubt whatsoever that Dave Edmundson has a great deal to be proud of.

Dave left after four years of extremely hard work and dedicated service, and his successor in 2011 was **Mike Evans** (who had previously been a Regional Manager working under Dave since February 2008). Mike was eventually appointed as Chief Executive of the EFL Trust during the 2019/2020 season. He has done a tremendous job in guiding the Trust to become a key player and supporter in the further development of club-based community schemes. Indeed, with the support of a significantly enhanced management team of colleagues, he has played a key role in accessing and introducing new external partnerships and funding to the EFL Trust which has hugely grown the organisation, together with the programmes that are promoted through the locally based EFL club schemes. Under Mike's leadership, the EFL Trust adopted a new five-year Strategy for 2019-2024 with the vision of "Stronger, healthier, more active communities". The EFL Trust has also adopted impressive values following consultation with partners, stakeholders, Board members and staff being:
- Leading by example
- Innovate and inspire
- Passionate about people
- Continually improve

These values confirm that a new generation of persons at the 'helm' of community operations retain the fabulous enthusiasm and passion necessary to keep driving forward football club-based community organisations.

The Premier League, who had been led by **Simon Morgan** as Head of their own internal community department for many years, are now 'headed up' by **Nick Perchard**. After joining the PL in 2014, Nick took up his new post as 'Head of Community' in 2015 having previously been Chief Executive of Hertfordshire CFA. Nick oversees an operation which now supports 20 PL club schemes, 72 EFL club schemes and 68 National League clubs. The Premier League 'Communities Strategy' focuses on using its reach and appeal to inspire children and young people to realise their potential. Their four key objectives are:
- Building stronger communities where everyone can achieve.
- Enhancing physical and mental well-being.
- Developing personal skills and positive relationships.
- Increasing sporting, educational and employment opportunities.

The three main national programmes which deliver this strategy are:
- Premier League Primary Stars
- Premier League Inspires
- Premier League Kicks (formerly 'Kickz')

In addition, the Premier League strives to deliver their objectives by supporting a wide range of organisations that enhance the game. Most notable is the PL's partnership with the FA and Sport England to enhance community sports facilities across England via their delivery partner, the Football Foundation. More details about the present-day involvement of some club community schemes is featured in the next Chapter.

CHAPTER 19 – 2008 TO THE PRESENT DAY

THE WAY IN WHICH PROFESSIONAL club-based community schemes have continued to develop and grow since 2007 is simply incredible. All 92 professional (PL and FL) clubs, plus several non-league clubs, now have community schemes that operate as registered charitable organisations. All of them offer wonderful community engagement via a huge range of activities, visits, events, extended involvement with the football club or any combination thereof.

In addition to community engagement, the present-day offer extends to Corporate Social Responsibility work (CSR)[52] and philanthropic work. The move from being 'Football in the Community' schemes operating as unincorporated associations to becoming charitable Community Trusts or Foundations has been hugely successful and has helped to facilitate the capacity-building that these organisations desperately craved.

Former FFE&VTS Community Programme Regional Director and PFA Director of Community, now PFA Director of Corporate Social Responsibility, **John Hudson**, said:

> *"Corporate Social Responsibility is no longer the best kept secret, but we must ensure that the influence of our pioneers back in 1986 – who saw that something had to be done during a dark time for the game, and had the vision and determination to tackle the problem – is sustained."*

Access to external funding has surged forward, stimulating and increasing turnover year-on-year.

Club community schemes, as registered charities, now have opportunities to access new and alternative sources of funding. In addition, massively increased PL funding has become accessible since the mid-2000's, largely (and cleverly) aimed at introducing new external funding based on encouraging "match" funding in order to enhance income and the range of projects.

Information made available by the Charity Commission confirms financial details of the accounts for most Football Club Community Charities. Total collective turnover is simply huge bearing in mind the initial efforts to raise funding in the early 1990's (see Appendix I for details of registered charity numbers and turnover for Club Schemes with year-end dates in 2017).

In addition, partnership working has been greatly extended to embrace key relationships with deliverers in the fields of education, health and social inclusion (together with sport development/participation).

The developing support of the PL (and the PL Charitable Fund) and the FL has also undoubtedly played a significant part in this continuing growth and development. Financial support from the PL is significant for member club's community work, but their now on-going support for clubs in the FL and, indeed, also in the National League, speaks volumes. Not

---

52. *In 2008, following on from Chelsea's CSR report in 2005/6, Manchester City produced a sizeable document entitled "Off the Pitch. Social Responsibility and Environmental Impact Report 2008". City therefore became the second club to spend considerable time and effort in producing a detailed analysis of the extent of the club's Corporate Social Responsibility work. Amongst organisations the club's community scheme were working with were 4CT (an East Manchester based voluntary sector organisation), Children in Need, East Manchester Youth College, Healthsure, Kickz, Manchester City Council, Manchester NHS Primary Care Trust, Tameside Metropolitan Borough Council, Willow Water (and Sportsmatch) and many, many others.*

only that, but the investment in the Football Foundation has continued and there is substantial evidence now of the impact and success of the Foundation's investment into community accessible facilities across the country. Having taken on what was established so well by the former Football Trust (then from funding from the Pools Companies), the Football Foundation is now a thriving organisation funded on the basis of the PL investment being matched by further investment from Government and by the FA.

The professional clubs themselves were somewhat reluctant to back the idea of increased involvement in their local communities going back to the 1980's and 90's, but, to their great credit, they now fully back the concept, and, perhaps more importantly, understand and appreciate the all-round benefits.

There is no doubt at all that 'Football in the Community' schemes at the professional clubs had evolved substantially by 2007 on the back of the pioneering work undertaken by the first Community Officers to be appointed – let's call them "ground breakers"! What is also clear, is that the only restrictions placed on the wider development of community schemes before 2007 was due to the reduced access to the mainly external funding that became significantly more available after 2007. That said, what needs to be recognised is that without the pioneering work of the "ground breakers" in the 1980's and 1990's, against a backdrop of much restricted access to funding and occasional unwillingness to become involved displayed by the clubs themselves, the work being done today would simply not be underway. In addition, of course, there are many thousands of people working directly or indirectly for or with club-based community operations whose jobs exist because of the success of the founding work undertaken prior to 2007.

Post 2007, Community Officers took on board the offer of accepting different support, coming as it did from the PL, FL and from the PFA rather than had been the case with the previous lower amount of financial support offered by the former FFE&VTS Community Programme. Available funding from the PL increased significantly, especially for their own club community schemes.

FL support[53] (often routed to them from the PL) became available at different levels based on the achievement of club schemes in quality assurance matters and including bronze, silver or gold standard definitions. The PFA offered as much support as they could to Community Officers in order to continue to encourage their club's players to attend and to support local community activities. Indeed, the PFA set out to record this player support on an annual basis and their annual reports on this subject make impressive reading[54]. The PFA have also spent considerable time and effort to support the formation of player foundations such as those established by **Jermain Defoe** (ex-Tottenham Hotspur), **James Milner** (ex-Leeds United), **Jason Roberts** (ex-Blackburn Rovers) and **Alan Shearer** (ex-Newcastle United). In acknowledging some of the early pioneering work done in the name of 'Football in the Community', it is worth looking at where some of the involvement has now extended.

One of the huge successes, of course, has been the impressive growth in the number of girls and women playing, and watching, football. The idea, first established through community schemes way back in the 1980's of establishing women's teams in the name of the parent professional football club, is now here to stay and women's teams operating as part of the professional clubs are fairly commonplace. The womens' team at Manchester City's even celebrated thirty years of existence following their formation back in 1988 – and author, **Gary James**, has even written a best-selling book about the club's history. Manchester City are one of several clubs who invest in their women's teams in the present day. Great credit is due to all those people who have encouraged this huge upsurge in numbers playing and watching football. Female football, of course, was overseen by the WFA since 1969 (who first affiliated with the FA in 1983) but it has

---

53. *Significant parts of English Football League* club community scheme work were occupied by access to funding streams – e.g. in support of the National Citizens Scheme. *The Football League (FL) was renamed "The English Football League" (EFL) in 2016/17 season.*
54. *The PFA produce an annual 'Community Evaluation' booklet which includes a statistical analysis of player attendances at community activities and events.*

only operated under the auspices of the FA since 1983. Indeed, it is worth recalling that the FA only lifted their original ban of women's football in 1971.

The involvement of people aged over 50 has been extended far beyond 'tea-dances' and now encourages them to take part in (mixed) 'Walking Football', with all the physical and mental benefits that being more active brings. Indeed, the vast majority of Community schemes now offer opportunities (usually for over 50's men and women) to play 'Walking Football' on a weekly basis.

Opportunities for people with disabilities were extremely limited until community schemes began offering people the opportunity to play, irrespective of their disability. Community schemes first worked alongside Mencap back in 1987, but now, and following some wonderful and devoted work by the FA's **Jeff Davis**, there are terrific opportunities to play football for people who are blind and/or are partially sighted, have cerebral palsy, people who are deaf, people with learning difficulties, people for whom restricted growth conditions apply, amputees etc. There are 'Ability Counts' schemes within most County FAs (first launched in 1999), and there have been pan-disability leagues established in most areas of the country. The icing on the cake for footballers with disabilities is that there is now in place a genuine player pathway for elite performers leading to recognition in England's national disability squads.

Work with people who are out of work or are ex-offenders continues. It is, however, fair to say that the sort of training and career opportunities previously available through the Government's Community Programme, Training for Work and Employment Training employment programmes are less available.

Match day attendances continue to rise (see Appendix II. Since the low point of season 1985/6, attendances have – incredibly - just about doubled from 16.4 Million in season 1985/6 to 32.6 Million in season 2017/18).

Player involvement in attending all community activities is positively encouraged by virtually everyone involved in the game (there are now no longer any managers in the professional game who are allowed to impose their own ideas of whether women should be playing football, or whether players should be attending community activities at all).

Looking at some of the club community schemes in the present day, it is fair to say that the original six clubs that set out up those 'pilot', tentative community schemes in 1986, have continued to be successful and remain very different not just in size and turnover, but also in the ways in which they operate. The Bury and Oldham charities remain the smallest of the original six operators (turnover in the Bury FC Community Trust was just over £420k, whilst the Oldham Athletic Community Trust turned over just under £230k); the Bolton and Preston charities are "mid-range" (the Bolton Wanderers Community Trust turned over more than £850k; the Preston North End Community and Educational Trust just under £770k) whilst, as you'd probably expect, and with significant support from the PL, the Manchester City FC City in the Community Foundation (turnover just short of £2.7 million) and the Manchester United Foundation (turnover well over £3.8 million) are the largest of the original six 'founding' club community schemes.

The Bury Trust *"utilises the power of sport to engage the community and the surrounding areas in activity with the aim of improving health, education, inclusion and social well-being"*. New monies and support during the financial year ending in 2017 saw new projects underway with funding from PL Schools, the English Sports Council Lottery, the Armed Forces, Awards for All and Children in Need (the latter for a second year). The accounts for 2017 saw two football club directors also acting as Trustees of the Charity, whilst long-serving Club Secretary, **Jill Neville**, also became a Trustee in January 2018. Following the clubs' difficulties and expulsion from the EFL, it remains to be seen whether a new club can be established which might work with the Bury FC Trust in future.

The Oldham Athletic Community Trust has clearly moved to secure representation on the Board of Trustees from key local strategic partners including Greater Manchester Police, Manchester County FA, Oldham Community Leisure, Oldham Council, Oldham Primary Care Trust and The Oldham College. The Oldham Athletic Trust benefits from significant funding from the PL (PL Charitable Fund) and operates PL Kicks, PL Women and Girls and PL Primary Stars. The six main 'themes' under which it operates are education & school sport, health, inclusion, Oldham Athletic, participation and women & girls.

> The Bolton Wanderers Community Trust has a mission statement "to inspire people and raise aspirations". "We provide quality experiences to the wider community that focus on narrowing the gap of disadvantage in health, education, disability and inclusion". The Annual Report for 2017 comments on the fact that the Trust "played a significant role in helping to shape and develop the new Bolton Vision 2030, the new, long-term community strategy for Bolton".

The Bolton Trust continues to deliver and expand several PL-funded initiatives including PL Enterprise, PL Kicks, PL Girls, PL Primary Stars and PL4Sport (though this has now merged with PL Kicks). Other programmes operating include 'Aspirations' for 400 x year 5 and 6 pupils at 13 classes in 9 schools and the 'Positive Chances' programme working with some of the most disadvantaged looked-after children and young people (aged 3-21) which also sees the operation of a weekly youth club. This project won "Initiative of the Year at the 2017 North West Football Awards. Support for Bolton Wanderers Ladies FC also continues. The Trust appreciates the importance of partnerships including those with the University of Bolton, Bolton College and Bolton Council. Of the trustees in place, ex-Wanderers player, **John McGinlay**, continues to give his support to this wonderful charity.

Like the Oldham Trust, the Preston North End Community and Education Trust has 6 "focus areas" which are community, education, health, inclusion, the National Citizen Service[55] (NCS) and sport. Regarding the NCS, the Preston Trust claims to be *"one of the biggest providers of this service within the FL clubs operating in the North West"*. Indeed, of total turnover for the Trust for the year ending in 2017, NCS income of £425,992 represented over 55% of total turnover, underlining the importance of this programme of work as a key theme. PL income, mainly relating to PL Girls and PL Kicks, totalled just under £100k.

The Preston North End Trust, which continues to be supported by Club Secretary, **Ben Rhodes**, after many years of personal support for the club's community involvement, stays loyal to its original "core" roots by offering holiday soccer camps/activity clubs, a range of match-day activities and an after-schools programme of activity including multi-sport in engaging and fun sports.

Ex-City favourite as a player, **Alex Williams**, retains an involvement in the Manchester City FC City in the Community (CITC) Foundation as an ambassador. The City Foundation boasts in its 2017 Annual Report that *"over the past five years alone, CITC has invested over £8 million into local communities within Manchester"*. The Report also reports that 2016 *"marked the 30th anniversary of the charity and the wider Football in the Community initiative supported by "30 years of giving Manchester Kids a better shot at life"*.

CITC concentrates on three key social issues: education, health and inclusion. It has grown in recent years and the 2017 Annual Report comments on a staffing re-structure which embraced the creation of new posts including Senior Operations Manager, Senior Partnerships Manager, Insights Manager and Insights Officer. Some of the growth was encouraged by a *"significant growth of PL funded projects"* including PL4Sport, PL and BT Disability Sports, PL Kicks, PL Primary Stars and PL School Sports (totalling over £700k). Further growth arose following the award of a major Big Lottery grant of £500k to roll out a family lifestyle programme. Some of the key partnerships are also acknowledged including links with Lancashire County Cricket Club Foundation, Manchester Metropolitan University, Manchester United Foundation and Sale Sharks in the Community Trust all of whom support the "Coach Core" apprenticeship programme as Employers. Hopwood Hall College also support the provision of a BTEC Level 3

---

55. *The National Citizen Service is a national campaign for 16-17 year-olds that helps build skills for work and for life.*

Extended Diploma in Sport course for 16-19 year-olds.

The Manchester United Foundation has the largest turnover of the original six club-based community schemes, boosted by what is now a two-year cycle of staging fund-raising matches at Old Trafford. In the case of the accounts for 2017, it is clear that the 2017 match between a Manchester United 'legends XI' and a team comprising FC Barcelona 'legends' raised a significant amount of money for the Foundation. The Foundation continues to operate with a Board of Trustees which includes two United (club) Directors, one of whom, **Michael Edelson**, attended the original United Board Meeting held way back in 1986.

The Chairman of the United Foundation speaks in the 2017 Annual Report of the *"partnerships with high schools and local community initiatives"* which have helped to ensure the continued success of the Foundation's work. This is underlined by the amounts of monies generated from 'High School Delivery' (£1,077,988) and 'Primary School Delivery' (£176,308).

Its aims are to use *"football to engage and inspire young people to build a better life for themselves and unite the communities in which they live"*.

United's community engagement work is almost all undertaken under their own branding so, amongst some of the successful programmes in which the Foundation is involved, are the following:

- The Manchester United Enterprise Academy
- "Inclusive Reds" (a disability sport initiative supported by the PL and BT Disability Sports Fund)
- "Street Reds" (and "Carrick's Street Reds" funded by 3 years of funding from the Michael Carrick Foundation – set up following his Testimonial held in June 2017).

The Foundation, like many of the larger community charities, also has a trading subsidiary which includes income derived from matchday lotteries.

John Shiels was appointed as Head of the Manchester United Foundation in 2008 and clearly has huge knowledge about the growth and development of community schemes at professional clubs:

> *"They are now sophisticated, well run charities that are effectively 'social enterprises' in their own right. Their workforces have changed too. Managing at the top level are trained managerial staff rather than former players with coaching experience as was the case in the early days."*

It's worth recalling at this point that one of the original aims of the Community Programme scheme in the mid-1980's was to create jobs for former players – hence why so many former players were full time "Activity Organisers" or "Supervisors" in the very early days. They 'opened doors' into the wider community for the clubs where they worked – and still do!

A quick run around some of the other charitable community schemes operating across the UK reveals that the huge growth of community schemes in recent years is at least partly down to the significant investment of the PL in community projects and, indeed, to the hard work of PL and EFL Trust officers in encouraging increased partnership working and investment. The National Citizens Service (NCS) work alone sees sizeable income across the vast majority of EFL club community schemes. Indeed, in the EFL Trust accounts for the year ended 30th June 2018, total income rose to over £18.6 million, of which over £13 million came directly from the NCS programme. £2.8 million also came to the Trust from the PFA. Income is also forecast to increase to exceed approximately £20 million in the next year's accounts.

The Blackpool FC Community Trust saw turnover go fractionally over £1 million during the year ended 30th June 2017. In the Annual Report, the Trust proudly states that they have delivered *"in excess of 10,000 sessions which involved over 200,000 visits"*. The Trust has an excellent balance of original 'core' activities (including soccer schools and after-schools work) which generated 49% of income during the year together with PL funded initiatives (such as PL Girls, PL Kicks and PL Enterprise the latter of which first started following the club's promotion to the PL in 2010) which generated just over 20% of total turnover. Of interest too is the fact that the Annual Report includes a statement confirming that the offices in the stadium offered for the use of the Community Trust are *"free of rent"* and that the club also supports the Trust with *"central administrative and financial functions"*. It is also true that the club offer significant support to the Trust through the work of Disability Liaison Officer, **Chris Beveridge**, who also continues to offer wonderful "dream days" for young supporters who have had a tough time for one reason or another. Having done a fantastic job for so many years, it is important to acknowledge the contribution made by former Blackpool striker, **Derek Spence**, who announced his retirement from the Community Trust in December 2016 (not forgetting his wife **Lyn** who continues to work for the Trust after many years in post). Another key contribution came from former Trust Chairman, **Gavin Steele**. Under his chairmanship, the Trust grew significantly from season 2010/2011 when turnover increased hugely following Gavin's decision to restructure the Trust.

Also continuing to operate, in the North West of England, are the Everton and Liverpool community charities. Concentrating on *"Merseyside and surrounding areas"*, Everton's community scheme, "Everton in the Community" (EITC) recently saw their Chief Executive (**Dr Denise Barrett-Baxendale**) leave in order to become Chief Executive and a Director of Everton Football Club. This is a huge tribute to her work for the Community charity, and a huge endorsement of the talent and skill of a senior Community Officer. Denise continues to be Executive Chair of the Board of Trustees of Everton in the Community too. (Interestingly enough, exactly the same thing happened in February 2019 at Tranmere Rovers where the former Managing Director of Tranmere Rovers in the Community, **Dawn Tolcher**, was appointed as Managing Director of Tranmere Rovers Football Club).

Everton's excellent and wide-ranging community work has won many awards in recent years, but arguably one of their best and long-term programmes sees their continuing work with people with disabilities. Indeed, in 2017, the Everton charity operated 9 disability teams across all key disability areas. Other work includes on-going work with Alder Hey Children's Hospital in Liverpool, including the delivery of fun activity workshops actually on the wards! The EITC apprenticeship programme was noted to be successful as were the delivery of soccer schools in China, Germany and Hong Kong!

Financial contributions to the Everton charity included over £400k from the NCS and over £650k from the PL.

Liverpool's community work carries on predominantly in much the same operating areas as Everton's. As with the Manchester United Foundation, the Liverpool FC Foundation saw the proceeds of over £1 million raised from a Liverpool Legends game against a Real Madrid Legends XI (held in March 2017) go exclusively to the Foundation. The Liverpool FC Foundation enjoys the support of all the PL programmes, offering PL Kicks in 10 areas of Merseyside plus the new Kicks Football+ scheme (in conjunction with Merseyside Fire and Rescue Service). PL Employability Works engaged 29 unemployed young people, PL Enterprise, PL Girls, PL Primary Stars, PL School Sports and even a 'winding down' PL4 Sports scheme which saw delivery across 6 different sports (badminton, basketball, boxing, netball, table tennis and volleyball). The Foundation also continues to offer the original 'core' of activities under what is headed up as work in "Community Programmes". The Foundation college also offered access to GCSE's, Foundation degrees and FA coaching qualifications for 16-19 year-olds at the time, although the college now no longer operates. The Foundation is now ably led by **Matt Parish,** previously a long-term assistant working with **Jason Morgan** at Charlton Athletic.

The work of "Tranmere Rovers in The Community" continues to be well received on the Wirral where **Steve Williams** has been doing a super job as the club's long-serving Head of Community having completed over 30 years in post in 2018. What is particularly encouraging is that the devotion of the scheme towards female football continues and, indeed, Steve also acts as Chairman of Tranmere Rovers Ladies FC where long-serving officers, **Louise Edwards** and **Shirley Waring** also continue to be involved. The Tranmere Rovers Community charity is an approved centre of delivery/approved training provider on the Register of Training organisations and is sub-contracted by Wirral Metropolitan College to deliver a vocational educational programme (college income contributed approximately just under 50% of total income during the year ended 30th June 2017).

Despite relegation from the PL after 8 consecutive seasons in 2013, Wigan Athletic's community operation continues to thrive under the management and leadership of Head of Community, **Tom Flower** (previously with Manchester City). Indeed, 2017 proved to be an excellent year for the Wigan Athletic FC Community Trust as it won the EFL 2017 North West Checkatrade Community Club Award in March and was named the Leesa North West Football Awards Community Club Winner in November 2017. This followed a 'realignment' of its programme of activities to cover 3 main areas of operation being: Schools, Community Development (including various healthy projects and the NCS scheme) and Training & Skills (including apprenticeships, traineeships and a foundation degree provision in conjunction with the University of South Wales).

The Trust also continues to operate several PL projects including PL Kicks, PL Primary Stars, PL Enterprise and PL Girls Football (plus PL 4 Sport up to 2017). Indeed, by 2018, PL income accounted for one third of total turnover. Major income sources in 2017 included PPA working (over £69k), Soccer schools and after school-work (over £130k) and a grant from the Big Lottery Fund of over £138k. Former player, **Emmerson Boyce**, is a current trustee.

Across the Pennines in Yorkshire, several of the community schemes that got underway way back in 1988 continue to thrive and flourish. For example, under ex-player **Wayne Bullimore**, the Barnsley community charity ("Reds in the Community"), like many EFL club-based charities, has grown hugely in recent years. Like most of the FL community charities, the Barnsley charity offers 4 key themes to their work being education, health, social inclusion and sports participation. It also attracts PL funding via their PL Kicks and PL Primary Stars programmes and for the delivery of the National Citizens Service (NCS) programme on behalf of the EFL Trust. In addition, the original 'core' areas continue to be delivered, raising over £120,000 towards total income. Key support also comes from Barnsley Metropolitan Borough Council and from 'Every Player Counts' (from the EFL Trust). After an extensive involvement in community schemes in the past, former Area Manager, **Dick Krzywicki**, also continues to act as a Trustee on the charity Board.

Also, in South Yorkshire, the Doncaster Community Sports & Education Foundation embraces a number of different partnerships, e.g. with Doncaster Rovers FC, the Dons Rugby League Club, Doncaster Metropolitan Borough Council, Doncaster Culture and Leisure Trust, South Yorkshire Police, St. Leger Homes and with Selby College (South Yorkshire Police and St Leger Homes support the delivery of the PL 'Kicks' programme. Working with the College, the Foundation offered full-time further and higher education for 137 young people during the 2017 year. NCS opportunities were also provided for over 700 young people.

The Rotherham United Community Sports Trust also moved into a new and exciting era, taking over the brand-new, state of the art, "Goal Zone" facility based at the Millers New York Stadium. The 'Goal Zone' facility includes 3 classrooms together with office and health space. The Trust also attracted funding the PL in order to deliver the PL Girls, PL Kicks and PL Primary Stars programmes and saw the delivery of a simply huge NCS programme with income from NCS alone accounting for just under 50% of total income for the year.

Leeds United's community operation, the Leeds United Foundation, works closely with the PL on the delivery of certain PL programmes (including PL4 Sport) and with the EFL Trust concerning the delivery of the NCS programme whilst maintaining their commitment to the original 'core' of activities with a huge programme of soccer schools and coaching work.

In the North East, community schemes at Middlesbrough and Newcastle United both offer some fantastic community engagement opportunities across many widely varying programmes, including the many various PL programmes (PL Disability, PL Enterprise, PL Girls (and Women), PL Kicks, PL Primary Stars, PL4 Sport, PL Employability Works etc.)

Middlesbrough's long-established and highly successful scheme (The Middlesbrough Football Club Foundation) also runs the multi-sports facility, the Herlingshaw Centre on Normanby Road in Eston, Middlesbrough. The Foundation supports 4 key themes being education, health, social inclusion and sports participation.

The Newcastle United Foundation took over the running of the Newcastle United Women's Football Club (which operates as a separate legal entity but is wholly owned by the Foundation). Looking forward after over ten years excellent work under Head of Community, **Kate Bradley**, the Foundation openly looks forward in their 2017 Annual Report to looking at developing community accessible facilities in Newcastle, hopefully alongside Northumberland CFA as part of the creation of possible Park Life community hubs to be established in the city.

In the Midlands, community schemes at Coventry City, Stoke City and West Bromwich Albion continue to be successful despite their respective parent clubs relegation from the PL.

Coventry City's "Sky Blues in the Community" continues to be successfully led by ex-player, **David Busst** (who also acts as the charity's Secretary). Like many EFL clubs, they have adopted 4 core themes in education, health, inclusion and sport. The scheme offers unique programmes including the healthy school projects "Move and Learn" and "Fit 4 Life". Also, in place is a unique link with the Jimmy Hill Legacy Fund, supporting *"a number of causes that were close to his heart"* including work with children and adults with disabilities and with disadvantaged children and young people. Sky Blues in the Community also boast of securing funding from 17 different "principal funders".

The Stoke City Community Trust continues to see Chief Executive, **Tony Scholes**, act as a Trustee, with the hard-working, **Adie Hurst,** continuing in post as Head of Community. 2017 saw the Trust grow its business by approximately 24% thanks largely to the continued support of the PL. The Trust also undertook some work overseas as far afield as Canada, China and the USA.

Rob Lake still leads West Bromwich Albion's 'Albion Foundation'. Rob has done a fantastic job over many years and also acts as Charity Secretary. The Albion charity continues to offer hugely wide-ranging programmes of community engagement (including a continuation of many PL programmes such as PL Employability Works) and delivering an exceptional disability sport programme working with more than 800 people with disabilities. It is good to see that the charity celebrated its 25th anniversary during the 2016/17 season (having been first set up in October 1989) and that it continues to work overseas in Australia, Canada, China, India and Kenya.

In the East Midlands, the vastly experienced **Allison Tripney** has been Community Director at the Leicester City Football Club Trust since October 2017 having previously been a dynamic and active force as Education and Learning Manager at West Bromwich's highly successful Albion Foundation. The Leicester Trust, which operates with the club's Chief Executive and a club Director on the Board of Trustees, works in three key areas (community, education and inclusion) and has extensive involvement, as you'd expect, in delivering all the PL programmes. The Trust also saw huge growth from 2016 to 2017 with turnover alone increasing by just under 50%. The Leicester City Football Club Trust carries on its long tradition of excellent and wide-ranging community engagement dating back to the very early days.

Simon Carnall remains in post as Head of Community at the Derby County Community Trust where PL programmes and the NCS scheme are well-established. The Trust grew by approximately 18% during the year ended June 2017.

Northampton Town's Football in the Community Programme works well and saw the club's Chief Executive, **James Whiting**, appointed to the Board of Trustees in January 2018.

In Nottingham, both Nottingham Forest and Notts County boast excellent and wide-ranging community operations. The Nottingham Forest Community Trust is led up by the popular **Graham Moran** (previously with Notts County) who is assisted by **Calum Osborne** as Chief Operating Officer.

Graham, by the way, received a well-deserved life-time achievement award from the City of Nottingham for services to professional football and community engagement in November 2018.

Of interest during the year ended 31st December 2017 is the fact that Nottingham Forest Football Club made a donation of £150,000 to the Trust (more or less representing the growth in turnover on the previous year). Income from PL programmes continues to be important for the Forest Trust, which also secures significant income from the EFL Trust based on delivery of the NCS scheme (365 young people graduated during the year).

On the other side of the River Trent, whilst Notts County Football Club now find themselves in the National League, nevertheless the Notts County FC Community Programme continues to boast of many varied community engagement programmes funded from many different sources of revenue and by many different partners. The ever so successful "Heading for Goal" project (the classroom-based project for hard-to-engage teenagers aimed at helping to maximise their potential) continues to be as successful as ever. Indeed, despite the parent club's relegation from the Football league in 2019, the Notts County FC Community Programme continues to do great things based on a wide range of programmes and a huge number of partners. The NCS programme is one of those successful programmes, with just under £440,000 of income generated in the year ended 31st December 2017. Many congratulations too to the long-serving **Colin Slater** who continues to act as a Trustee after many years' service.

In the South West of England, the Swindon Town Football in the Community Trust is now solely managed by **Jon Holloway**, as Head of the Trust, following the retirement of former joint-Head, **Clive Maguire,** in April 2019, after 24 years loyal and successful service. Talking in the Swindon Advertiser, Jon said *"Clive has worked tiresomely over the years to ensure that our projects and programmes could have a positive effect on as many participants as possible".* The Swindon Town Trust works closely with key partners such as Swindon Borough Council, Wiltshire Police and Probation Services. The Trust also deliver the 'Extra Time' project for over 50's and offers 'Walking Football' as an opportunity for that age group.

Mark Lovell is Head of Community at the Plymouth Argyle Football in the Community Trust where the club have two directors and one associate director acting on the Board of Trustees. The Trust attracts funding of over £250,000 from the PL for programmes including PL Girls, PL Kicks, PL Primary Stars and School Sports plus PL4 Sport. In addition, the Trust offers PPA support opportunities to 40 schools and, via their huge NCS programme, to 630 young people in the summer and autumn. The Plymouth Trust has over 30 partnerships in place across Devon and Cornwall and saw a sizeable increase in growth of about 25% from 2016 to 2017 which was based largely on a huge increase in income from the NCS programme (from £464,599 the previous year to £761,626 in 2017).

In Exeter, the Exeter City Community Trust operates across Devon and Somerset and works in four key areas being: education, health, multi-sports development & participation and social inclusion. As with the Plymouth community scheme, the Exeter programme includes a "rapidly" expanding NCS programme which accounts for approximately 45% of turnover (income generated) during the year. **Jamie Vittles** still does a sterling job as Head of Community for the Trust which also takes a charity executive box at St. James Park for matchday/promotional use.

The South East continues to see the biggest operators in community engagement work, most notably at Charlton Athletic and Chelsea. Indeed, by far and away, the biggest single community scheme operators (based on turnover and numbers of staff) are at Chelsea and at Charlton Athletic.

Chelsea's Foundation sees Chelsea Football Club Chairman, **Bruce Buck**, involved as a Trustee, together with former Kick It Out Head, **Piara Powar** and **John Devine** (now a partner with the North East-based law firm Muckle LLP). In 2017, the Club Foundation worked with an amazing total of 57,000 'unique participants'. Former player, **Shaun Gore** (now "Head of Community") has done an incredible job in growing the work of the charity over so many years and he is now assisted by Head of Foundation, **Simon Taylor**. The Foundation uses sport *"as a catalyst for positive change in the lives of people of all ages at home and abroad"* (the Foundation also continues to engage audiences overseas through their international department). Interestingly, turnover at the charity grew again in 2018, going up by 22% (from £6,493,857 in 2017 to £7,944,647 in 2018).

The community scheme at Charlton is now so wide ranging it embraces disability working, education, equality and diversity, football (and sports) development, health improvement, social inclusion and youth service work (Charlton now run the local youth programme, including disability youth services, on behalf of The Royal Borough of Greenwich Council). Indeed,

Charlton Athletic's community work in 2017 saw several highlights including:

- Total income reached £6,956,000 in 2017 (turnover was £5,513,000 in 2016, reflecting an increase in income of over 25% based largely around a legacy donation of approximately £1.5 million generously left by the late **Tom Mackie**, a former Trustee).

- Delivery of a total of 62 separate NCS events (income from NCS alone exceeded £600,000).

- The development of a 2-year Foundation degree in partnership with the University of Greenwich.

- The creation of a Charlton v Homophobia football tournament to help raise awareness of discrimination against the LGBT community.

The vast extent of the community work in which Charlton Athletic are fully immersed is impossible to summarise in brief though one or two further aspects can be described here. A 9-year partnership with Kent and Medway NHS Trust delivering a mental health early intervention project has been commissioned for a further 3 years. The executive team has been re-structured following the departure of long-serving Chief Operating Officer, **Matt Parish** (Matt joined the Liverpool FC Foundation as their new Director in March 2019, having originally left Charlton in 2016 to move to the North West in order to take up the post of Deputy Community Director with Burnley's community operation), and now embraces the Chief Executive, a Director of Finance and Support Services, a Director of Youth and Inclusion and a Director of Education, Sport and Health. New community facilities including offices and a full size 3G artificial pitch have been established at Footscray Rugby Club in New Eltham. The 'One Goal' project (run alongside 8 other London-based community schemes) successfully engages young people aged between 5 and 21 into positive activities to improve social and emotional wellbeing and future prospects. In terms of income generated, the main income streams include over £550,000 from the Royal Borough of Greenwich for health improvement services and over £370,000 from the L & Q Housing Association.

Further evidence of the success of Charlton Athletic's highly successful community work came in December 2013 when **Jason Morgan**, long-serving Head of their highly successful community operation, was awarded an MBE in recognition of all his work and extensive commitment to the Charlton cause.

Two of the earliest London-based community schemes to be established were at Brentford and Millwall. The Brentford FC Community Sports Trust still has the highly successful **Lee Doyle** at the helm. The Trust has devised four new "global outcomes":

- Improved health
- Improved access to educational opportunities
- Improved employment prospects
- Improved community cohesion

Strategic partners are the London Boroughs of Ealing and Hounslow. The Trust continues to offer much of the original 'core' of activities and remains predominantly sports participation based (turnover in sports participation increased from £674,675 in 2016 to £1,240,176 in 2017). Indeed, over 100 sessions per week are offered by the Trust across Ealing, Hounslow, Hillingdon and Richmond.

Millwall's Community Trust evolved from the Millwall Football in the Community programme that was originally established in 1985 and now boasts:

- Contracts with Housing Associations across the London Boroughs of Lewisham and Southwark (and strong relationships with the Boroughs of Lewisham and Southwark)

- Links with the Metropolitan Police and PL Charitable Foundation in support of the Kicks programme

The Trust also operates the Lions Centre adjacent to the ground and, since 2016, has taken management responsibility of the St. Paul's Community Sports Ground in Rotherhithe, Southwark, where the Millwall Lionesses play all their Women's League fixtures.

The Millwall Trust continues to offer a range of many different ways of engaging with the local community, including the original 'core' provision of schools coaching and sports participation (including holiday courses). The Trust also attracts a wide range of grants towards its hugely diverse work with key funders including the PL Kicks programme, the L & Q Housing Association (a leading housing association and residential developer) and the EFL Trust who offered core and infrastructure grant support during the financial year of just over £35,000. Millwall Football Club Chief Executive, **Steve Kavanagh**, joined the Board of Trustees in October 2017, thus maintaining a clear link to the parent football club.

The QPR in the Community Trust continues to be led by Head of Community, **Andy Evans**, and sees the club represented on the Board of Trustees with a club Director, the club's Chief Executive and Commercial Director. The Trust works across seven London Boroughs and, as if to emphasise its "cradle to the grave" work, its Annual Report mentions the Trust's youngest participant as being a 2 year-old involved in the 'Mini Footballers' programme and their oldest participant an 89 year old involved in the 'Extra Time' project! Illustrating the club's 'big heart', the Trust also worked closely with the club in setting up a 'Game4 Grenfell' just a few months after the tragedy of the fire at the nearby Grenfell Tower block of flats in North Kensington in June 2017. All the proceeds from the game which attracted a gate of over 17,000 went back to the local community.

Of the former football clubs that are now non-league clubs, there are a number who continue to operate community schemes with the now well-established support of the National League. It was back in 2010 that the PL committed the sum of £800,000 per year for an initial three years to allow the National League to support community projects at their member clubs. It is worth mentioning that **Brian Lee** himself (then Chairman of the Football Conference) was a key personality involved in these new arrangements – Brian being the first person ever to write about 'Football in the Community'). **Susan O'Brien** set up a grant-based funding system for National League clubs, together with a training programme to encourage clubs to develop the skills to manage community projects, create partnerships and to make grant applications. A charity was created in 2012 to manage the funding (renamed the National League Trust (NLT) in 2016) and the PL generously increased their funding to £1.2 million also in 2016. Since the Trust was first set up, 95 different clubs have received funding support for community projects. Many of these clubs have been promoted to the EFL and many are former EFL clubs.

Amongst the former Football League clubs now supported by the NLT are Hartlepool United, Stockport County, Torquay United (in the National League) and York City (in the National League North).

The Hartlepool United Community Sports Foundation continues much as it was set up whilst the club were members of the Football League (FL). It operates with 4 key 'themes' and works closely with key partners Hartlepool Borough Council, Hartlepool Primary Care Trust, the Duke of Edinburgh's award scheme, the Prince's Trust and Durham CFA. Ex-player, **Keith Nobbs**, is still Manager of the charity, whose main projects include events organised with Show Racism the Red Card and Kick It Out, plus a girl's engagement programme funded by the PL Charitable Fund and the FL Trust, the latter of which saw 5 girls satellite centres established. Perhaps the largest single project in which Hartlepool's community scheme is involved, however, is the NCS programme, income from which accounts for 50% of total turnover. One quick footnote about the scheme and that is simply to say that the accounts continue to be prepared by Sheffield-based **Nigel Sharpe** many years after his first involvement in preparing accounts for the fledgling community schemes in the 1980's.

To give its full title, the Stockport County Community Sports & Education Foundation still operates most effectively despite the loss of significant PL and FL financial support. That said, the Foundation receives excellent support from the National League (£44,217 in the 2017 accounts, increasing to £71,345 in 2018). The bulk of County's community work is still based around the original 'core' activities, predominantly schools work, which accounts for just under 80% of all revenue. Interestingly enough, the Foundation's income increased again in 2018 by a further 20% even without the significant 'core' funding offered to PL and EFL clubs. Head

Officer, **Dave Wardle**, leads the Foundation's excellent work under a Board of Trustees headed up by Chairman, **Ian Lees** (once an Activity Organiser with Manchester City's community scheme in the early days).

The work of the Torquay United Community Sports & Education Trust continues following the retirement of long-serving Community Officer, Frankie Prince, at the end of 2014. As at Stockport, Torquay's main business continues to be the original 'core' activities (predominantly school's engagement work in the South Devon area). The operation increased in 2018 following access to additional funding grants, leading to an increase in turnover of approximately 45% – incredible growth for the charity.

York City's community scheme was initially brought "in-house' as a department of the club before being established as a Foundation which secured charity status in November 2014, following the closure of the former York City Football in the Community Programme. With a Foundation Manager and an Operations Manager now in post, significant success has been enjoyed by the newly-established Foundation based on new local partnerships and an increase in access to new funding streams, notably grants (which went up from just under £45,000 to over £140,000 in 2017).

Community schemes across the top levels of the football 'pyramid' continue to do wonderful things across England and Wales. Indeed, back in 1987, television personality, music entrepreneur and Factory Records owner, **Tony Wilson**, was correct when he described Football in the Community schemes as *"doing good for people, doing good for the community and doing good for football."*

If truth be told, community schemes now go way beyond simply "doing good" with serious investment in health, education and well-being programmes. Most clubs accept that they have a responsibility to play a key role in their local communities, and, in many cases, they are delivering life-changing opportunities for local people.

It is only right and proper that the terrific work that has been carried on since 1979 is properly acknowledged, and it is hoped that this book pays appropriate respect to those people, and certainly to the early pioneers, for "pioneers' (or "ground breakers") they certainly were. Following on in their footsteps, so many thousands of people in the past and present have contributed and will continue to contribute to making football's community engagement programmes so very successful, leading to 'Football in the Community' schemes at clubs being much valued, and, more importantly, here to stay. Here's to a rosy future for all!

APPENDIX I - LIST OF CLUB COMMUNITY CHARITIES RECENT ACCOUNTS

SOURCE: THE CHARITY COMMISSION

COMMUNITY CHARITY	CHARITY NUMBER	LATEST YEAR END ACCOUNTS	TURNOVER (INCOME)
Accrington Stanley Football in the Community Trust	1139575	30.9.2017	£493,397
Aldershot Town and District Football in the Community Trust*	1135131		
AFC Bournemouth Community Sports Trust	1122693	30.11.2017	£1,017,230
The Arsenal Foundation	1145668	31.5.2017	£1,578,877
Aston Villa Foundation	1152848	31.5.2017	£503,980
(Barnet) The Hive Foundation	1132710	30.6.2017	£267,853
(Barnsley) Reds in the Community	1118735	30.6.2017	£893,341
Birmingham City Football Club Community Trust	1086631	31.12.2017	£402,177
Blackburn Rovers Community Trust	1117122	31.12.2017	£1,350,126
Blackpool F.C. Community Trust	1128235	31.8.2017	£1,000,920
Bolton Wanderers Community Trust	1090753	30.6.2017	£856,071
Boston United Football Club Community Foundation[1]	1174561		
Bradford City FC Community Foundation	1122310	30.6.2017	£843,458
Brentford FC Community Sports Trust	1112784	31.3.2017	£1,773,663
(Brighton and Hove) Albion in the Community	1110978	30.6.2017	£3,507,315
Bristol City Community Trust	1093059	31.5.2017	£763,142
Bristol Rovers Community Trust	1088148	30.6.2017	£324,386
(Burnley) Clarets in the Community	1155856	30.6.2017	£1,689,334
Burton Albion Community Trust	1142920	31.5.2017	£1,105,353
Bury FC Community Trust	1121232	31.12.2017	£422,762

Cambridge United Youth and Community Trust	1137275	31.5.2017	£198,767
Cardiff City FC Community Foundation	1128443	31.8.2017	£1,430,491
Carlisle United FC Community Sports Trust	1126600	30.6.2017	£360,381
(Charlton Athletic) South of England Foundation Formerly Charlton Athletic Community Trust	1096222	31.3.2017	£6,956,000
Chelsea FC Foundation	1129723	30.6.2017	£6,493,857
Cheltenham Town Community Education and Sporting Trust[2]	1124119 1180210	30.4.2017	£280,399
Chester City*			
Chesterfield FC Community Trust	1136235	30.6.2017	£558,266
Colchester United FC Football in the Community	1159381	30.6.2017	£458,439
(Coventry City) Sky Blues in the Community	1127014	31.12.2017	£954,188
Crawley Town Community Foundation	1149113	30.6.2017	£609,397
(Crewe) Alexandra Soccer and Community Association	1113503	30.6.2017	£319,123
(Crystal) Palace for Life Foundation	1125878	30.6.2017	£1,700,688
Dagenham and Redbridge FC Community Trust	1141511	30.6.2017	£49,327
Darlington*			
Derby County Community Trust	1123520	30.6.2017	£1,871,771
Club Doncaster (Rovers) Community Sports and Education Foundation	1122676	31.8.2017	£1,630,547
Everton in the Community	1099366	31.5.2017	£4,385,340
Exeter City Community Trust	1121596	31.1.2017	£1,127,601
Fleetwood Town Community Trust	1146037	30.6.2017	£562,618
Forest Green Rovers*			
Fulham Football Club Foundation	1111639	30.6.2017	£1,961,055
Gillingham Football Club Community Trust	1125163	31.5.2017	£1,395,674

Grimsby Town Football in the Community Sports and Education Trust	1123447	31.5.2017	£757,575
FC Halifax Town*			
Hartlepool United Community Sports Foundation	1124207	31.1.2017	£190,196
Huddersfield Town Foundation Limited	1146501	30.6.2017	£194,879
(Hull City) Tigers Sport and Education Trust	1092287	31.7.2017	£1,743,287
Ipswich Town Charitable Trust / Ipswich Town Community Trust renamed "Inspire Suffolk Ltd"	1101519	31.12.2017	£1,284,337
Kidderminster Harriers FC Football in the Community	1092877	31.7.2017	£117,329
The Leeds United Foundation	1137703	30.6.2017	£847,668
Leicester City Football Club Trust	1126526	30.6.2017	£1,038,613
Leyton Orient Trust (SCORE)	1071766	31.3.2017	£787,665
Lincoln City Foundation	1128464	31.8.2017	£452,704
Liverpool FC Foundation	1096572	31.5.2017	£2,802,078
Luton Town FC Community Trust	1123078	31.3.2017	£659,174
Macclesfield Town Community Sports Trust Limited	1136526	30.6.2017	£78,515
Manchester City FC City in the Community Foundation	1139229	31.8.2017	£2,686,799
Manchester United Foundation	1118310	30.6.2017	£3,888,468
Mansfield Town Football in the Community Limited	1124621	31.3.2017	£187,022
Middlesbrough Football Club Foundation	1059418	31.8.2017	£1,873,998
Millwall Community Trust	1082274	31.3.2017	£1,068,528
Milton Keynes Dons Football Club Sports and Education Trust	1123762	30.6.2017	£1,292,710
Morecambe FC Community Sports	1155802	31.5.2017	£202,802
Newcastle United Foundation	1124896	31.7.2017	£2,711,266
(Newport) County in the Community Trust*	1172602		
Northampton Town FC Football in the Community Programme	1092502	31.12.2017	£238,004

Norwich City Community Sports Foundation	1088239	31.12.2017	£4,269,210
Nottingham Forest Community Trust	1139561	31.12.2017	£1,359,535
Notts County FC Community Programme	1091927	31.12.2017	£1,568,393
Oldham Athletic Community Trust	1120894	31.12.2017	£229,767
Oxford United Community Trust*	1165761		
Peterborough United Foundation	1132364	31.8.2017	£430,918
Plymouth Argyle Football in the Community Trust	1128906	31.12.2017	£2,172,981
(Portsmouth) Pompey in the Community	1126118	31.5.2017	£2,002,549
Port Vale Football Club Foundation	1161401	30.6.2017	£158,517
Preston North End Community and Education Trust	1130773	30.6.2017	£767,400
QPR in the Community Trust	1127806	31.5.2017	£1,542,603
Reading FC Community Trust	1125817	30.6.2017	£1,116,461
Rochdale AFC Football in the Community Trust	1121850	31.12.2017	£240,683
Rotherham United Community Sports Trust	1123692	31.8.2017	£1,289,015
Scunthorpe United FC Community Sports and Education Trust	1125158	30.6.2017	£585,378
Sheffield United Community Foundation	1126620	31.8.2017	£1,100,078
Sheffield Wednesday Football Club Community Programme	1108538	31.12.2017	£1,704,437
Shrewsbury Town in the Community	1125101	31.12.2017	£573,988
(Southampton) Saints Foundation SFC	1090916	30.6.2017	£2,256,228
Southend United Community and Educational Trust	1105515	31.8.2017	£748,329
Stevenage Football Club Foundation Limited	1140006	31.8.2017	£293,513
Stockport County Community Sports and Education Foundation	1125117	30.6.2017	£221,436
Stoke City Community Trust	1104006	31.8.2017	£1,663,394
(Sunderland) Foundation of Light	1089333	31.12.2017	£3,853,431
Swansea City AFC Community Trust	1126933	31.12.2017	£1,023,005

Swindon Town FC Foundation	1121820	31.12.2017	£771,752
Torquay United Community Sports and Education Trust	1125138	30.6.2017	£245,027
Tottenham Hotspur Foundation	1113725	30.6.2017	£4,310,077
Tranmere Rovers in the Community	1117749	30.6.2017	£409,612
Walsall FC Community Programme	1087147	31.12.2017	£307,510
Watford FC's Community Sports and Education Trust	1102239	30.6.2017	£3,034,604
(West Bromwich) The Albion Foundation	1081948	30.6.2017	£2,258,456
West Ham United Foundation	1114458	31.5.2017	£2,605,242
Wigan Athletic FC Community Trust	1120745	31.12.2017	£1,094,197
AFC Wimbledon Foundation	1154198	30.6.2017	£207,411
(Wolverhampton Wanderers) Wolves Community Trust	1126799	31.5.2017	£1,004,164
Wrexham*			
Wycombe Wanderers Sports and Education Trust	1119794	30.6.2017	£528,558
Yeovil Town Community Sports Trust Limited	1127710	30.6.2017	£204,298
York City Football Club Foundation	1159325	30.6.2017	£331,269
	TOTAL	(98 schemes)	£125,684,357

* *No accounts available*
1. First registered in September 2017 so no accounts available at time of going to print
2. The Cheltenham Town Community Trust was registered with the Charity Commission in October 2018

APPENDIX II - TOTAL FOOTBALL LEAGUE ATTENDANCES SINCE THE SECOND WORLD WAR

SEASON	TOTAL	FOOTBALL LEAGUE ONLY (SINCE 1992/3)	FA PREMIER LEAGUE ONLY (SINCE 1992/3)
1946/7	35,604,606		
1947/8	40,259,130		
1948/9	41,271,414		
1949/50	40,517,865		
1950/1	39,584,967		
1951/2	39,015,866		
1952/3	37,149,966		
1953/4	36,174,590		
1954/5	34,133,103		
1955/6	33,150,809		
1956/7	32,744,405		
1957/8	33,562,208		
1958/9	33,610,985		
1959/60	32,538,611		
1960/1	26,619,754		
1961/2	27,979,902		
1962/3	28,885,852		
1963/4	28,535,022		
1964/5	27,641,168		
1965/6	27,206,980		
1966/7	28,902,596		
1967/8	30,107,298		
1968/9	29,382,172		
1969/70	29,600,972		
1970/1	28,194,146		

1971/2	28,700,729		
1972/3	25,448,642		
1973/4	24,982,203		
1974/5	25,577,977		
1975/6	24,896,053		
1976/7	26,182,800		
1977/8	25,392,872		
1978/9	24,540,627		
1979/80	24,623,975		
1980/1	21,907,569		
1981/2	20,006,961		
1982/3	18,766,158		
1983/4	18,358,631		
1984/5	17,849,835		
1985/6	16,488,577		
1986/7	17,379,218		
1987/8	17,959,732		
1988/9	18,464,192		
1989/90	19,445,442		
1990/1	19,508,202		
1991/2	20,487,273		
1992/3	20,657,327	10,897,954	9,759,809
1993/4	21,683,381	11,041,283	10,644,551
1994/5	21,856,020	10,642,852	11,213,168
1995/6	21,844,416	11,375,309	10,469,107
1996/7	22,783,163	11,978,401	10,804,762
1997/8	24,692,608	13,600,502	11,092,106
1998/9	25,452,964	13,832,638	11,620,326
1999/2000	25,371,634	13,703,137	11,668,497
2000/1	26,018,818	13,546,724	12,472,094

2001/2	27,759,280	14,716,162	13,043,118
2002/3	28,340,946	14,871,981	13,468,965
2003/4	29,553,453	16,250,320	13,303,133
2004/5	29,451,254	16,569,486	12,881,768
2005/6	29,301,197	16,446,784	12,876,182
2006/7	29,800,222	16,707,466	13,094,307
2007/8	30,175,435	16,440,598	13,734,837
2008/9	30,214,675	16,662,673	13,552,002
2009/10	30,321,804	17,320,188	13,001,616
2010/11	29,627,877	16,192,665	13,435,212
2011/12	29,638,860	16,473,444	13,165,416
2012/13	29,368,088	15,724,815	13,643,273
2013/14	29,813,436	15,870,977	13,942,459
2014/15	30,117,661	16,375,679	13,741,982
2015/16	30,299,124	16,433,019	13,866,105
2016/17	31,838,537	18,219,941	13,618,596
2017/18	32,649,065	18,143,156	14,505,909

Sources: Football League and FA Premier League

APPENDIX III - TABLE OF TRAINEES IN POST YEAR BY YEAR 1994-2002

CLUB-BASED COMMUNITY SCHEMES	AV NO. OF TRAINEES IN POST							
	1994/95	1995/96	1996/97	1997/98	1998/99	1999/00	2000/01	2001/02
Accrington Stanley								
AFC Bournemouth								
Arsenal								
Aston Villa								
Barnet				0.30				
Barnsley	3.00	3.07	3.20	3.53	3.75	2.33	2.08	1.92
Birmingham City		0.20			0.16	2.50	3.33	2.33
Blackburn Rovers	4.00	4.00	2.50	2.92	2.08	1.25	2.50	2.75
Blackpool	4.40	4.46	1.70			0.50		1.00
Bolton Wanderers	5.90	5.90	5.50	3.69	2.58	4.92	4.75	2.83
Boston United								
Bradford City	2.00	2.00	2.30	0.46	1.25	2.42	3.08	2.67
Brentford	2.00	2.00	0.30		0.16	0.33		0.58
Brighton & Hove Albion					0.58	0.33		
Bristol City	1.80	1.80	0.90	0.46				
Bristol Rovers	1.80	1.80	3.50	0.30				
Burnley	3.80	3.84	5.20	4.76	2.08	3.50	1.42	2.92
Bury	3.00	3.07	3.50	2.23	1.00	1.08	1.25	3.33
Cambridge United								1.75
Cardiff City		0.50			0.08	1.00	1.00	0.16
Carlisle United	3.20	3.20	2.20	1.07				
Charlton Athletic								

Chelsea		0.38	0.30					0.25
Cheltenham Town								
Chester City							0.58	0.25
Chesterfield	5.90	5.90	4.10	2.46	3.66	1.92	4.92	2.00
Colchester United		0.30	2.60	0.23			0.25	
Coventry City	1.70	1.69	2.50	1.53	2.75	3.66	2.33	0.50
Crewe Alexandra	4.00	4.00	3.60	4.46	2.33	3.50	3.92	3.16
Crystal Palace	3.00	3.07	1.80	2.68	1.00			
Darlington	1.70	1.76	3.00	3.00	2.75	3.08	4.42	3.58
Derby County								
Doncaster Rovers	3.40	3.46	1.50	2.07	1.33	1.75	2.75	2.33
Everton								
Exeter City								0.67
Farnborough Town		0.46	0.50	0.07	0.25			
Fulham	2.00	2.00	1.00					
Gillingham		0.40						
Grimsby Town				1.00	0.41	0.50	1.00	1.58
Halifax Town	2.40	2.46			0.16	3.17	4.00	3.66
Hartlepool United	2.80	2.84		1.15	0.33	2.66	2.50	1.33
Hereford United								
Huddersfield Town	4.00	4.00	5.50	3.84	4.10	4.75	4.75	6.00
Hull City	4.30	4.38	4.50	3.76	3.00	4.00	3.25	3.25
Ipswich Town								
Kidderminster Harriers	2.40	2.38	0.70	1.07		1.42	0.50	0.58
Leeds United	5.60	5.69	6.00	5.92	1.25			
Leicester City	1.70	1.76	1.20	0.92	2.58	3.08	0.58	

Leyton Orient		0.30	0.50					
Lincoln City					0.33	1.00	1.00	0.08
Liverpool								
Luton Town								
Macclesfield Town						0.42	0.33	0.41
Manchester City	5.60	5.69	5.00	4.92	3.75	4.50	4.75	0.83
Manchester United								
Mansfield Town	4.10	4.15	3.40	2.46	1.66	1.50	1.75	0.67
Middlesbrough	3.80	3.84	3.50	3.00	2.00	5.17	2.33	2.25
Millwall								
M K Dons								
Newcastle United	1.80	1.84	0.20					
Northampton Town		0.46						
Norwich City							0.83	2.25
Notts County	2.40	6.15	7.40	6.00	5.33	1.92	1.42	1.92
Nottingham Forest	6.10	2.46	3.30	3.00	1.08	3.25	4.67	2.83
Oldham Athletic	2.20	2.23	2.30	0.38	0.25	0.42		0.33
Oxford United								
Peterborough United								
Plymouth Argyle								
Portsmouth		0.23	0.20					
Port Vale		0.38	1.30	1.46	1.66	4.17	2.08	1.50
Preston North End	3.40	3.38	1.70			0.75	4.92	1.58
Queens Park Rangers	1.00	1.00	1.40	0.53	0.50			
Reading	1.40	1.46	0.50	0.46				
Rochdale	3.00	3.00	2.80	2.53	1.75	3.25	2.00	1.66

Rotherham United	2.00	2.07	1.60	1.61	1.91	0.08	1.17	0.50
Scarborough						0.92	0.33	
Scunthorpe United	2.70	2.76	2.50	1.84	1.41	0.92	2.25	3.42
Sheffield United	3.30	3.38	3.80	4.84	4.75	4.75	3.17	3.67
Sheffield Wednesday	1.10	1.15	1.20	0.23	1.00		0.50	1.00
Shrewsbury Town								1.16
Southampton					0.67	0.66	0.17	1.00
Southend United	2.20	2.20	0.70	1.23	1.41		0.08	
Stockport County	2.70	2.76	2.80	3.69	2.75	1.42	2.42	3.08
Stoke City	1.00	1.00	3.40	4.30	3.58	7.58	7.17	5.33
Sunderland				1.07	2.00	0.83		
Swansea City								
Swindon Town				0.61	1.00	0.58		0.41
Torquay United								
Tottenham Hotspur								
Tranmere Rovers							0.42	0.91
Walsall	0.80	0.84	1.30	1.84	1.08	1.42	1.34	2.83
Watford								
West Bromwich Albion	5.90	5.92	5.50	4.69	5.75	6.75	6.17	5.08
West Ham United								
Wigan Athletic	4.00	4.07	3.20	4.38	2.50	3.33	5.08	1.92
Wimbledon		0.15	0.30					
Wolves	1.60	1.61	1.60	0.30				0.50
Wrexham	1.30	1.30			0.16	0.58	2.25	2.25
Wycombe Wanderers				0.30	1.08	1.00	1.42	1.00

Yeovil Town								
York City	.					0.75	1.00	0.25
Average Number of Trainees in Post at any one time	**143.20**	**148.55**	**131.00**	**109.55**	**88.98**	**111.57**	**116.18**	**102.00**

TABLE OF TRAINEES IN POST YEAR BY YEAR 2002-2007

Club-based Community Schemes	Av No of trainees in post 2002/03	Av No of trainees in post 2003/04	Av No of trainees in post 2004/05	Av No of trainees in post 2005/06	Av No of trainees in post 2006/07
Accrington Stanley					
AFC Bournemouth		0.92	1.00	0.08	
Arsenal					
Aston Villa					
Barnet					
Barnsley	3.42	1.83	2.42	1.00	
Birmingham City	2.17	1.33			
Blackburn Rovers	4.50	3.92	7.00	2.92	0.25
Blackpool	0.08	0.75	1.00		
Bolton Wanderers	4.50	4.00	6.66	7.00	2.08
Boston United			0.83	2.42	1.92
Bradford City	2.17	1.58	1.92	2.42	1.08
Brentford	0.50		1.16	3.75	1.08
Brighton & Hove Albion					
Bristol City	0.75	1.00	1.00	1.17	
Bristol Rovers					
Burnley	5.17	3.58	3.42	5.00	2.41
Bury	3.42	1.58	1.08	2.00	1.00
Cambridge United	2.75	2.17	1.50	0.92	0.92
Cardiff City	0.58				
Carlisle United			2.00	2.00	0.58
Charlton Athletic	0.16	1.00	0.58		
Chelsea	0.58	1.00	1.00	0.92	0.92

Cheltenham Town					
Chester City					
Chesterfield	2.33	2.17	1.58		
Colchester United	2.58	4.33	3.17	2.75	
Coventry City	1.17	2.00	2.00	2.25	0.92
Crewe Alexandra	2.25	0.75	1.00	0.25	
Crystal Palace		0.42	2.00	0.50	
Darlington	3.16	1.58	1.41	2.00	0.67
Derby County				1.50	1.33
Doncaster Rovers	3.67	3.33	3.92	3.25	0.50
Everton					
Exeter City	0.92	0.17	0.41	1.00	0.67
Farnborough Town					
Fulham	0.58	1.50	1.33	0.17	
Gillingham		0.83	1.75		
Grimsby Town	3.42	2.67			
Halifax Town	2.00	2.00	0.66		
Hartlepool United	1.00	1.50	1.00	1.58	1.00
Hereford United					
Huddersfield Town	5.42	5.33	7.58	9.00	4.91
Hull City	4.50	6.42	2.33	2.17	1.83
Ipswich Town					
Kidderminster Harriers	0.50	0.25			
Leeds United					
Leicester City					
Leyton Orient					
Lincoln City					
Liverpool					
Luton Town					
Macclesfield Town	1.25	2.00	1.00	1.00	

Club					
Manchester City	1.25				
Manchester United	0.50	1.00	0.16		
Mansfield Town	3.33	3.00	0.16		
Middlesbrough	1.67	2.67	3.08	0.92	
Millwall					
M K Dons			0.16	2.00	1.83
Newcastle United	1.75	3.83	2.66	2.08	0.83
Northampton Town	0.83	1.75	0.16		
Norwich City	1.67	2.17	6.25	2.83	0.17
Notts County	3.50	5.17	4.92	1.42	
Nottingham Forest	4.42	4.50	2.58	1.00	0.17
Oldham Athletic	0.08	0.75	2.33	0.75	
Oxford United			0.83		
Peterborough United					
Plymouth Argyle	0.75	1.00	1.00	1.00	
Portsmouth		0.50	3.08	3.58	1.92
Port Vale	2.00	2.08	2.50	5.50	3.00
Preston North End	1.50	2.00	2.33	2.00	
Queens Park Rangers		0.33	1.00	0.42	
Reading	1.17	2.00	0.16		
Rochdale	2.42	2.42	1.33	2.08	0.92
Rotherham United	1.33	1.75	2.66	3.33	1.00
Scarborough	0.16	1.00	1.08	1.00	0.58
Scunthorpe United	2.17	2.08	3.50	2.33	1.42
Sheffield United	4.33	2.58	1.08	0.50	
Sheffield Wednesday	1.00	1.08	3.58	3.00	1.92
Shrewsbury Town	1.08	0.08			
Southampton	1.00	1.50	2.00	1.08	
Southend United		1.17	2.00	1.00	
Stockport County	2.00	1.67	1.16		

Stoke City	3.25	4.17	7.58	7.34	2.17
Sunderland		2.83	1.08		
Swansea City				1.00	0.08
Swindon Town	0.50	0.25	0.66	1.83	0.92
Torquay United	0.58	1.00	0.58		
Tottenham Hotspur					
Tranmere Rovers	0.33		1.00	1.00	
Walsall	3.42	2.42	4.83	4.83	2.24
Watford					
West Bromwich Albion	4.08	2.42	1.83	3.85	1.42
West Ham United					
Wigan Athletic	3.50	1.00	3.00	3.50	1.92
Wimbledon					
Wolverhampton Wanderers	2.58	1.75	5.00	3.00	0.75
Wrexham	3.42	3.58	2.42		
Wycombe Wanderers	1.08	0.58	1.83	3.83	2.00
Yeovil Town					
York City	0.75	0.75			
Average Number of Trainees in Post at any one time	**128.90**	**130.74**	**145.27**	**127.02**	**49.33**

APPENDIX IV
APPROXIMATE START DATES FOR FOOTBALL IN THE COMMUNITY SCHEMES

1986	1987
Manchester City 21st July Bury 4th August Oldham Athletic 25th August Preston North End 25th August Bolton Wanderers 6th October Manchester United 13th October	Crewe Alexandra 1st June Chester City 22nd June Burnley 13th July Blackburn Rovers 27th July Blackpool 3rd August Wigan Athletic 10th September Rochdale 14th September

1988	1989
Barnsley 1st February Everton 1st February Liverpool 1st February Sheffield United 1st February Bradford City 29th February Grimsby Town 29th February Rotherham United 29th February Sheffield Wednesday 29th February Doncaster Rovers 14th March Huddersfield Town 25th April Halifax Town 13th June York City 3rd July Port Vale 4th July Scunthorpe United 4th July Newcastle United 6th October Tranmere Rovers 10th October Hartlepool United 18th October Sunderland 20th October West Bromwich Albion 23rd October Leeds United 31st October	Darlington 9th January Stockport County 26th April Northampton Town 26th June Leicester City 3rd July Nottingham Forest 3rd July Stoke City 31st July Carlisle United July * Notts County 7th August Scarborough 14th August Birmingham City 23rd October Walsall 4th December

1990	1991
Mansfield Town 15th January	Fulham 29th July
Aston Villa 12th February	AFC Bournemouth July *
Hereford United 12th February	Cambridge United 5th August
Wrexham 30th April	Southend United 19th August
Hull City 30th July	Swansea City 2nd September
Wycombe Wanderers 2nd September	Swindon Town 16th September
Chesterfield 8th October	Wolverhampton Wanderers 23rd September
Peterborough United November *	Coventry City 7th October
	Wimbledon 7th October
	Bristol City 2nd December
	Middlesbrough 16th December

1992	Others (after 1992)
Oxford United 1st January	Colchester United 4th January 1993
Gillingham 20th January	Kidderminster Harriers 11th January 1993
Exeter City 27th January	Barnet 6th January 1997
Lincoln City 17th February	Macclesfield Town 1st December 1997
Watford 9th March	Derby County 1st October 1998
Bristol Rovers 16th March	Cheltenham Town May 2000 *
Farnborough Town March *	Boston United July 2003 *
Plymouth Argyle March *	MK Dons September 2003 *
Queens Park Rangers 1st May	
Reading 4th May	
Torquay United 18th May	
Portsmouth June *	
Norwich City 10th August	
Charlton Athletic 20th August	
Tottenham Hotspur 14th September	
Yeovil Town September *	
Luton Town 5th October	
Chelsea 19th October	
Shrewsbury Town 19th October	
Cardiff City 7th December	

Exact start dates of Community Schemes at AFC Bournemouth, Boston United, Carlisle United, Cheltenham Town, Farnborough Town, MK Dons, Peterborough United, Plymouth Argyle, Portsmouth and Yeovil Town are unknown. Exact start dates of Community Schemes at Arsenal, Brentford, Brighton & Hove Albion, Crystal Palace, Ipswich Town, Leyton Orient, Millwall, Southampton and West Ham United are also unknown as they were all underway prior to being approached by representatives of the FFE&VTS Community Programme.

APPENDIX V – DETAILS OF THE VARIOUS NATIONAL COMPETITIONS RUN BETWEEN 1987 AND 2005

THE UNDER 11'S SCHOOLS 6-A-SIDE "ROLL OF HONOUR"

YEAR	WINNERS	LOCAL COMPETITION/ CLUB REPRESENTED	SPONSORS
1987	St. Edwards RC Primary School	Manchester City	-
1988	Drighlington Primary School	Leeds United	-
1990	Guardian Angels Primary School	Bury	-
1991	St Joseph's School	Stockport County	Crime Prevention Scheme & Thorn Home Security
1992	Grove Vale Junior School	West Bromwich Albion	Crime Prevention Scheme & Thorn Home Security
1993	Braybrook Primary School	Peterborough United	NCP
1994	Grosvenor Road Junior School	Manchester United	Refuge Assurance
1995	Brinsworth Manor Junior School	Rotherham United	Refuge Assurance
1996	Kingmoor Junior School AND Oliver Goldsmith Primary School	Carlisle United Millwall	Refuge Assurance
1997	High Oakham Middle School	Mansfield Town	Panini
1998	Fernwood Junior School	Nottingham Forest	Panini
1999	Inmans Junior School AND Penyrenglen Junior School	Hull City Bristol Rovers	Adidas (Predator)
2000	Headington Middle School	Oxford United	Adidas (Predator)
2001	Headington Middle School	Oxford United	Railtrack "Play Safe"
2002	Farnborough Road Primary School	Everton	Railtrack "Play Safe"
2003	Woodchurch CE Primary School	Tranmere Rovers	Network Rail (previously Railtrack)
2004	The Avenue Primary School	Middlesbrough	Kellogg's Frosties
2005	Tidemill Primary School	Millwall	Kellogg's Frosties

APPENDICES

THE UNDER 13'S GIRLS SCHOOLS 6-A-SIDE "ROLL OF HONOUR"

Year	Winners	Local Competition/ Club represented	Sponsors
1999	Collegiate High School	Blackpool	Adidas (Predator)
2000	Cator Park School for Girls	Crystal Palace	Adidas
2001	Cator Park School for Girls and St. David's School	Crystal Palace Middlesbrough	Adidas
2002	Trinity School	Blackburn Rovers	Adidas
2003	Kesteven & Sleaford High School	Lincoln City	Adidas
2004	Ivy Bank Business & Enterprise College	Burnley	Adidas
2005	Estover Community College	Plymouth Argyle	Adidas

THE SMOBY MONNERET TABLE FOOTBALL "ROLL OF HONOUR"			
Year	Winner	Local Competition/Club represented	Venue
1998	Martin Hiley	Southampton	Football Football (restaurant)
1999	Birsher Pattar	Wolverhampton Wanderers	Wembley Stadium
2000	Peter Freeman	Grimsby Town	Millennium Dome
2001	Max Waters	Wimbledon	Anfield
2002	Daniel Ellis	Derby County	Anfield
2003	Brandon Daniels	Port Vale	Elland Road

SOURCES OF REFERENCE: BIBLIOGRAPHY

"Behind the Glory – 100 years of the PFA" (John Harding)

"Celebrating 30 years of the PFA's Community Programme. The PFA."

"Corporate Social Responsibility Report for the 2005/6 Season. Chelsea Football Club"

"EFL Trust – Strategy 2019-2024. Stronger, healthier, more active Communities"

"Football and its Communities. Baseline Analysis of Case Study Football and Community Initiatives. For the Football Foundation" (Mellor, Brown, Blackshaw, Crabbe and Stone)

"Football Confidential" (Ian Bent, Richard McIlroy, Kevin Mousley and Peter Walsh)

"Football Confidential 2" (David Conn, Chris Green, Richard McIlroy and Kevin Mousley)

"Football into the 1990's" (a conference transcript)

"Football Nation" (Andrew Ward and John Williams)

"For the Good of the Game" (John Harding)

"From the Troubles to the Tower" (Derek Spence)

"Off the Pitch. Social Responsibility and Environmental Impact Report 2008. Manchester City Football Club".

"PFA Awards 2003 Brochure"

"The Beautiful Game? Searching for the Soul of Football" (David Conn)

"The Blueprint for the Future of Football" (Football Association - June 1991)

The Charity Commission – website: https://www.charitycommission.blog.gov.uk

"The FL Trust – Community Strategy – Make Every Goal Count"

"The National Football and the Community Programme: A Research Report" (John Williams and Rogan Taylor, University of Leicester)

"The PFA Awards Brochure 1987"

"The PFA Premier & Football League Players' Records 1946-2005" (Edited and Compiled by Barry J. Hugman)

"Twin Strikers. Guidelines for Football and Community Schemes" (Brian Lee)

Watson Burton Charity Commission binder

"Women on the Ball: A Guide to Women's Football" (Sue Lopez)

The Training & Enterprise Directory 1995

"Youngy – The Autobiography of Alan Young" (Alan Young and Simon Kimber)

"20th Annual Presentations – The PFA Awards Brochure 1993"

"34th Annual PFA Awards 2007 Brochure"

Research Surveys:

"Let the ball do the work" (Rachel Barnes)

"Community Education – What is the Impact of Professional Football on Community Education" (Helen Boulton)

"It's a money old game" (transcript by James Cooper)

"Sport and Recreation with special reference to ethnic minorities" (Professor Gajendra K. Verma – supplied by Jas Bains)

"Football in the Community – implications for Primary Schools" (Phil Eardley)

"Sports Council Study of Public and Commercial Use of Football Grounds" (Eileen Hinson/Mike Bonner)

"Football and the Community – Monitoring Project Phase Two" (Roger Ingham)

"The Community Scheme – a survey into the percentage of return visits from the free ticket allocation to local schools" (Anthony McKenna – supplied by Dave Capper, Club Secretary at Sheffield United FC)

"Alleviating Recreational Needs through Professional Football – the Potential Role of Plymouth Argyle FC" (Neil Massey)

"European Conference on Football Violence" (edited by Tim O'Brien)

"Football in the Community – Finance and Marketing at Club, Regional and National Levels" (Liam Roberts)

"The Community Aspects of Football" (Tim Rogers)

"The Development of the Football in the Community Scheme in its original six members" (Christian Smith)

"A Critical Analysis of the Impact that new technology has had on crowd control and ticketing at English Football grounds, its likely future extent and an evaluation of how this will affect the clubs involved" (Jeremy Wong)

"Resources and Opportunities" (Rick Fenoglio and Brendon McGuire - Manchester Metropolitan University)

ACRONYMS AND INITIALS

ACAS	Advisory, Conciliation and Arbitration Service
AFC	Association Football Club
AMA	Association of Metropolitan Authorities
BA	Bachelor of Arts
BBC	British Broadcasting Corporation
BT	British Telecommunications
BTEC	Business and Technology Education Council
CFA	County Football Association
CSR	Corporate Social Responsibility
CV	Curriculum Vitae
DCMS	Department of Culture, Media and Sport
DfEE	Department for Education and Employment
EFDS	English Federation of Disability Sport
EFL	English Football League
ESFA	English Schools Football Association
ET	Employment Training
FA	Football Association
FC	Football Club
FEFC	Further Education Funding Council
FFE&VTS	Footballers Further Education and Vocational Training Society
FL	Football League
FSC	Federation of Stadium Communities
GMEX	Greater Manchester Exhibition Centre
HRH	His Royal Highness
ICT	Information & Communication Technology
IFC	Independent Football Commission

IIP	Investors in People
IMA	Integrated Marketing and Advertising
LDV	Leyland Daf Vans
LSC	Learning & Skills Council
MASE	Modern Apprenticeships in Sporting Excellence
MBE	Member of the British Empire
MEP	Member of European Parliament
MMU	Manchester Metropolitan University
MP	Member of Parliament
MSC	Manpower Services Commission
NASL	North American Soccer League
NCP	National Car Parks
NCS	National Citizen Service
NLT	National Literacy Trust
NPFA	National Playing Fields Association
NROVA	National Record of Vocational Achievement
NSPCC	National Society for the Prevention of Cruelty to Children
NVQ	National Vocational Qualification
PAG	Programme Advisory Group
PAT	Policy Action Team
PC	Personal Computer
PCA	Professional Cricketers Association
PCT	Primary Care Trust
PFA	Professional Footballers Association
PL	Premier League
PR	Public Relations
QISS	Quality in Study Support
SCIP	School Curriculum Industry Partnership
SRB	Single Regeneration Budget
SWOT	Strengths, Weaknesses, Opportunities, Threats
TEC	Training and Enterprise Council
TES	Times Educational Supplement

TFW	Training for Work
UEFA	Union of European Football Associations
VAT	Value Added Tax
WFA	Women's Football Association
YT	Youth Training

COVER CAPTION

" "The United Colours of Football in the Community" was the caption for the iconic photograph taken at the Pizza Hut launch event at Arsenal's Highbury in 1993 when virtually every professional club's Community Officers was photographed together in one picture wearing their own club colours....

The photograph shows:

Front row (all left to right): **Barry Powell** (Coventry City), **Pete Devine** (Blackburn Rovers), **Chris Walters** (Crewe Alexandra), **Kirk Wheeler** – standing in for **Mickey Cook** (Colchester United), **Jim Lowther** (Wimbledon), **David Geddis** (Middlesbrough), **Dean Wheatley** (Lincoln City), **Fraser Foster** (Rotherham United), **Geoff Lomax** (Bolton Wanderers), **Brian Hall** (Liverpool), **Ces Podd** (Leeds United), **Peter Mendham** (Norwich City), **Julie Helmsley** (Brighton & Hove Albion), **John Davies** (Hull City), **Peter Rhoades-Brown** (Oxford United), **Dave Harper** (Bristol Rovers), **Shaun Parker** (Bristol City), **Steve Rogers** (Plymouth Argyle), **Jonathan Trigg** (Swindon Town), **Tommy Hutchison** (Merthyr Tydfil/ Taff Ely Council), **Gary Mulcahey** (Fulham), **Grant Cornwell** (Leyton Orient), **Phil Attfield** (Gillingham), **Martyn Spong** (Brentford).

Second Row: Frankie Banks (Southend United), **Alan Young** (Notts County), **Neville Hamilton** (Leicester City), **Jason Withe** (Birmingham City), **Warwick Adams** (Aston Villa), **Nick Griffiths** (Kidderminster Harriers), **Tony Evans** (Wolverhampton Wanderers), **Jim Cooper** (Port Vale), **Richard Angus** (Bradford City), **Eric Randerson** (Doncaster Rovers), **John Cockerill** (Grimsby Town), **Adrian Shaw** (Chesterfield), **Rick Passmoor** (Scunthorpe United), **Paddy Roche** (Halifax Town), **Steve Lister** (Barnsley), **Charlie Williamson** (Sheffield Wednesday), **Gordon Staniforth** (York City), **Ian Kerr** (Scarborough), **Louise Waller** (Millwall), **Jason Morgan** (Charlton Athletic), **Trevor Lewin** (West Ham United), **John Kerr** (Chester City), **Brian Taylor** (Bury), **Neil Mather** (Stockport County), **Ted Sutton** (Everton).

Third Row: Shaun Gore (Chelsea), **Steve Bradshaw** (Arsenal), **Richard Hill** (Reading), **Mike Cook** (Cambridge United), **Dave Bentley** (Mansfield Town), **Jason Fletcher** (Nottingham Forest), **Frankie Prince** (Torquay United), **Chris Whalley** (Yeovil Town), **Mick Kearns** (Walsall), **Mark Ashton** (West Bromwich Albion), **Brian Williams** (Hereford United), **Dick Pratley** (Shrewsbury Town), **Mick Ferguson** (Sunderland), **Ian Johnstone** (Preston North End), **Steve Williams** (Tranmere Rovers), **Russell Lewis** (Northampton Town), **Jamie Houchen** (Norfolk CFA), **Gary Hooper** (Luton Town), **Domenico Genovese** (Peterborough United), **Alan Smith** (Southampton), **Mark Lillis** (Huddersfield Town), **Craig Madden** (Blackpool), **Bob Oates** (Burnley), **John Halpin** (Carlisle United), **Len Julians** (Tottenham Hotspur).

Fourth Row: Paul Johnson (Stoke City), **Frankie Bunn** (Wigan Athletic), **George Kent** (Exeter City), **Tony Currie** (Sheffield United), **Ray Hankin** (Newcastle United), **Terry Bainbridge** (Hartlepool United), **Iain Leckie** (Darlington), **Dave Ryan** (Manchester United), **Alex Williams** (Manchester City), **Mike Rigg** (Wrexham), **Jason Mahn** and **Andy Evans** standing in for **Emlyn Brown** (Queens Park Rangers), **Geoff Noonan** (Farnborough Town), **Jimmy Gilligan** (Watford), **Alan Curtis** (Swansea City), **Glyn Jones** (Cardiff City), **Gary Holland** (Portsmouth), **John Platt** (Oldham Athletic), **Keith Hicks** (Rochdale), **Darren Hare** (Kent CFA), **Dave Armstrong** (Weymouth/Dorset CFA).

Fifth and Back Row: Peter Withe, Dick Krzywicki, John Seasman, Gordon Coleman (Area Managers), **Kevin Glendon** (Regional Director), **Julian Hayes, Paul Power** (Area Manager), **Mark Holroyd, Andy Welsh** (Area Manager), **Gordon Taylor** (Chief Executive - PFA), **Mickey Burns** (Chief Executive – FFE&VTS), **Roger Reade, John Relish** (Regional

Director), **Dave Palmer** (Area Manager), **Brendon Batson** (Deputy Chief Executive – PFA), **George Berry** (Commercial Manager – PFA), **Dennis Leman**, **Richard Finney** (Regional Director), **Kay MacMillan**, **Tracey Parkinson**, **Adele Scott**, **Clive Baker** (Chairman – PFA), **Jim Hicks** (Area Manager), **Brian Marwood** (Commercial Director – PFA)

Those unable to attend the launch event due to other commitments included Training Officer **Kevin Jardine**, **Tommy Spencer**, **Dave Bell**, plus representatives of Crystal Palace, Durham CFA and Sheffield & Hallamshire CFA. Club Officers unable to attend included **Ron Wylie** (Aston Villa), **Lee Doyle** (Brentford) and **Mickey Cook** (Colchester United). Arrangements were, however, made for Ron and Micky to be represented by other officers. Those clubs not working alongside the FFE&VTS Community Programme at the time were AFC Bournemouth, Barnet, Derby County and Ipswich Town.

INDEX

INDEX

SUBSCRIBERS

COMMENTS

MARK ABRAHAMS

Former Head of Community now Director of Business and Community Development, Southampton FC

The FITC scheme created a career path for so many people from inside and outside the game. Having joined as the Head of Community in 2003, it has proved to be the cornerstone of my career in the football industry and continues to help so many people in the community.

DEREK ALLAN

Former Secretary Preston North End and, later, Brighton and Hove Albion

The little acorn, in 1986, that was the pilot scheme for FITC has now grown beyond belief into a huge oak! Preston NE were one of the initial six clubs chosen to take part and immediately appointed Mick Baxter as their community officer. What a first-class partnership this turned out to be! Whilst tragically Mick is no longer with us, the fantastic work he did during his time at Deepdale laid the foundations for the huge success of the scheme, both at PNE and beyond. The FITC has since branched out considerably to become an integral cog in the wheels of every professional club in the country. Millions of people have been made to feel a part of their community and this is all due to the little acorn that was nurtured all those years ago. Well done to the PFA and all the clubs involved.

JACKIE ARMSTRONG

Former Secretary, Rochdale AFC now Business Owner

Rochdale were delighted to be one of the first league clubs to support FITC. From its inception the scheme was a great success, engaging the local community and making a positive impact in what were difficult and challenging times.

MARK ARTHUR Former Chief Executive, Nottingham Forest now Chief Executive, Yorkshire County Cricket Club

MARK ASHTON Former Head of Community, West Bromwich Albion, now Chief Executive, Bristol City FC and Board Director at EFL.

FRANCISCO BAEZA

Former Principal Lecturer, Buckinghamshire New University.

I met Roger a number of years ago when I was a principal lecturer in the sports department at Buckinghamshire New University. Our professional and personal relationship grew over the years due to our passion for improving peoples' lives by combining education and football. Roger was a great supporter of our work-related foundation degrees. Some of his FITC colleagues were some of my first students. I am very proud of having been a part of a team that recommended Roger for an honorary doctorate from the university in 2006 for his work in the field of FITC. If there is one person who knows and has extensive experience in the field it is Roger Reade!

ANTHONY BARLOW Former Community Development Manager, Blackburn Rovers now living and working in Australia	A great initiative I was fortunate enough to be a small part of! Wow, looking back we did some great work. A big shout out and thanks to the PFA, the football club itself my work colleagues, and the communities themselves for making it the most enjoyable time of my career
PROFESSOR DENISE BARRETT-BAXENDALE	Chief Executive Officer, Everton FC
BRENDON BATSON Former Deputy Chief Executive, The Professional Footballers' Association	Roger Reade, author! Who would have thought it! It was a pleasure working with you. Well done mate.
DARREN BERNSTEIN Former Commercial Manager, The Football League and The Football Association, now Director at Bury AFC.	FITC has impacted on most football fans lives in one way or another. As a kid I spent many a summer on Bury's Summer Coaching courses, then when I was a bit older doing a bit of work experience with the community programme. It undoubtedly shaped my thoughts that football clubs are so much more than those 90 minutes on a Saturday. It's so good to, at last, have the story told by the man at the centre of driving FITC forward for so many years. Well done Roger.
DAVE BENTLEY Former Head of Community, Mansfield Town	Really enjoyed the experience working with some great people. It also helped me in gaining my coaching licence.
MARK BLACKBOURNE Former Club Secretary, Oldham Athletic, Burnley FC and Sunderland AFC, now Freelance Sporting Event Consultant	The community programme has shown it is possible to change the trajectories of hard-to-reach communities. From inception to delivery and then with further evolving, Roger can be extremely proud of his programme outcomes. That much used term 'sport has the power to change lives' sits neatly into Roger's career milestones… thank you Roger for showing football the way forward.
MIKE BRENNAN Former Head of Community, Blackburn Rovers, now Director at IHM International Football Academy	The FITC programme was everything to me, it enabled me to start my career in the game with the club I loved and over 20 years later I'm still working in football. The education and the start in my career it gave me was fantastic and the times working with the programme remain fond memories.
JAMIE BUNCH Former Head of Community, West Bromwich Albion, now Freelance Sports Professional	Joining the FITC scheme at my boyhood Club 'The Albion' in 1999 gave me a unique opportunity at a very vulnerable time in my life after I walked out on playing full time. I never imagined it would provide the life experiences and a platform to my career remaining in the game and into wider sporting development. The foundations of FITC were a blueprint for modern community sport development and the programmes we are now seeing at all levels of the game from Premier league down to the National League System Football Clubs. A huge personal thank you to Roger et al and also The PFA.

DAVE CHALMERS Managing Director, Radcliffe Borough FC	A great venture which has been and still is extremely well organised by the dedicated staff. It has provided many benefits to many communities around the UK.
JERRY CHARTER Former Marketing Director, Burtons Biscuits, now Freelance Sales and Marketing Consultant	Working with Roger and his team was genuinely one of the most rewarding in my career. A great combination of enthusiasm and commercialism – and a real can-do attitude. A terrific enterprise I wish every continued success!
JOHN CLUBB	Former Community Officer, now Clubb Sports Consultancy
DEREK CLYDESDALE	Former Community Officer and Area Manager, FITC
PHIL CRITCHLEY Former Commercial Manager, Manchester City	MCFC in the 80s were unrecognisable from the modern-day giant of the game they have become but I'm proud we led the way in helping to establish FITC as a vital contributor to clubs and communities throughout the country
TONY CURRIE Former Community Officer, Sheffield United	FITC was a lifesaver for me. It got me working again after a really bad time mentally. The 20 years serving FITC and SUFC taught me to be a boss; organising activities, book-keeping, doing reports, appraisals of staff etc. It was very satisfying and I'm very proud of what I achieved.
ALAN CURTIS former Swansea City Head of Community and manager, now President, Swansea City	I'm particularly grateful to the community scheme for bringing me back into professional football and specifically Swansea City FC. I loved taking the club into schools, special schools, to the unemployed and even training sessions for young offenders in Swansea prison. It's been wonderful to see the scheme go from strength to strength.
KEITH DANIELL International Personal Development Expert, Company Owner and Presentations Skills Coach	FITC was ahead of its time. It was about giving back and using the power of football. The world has moved on, the riches that football has now were inconceivable when FITC kicked off but the mission, amongst the community projects across the country, remains. Arsene Wenger's recent Desert Island Discs was a revelation: the young man from the French-German border who loved football and lived the dream. He talked about loyalty, humility and the importance of football and footballers realising they can make a difference and give back. In a way Wenger summed up FITC. The FITC legacy is strong and those involved should be hugely proud that they touched so many lives in such a positive way.
ADAM DAVY Community Director, Walsall FC	I joined Walsall FC in 1994 as an 18 year-old and fresh out of college. I have done every job going in the scheme from an FFE & VTS Trainee to Head of Scheme, and everything in between. My entire working life, to date, has been at the club. I am so fortunate to have a 'hobby for a job' and it remains a role that excites and enthuses me to achieve even more, through the power of football, in our local community.

ANDY DAYKIN

Former Commercial Manager, Sheffield United now Director at Andy Daykin Associates

A fantastic initiative which has come a long way in 35 years thanks to the PFA along with Roger Reade and the team which established it throughout the professional game.

DAVE EDMUNDSON

Former Chief Executive, Burnley and former Chief Executive, The Football League Trust, now Chair at Spring North

The decision to create the FITC to combat hooliganism at football grounds has proved visionary. Now it is much more than football – under the management of the EFL trust, 72 football club charities deliver a variety of programmes in their communities in health, education, social inclusion and multi sports. Truly the beating heart of Football League towns and cities.

ANDY EVANS   Head of Community, Queens Park Rangers

LUCY FAULKNER   Formerly with The FA, now Board Member, Netball Scotland

---

TOM FINN   Former Club Secretary at Oldham Athletic, West Ham United and Blackburn Rovers, now Sports Professional

---

RICHARD FINNEY

Former Regional Director and Marketing Director, FITC

FITC was a brilliant concept. Rolled out by Mickey Burns from the offices of the PFA in 1986 and looking to utilise former professional players to help bring clubs closer to their local communities, the spirit of familiarity and trust that existed between club officers was simply brilliant. As part of the management team, initially my task was to establish projects at football clubs in Yorkshire and the north east and then the East Midlands out as far as Norwich City. The scheme continued to expand, and I took up a new specific role of co-ordinating the national sponsorships and competitions including working closely with Sportsmatch. I was fortunate... I had 20 years of working with some fantastic individuals, projects, clubs and organisations. The experience was a privilege and a pleasure.

TOM FLOWER   Head of Community, Wigan Athletic

FRASER FOSTER   Former Regional Director, FITC now Director of Soccer Development Massive Soccer Coaching (USA)

MIKE FOSTER

Former Assistant Secretary, The Football League and Secretary, The FA Premier League

Among the current generation of footballers we seem to have a significant number who contribute to society in a wholesome and self-effacing manner, more so than in any era in the past. Why is that? This book might well provide a clue. These players have grown up and developed in a culture where football clubs have reached out to their communities and provided support and opportunities for a variety of groups in so many different ways. The author was at the sharp end when the concept of footballers engaging with their local communities was first mooted and he played a central role in laying the foundations and developing what has become a nationwide success story. The book faithfully chronicles the difficulties the scheme had before gaining acceptance and recognises the many people involved in helping it become established, Everyone involved can be proud of their efforts.

ELSPETH GILFILLAN Former Senior Development Manager (Sport), NSPCC, now Philanthropy Consultant	It was a pleasure and a privilege to work with Roger Reade and all the various FITC schemes across the country in support of the NSPCC's Football FULL STOP Campaign. It was amazing to see the world of football come together in support of helping bring child abuse to an end.
JOHN HALPIN Head of Community, Carlisle United	Huge changes have taken place over my 30 years working in the community from small projects to now vast foundations and trusts. I have met some fantastic people along the way and formed friendships that are still as strong today as they were in the 90s.
MATT HANCOCK Head of Community, Burton Albion Community Trust	Football and the difference it can make within communities has never been so apparent. It's important to remember that football has always been about bringing people and communities together.
THE HANNAH FAMILY Family of the late Mr Frank Hannah	This book not only recognises the hard work and contribution of individuals within community football but also confirms how grassroots football lays the foundation for the whole game, for all. Long may it continue.
ROB HALSALL	Former Research Director, Manchester Metropolitan University
NIGEL HARGREAVES	Former Head of Strategic Development, The FA, now Group Sales Director Westlab Ltd.
JON HOLLOWAY Head of Community, Swindon Town FC	FITC has been a huge part of my life for the past 30 years and I am extremely proud to have played my part in the history of Swindon Town FC FITC
MARK HOLROYD Former Finance Officer, FITC	The FITC scheme harnessed the universal splendour of football to transform and enhance the lives of thousands of people for whom a desire to work in the world of sport was previously too easily dismissed.
GARY HOOPER Former Head of Community, Luton Town, now Director at Footmark Sports Ltd.	As the first FITC Manager at Luton Town, I am very proud to have been involved in the project and have watched it grow over the years into what it is today and how it effects all manner of lives
JAMIE HOUCHEN Former Community Officer, Norwich City/Norfolk County FA Community Scheme, now Director of Football Education Ltd.	I will remain forever grateful to FITC for providing me with the opportunity to develop the game I love, ultimately at a local level, then national, then European and now worldwide. The experience I gained over 10 years has equipped me to work for a lifetime in football – never a job, always a passion.
ADRIAN HURST	Head of Community, Stoke City
CALLUM IRVING	Former Regional Director, The Football Association, NOW Football and Sport Consultant
GARY JAMES	Honorary Research Fellow at De Montfort University
IAN KNIGHT Former Community Officer, now Football Services Provider (Canada)	The FITC scheme gave me hope and likely saved my life following retirement as a player/ It enabled me to find a new path to remain in the game that has meant so much to me. I am forever grateful to Roger et al at FITC

DICK KRZYWICKI Former Regional Director FITC	The book certainly gives a great insight into how FITC has made an impact in promoting good relations between the community and football clubs in particular but more specifically young people in terms of education and developing their football skills
ROB LAKE Head of Community, West Bromwich Albion	
IAIN LECKIE Former Head of Community, Darlington FC, now Sports Lecturer and football coach	As Darlington FITC officer in the early 90s it was fantastic to see the scheme develop into what it is today. A real positive influence for the game.
IAN LEES Former Activity Organiser, now Chairman Stockport County Foundation	15th June 1986 I will always remember this quote by Roger "If this project lasts 12 months I will be happy". 35 years later, well pal what a good 12 months that was!
MARK LOVELL Head of Community, Plymouth Argyle	
ALISON LOVETT Former Assistant to the Chairman, West Ham United	"The sense of community that we've all been experiencing during 2020 has its roots deep set. Football clubs, both at grass roots and professional level up and down the country, have been working in their local communities for many years. That involvement is so well embedded nowadays that it has really helped to build that sense of community even more."
ALISON LUCAS Former Marketing Controller, Burton's Biscuits, now Director at Randolph Partnership	Having worked with Roger and FITC in the 90s I am really look forward to revisiting this enjoyable part of our history. It was always a pleasure working with Roger.
BRENDON MCGUIRE Former Senior Lecturer in Physical Education, Sociology of Sport, now author	FITC is a football 'good news' story that has long been needed to be told. To me, it remains football's best kept secret. I am so pleased to that the person recalling the history of events is Roger Reade, who was central to so much of the scheme's growth. This is a much-needed analysis that I can't wait to read!
NEIL MATHER Former Activity Organiser and Community Officer, now Schools Coordinator, Manchester City Academy	What does FITC mean to me? Everything. It simply made me who I am today. It gave a young man who wasn't quite good enough to make it as a player the chance to stay in the game and make a career doing something he loves. It gave me lifelong friendships and treasured memories. It also played a huge part in the development of women's football and meant people like me could lay the foundations for clubs like Manchester City Women. FITC was absolutely ground-breaking and I will be forever grateful for it.
PETER MENDHAM Former Head of Community, Norwich City	The greatest concept ever! The sport of football is massive across the UK and what better way to bring the Community closer to their Clubs. I was so proud and honoured, after a long career at Norwich city as a player, to become their first FITC Officer.

GRAHAM MORAN

Chief Executive Officer,
Nottingham Forest
Community Trust

Great that Roger Reade has devoted the time, energy and passion to capture the rise and positive impact in our communities of what many used to call the 'best kept secret in professional football'. The ability of Football Clubs Community Organisations to respond on a massive scale nationally to the 2020 Covid-19 Pandemic is testament to the pioneering vision of the PFA and all those who played a key role in the formation and development of the 'Community Programme in Professional Football'

GARRY NELSON

Former Senior Commercial
Executive, PFA, now Group Head
of Marketing, AllClear Insurance
Sevices

Enjoyed a great working relationship with Roger and his team at the FITC up in Manchester. Roger's infectious enthusiasm and positive outlook often in the midst of football's complex politics was a great example to us all. Great to see you published Rog - wish you deserved success.

GARY NAVEN   Former Head of Adult and Youth Training, FITC, now Business Owner

PAUL NEWMAN   Chief Operating Officer, Derby County Community Trust

IAN NIVEN

Former Assistant Secretary, Manchester
City and Admin Officer, FITC

After 29 years service at MCFC, I never thought I would find the same rapport and job satisfaction again, but after 7 years at FITC I certainly did. It was a pleasure to go to work at a great organisation with some of the nicest people you could meet. I made many friends for life.

BOB OATES

Former Regional Director, FITC and
ex-Head of Community at Burnley
and Sunderland

I feel privileged to have worked for FITC, in my opinion one of the best off the field developments we have ever had in football. It deserves to go on record – and no-one is better qualified to tell the story than Roger

IAN ORMONDROYD

Chief Executive, Bradford City FC
Community Foundation

RICK PARRY

International Football Consultant,
Chairman, English Football League
and former Chief Executive of the FA
Premier League

Having played a small part in the history of community football many years ago, I'm looking forward to reading what is sure to be a fascinating and comprehensive account of its history.

RICK PASSMOOR

Former Community Officer,
now Youth Development Officer,
Scunthorpe United

I hope today's generation recognise the incredible work done by many for the love of the game from Bishopsgate to the Community Officers who were simply the pioneers and trailblazers!

LAWRIE PEARSON   Former Community Officer

JOHN PLATT

Former Community Officer,
Oldham Athletic

Back in the summer of 1986 after having just been released as a player by Preston NE, I was delighted to be appointed as the first ever community officer at Oldham Athletic having previously played for them for 10 years. I was helped by a large number of community officers (from an initial 6 to over 90) over the years by their advice and ideas for various initiatives involving the local community. All were dedicated and hard-working people, including many ex-professionals wanting to give something back to their local community. Most of the time it didn't feel like work because we were involved in football at clubs we had a still have a great deal of feeling for. I was so grateful for the chance to be part of something special for nearly 25 years/

PAUL POWER   Former Area Manager, FITC

FRANK PRINCE   Former Head of Community, Torquay United

KEVIN REEVES

Former Community Officer, Crewe Alexandra

In my time as a Supervisor at Crewe Alexandra and Chester City I really enjoyed developing the staff under and going out into the community. On a personal level was able to develop and re-educate myself through various courses which helped develop my coaching career.

JOHN RELISH

Former Regional Director, FITC and Regional Manager, EFL Trust

It has been a huge honour and privilege to play a small part in the establishment and development of the FITC programme over the last thirty five or so years. Starting out as a project to make the football stadium the focal point for its local community, it has grown enormously over the ensuing years.

I would like to pay tribute to the countless FITC officers over the years who have realised that the power of our national game can enable us to address some of the most difficult social issues of the day. Today, ground-breaking programmes to tackle Mental Health, Wellbeing, Disability, Employability, Homelessness and endless other initiative are to be found throughout the country. In my opinion it is the greatest success story that football as an industry and sport, has had over the last three decades.

NIGEL ROTHBAND

Hertfordshire County FA Referee, Host "The Man City Show" podcast and Business & Leadership Coach

It was a pleasure to play a very small part in FITC's journey by refereeing a number of the competition finals. An outstanding initiative that has made and continues to make a significant impact.

ROBIN RUSSELL   Football Development Consultant at UEFA

JOHN SEASMAN

Former Area Manager, FITC

Great scheme, great success, great experience! Congratulations and best wishes to all those involved.

NIGEL SHARPE   Business Owner and Accountant

ROB SMITH Head of Community, Watford FC	From little acorns... FITC – what a fantastic success story. Great to see how these pilot schemes at clubs have led on to such a strong network of club community organisations all making positive differences in their communities. We are proud to have been able to play our small part in this - the football family at its best.
STUART SMITH Former Head of Community now Youth Football Coach, Luton Town	I reflect on my time with FITC programme with great fondness. Roger Reade, Dennis Leman and Dave Palmer provided me with great support while setting up the programme at Luton Town. Also, the PFA's support in developing my coaching to A licence through their courses will be forever appreciated.
TOMMY SPENCER Former Area Manager, FITC	As my role involved going to the clubs to make sure things were running well, I popped in to see Tony Currie. His staff were out at schools and were late back. He set off down to reception and then shouted "Tom – come and see this!" There in the car park was one of the staff trying to do keepy uppies. There were quite a few cars and the ball was bouncing all over them. I've never seen TC move so fast – a few choice words came out too!
DALE SPIBY	Chief Executive, Southend United Community & Educational Trust
LESLEY SPUHLER	Chief Executive, Foundation of Light, Sunderland AFC
GORDON STANIFORTH	Former Head of Community, York City and FA Regional Coach
NEIL TAYLOR Chief Executive, Leyton Orient Community Sports Programme	My own FITC journey began in 1991 when I started going to Leyton Orient matches and becoming aware of the Leyton Orient scheme led by the imperious Neil Wilson. I had the opportunity of getting involved with the scheme in 1997 bringing in grant funding for an Education Officer through the Foundation I worked for at the time. As the scheme became a registered charity, I joined the team and am still here enjoying every minute helping place the Trust at the heart of the community.

IAN & JACKIE THORNTON

Head of Community and Head of Development, Norwich City Community Sports Foundation

I never thought attending my Work Experience on a Norwich City Soccer Schools would shape my life so much. There are many inspiring and supportive people that have all played their part to get to this point. The strategy and the science of the good' ole FITC days have certainly worked. Credit to Roger and all the team at the PFA and all the local clubs and in our case the County FA for its creation. To this day many of us of have grown and transitioned to Charitable Foundation's delivering so much more than Football. Across the circuit some impressive, life impacting work is taking place.

For me, 28 years on. As one of the early Assistant FITC Officer's I married our Girls FDO. Today, we are married with two children. To this day we have 80 full time staff, over 50 initiatives with an excellent and talented workforce. We are currently building our second facility, The Nest, (please take a look). May this book bring about all the successes, challenges and stories that have made many smile.

LEE TURNBULL

Former Head of Community, Scunthorpe United, now business owner, LT9 Limited

After 16 years working as the manager of community trust at Scunthorpe United, I'm sure Roger's book will inspire and intrigue the readers.

JAMIE VITTLES

CEO at Exeter City Community Trust

From the beginning, it was apparent to me how impactful the FITC programme could be, but over the past 35 years, the impact and reach of Club Community Organisations across the country continues to impress and inspire me. Since 1991, our work in Exeter has developed and evolved from school holiday football clubs and match day activities into a varied portfolio of projects in areas including physical activity, education, health & wellbeing, and social inclusion. Both ourselves and other Club Community Organisations have perhaps evolved more in the last year than the last 25+ combined, stepping up to help our communities through the Covid-19 pandemic in any way we can. I am confident that football and the work we do alongside the game will continue to play an important part in supporting our communities for years to come, and I am immensely proud to be a part of that journey.

DEAN WHEATLEY Former Head of Community at Lincoln City FC

KIRK WHEELER

Former Head of Community at Watford FC and Aldershot Town

Privileged to work on various FITC projects since their inception and shared the journey and huge success with so many passionate and inspirational characters. Also glad to see that most us haven't aged a day since that cover photo at Highbury.

RAF WILLEMS

Independent Writing and Editing
Professional

I first visited FITC in 2002. It felt like coming home: the combination of my social education with my football passion. From then on I gave myself a mission: to spread the idea of FITC in Belgium and the Netherlands. Both the Dutch KNVB and the Belgian RBFA eventually sought my views – so, without FITC there would be no social football organizations in either the Netherlands or Belgium. It is my honest opinion that since the inception of football, FITC has been the most beautiful thing that our beloved sport has produced. 35 years is not the end, it is only the beginning!

STEVE WILLIAMS

Head of Community,
Tranmere Rovers

A truly ground-breaking initiative, now fully embedded in the fabric of football

JULIAN WINTER

Former Regional Director, FITC,
now CEO at Swansea City

FITC was, & remains, although in many different guises these days, a unique football proposition. From concept to delivery, it took tremendous effort from the key people involved at the time, not least Roger Reade, to drive forward a programme of activity in partnership with all the key football agencies & the clubs themselves to transform the football landscape for clubs. I for one will never forget the story that Roger describes & my small part in its history. I always felt that the work done here in England & Wales through FITC should have been promoted to the world as a means of truly demonstrating the power of football at community level. Maybe this book will travel far & wide & show the world just how much hard work & commitment went into creating, maintaining & developing a truly special programme of work - the legacy of which is maintained today in all our football clubs & their communities.